**palgrave advances in
european union studies**

Palgrave Advances

Titles include:

Michele M. Betsill, Kathryn Hochstetler and Dimitris Stevis (*editors*)
INTERNATIONAL ENVIRONMENTAL POLITICS

Terrell Carver and James Martin (*editors*)
CONTINENTAL POLITICAL THOUGHT

Michelle Cini and Angela K. Bourne (*editors*)
EUROPEAN UNION STUDIES

Jeffrey Haynes (*editor*)
DEVELOPMENT STUDIES

Palgrave Advances
Series Standing Order ISBN 1–4039–3512–2 (Hardback) 1–4039–3513–0 (Paperback)
(*outside North America only*)

You can receive future titles in this series as they are published by placing a standing order. Please contact your bookseller or, in the case of difficulty, write to us at the address below with your name and address, the title of the series and the ISBN quoted above.

Customer Services Department, Macmillan Distribution Ltd, Houndmills, Basingstoke, Hampshire RG21 6XS, England

palgrave advances in european union studies

edited by

michelle cini

department of politics
university of bristol

and

angela k. bourne

department of politics
university of dundee

First published 2006 by
PALGRAVE MACMILLAN
Houndmills, Basingstoke, Hampshire RG21 6XS and
175 Fifth Avenue, New York, N.Y. 10010
Companies and representatives throughout the world

PALGRAVE MACMILLAN is the global academic imprint of the Palgrave
Macmillan division of St Martin's Press LLC and of Palgrave Macmillan Ltd.
Macmillan® is a registered trademark in the United States,
United Kingdom and other countries. Palgrave is a registered
trademark in the European Union and other countries.

ISBN-13   978–0–333–99762–8 hardback
ISBN-10   0–333–99762–X hardback
ISBN-13   978–0–333–99763–5 paperback
ISBN-10   0–333–99763–8 paperback

This book is printed on paper suitable for recycling and
made from fully managed and sustained forest sources.

A catalogue record for this book is available from the British Library.

Library of Congress Cataloging-in-Publication Data
Palgrave advances in European Union studies / edited by Michelle Cini and Angela Bourne.
    p. cm.
Includes bibliographical references and index.
ISBN 0–333–99762–X (cloth) — ISBN 0–333–99763–8 (pbk.)
    1. European Union. 2. European Union countries—Politics and government. I. Cini,
Michelle. II. Bourne, Angela K.

JN30.P335 2005
341.242'2—dc22

2005052294

10 9 8 7 6 5 4 3 2 1
15 14 13 12 11 10 09 08 07 06

Printed and bound in Great Britain by
Antony Rowe Ltd, Chippenham and Eastbourne

contents

list of figures and tables **vii**
preface **ix**
notes on contributors **x**
list of abbreviations and acronyms **xii**

1. introduction **1**
angela bourne and michelle cini

2. rational institutionalism and liberal intergovernmentalism **19**
roger scully

3. constructivism and sociological institutionalism **35**
antje wiener

4. europeanization: solution or problem? **56**
claudio m. radaelli

5. conceptual combinations: multilevel governance and policy networks **77**
alex warleigh

6. the study of eu enlargement:
theoretical approaches and empirical findings **96**
frank schimmelfennig and ulrich sedelmeier

7. conceptualizing the european union's global role **117**
ben tonra

8. european identity: theory and empirics **131**
paul gillespie and brigid laffan

9. eu legitimacy and normative political theory **151**
andreas føllesdal

10. political economy and european integration   **174**
amy verdun

11. from state to society? the historiography of european integration   **190**
wolfram kaiser

12. knowing europe: metatheory and methodology
in european union studies   **209**
joseph jupille

13. cleavages, controversies and convergence
in european union studies   **233**
wolfgang wessels

references   **247**
index   **289**

figures and tables

figures

2.1 A simplified model of the EU policy space **28**

3.1 Core theoretical positions **41**

3.2 Establishing the middle ground **42**

3.3 Stations on the bridge **42**

4.1 Three approaches: European integration, top-down Europeanization, and bottom-up Europeanization **60**

8.1 Dimensions of identification **136**

12.1 EU articles in selected US subfield journals, 1968–2003 **222**

12.2 Methodological content of EU journals **225**

12.3 Methodological trends in EU Studies, 1952–2002 **227**

12.4 The fish-scale model of omniscience **230**

tables

3.1 Three phases of institution-building **47**

3.2 Leading research questions **48**

4.1 Modes of governance, mechanisms, and explanations **69**

5.1 Marks and Hooghe's new typology of multilevel governance **85**

5.2 Rhodes' typology of policy networks **89**

5.3 The theoretical use in combining multilevel governance and policy networks **91**

6.1 Theoretical approaches and key explanatory factors for enlargement **102**

8.1 Political order, theory and identity   137

9.1a Conceptions, mechanisms and objects of legitimacy (I)   155

9.1b Conceptions, mechanisms and objects of legitimacy (II)   155

12.1 Possibilities for metatheoretical combination   212

12.2 Practical metatheoretical–methodological combinations   215

12.3 Journals surveyed   224

12.4 EU Studies methodology in US and European journals   226

preface

The original idea for this book arose from a discussion between the two editors sitting in a café on Park Street in Bristol back in 2001. Bemoaning the time and effort needed to keep up with the immense literature on the European Union and European integration, we recognized a puzzling gap in that literature. We could think of no book that sought to stand back from the EU to review the 'state of the art'. When we first discussed how we might turn this undeveloped insight into a book proposal, our original ambition was to put together a series of interwoven review essays. However, this idea soon evolved into something quite different. Thus, although most of the contributions in this volume do incorporate mini literature reviews and explain recent developments in their respective research fields, they also make a contribution to that literature in their own right, pushing at the boundaries of their field, and identifying for the reader just where the (or a) 'cutting edge' is.

As is the case for many edited volumes, this book had a gestation period which was rather longer than we had originally intended. We would like to thank Alison Howson and Guy Edwards for their forbearance in this, and for their non-intrusive support during the production of this book. In a similar vein, we would like to express our appreciation to our contributors, and particularly those who submitted their drafts early and waited patiently for the book to appear. I'm certain that some wondered whether it ever would! Our gratitude also goes to Machiko Miyakoshi for her excellent and timely research assistance. Finally, we thank our friends and partners for the misery that they (must have) endured at various stages of this book project – and particularly in the final weeks leading to the submission of the typescript. We hope very much that both the wait and the effort were worthwhile.

Michelle Cini and Angela K. Bourne
June 2005

notes on contributors

Angela K. Bourne is Lecturer in European Politics in the Department of Politics, University of Dundee, UK.

Michelle Cini is Senior Lecturer in Politics and Jean Monnet Lecturer in European Community Studies in the Department of Politics, University of Bristol, UK.

Andreas Føllesdal is Professor of Political Philosophy and Director of Research at the Norwegian Centre for Human Rights, Faculty of Law, University of Oslo, Oslo, Norway.

Paul Gillespie is Foreign Editor of the *Irish Times*, Dublin, Ireland.

Wolfram Kaiser is Professor of European Studies in the School of Social, Historical and Literary Studies, University of Portsmouth, UK and Visiting Professor at the College of Europe in Bruges, Belgium.

Brigid Laffan is Jean Monnet Professor of European Integration in the Department of Politics, and Research Director of the Dublin European Institute, University College Dublin, Ireland.

Joseph Jupille is Assistant Professor in the Department of Political Science at the University of Colorado, Boulder, USA.

Claudio M. Radaelli holds the Anniversary Chair in Political Science in the Department of Politics, University of Exeter, UK.

Ulrich Sedelmeier is Marie Curie Fellow at the European University Institute, Florence and Senior Lecturer in International Relations at the London School of Economics.

Frank Schimmelfennig is Research Fellow at the Mannheim Centre for European Social Research, University of Mannheim, Germany.

Roger Scully is Senior Lecturer in European Politics and Director of the Jean Monnet Centre for European Studies, University of Wales, Aberystwyth, UK.

Ben Tonra is Jean Monnet Professor of European Foreign, Security and Defence Policy and Senior Lecturer in the Department of Politics, and Academic Director of the Dublin European Institute, University College Dublin, Ireland.

Amy Verdun is Jean Monnet Chair in European Integration Studies and Professor of Political Science, University of Victoria, Canada.

Alex Warleigh is Professor of International Politics and Public Policy in the Department of Politics and Public Administration, University of Limerick, Ireland.

Wolfgang Wessels is Professor and Jean Monnet Chair of Political Science at the University of Cologne, Germany.

Antje Wiener is Professor of International Relations, Jean Monnet Chair and Director of Jean Monnet Centre of Excellence in the School of Politics and International Studies, Queens University Belfast, Belfast, UK.

abbreviations and acronyms

AJPS	*American Journal of Political Science*
APSR	*American Political Science Review*
BDI	Bundesverband der Deutschen Industrie
BJPS	*British Journal of Political Science*
CAP	Common Agricultural Policy
CEES	Central and Eastern European States
CFSP	Common Foreign and Security Policy
CONNEX	Connecting Excellence on European Governance
CP	*Comparative Politics*
CPS	*Comparative Political Studies*
DFG	Deutsche Forschungsgemeinschaft
EC	European Community
ECPR	European Consortium of Political Research
ECSA	European Community Studies Association
ECSC	European Coal and Steel Community
EDC	European Defence Community
EEC	European Economic Community
EFTA	European Free Trade Association
EJIR	*European Journal of International Relations*
EMU	Economic and Monetary Union
EP	European Parliament
EPC	European Political Cooperation
epsNET	European Political Science Network
EPU	European Payments Union
ESDP	European Security and Defence Policy
ESRC	Economic and Social Research Council
EU	European Union
EUP	*European Union Politics*
IA	*International Affairs*

IDNET	Europeanization, Collective Identities and Public Discourses Network
IGC	Intergovernmental Conference
IO	*International Organization*
ISA	International Studies Association
ISQ	*International Studies Quarterly*
JCMS	*Journal of Common Market Studies*
JCR	*Journal of Conflict Resolution*
JEPP	*Journal of European Public Policy*
JOP	*Journal of Politics*
JPR	*Journal of Peace Research*
JSTOR	The Archive of Journal Storage
LSQ	*Legislative Studies Quarterly*
MEP	Member of the European Parliament
NATO	North Atlantic Treaty Organization
NGO	Non-Governmental Organization
OECD	Organization for Economic Cooperation and Development
OEEC	Organization for European Economic Cooperation
OLS	Ordinary Least Squares
PRQ	*Political Research Quarterly*
PSQ	*Political Science Quarterly*
QMV	Qualified Majority Voting
SEA	Single European Act
SSCI	Social Science Citation Index
TEU	Treaty on European Union
US	United States
WP	*World Politics*

1

introduction: defining boundaries and identifying trends in european union studies

angela k. bourne and michelle cini

introduction

Over the past twenty years or so, research on European integration and on the European Community/European Union has expanded dramatically. When the elder of the two editors of this volume chose to take a first degree in European Studies in the early 1980s, (a component of which was the study of European integration), some of her peers thought her decision unconventional. A more traditional disciplinary choice was still very much the norm for prospective undergraduates. However, by the mid-1990s, when the younger of the two editors began research on the European Union (EU), the subject was much better established, and was no longer considered an unusual choice for either undergraduates or postgraduates.

Reflecting on the broad parameters of what was studied in courses on European integration and the (then) European Community (EC) more than twenty years ago, there seems at first sight to be a great deal of continuity. For instance, theories of European integration – neofunctionalism in particular – were, and are still, included in many courses that engage with the conceptualization of the European integration process; policies, such as the Common Agricultural Policy, continue to be critiqued by undergraduate and postgraduate students; and the dynamics of market integration, which may now focus on Economic and Monetary Union more than the Single Market Programme, is still a central topic in courses on the EU. Where there has been change, it has come from two discrete sources. First, new ideas and theories – some might, rather disparagingly, call them fads and fashions – have led to the application of new perspectives on European integration and the EC/EU. Thus the EU is seen through new conceptual lenses, and insights not previously obvious to the student of European integration now become glaringly so. Second, developments in European integration and in the evolution of the EC/EU have triggered new avenues for research and teaching. This has not only contributed to original empirical research, but has also fed directly into theorization of the EU.

The genesis of this book lay in our view that although there is now a large and very diverse literature on the EU, there is still room for work which stands back from the literature to identify trends and to define the boundaries of this field of research. More practical objectives were also in our minds as we began to think about the kind of contributions we wanted to commission. First, we wanted a book that would be more advanced than a textbook, but which would also offer a helping-hand to those new to this particular subject area, albeit at an advanced level. In other words, our target market was new research postgraduates beginning work in this or related fields, as well as more established academics, who, though non-specialists in, or out-of-touch with, research on the EU, would like to know more about the key advances. We expect, however, that the book will also be of interest to many others, not least advanced undergraduates, masters students and researchers currently working on the EU, who we hope will also find much that is new in the chapters that follow.

Before launching into the individual contributions, this introductory chapter highlights some of the ideas and trends that we found most stimulating in the chapters that follow. In so doing, we do not want to pre-empt the discussions and arguments below, nor to set out a model or framework, but simply to engage thoughtfully with some of the cross-cutting themes and contentious issues that seemed to us, at the time of writing, to be most pertinent. Our primary aim is to identify trends in the field of EU Studies, particularly those that suggest either a fragmentation of research interests or a concentration of that research around various themes and orientations.

We begin this introductory chapter by saying a little more about the organizing rationale of the book and the contributions therein, with the aim of explaining where we have drawn the boundaries around what, in this volume, we call 'EU Studies'. The second section examines the alleged disciplinary dominance of political science in the field and contrasts this against the interdisciplinary characteristics and aspirations that go hand-in-hand with the study of the European Union. The third section develops a theme identified in the second section, that of divergence and convergence in research in EU Studies, to explore further centrifugal and centripetal trends in the literature. The final section provides a brief overview of the key arguments found in the chapters that follow.

why 'eu studies'?

The title of this volume, *Advances in European Union Studies*, begs a number of obvious questions: first, what do we understand by the term 'EU Studies'?; and second, how might we identify key advances in this research area? Although problematic in certain respects, we intentionally chose the term 'EU Studies' as a way of signalling what we consider to be the primary substantive research focus of the field. Three points are worth emphasizing here: first, we decided to distance ourselves from the term 'European Studies', which we understand to encompass a much broader range of subject matter than our own focus on the EU. Second, we use the word 'studies' to draw attention to our interest in questions of disciplinarity and interdisciplinarity, which we believe to be important. Third, throughout the rest of the chapter, and where appropriate in the book, we refer to the EU, and not to European integration or the EC/EU. This is a way for us to emphasize the contemporary character of the contributions below. However, it does not mean that we ignore the pre-1993 EC, nor the long view of the European integration process. A satisfactory inclusive term, which captures this field of study, and which reflects a composite of research on the EU and the EC, as well as into European integration and Europeanization (see Chapter 4), is yet to be coined as far as we are aware: until it is, we are settling for 'EU Studies'.

It is not only the naming and defining of the field of study that is problematic, however. Identifying key advances in EU Studies is also a rather subjective exercise. What we tried to do was to select a range of empirical and theoretical topics which we felt, together, would provide the reader with an excellent feel for new developments in EU research over the past ten-to-fifteen years. We make no claim that we have been comprehensive in making our selection, not least as the choice of chapters and contributors reflect our own interests and biases. For example, despite our openness to and interest in EU research undertaken within a broad range of disciplines, we, as editors, have to lay our cards on the table and admit our bias for political research on the EU. By this we mean the use of 'political analysis' (Hay, 2002, 2), rather than just a specific focus on (EU) politics as a dependent variable or research object (see Huysmans, 2005), though in practice the two often go hand-in-hand. Although we did not impose this bias on our contributors, and several chapters explictly address non-political literatures and approaches (see, for example, Chapters 10 and 11), there does seem to be an unstated assumption in the contributions to this volume that political approaches constitute a mainstream of some sort (though this is hardly surprising given that most of the contributors are indeed political scientists). We return to this question in the section that follows. Suffice to say at this point that those contributions exploring key approaches to what from our perspective looks like the mainstream of contemporary EU Studies provide the point of departure for this volume. For this reason, we begin the book with chapters on rational institutionalism and liberal institutionalism (Roger Scully), sociological institutionalism and constructivism (Antje Wiener), Europeanization (Claudio M. Radaelli), and multilevel governance and policy networks (Alex Warleigh) approaches to EU Studies. While not exclusively 'political', such approaches are primarily used by political researchers interested in the EU.

These first four chapters reflect upon the concepts, methods and the foundational assumptions of approaches that we consider to be central reference points for contemporary intellectual debate and empirical research on the EU. They do not provide a summary of all aspects of EU theory nor, indeed, do they confine themselves to theoretical discussion. However, they comment on research programmes and empirical findings generated by these approaches. We recognize that isolating these, rather than other, approaches for detailed analysis may be controversial. We took the conscious decision, for instance, not to include a chapter explicitly dedicated to 'classical' theories of integration such as transactionalism, neofunctionalism and early intergovernmentalism, as these do not fit with our conception of 'advances'. In taking this line, we may face the criticism that we have failed to appreciate (and consciously so) the continuing relevance of seminal works within the field; or that we do not acknowledge just how much contemporary analysis draws on or recycles earlier concepts and arguments (see Cram, 1997 for examples of this kind of work; and Schmitter, 2004). We respond by noting that the origins, evolution and legacies of classical integration theories are well charted elsewhere (Wiener and Diez, 2003; Rosamond, 2000a) and that our aim is not to provide another textbook on EU theory. Rather, we aim to present a snapshot of academic research on the EU as of the middle of the first decade of the twenty-first century and to reflect upon possible future developments.

As mentioned at the start of this chapter, advances within academic fields of study may be prompted on the one hand, by new ideas, polemics and trends in intellectual thought, and, on the other, by 'real world' developments. Established narratives on the evolution of EU integration theory offer myriad examples of both (see Wiener and Diez, 2003; Rosamond, 2000a; see also Chapter 13 of this volume). The impact of International Relations theories such as 'realism', 'institutionalism' and 'social constructivism', and the rational choice 'revolution' in political science, are clear examples of the former; the implications of 1960s Gaullism on the rise of early intergovernmentalism, the prompt provided by the single market programme to Comparative Politics and the new 'governance' approaches, and the impact of the constitutionalizing agenda of the Maastricht and post-Maastricht period on the development of normative and constructivist approaches in EU Studies, are important examples of the latter. Many of the contributors to this book discuss the intellectual influences on developments within their field. However, anticipating that specifically addressing important developments in EU Studies would offer fertile ground for the presentation of innovative research, we sought also to include a series of chapters reviewing recent academic work on enlargement (Chapter 6), the EU's global role (Chapter 7) and identity politics in the EU (Chapter 8). Other chapters include sustained reflection upon recent events, notably Andreas Føllesdal's chapter on normative political theory, which addresses the responses of political theorists to the Constitutional Treaty (Chapter 9), and Amy Verdun's chapter on political economy approaches (Chapter 10), which includes some discussion of Economic and Monetary Union.

disciplinary dominance and interdisciplinary aspirations

Academic research on the EU takes various disciplinary shapes and forms. The application of disciplinary approaches has clearly produced a wealth of literature on the EU and on European integration. Adopting such an approach clearly has its advantages. For example, it allows the researcher to tap into a well-defined body of literature, complete with its seminal works, authorities in the field, and its intellectual shorthand.

The contribution made by lawyers to our understanding of the EU, for example, has been immense. While much legal research speaks directly to the legal community alone, and adopts a conventional disciplinary approach to the study of the EU (see amongst many others texts by Hartley, 1998; and Trimidas, 1999), others, especially those whose research might be termed socio-legal, or that falls under the rubric of 'law in context', have produced studies that appeal as much to non-lawyers as they do to the legal community (see for example, Weiler, 1999b; Shaw, 2003). Work of this kind can be found in excellent journals like the *European Law Review*.

Economists, too, have written extensively on the EU. From the early days of the Community, research has helped to explain the drivers of economic integration (for example, studies by Viner, 1950; and Balassa, 1961). While some of the economics literature may be difficult for non-specialists to grapple with, there are a number of economists working on the EU who are able to speak to a much wider audience (Tsoukalis, 1997 and Begg and Grimwade, 1998 for example). The *Journal of Common Market Studies* has been particularly influential in bringing recent work of this kind into the mainstream since the late 1990s, rediscovering an earlier editorial focus of that journal.

Sociologists have been much less visible in EU Studies than lawyers and economists, and their direct contribution to EU Studies has been somewhat limited (see, however, Rumford, 2002). The same is true of social psychologists. Both, indirectly, have begun to influence the EU literature, however, through their work on European identity (see Chapter 8 in this volume). Studies in the geography of the EU are also rather thin on the ground, though again there are a small number of studies that might be of interest both to geographers and non-geographers, especially covering subjects such as population, regional disparities and social inequality (for example, Cole and Cole, 1997). Cutting across the sociology/geography divide, Rodriguez-Pose's

(2002) textbook makes an important and novel contribution to this literature. More visible have been anthropological studies of the EU, largely because of Maryon McDonald's research on the European Commission (2005), both alone and with French researchers Marc Abélès and Irène Bellier (1993). Chris Shore's anthropological research into the cultural politics of European integration also brings anthropology to a public beyond his own discipline (Shore, 2000).

As one of our contributors, Wolfram Kaiser, discusses at length below (see Chapter 11), historians, too, have had something to say about the EU (or, perhaps to be more specific in this case, about the early EC and European integration process). Interestingly, Kaiser charts how historians have drawn on social science research in their work on European integration, an example of which is Alan Milward's application of intergovernmentalism (for example, Milward, 1984 and 1992). The scope for historians to contribute to the EU Studies literature has increased in the last couple of decades. Once they were able to look back over more than thirty years or so of history, the potential for engaging in research – and particularly archival research – increased substantially.

Political researchers working on the EU have been extremely prolific in publishing their research, and there is a huge body of literature, incorporating work from various key sub-disciplines, such as International Relations (Moravcsik, 1998a; Pollack, 2001), Comparative Politics (Hooghe and Marks, 2001a; Hix, 1998 and 1999) and Public Administration (Levy, 2003). Even though the proliferation of research of this kind really kicked off in the 1980s, accusations of the dominance of political approaches in the study of the EC/EU and the European integration process have long been made by researchers in other disciplines. However, 'politics' or 'political science' is such a broad church that many studies that are said to fall into the category are not grounded in any particular disciplinary tradition. Where this is the case, one might say that these works are really only in the politics 'box' by default, with the politics label serving as a kind of residual category for research that does not fit neatly into any other discipline.

An early preference for case studies of decisionmaking, which were ostensibly *about* politics, but did not make explicit what (political) research tools and theories they used, helped to bolster accusations that other disciplines were underrepresented in the field of EU Studies. These case studies, though informative and interesting, tended towards the descriptive and atheoretical, and as such, often seemed detached from any disciplinary heritage. Although some were grounded in the 'old' institutionalism, the absence of an explicit theoretical component allowed researchers using the case study approach a freedom to see their work as interdisciplinary. In reality a more accurate description of much of this research would have been 'non-disciplinary'.

What was previously identified as interdisciplinary in EU Studies really formed part of an 'area studies' approach in the social sciences. This approach rested on a belief that effective research could only be accomplished where the researcher possessed an empirically rich knowledge of one geographical region. This usually involved linguistic skills, immersion through first-hand experience of living in the region, and a knowledge which cut across traditional disciplinary cleavages to encompass subjects such as economics, history, geography and politics, whilst often rejecting the dividing lines between these categories and the disciplines that explained them (see also Calhoun, 2003).

'Area studies' has suffered from a loss of credibility as a way of undertaking research, which paralleled the rise of generalizable, comparative social science (and not just in the field of political science). Area studies became associated with empirically detailed, but theoretical underspecified research, which failed to contribute to the creation of more general 'laws' of social science (see for instance Bates, 1997). The latter was taken more seriously, particularly in the US, in the 1990s, and this was where the demise of area studies was most painful. Area studies institutes closed or found resources being transferred to disciplinary departments, and the term 'area studies' at times was used disparagingly.

It is paradoxical, then, that many students of the EU today claim to adopt an interdisciplinary approach in their work. Indeed, interdisciplinary has become one of the clarion calls of contemporary social science. Unlike the interdisciplinarity of the past, the contemporary version of interdisciplinarity in EU Studies aspires to be theoretically informed. In practice, though, what many researchers take to be interdisciplinarity is more accurately described as multidisciplinarity. The latter suggests a parallel or even an eclectic use of disciplines within one research project or in addressing one research question. The former suggests something much more ambitious – a kind of merging of the disciplines, in a manner that seems to us to be overly demanding for individual researchers (both practically and intellectually). While there are numerous examples of multidisciplinary studies, evidence of interdisciplinarity, at least as we understand and define it, is much rarer.

In the section that follows, we look more closely at what we defined above as mainstream research on the EU and European integration. Some of the trends we identify below have arisen as a consequence of a kind of intellectual osmosis across disciplinary boundaries. Others have come about as a consequence of efforts to construct a body of political science literature on the EU, addressing criticisms that EU Studies have in the past failed to export theories, concepts and ideas outside their own field (see Chapter 13 on this). It is perhaps ironic that a solution to the intellectual isolationism of EU Studies has contributed to a strengthening of the field's disciplinary credentials. However, it would seem that what we have witnessed is part of a trend which takes us from an 'area studies' approach (often the term interdisciplinarity was used to signal this), to a disciplinary strengthening of the field, to, ultimately, a multidisciplinarity which hides behind demanding aspirations for a new interdisciplinary approach to EU-focused research.

divergence and convergence in the eu studies mainstream

Much of the conventional, or mainstream, narrative on theorization and conceptualization in EU Studies emphasizes differentiation and competition among alternative approaches. This has involved a variety of combatants. The struggle between neofunctionalists and intergovernmentalists in the 1960s and 1970s was supplemented, and some might say supplanted, by a similar dichotomy which appeared between Comparative Politics and International Relations scholars in the 1980s; and, more recently, a rationalist–constructivist divide has become increasingly important from the 1990s on (Pollack, 2001). These narratives do not assume the 'victory' of one particular approach over the other, however; and neither is this the end of the story for EU Studies. But it does provide the taken-for-granted starting-point for many of the contributions in this volume.

The narrative of the neofunctionalist–intergovernmentalist dichotomy is well-worn. Neofunctionalist theory explained regional integration as an evolutionary process, driven by the self-interest of societal groups, and by the active promotion of integration by supranational elites. This was to be achieved through a process identified as spillover. The theory played down the importance of the nation-state and national actors, and viewed integration, once initiated, as an inevitable process, which might ultimately lead to the formation of a new kind of political community. Though dominant in explaining the European integration of the 1950s and early 1960s, by the middle of that decade, such claims were being contested by intergovernmentalists, and especially by Stanley Hoffmann, who claimed that while spillover might be in evidence in areas of low politics, there could be no spillover in policy areas that touched the core of national sovereignty. While both approaches are in fact much richer in detail than this summary can communicate, the debate between the two was often reduced to one which emphasized a supranational dynamic (particularly supported by those in favour of European integration) on the one hand, and an international or intergovernmental dynamic (particularly supported by those less inclined to admit the novelty of Western Europe's post-1945 integration experiment), on the other. Competition between the two remains to this day, albeit drawing on newer variants of supranational and intergovernmental theorizing that have to some extent become subsumed within newer academic/intellectual rivalries.

The most important of these rivalries, at least up until the 1990s, comprised a new dichotomy separating International Relations scholars from those researching specific aspects of EU politics. The latter was theoretically informed, and the object of their research was 'European integration'; in certain manifestations the EU was studied as if it were a kind of international regime. By contrast, the former was largely empirical and less theoretically and conceptually defined, with the 'Community' studied as though it were a unique kind of political system. This initial characteristic of the approach has been changing, however, since the 1980s, as scholars of political science sought to combat the dominance of 'European integration theory' by applying (largely) mid-range political science theories to explain particular aspects of EU politics. By the mid-1990s, yet another dichotomy supplemented those discussed above – the rationalist–constructivist divide in EU Studies. More will be said about these approaches in Chapters 2 and 3.

Understanding the changing nature and salience of scholarly cleavages in EU Studies, which is central to the conceptualization of phases or periods in the evolution of this field, helps to define the 'state of the art' and to differentiate innovative, 'publishable' and 'fundable' research from that considered dated or irrelevant. It allows those researching in the field to understand the sociology of their own profession, and to be reflective when it comes to acknowledging how and why certain themes, questions, or approaches become fashionable. Those who undertake such reviews bear no small measure of responsibility. It is all too easy to fall to the temptation of defining the field in a way that makes one's own research appear crucial and cutting-edge.

The differentiation, rivalry and competition which can be identified in the field of EU Studies may help explain why Donald Puchala's (1972) description of international integration theory, as the story of blind men trying to understand an elephant, is so widely repeated by scholars in the field. The vividness of the metaphor makes it worth reproducing here:

> The story of the blind men and the elephant is universally known. Several blind men approached an elephant and each touched the animal in an effort to discover what the beast looked like. Each blind man, however, touched a different part of the large animal, and each concluded that the elephant had the appearance of the part he had touched. Hence the blind man who felt the animal's trunk concluded that an elephant must be tall and slender, while the fellow who touched the beast's ear concluded that an elephant must be oblong and flat. Others of course reached different conclusions. The total result was that no man arrived at a very accurate description of the elephant yet each man had gained enough evidence from his own experience to disbelieve his fellows and maintain a lively debate about the nature of the beast. (Puchala, 1972, 267)

The metaphor has survived in the collective memory of the EU Studies community because it so aptly identifies the problems that can arise when competing theories and approaches become crystallized into non-communicating schools of thought. In this volume, however, we observe that many contemporary scholars are increasingly sensitive to the lessons of the metaphor. Many are open to the possibilities of learning from, combining or even synthesizing what might otherwise be considered conflicting approaches to the study of the EU. With this openness comes an increasing tolerance for, or propensity to accept, the validity of claims made by alternative approaches. We find some evidence of this kind of 'centripetal' tendency in almost every chapter of this book.

Thus, it is not too difficult to piece together a counter-narrative to the argument that mainstream EU Studies has been characterized by the emergence, reproduction and eventual evolution of academic battle lines. For example, O'Neill (1996) has argued that the interdependence theories of the 1970s were truly syncretic in their application to regional integration (O'Neill, 1996). There have also been notable attempts to create explanatory or conceptual frameworks that combine more than one theoretical approach in an effort to capture the complexity of the EU. In other words, the aim of this kind of exercise, to draw on Puchala's metaphor, is to create a framework for research into the EU, which allows the scholar to take evidence of the elephant's trunk, ears and other parts and work them into an understanding of the whole animal. John Peterson's attempts (1995; 2001) to bridge the gap between theories of European integration and policymaking approaches offer an excellent example of this kind of approach. The rationale behind Peterson's efforts is that 'different theoretical models may offer "best" explanations for decision-making at different levels of analysis' (1995, 93): that is, macro theories, such as neofunctionalism or neorealism may be appropriate for the analysis of 'history-making decisions', whereas Comparative Politics and institutionalist approaches better explain 'policy-setting decisions', and policy networks approaches policy-shaping decisions. Another example of a framework approach combines middle-range theories. Andrew Moravcsik's liberal intergovernmentalism is the best-known example of such an approach in EU Studies. Liberal intergovernmentalism brings together three theories: a liberal theory of national preference formation; an intergovernmental theory of bargaining; and a theory of institutional choice, to form a rationalist theory of European integration (Pollack, 2001, 232). The approach allows the different dynamics involved in European integration to be incorporated within the overarching structure.

In this volume, Warleigh's contribution (Chapter 5) on multilevel governance and policy networks applies a still different take on this approach by combining multilevel governance and the policy network literature into a single explanatory framework. Also in this volume, but at a looser, more general level, Radaelli implies that the concept of Europeanization combines a wide variety of mid-level concepts, so that while Europeanization is not a theory in itself, it performs an important role as an 'orchestrating approach'. Thus, although it does not serve as a 'framework' itself, it does provide a conceptual umbrella that may encourage a more eclectic approach to theory-building.

Recent attempts to bridge, or at least to narrow the gap between rationalist and sociological approaches (for example, Aspinwall and Schneider, 2000;

Jupille *et al.*, 2003) also suggest a centripetal tendency in EU Studies. For better or for worse, the differences between 'rationalists', particularly liberal intergovernmentalists and rational institutionalists, on the one hand and, academics who advocate the adoption of 'sociological' approaches, particularly constructivists and sociological institutionalists, on the other, have often been pitched as the great debate of contemporary EU Studies (Pollack, 2001; Wiener and Diez, 2003), reflecting trends in International Relations theory, which have found their way over time into the EU Studies literature. This debate has inspired scholars to rethink the battle lines of their field, and has meant that there has been a potential for former rivals to join together to become part of a new team. Once grouped within the rationalist *genus*, for example, intergovernmentalists, neofunctionalists and multilevel governance theorists suddenly seemed to have more in common than when they belonged to the rival paradigms of regional integration theory. The categories of 'rationalist' and 'sociological' became the new lens through which researchers could develop new approaches, most notably within the broad field of 'institutionalism' (see, for instance, Aspinwall and Schneider, 2000). Here too, developments outside EU Studies, and most notably driven by the work of March and Olsen (1989) on what came to be called the 'new institutionalism', had a major impact on trends within the field.

Although this redefinition of the boundaries of scholarly debate has now become almost hegemonic, there has been evidence of restraint in certain quarters. Some rational institutionalists, for example, have sought to apply concepts within their work that are more often at home in sociological studies. One example of this is the way in which the language of 'ideas' has been imported into this literature. For Garrett and Weingast (1993), for example, ideas serve as 'focal points' that can guide decisionmakers to certain outcomes where there are multiple optimal (or equilibrium) outcomes. One must note, however, that they use 'ideas' as independent or intervening variables in a way that most constructivists would not. Similarly, some constructivists, namely those labelled 'soft' constructivists, have made space for rationality within their frameworks, defining it as one form of 'appropriate' behaviour. Some have gone even further to question the permeability of the boundaries between the 'rationalist' and 'sociological' approaches (Jupille *et al.*, 2003, for example). Still others found it useful to employ both rationalist and constructivist arguments and concepts in tandem, drawing from them competing hypotheses to account for the complexity of EU processes. An example of a topic on which work of this kind has been undertaken is EU enlargement (see Sjursen, 2002; Chapter 6 in this volume).

But it is not only in theorizing or conceptualizing the EU that there is a centripetal tendency of the kind identified above. There is also some evidence of a similar, though perhaps less developed, trend in evidence methodologically. In other words, it is not only the theoretical, but also the methodological cleavages, that are breaking down or being redefined in EU

Studies. Jupille presents himself as an advocate of this kind of methodological eclecticism. This point is further explored in Chapter 12. While not all scholars working on the EU are open to new or alternative ideas, these examples do represent what we identify as a centripetal tendency in EU Studies. This tendency involves openness to and an acknowledgement of the validity of claims generated by various approaches; what some have characterized as a kind of pluralism in the field (Jupille *et al.*, 2003). It involves a search for commonality among approaches, rather than just the identification of difference. This tolerance for theories, concepts and ideas is taken from a variety of sources and the discovery of commonalities among ostensible differences can be built into more comprehensive theoretical frameworks that explicitly aim to combine or merge different approaches. In all these different ways, contemporary EU scholars appear to be taking on board the lessons of Puchala's metaphor.

summary of chapter content and key arguments

We conclude this introductory chapter by summarizing some of the key arguments presented in the chapters that follow below. We begin with two chapters that pick up what is now considered to be the key dividing line in the EU Studies literature: that between rationalist and constructivist approaches to the study of the EU.

In Chapter 2, Roger Scully reviews contributions to and critiques of rationalist research on the EU, including liberal intergovernmentalism, delegation theory and legislative power models (for example, Tsebelis and Garrett, 1996). Drawing on studies of the European Parliament to illustrate his point, Scully demonstrates how rationalist ideas inform important scholarship on the EU, work that attempts, amongst other things, to understand the reduction in ideological dogmatism within the European Parliament's party groups (Kreppel, 2002); MEPs' tendency to follow their domestic party's political line (Hix, 2004); and why MEPs fail to 'go native' (Scully, 2005). No longer an 'eccentric import from various branches of macro-economics', he argues, rationalist approaches are claiming an indispensable role for themselves in EU Studies.

Antje Wiener's chapter focuses on constructivist and sociological institutionalist theory, and its application to the EU. She argues that a close interdisciplinary relationship exists between constructivist political science and organizational sociology. The 'constructivist turn' in EU Studies has thus arisen out of a fairly recent interest in 'the social' by researchers working on the EU, and offers an important tool for the analysis of European integration. Wiener's chapter summarizes the theoretical background to constructivism and sociological institutionalism and provides some pointers to interesting empirical research on the EU.

Chapters 4 and 5 pick up two conceptual approaches, Europeanization and multilevel governance, both of which have become focal points for research on the EU over the past decade or two. The provenance of Claudio M. Radaelli's chapter on Europeanization is the more recent of the two. It questions whether there is any coherence to the literature on Europeanization, and whether this is a new theoretical orientation, or just a fad. In seeing Europeanization as a problem, a set of puzzles or as something to be explained, Radaelli argues that it can help to bring EU Studies into mainstream political science by providing new insights, original explanations and interesting questions that link directly into the research agendas of International Relations, Policy Analysis and Comparative Politics. After introducing the concept, the chapter analyses various perspectives on Europeanization, considers how to make sense of Europeanization when designing research, explores the main mechanisms of the concept and summarizes the principal findings of empirical research. In concluding, Radaelli calls for conceptual clarity when using the concept of Europeanization.

Alex Warleigh's chapter closely ties multilevel governance to the concept of policy networks to argue that the two concepts are most useful when used in tandem. Together, he argues, they provide an understanding of the EU and how it works, whilst helping to fill, as he puts it, a 'theory-shaped hole' in the literature, and accommodating changing understandings of state power. The chapter examines multilevel governance as a concept, its evolution and its application to the EU. While essentially rationalistic, multilevel governance has been reformulated to stress a normative dimension (for example, in work on the democratic deficit). Warleigh then assesses the policy networks literature. The chapter concludes by arguing that multilevel governance and policy networks are complementary, though they perform different analytical tasks, and by constructing a 'working theory of EU governance', before evaluating the strengths and weaknesses and recognizing the limits of such an approach.

In the next pair of chapters, two empirical external relations topics provide a testing ground for some of the theoretical ideas covered in the earlier chapters of the book. Frank Schimmelfennig and Ulrich Sedelmeier begin their chapter on EU enlargement by establishing that this subject was long neglected as a research focus for scholars interested in European integration. Although there are many descriptive case studies, the dearth of theoretical and comparative research on enlargement remains a weakness in the literature on EU Studies. In addressing this weakness, the authors begin their chapter by defining enlargement as 'horizontal institutionalization'. They identify four main dimensions of enlargement (realism, liberal intergovernmentalism, sociological institutionalism and constructivism), and identify key research questions and key explanatory approaches for each of these. Finally, the chapter provides an overview of research into EU enlargement, as a way of demonstrating the utility of the four approaches for structuring the debate in this area. Schimmelfennig and Sedelmeier argue that structuring the debate in this way – that is, using existing analytical tools in International Relations and EU Studies – is preferable to trying to create a grand theory of enlargement. They also conclude that rationalist and constructivist perspectives are both useful frameworks for analysis, and are not necessarily mutually exclusive.

In his chapter, Ben Tonra explores the difficulties associated with conceptualizing the EU as an international actor, and how this exercise has challenged assumptions about what the EU is. By examining different approaches that can be used to rethink the EU's role, he argues that both traditional theories of integration and traditional International Relations theories failed to provide an adequate explanation of the emergence of an EU-level foreign policy. As a consequence of weaknesses in the existing theoretical literature, analysts of the EU's international role were driven to reconceptualize the EU, using both rationalist/positivist and more normative approaches. He concludes his chapter by providing a number of examples of how theorists see the EU's global role and by acknowledging that there are many routes to understanding the EU.

Tackling two key concepts in contemporary EU Studies, identity and legitimacy, the next pair of chapters touch on how sociological (or social-psychological) and philosophical (or political theory) approaches have come to shape this field. Paul Gillespie and Brigid Laffan's chapter looks at the relevance of the concept of identity for the study of European integration and the EU. They argue that political identity is a necessary lens through which to analyse contemporary European integration, and that it forms part of the 'discursive explosion' of recent years. The chapter begins by considering why identity has become so salient in both theoretical and empirical debates about the EU. This, Gillespie and Laffan argue, is linked not only to developments in the EU itself, but also to wider international changes in the 1990s (notably the consequences of the end of the Cold War). The concept of identity remains contested, however. The chapter thus explores different understandings of identity, which in turn are reflected in the ways in which the EU deals with this topic. With political identity so tied up with notions of homogeneity in the modern European state, the authors argue, it is hard to see how it might be possible to apply it to a heterogeneous EU. To do this requires what they call a 'double conceptual disengagement': citizenship from nationalism and ethnicity on the one hand, and democracy from territory, on the other – difficult as this may be to do in practice. The authors go on to reflect on the advantages of engaging in research on identity, not least that this opens the door to new debates about the EU's political order. They emphasize, in particular, the importance of 'cross-disciplinary' work in teaching us more about political identity, though they acknowledge that there is a lot of work still to be done in this area.

Andreas Føllesdal, in his chapter, presents a normative approach to the study of the EU, focusing on the theme of legitimacy, and how the EU (or EU institutions) should be governed. Føllesdal explains why this field of research has become so important in the post-Maastricht period. He does so by reviewing the literature on the legitimacy deficit. To understand the complexities involved in resolving this deficit, Føllesdal then sets out four different conceptions of legitimacy (legality; compliance; problem-solving; and justifiability) and four mechanisms for resolving the problem (participation; democratic rule; actual consent; and output). He explores how researchers might reconcile these alternative conceptions/mechanisms, arguing for a 'unified account' to guide the trade-offs that will inevitably occur when seeking a solution to the legitimacy deficit. To that end, Føllesdal draws on his own work on trust and trustworthiness, and uses the Constitutional Treaty as a focal point for exploring various strategies for enhancing legitimacy. Finally, Føllesdal considers the contribution that normative political theorists may make, through the research they do, to help to legitimize the EU. But he is understandably cautious on this point, as it may well be that the research finds that there is no common good arising out of the EU. If that were the case, then normative political theory could contribute to a weakening rather than a legitimizing of the EU.

In the next two chapters, two further influences on mainstream EU Studies – economics and history – are examined. Amy Verdun's chapter examines political economy approaches that have been used to explain the EU. These, Verdun notes, are situated at the 'intersection of International Relations and Comparative Politics', so that they take on board insights from International Relations debates at the same time as being sensitive to economic structures, institutions and international, national and transnational actors. She argues that political economy has something important to offer EU Studies, not least as it is 'interdisciplinary' and can draw on a wide variety of methodological approaches. Verdun's chapter examines the role of theories and methods in this field. It considers the value of drawing on both political science and economics, and provides some illustrations of the kinds of studies that have adopted a political economy approach.

Wolfram Kaiser's chapter identifies a new interest in the historiography of European integration and the EC institutions, which has its origins in work undertaken in the 1970s. The chapter charts these developments, noting their shortcomings. It explores the relationship between history and social science theorizing in EU Studies, showing how historians have used mainstream EU theory in their own work. Finally, the chapter points to new historical research which acts as a counterpoint to the kind of traditional (mainstream) social science theorizing which pits intergovernmental bargaining against supranational policymaking, notably in the fields of cultural history, transnational relations and socialization research. In making this point, Kaiser's chapter demonstrates that an historical approach to research on the

EU (including European integration) can help the field of EU Studies to evolve theoretically in new directions. Rather than simply 'taking' theory from the mainstream, historians have the potential to help recreate the mainstream at least partially in their own image.

The final two chapters on metatheory and methodology (Jupille) and cleavages, controversies and convergence in EU Studies (Wessels) allow us to stand back from the literature on EU Studies to address some important questions about the nature of this research field. Jupille identifies the principal metatheoretical debates in EU Studies and the various methodologies of choice. This analysis is undertaken with an eye to identifying the limits and opportunities for dialogue and mutual learning among different approaches to the study of the EU. He concludes that there are fewer barriers to such an ambition than some may imagine and he notes that substantial scholarly progress in the direction of bridging work within and across stylistic, social-theoretic, disciplinary, methodological and even ontological dimensions of research has already taken place.

Of all the chapters in this volume, Jupille's work explores in the most extensive and systematic manner the opportunities for synthesis that can arise out of an eclectic or pluralistic approach to EU research. Addressing the possibility for metatheoretical and methodological synthesis, for example, he concludes that EU Studies operates within a 'permissive environment within which a thousand flowers might bloom'. Defining metatheory as the set of general architectural principles guiding the conduct of scholarly enquiry, he identifies five principal dimensions of EU Studies within which lie a number of cleavages and which may or may not be susceptible to synthesis: in the ontological dimension the material is pitted against the social; in the epistemological dimension, a positivist versus post-positivist divide is identified; in the social theoretic dimension, rational choice and constructivist accounts compete; in the disciplinary dimension, we find, for instance economic approaches opposing those of sociology or politics; and in the 'scholarly style' dimension, Jupille pits generalizing against particularizing theories. Abstract reflection and analysis of recent research in the field suggests to Jupille, however, that with some exceptions (most notably in the epistemological dimension) there is wide scope for combining or reconciling what have sometimes been regarded as 'incompatible' approaches.

Interestingly, Jupille raises and addresses two major difficulties with this enterprise: how one might avoid too much consensus which could inhibit debate and restrict the development of the field; and the sheer impossibility for individual scholars to attain expertise in all relevant fields. His answer, following Campbell (1969), is to aim for a 'fish-scale model of omniscience' where in the 'ideal-typical case, each individual becomes specialised in an area of knowledge unique to her' and where there is 'a continuous texture of narrow specialities which overlap with other narrow specialities' (Campbell, 1969, 328 and see Figure 12.4).

Finally, we turn to Wolfgang Wessels' chapter. This chapter is unique in the volume as it is the only contribution that explicitly addresses the teaching of, as well as research into the EU. Moreover, it is fitting, if somewhat ironic, that while our emphasis in this Introduction has been on the propensity for convergence and the centripetal tendencies we are witnessing in EU Studies, Wessels begins this concluding chapter by stressing the confusion and fragmentation that prevails in the field. He paints a picture of the 'state of the art' or as he terms it, the *acquis académique* in EU Studies, as riven by cleavages and as having a market for academic ideas that is not clearly demarcated. However, Wessels also acknowledges that fragmentation and even anarchy in the field of EU Studies is, to a certain degree, the flipside of the openness and pluralism that we, as editors, have identified in this Introduction. Indeed, he explicitly refers to trends in the state of the art as being defined by 'differentiation and pluralistic coexistence'. He calls for a didactic review of the literature on the EU, as a way of revealing more about how the field has developed. At the same time, however, he recognizes the danger inherent in such an exercise, that is, the reification of a subjective interpretation of the literature, which has more to do with what Wessels calls 'footnote cartels', or personal battles and ambitions, than with potential intellectual ends.

Wessels charts the 'pull' from the EU and the 'push' from the discipline, both of which have influenced the growth of activity in EU Studies. On the 'pull' side, he points to new trends in the field, driven by the increasing political relevance of the EU. He points, in particular, to the fact that the EU is now studied as a political system, and that, as such, it makes increasing sense to use political science tools when researching the EU. Applying the term 'governance' has also helped further new research, by side-stepping tensions in the earlier literature between researchers who possessed a *sui generis* view of the EU (that is, assuming the EU to be unique), and those whose primary interest was comparative (that is, those who saw the EU as a case of something, usually other international regimes or organizations). Though these developments are promising for EU research, Wessels cautions against moving away from European integration as an object of study, as the latter provides a sure-fire way of ensuring that research possesses a dynamic element. In other words, researchers working on the EU should not give up on searching for a general theory, but should also, alongside research on specific aspects of the EU, continue to adopt a macro-perspective on the EU.

Wessels goes on to consider how academics might contribute to political debate on the EU, calling for more critical (theoretical) work to be done by academics, work that could feed into the political process. In this respect, he points to the potential of the themes of constitutionalization and enlargement as providing a testing ground for new theories and methodologies. (Interestingly, these are the two case studies examined by Antje Wiener in her chapter – Chapter 3 – on constructivism and sociological institutionalism.)

How research into the EU will evolve is open to question. Wessels is unsure, but identifies three potential futures. The first rests on a slightly modified version of what he calls the 'West European canon'. This suggests more of the same, with only incremental change. The second builds on new dividing lines in the EU – research generated in old versus new states or small versus large states, research which might pick up themes of fragmentation and opposition to the EU. The third constitutes a more substantial change, and is characterized by a deep paradigm shift, which though as yet unidentified, arises out of the emergence of a new post-community Europe.

Finally, Wessels turns to examine the 'pull' of trends within the discipline. Here, the discipline to which he is referring is political science. He identifies what was the marginal position of work on the EU and European integration in political science, though this may be changing. Likewise, he notes that political science trends are now leading to new theoretical directions in and methodological approaches to research in this field – which also contribute to new insights into the EU.

Although Wessels does not say as much, it is not just in political science that disciplinary pushes are likely to have an impact on EU research. As we, the editors, suggest earlier in this introductory chapter, the drive towards an albeit illusive interdisciplinarity is likely to ensure that more than one disciplinary push will impact on the field of EU Studies. Although we accept that this volume privileges political research, and does not aim to set an example by (over) emphasizing non-political perspectives and approaches, we do hope all the same that in fulfilling our more limited ambition of charting some of the mainstream advances in the field, that we can, at the same time, show ourselves to be open to new approaches in what in this volume we have called not European Union Politics, but *European Union Studies*.

2

rational institutionalism and liberal intergovernmentalism

roger scully

introduction

Explicitly 'rationalist' approaches to the study of politics have become an increasingly important part of mainstream political science in recent times. Whereas twenty years ago, rationalist studies of politics might still have been viewed as an assortment of eccentric imports from various branches of microeconomics, such a view is no longer credible. Given the substantial development in rationalist scholarship, it is unsurprising that work in this tradition has achieved increasing prominence in study of the EU. Nor is it surprising that advocates of rationalist approaches claim an indispensable role for themselves in explaining European integration and EU politics.

This chapter reviews the contribution of rationalist scholarship to EU Studies. There are three parts to this review. First, the chapter briefly addresses what is generally meant by 'rationalist' work, and identifies its core claims. Second, the chapter examines where rationalist work has made an important contribution to contemporary understandings of the EU. The discussion here will be critical – the aim is not merely to state what have been the key claims of rationalist works, but also to evaluate their explanatory adequacy. Finally, the chapter will conclude with some general reflections about the current and future contributions of rationalist work in this field of study.

One final introductory comment. For much of their (approximately) fifty years of existence, rationalist approaches to the study of politics have excited controversy amongst scholars.[1] Some have advocated rationalist approaches as indispensable in making the study of politics a properly scientific enterprise (for example, Riker, 1982 and 1990), with the implication that other forms of scholarship are innately inferior; others view rationalist work as an abomination, or at least as having only a very marginal contribution to make in understanding the political world.[2] The position from which I write this chapter is located between these extremes: neither 'rational choice down to my DNA' (Fiorina, 1996, 85), nor abhorring rationalist work as irredeemably misconceived. Moreover, to argue, as I will, that rationalist scholarship has made, and should continue to make, an important contribution to the study of the EU does not mean that all rationalist contributions are important or that all important contributions must be rationalist.

defining rationalism

All human beings are, in an important sense, rationalists. In understanding why people do things, we commonly resort to explanations based on a rational link between ends and means: for example, X did A because they sought to achieve goal Y – A being a reasonable, rational means by which to achieve Y. It appears to be a universal feature of human thought to believe that people's actions can often be understood as a means of achieving particular aims (Pinker, 1999). Few, if any, of us would contend that this is the whole story, however. Emotions are also a powerful influence on our actions; so too are humans' limited (and in some ways systematically biased) cognitive capabilities; and our actions are also inevitably shaped by numerous features of the context in which we find ourselves, including the behaviour of other people. But the basic idea regarding the rational pursuit of objectives seems to be a universal part of 'common sense' understandings of human behaviour, and it is as relevant to politics as to any other aspect of life. To give a familiar example: understanding why the British Labour party in the mid-1990s went through the changes that transformed it into 'New Labour' cannot be accomplished *solely* through focusing on the desire of party leaders to maximize their electoral appeal and so win the 1997 UK election; but this factor is surely integral to any serious understanding of that leadership behaviour.

In essence, rationalist approaches are basically a development and extension of this basic idea: that if people in certain contexts are seeking certain ends, some actions will be a more rational means of achieving those ends than others. As such, there is a rationalist element to virtually all analyses of political life, and this element has been particularly evident in many famous works.[3] The key distinction in contemporary rationalist scholarship is that, following the tradition developed in microeconomics, it seeks to be highly explicit and rigorous in the definition and analysis of some key factors, including:

- *The actors under consideration.* Among the important questions here are whether we are examining individuals or collective entities, and whether we are concerned with understanding their behaviour considered separately or in a situation of strategic interaction.[4]

- *The nature of the goals sought.* As stated above, we commonly assume that people act in the pursuit of goals. But rationalist scholarship generally seeks explicitness about the goals that actors are presumed to be seeking: for instance, by distinguishing between the primary interests of political parties in winning votes, winning political office, or achieving policy goals (e.g. Strom, 1990).

- *The information available to actors.* Much work proceeds on the simplifying assumption that actors have 'perfect information' about the consequences of choosing between alternative courses of action, and/or about the preferences of other actors. Other rationalist work tries to develop models based on more realistic assumptions of information that is limited in some respects.

- *The options available and actors' preferences among those options.* Actors are usually presumed to be aware of available options and to have clear preferences between those options. A common further assumption made is that actors' preferences are *transitive* – that is, they are sufficiently consistent to ensure that if someone prefers option A to option B, and option B to option C, then they will also prefer A to C.

- *Other salient features of the context.* Rationalist work usually tries to be explicit about other aspects of the situation in which actors find themselves beyond those specified above. A sophisticated body of work known as *rational institutionalism* is concerned with how features of the context – such as the order in which multiple decisions are taken – can have important consequences for the final outcomes that are reached; rational institutionalism has therefore also considered that, anticipating the likely consequences of particular institutional arrangements for the sort of substantive decisions that will be made, rational actors will develop preferences for institutional arrangements likely to facilitate substantive decisions that they favour.[5]

The explicit and often highly complex treatment of the above factors through techniques such as extensive-form game theory and mathematical modelling of expected utility functions can render much rationalist work quite alien to many other scholars.[6] But such techniques are not in themselves a defining feature of rationalist work; and it is valuable to keep in mind the roots of rationalist scholarship as an 'extended common sense'.

The development of a serious and self-consciously rationalist study of politics dates from the 1950s. Probably the first landmark work was that of Arrow (1951), which made a huge contribution to the development of serious thinking about the problems of collective 'social choice'. Arrow suggested that the aggregation of individual preferences over different issues cannot be assumed to produce an objectively 'correct' outcome, but that collective choice is highly conditioned by the particular institutional rules employed. Arrow also demonstrated, making some basic and not unreasonable assumptions about individual preferences, that it was impossible to develop a system for collective preference aggregation guaranteed not to produce outcomes that are inconsistent or arbitrary.

A second major contribution, which has also spawned much subsequent work, was Downs' *Economic Theory of Democracy* (1957). Downs drew on a rather obscure branch of microeconomics – location theory – to examine how vote-seeking political parties should be expected to behave, concluding that they could be expected to become ideologically centrist, converging on the 'median voter'.[7] (In the 1950s era of 'tweedledum-tweedledee' politics in the US, and the 'Butskellist' consensus in the UK, this conclusion struck many chords!) However, Downs' work also produced puzzling paradoxes – for party competition if more than two parties were assumed, and also for understanding the behaviour of voters. Given the infinitesimally small chance of any single voter's ballot being decisive in an election, then if the act of voting imposed any significant costs at all on citizens, to vote appeared itself to be irrational: a rational citizen should 'free ride' on the votes of others. Much work since the 1950s has been devoted to trying to resolve these paradoxes.

A third highly influential work was Olson's (1965) examination of the functioning of interest groups in society. Reacting to work in many disciplines that assumed that people are motivated to join and participate in groups for the collective good, Olson examined these decisions from the perspective of the individual. He suggested that 'only a *separate and "selective" incentive* will stimulate a rational individual in a latent group to act in a group-oriented way' (1965, 51; emphasis in original). Like Downs' discussion of the rationality of voting, Olson pointed to the problems of people 'free riding' on collective goods supplied by the efforts of others, and his work has had enormous impact in developing both the theoretical and empirical study of collective action.[8]

While the rationalist work following on from the starting points listed above, and others, has come to be of great importance in the social sciences, it is fair to say that its impact on the study of the EU more specifically has been slow. There is little indication of rationalist influences in the landmark neofunctionalist study by Haas (1958) nor in much other work during the first decades of European integration. In the last ten years, however, this situation has changed, and in what follows, I will examine how.

choosing integration: liberal intergovernmentalism

Liberal intergovernmentalism is an approach to understanding the European integration process that has been developed principally by Andrew Moravcsik. In a series of major works (see particularly Moravcsik, 1991, 1993, 1998a and 1999), Moravcsik has developed an approach to the study of European integration that has proven highly influential: while a significant part of the agenda of EU Studies over the last decade has comprised scholars attacking (either implicitly or explicitly) some or other aspects of the liberal intergovernmentalism edifice, few if any have been able to match Moravcsik's work for theoretical clarity, empirical reach or rhetorical force. Although Moravcsik's work has developed considerably in theoretical subtlety and empirical scope over time, the core precepts of liberal intergovernmentalism have remained consistent from the beginning. European integration is argued to proceed primarily through a series of major decisions taken by national leaders, usually incorporated into treaty agreements. Notwithstanding the efforts of interest groups, other EU institutions (like the European Parliament) and supranational 'entrepreneurs' (such as notable Presidents of the European Commission, including Walter Hallstein and Jacques Delors), the agenda for and the negotiations leading towards these major decisions have remained dominated by national governments and national interests – with the efforts of the supranational 'entrepreneurs', lauded in other accounts, dismissed by Moravcsik as 'generally *late, redundant, futile and sometimes even counterproductive'* (1999, 269–70; emphasis in original). National interests themselves are regarded as being defined primarily by domestic economic factors and national leaders seeking economic advantage. Thus, just as Milward's earlier detailed research had suggested that Belgian support for the European Coal and Steel Community was motivated as much by the needs of the Belgian coal industry as by a fervent European-mindedness (Milward, 1992), so Moravcsik finds that President de Gaulle's European policy was shaped far more by the needs of French farming than traditional historiography – which has concentrated more on de Gaulle's ideas of French '*grandeur*' and his suspicions of the Anglo-American relationship – would suggest (1998a, chapter 3).

Moravcsik's more recent work (1998a) has developed his theoretical ideas on integration into an explicit three-stage model: the first being *National Preference Formation*, shaping what countries bring to the negotiating table; the second, *Inter-State Bargaining* between member states; and the third being the encapsulation of important parts of an agreement in *International Institutions*. Moravcsik's 1998(a) book is also his most methodologically advanced analysis: he applies his model of integration to the five major integration agreements from the 1950s through to the 1990s, and for every case tests his model against plausible counter-hypotheses at each of the three stages.[9]

Moravcsik's account is *intergovernmentalist* because national governments are viewed as controlling the process; and *liberal* in viewing economic issues (rather than military-strategic considerations) as the major drivers of international cooperation. It is also rationalist in several respects. First, it follows the broad approach of most rationalist work in grounding its explanatory framework in the rational pursuit of pre-defined interests (in this case, the broad economic interests of particular member states). Second, it understands the outcomes of international negotiations as being determined primarily by factors identified by rationalist theories of bargaining (such as the relative benefits to be obtained from an agreement by different parties, their realistic alternatives to an agreement, and their access to information and 'side-payments').[10] Finally, Moravcsik follows a rationalist approach in viewing international institutions as existing primarily to overcome problems of coordination among nation-states and to help embed 'credible commitments' where cooperation is potentially beneficial, but subject to breakdown owing to cheating.

While liberal intergovernmentalism has been described as 'compelling' (Puchala, 1999), there are a number of respects in which it can be, and often has been, subject to criticism. Moravcsik's most detailed and far-reaching account (1998a) draws on a considerable range of historical evidence, but it is certainly possible that his interpretation of parts of that evidence could be disputed. And while the range of his historical scholarship in *The Choice for Europe* has won widespread praise, his heavy concentration on only the preferences and behaviour of the EU's three leading states – (West) Germany, France and the UK – quite probably means that he gives insufficient attention at times to the role of other states. Moravcsik's fundamental aim of providing a general explanation of major steps in the integration process is not shared by all scholars – notably by those identifying with 'post-positivist' epistemological positions (for example, Diez, 1999). And even some accepting his rationalist premises find problematic the sharp analytic distinction that Moravcsik draws between the bargaining and institutionalization stages in his model (for example, Schimmelfennig, 2003b).

There are at least two further areas where the explanatory adequacy of liberal intergovernmentalism can be questioned. One concerns exactly what Moravcsik is trying to explain, and what evidence is relevant to it. Put simply, if one only examines instances of integration decisions taken by national governments, it is not particularly surprising that he draws the conclusion that the integration process is dominated by national governments. But for liberal intergovernmentalism to be a remotely adequate explanation of European integration as a whole, it must also be established that activities by entities other than national governments are of relatively limited importance to integration (Wincott, 1995). And yet other scholars have presented substantial evidence that other actors, such as the European Court of Justice, have had an impact on integration (Sandholtz and Stone Sweet, 1998; Scharpf, 1999; Stone Sweet, 2000). Moravcsik's ostensible solution to this problem in *The Choice for Europe* is to insist that he is not explaining the entirety of integration but only a series of important decisions: yet it is clear that he regards these decisions as central to the broader integration process.[11] Little attention is given to the possibility that the relevant causal arrow may run at least partly in the reverse direction – that much of the substance about which the governments negotiate might itself be shaped by other parts of the integration process. Relatedly, Moravcsik's account accords only limited attention to ways in which European integration may become self-sustaining. Some of these are readily incorporated into rationalist accounts – for example, the 'sunk-costs' of past integration deals may make further integration a more attractive solution to economic problems than other alternatives; but other factors are more difficult to 'rationalize' in this way – for instance, the possibility that integration begins to change the fundamental identities and preferences of actors.

The second issue that should be considered further is domestic politics. This is crucial to liberal intergovernmentalism in the sense that national preferences are believed to derive from reasons of national economic advantage, rather than imposed by some over-powering 'logic' of the international system. Yet Moravcsik has very little to say about domestic politics; indeed, it largely washes out of his account. It would appear that control of government by different political parties, or alternative political systems and structures, are essentially epiphenomenal to explaining major advances in integration: economic circumstances are what matter. Actually, this may well be largely true for the episodes that Moravcsik examines, episodes that occurred during an historic era in which integration was largely a consensual issue across most EU member states. But the irrelevance of domestic politics is almost certainly less true now, as integration has come to be increasingly a matter of partisan political contention. In this respect, liberal intergovernmentalism as currently formulated may be reflective of a particular time and place that is now passing; and further development of work in this tradition may well require a more substantial account of the political processes through which national preferences emerge.

choosing integration: delegation and agency

An increasingly important area of rationalist scholarship in political science in recent years has focused on the delegation of power. When do organizations devolve responsibilities to others, and how do they seek to avoid the dangers of 'shirking': that is, that 'agents' granted powers will pursue goals different from those of the 'principal' who has given them their task? In American political science, this approach has been particularly influential in the study of how elected politicians relate to government bureaucracies and other agencies that have major public power delegated to them (Moe, 1984; Epstein and O'Halloran, 1999). And more recently, this perspective has also been applied to the question of why political leaders in Europe have been willing to delegate substantial prerogatives to EU institutions.

The major scholar studying delegation and agency at the EU level has been Mark Pollack (2003a). Pollack has argued that the establishment and delegation of powers to supranational 'agents' like the Commission, European Court of Justice and the European Central Bank should be viewed as motivated 'primarily to lower the transaction costs of policy-making, in particular by allowing member governments to credibly commit themselves to international agreements and to benefit from the policy-relevant expertise provided by supranational actors' (Pollack, 2003b, 142). Although paralleling Moravcsik in the importance accorded to 'credible commitments', Pollack places substantially less emphasis than the former on the limits of integration and the extent to which national governments remain in control of the EU. Rather, he acknowledges that European integration is a far-reaching process in which some important powers have been ceded by national governments; his explanatory task is to explain where and why this has been done.

Pollack identifies four main reasons why delegation to supranational agents occurs. The first, *monitoring compliance with existing agreements* explains much about the important roles played by both the Commission and the European Court of Justice in operating as broadly independent arbiters, ensuring against defection from collective agreements. In a similar manner, the same two institutions also have an important task in *solving problems of 'incomplete contracting'* in EU treaties and other agreements: considerable powers are granted to the Commission to produce much secondary legislation, while the European Court of Justice produces much European law through its rulings. Third, Pollack points to the importance of *having credible regulation where principals may be ill-informed or biased*: in addition to its role in monitoring a government's compliance with regulations, the Commission has a more direct and immediate role in implementation and policy regulation in a few areas, such as competition and state aid policy, where problems are most likely to occur. Finally, he shows that powers may be delegated over *setting the legislative agenda* in order to forestall potential problems of legislative instability. Here, the monopoly of legislative initiative that has long been granted to the Commission, alongside the EU's restrictive legislative procedures, appears of great importance.

There are some important qualifications to Pollack's argument about delegation. A first is one explicitly developed by the author himself, following the line of argument taken in much of the American literature. Governments are not believed to be willing to delegate power indiscriminately, or without imposing some safeguards. In the context of the EU, as Pollack and others (for example, Franchino, 2000) have shown, mechanisms such as 'comitology' can be and are used to vary the degree of discretion given to, and oversight exercised upon, the Commission in particular.[12] A second limitation, one that Pollack again draws explicit attention to, is that the logics of delegation discussed above fare much less well in explaining the empowerment of the European Parliament. Here, as Pollack suggests and as Rittberger (2003) has elaborated on, concerns about the legitimacy of the EU as a whole appear far more relevant to the institutional reforms that have invested prerogatives in an EU body. Overall, Pollack's work is powerful and largely persuasive; its broad message on integration is best understood, I would suggest, not as contradictory to that of Moravcsik, but as one that offers a much more detailed and refined understanding of how and why integration is institutionalized. Nonetheless, as it stands, there are also some clear limitations to this body of work. Principal-agent frameworks, as acknowledged by Pollack, are for a number of reasons generally difficult to test empirically. While substantial empirical evidence has been uncovered that is consistent with claims that integration proceeds from a logic of delegation, there often seem to be either alternative interpretations of this evidence or other bodies of evidence that point in rather different directions. Thus, comitology can plausibly be viewed as explicable largely through Habermasian deliberative democracy and/or social constructivist premises (Joerges and Neyer, 1997a and 1997b); while Stone Sweet and Caporaso (1998) cast serious doubt on the explanatory reach of a principal-agent framework in explaining judicial politics in the EU. Pollack and others have not yet been able (to the extent that, for instance, Moravcsik does) to test their claims rigorously against plausible alternative explanations. This is the next obvious empirical step for work in this area.

A second potential line of critique is that it is not always clear that principal-agent approaches have yet been able to articulate with a high degree of precision both why powers should be delegated by governments in some areas, but also why they would not be delegated in other areas. While a highly plausible case can be, and often has been, developed to explain instances of delegation and some degree of variation in delegation, attention still appears focused heavily on a very limited range of the dependent variables, with the concomitant risks of producing biased causal inferences because it selects (see King *et al.*, 1994). Put more simply, a powerful explanation of delegation should also, and at the same time, contain within it an equally powerful explanation of *non*-delegation. It is not clear that this has yet been sufficiently accomplished.

legislating for europe

As Simon Hix has observed, 'the EU probably has the most formalised and complex set of decision-making rules of any political system in the world' (2005, 3). An important addition to the literature on the EU in recent years has been the detailed study of these rules and their implications. One body of work has examined countries in the EU Council in terms of their 'voting power' under Qualified Majority Voting (QMV; under unanimity voting rules in the Council, of course, all countries have effectively the same voting power).[13] Voting power is essentially defined as the ability to make or break a qualified majority. This work has been useful as a general summation of the implications of alternative voting weights and rules, but it takes no account of the increasing role in EU legislation of the European Parliament, nor of the political positions of particular states (states are assumed to be randomly distributed across the policy space) and thus their prior probability of occupying a pivotal voting position. Hence, the overall contribution of this work to understanding legislative institutions in the EU is quite small.

A more interesting and provocative body of literature has sought to examine the inter-institutional dynamics of the revised legislative procedures (cooperation and codecision) that the EU has employed over a growing amount of lawmaking since the Single European Act of 1986. This latter work draws explicitly on the analytical tradition in the US that, recognizing the potential for instability in collective choice processes, studies institutional rules for their role in shaping choices and generating 'structure-induced equilibria' (Shepsle, 1979; see Weingast, 2002 for an excellent summary review). The main pioneer in adapting these concepts and methods for use in the EU has been George Tsebelis (1994). Working mainly with Geoffrey Garrett (Garrett and Tsebelis, 1996; Tsebelis and Garrett, 2000), Tsebelis has written a highly influential series of papers that have sought to examine systematically the implications of variations in EU legislative procedures. This work has sometimes produced powerfully counter-intuitive findings.

Work in this tradition proceeds by explicitly stating assumptions about the type of policy space in which actors are assumed to operate (one-, two- or multi-dimensional), and then exploring the implications of alternative institutional rules while making certain other assumptions about the positions of the key actors within the policy space. For instance, much of Tsebelis' work has been based around the simple spatial representation in Figure 2.1.[14] Here, the single dimension of the policy space is usually assumed to be one of more or less integration; rather than try to represent all of the countries in the Council (15 at the time that most of this work was published) with their varying voting weights, the Council is represented in simplified form as seven states (the ideal policy positions of each represented by their location along the dimension) with equal voting weights, and with a 5/7 majority assumed to satisfy QMV requirements; the European Parliament and Commission are assumed (as unitary actors) to take more pro-integration positions than any of the governments, who are themselves supportive of varying degrees of further integration.

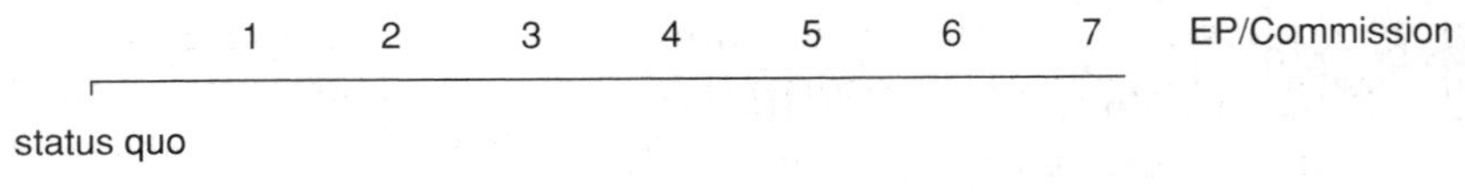

| 1 | 2 | 3 | 4 | 5 | 6 | 7 | EP/Commission |

status quo

Figure 2.1 A simplified model of the EU policy space

Based on such assumptions, Tsebelis (1994) suggested that the cooperation procedure gave the European Parliament more potential legislative power than had generally been realized: the rules of cooperation would allow the European Parliament to make a proposal that, if endorsed by the Commission (which, on the assumptions of the model, it would be) could be passed by QMV but only amended by unanimity in the Council. The pivotal government in this simplified Council is, under these circumstances, government 3; the European

Parliament, Tsebelis suggested, could offer this government a proposal (around the ideal point of government 5) that it would prefer to the status quo, and with no prospect of attaining better, government 3 should support this. Thus, the European Parliament would have the ability to make a 'take-it-or-leave-it' offer to government 3 to advance integration substantially. This ability Tsebelis termed 'conditional agenda setting'.

Tsebelis and Garrett (1996) went on to make the argument that the original version of the codecision procedure, included in the Maastricht Treaty, actually turned the tables and allowed the Council to become the conditional agenda setter. This argument was even more counter-intuitive than Tsebelis' work on cooperation, for it contradicted the conventional wisdom that had seen codecision as a substantial step forward for the European Parliament in granting it an irrevocable legislative veto. However, while Tsebelis' earlier work had been questioned (Moser 1996), the latter argument was criticized heavily on two fronts. A first, 'internal' critique suggested that even if the logic of Tsebelis and Garrett's model was accepted, the negative consequence of the Maastricht codecision procedure that they deduced did not follow: that codecision should never produce a worse policy outcome for the European Parliament than cooperation and it might even – if the ideal position of some actors was allowed to vary in the model – produce substantially better outcomes from the Parliament's perspective (Scully, 1997a and 1997b; Rittberger, 2000).[15] And secondly, several 'external' critiques observed that while Tsebelis probably had been correct in identifying cooperation as an important advance in the legislative influence of the European Parliament, a variety of qualitative and quantitative evidence converged on the conclusion that Maastricht had increased the European Parliament's 'clout' in EU lawmaking yet further (Garman and Hilditch, 1998; Rittberger, 2000; Tsebelis et al., 2001).

Other rather more general critiques of this work have also been developed. It has not escaped notice that the conclusions that these models of legislative procedures produce are usually highly dependent on very specific assumptions regarding the number of actors involved, their precise positions in the policy space and the dimensions of that space. Tsebelis and Garrett were never able to demonstrate satisfactorily that the assumptions that they made were even 'stylized facts' (that is, true in a general and approximate sense), but only that they seemed broadly appropriate as rough characterizations of EU politics. With far-reaching conclusions depending on quite arbitrary assumptions, it is unsurprising that some of those closely involved in legislative politics in the EU were dismissive about the extent to which this work actually captured many of the important political realities which they faced (Corbett, 2000).

Indeed, the work reviewed above brings into sharp relief a broader issue about the tradition of spatial modelling in political science within which this work sits. Practitioners in this intellectual tradition rarely acknowledge the extent to which their work is based on an analogy between the very precisely defined notion of a 'dimension' in mathematics and the much looser sense in which we can speak of a 'left–right' or an 'integration' dimension in the realm of politics. Much modelling work treats these with an equivalence that they do not possess. Even when carried out with a high degree of care, analysts are effectively applying mathematical precision to very imprecise concepts – or, put more crudely, doing mathematics on a metaphor. This suggests that while 'internal' arguments about the implications of a model are important to get right, they can still only grant us quite limited insight into the substantive political questions with which we are ultimately concerned.

representation in Europe

There are an increasing number of new areas where rationalist ideas are informing important scholarship on the EU. Several of these, which have produced important pieces of work, go beyond that reviewed immediately above, in looking not just at the growing importance of the European Parliament in EU policymaking, but also in considering aspects of the internal politics of the EU's unique, multinational elected chamber.

The increased powers received by the European Parliament are the point of departure for Amie Kreppel's excellent recent study (Kreppel, 2002). Her concern is with the impact of such exogenous change on the European Parliament's system of multinational party groups. The overall pattern, she finds, is one of 'movement away from egalitarian internal structures and strongly ideological coalitions toward increased internal centralization of power and ideological moderation' (2002, 10). Kreppel connects a 'macro' perspective (suggesting that institutions reform in response to important changes in the broader political context) with more detailed 'micro' hypotheses about the character of internal parliamentary reforms. As she observes, 'as the European Parliament acquired the power to impact legislative outcomes, the political groups could no longer afford ideological dogmatism if the European Parliament was to maximize its new powers' (Kreppel, 2002, 36). Kreppel's work constitutes an important advance in understanding the internal politics of the European Parliament.

Another major recent contribution has been made in Simon Hix's work on roll-call voting in the European Parliament. Hix has not only been involved in a major data-gathering exercise, with the entire corpus of votes in the European Parliament having been collected and made publicly available,[16] but has also pushed the analysis of voting in the European Parliament far further than any work conducted hitherto. He has used the immense body of voting data now available to develop and test theories of political behaviour in the context of the European Parliament. Hix (2002) applies a Principal-Agent model to the understanding of Member of the European Parliament's (MEP) voting, suggesting that MEPs operate with two principals – their national party and their European party group. Hix finds that in most votes, the two do not come into conflict; however, when they do, MEPs in general are far more likely to support their national party than their European one. In a more recent paper, Hix (2004a) pushes the analysis further by analysing voting patterns in relation to the electoral institutions under which MEPs are nominated and then elected. Hix finds that electoral systems that permit substantial candidate-based voting, and candidate selection procedures that are decentralized within member states, allow MEPs to be more responsive to the leadership of their European Parliamentary party group; however, when MEPs are elected under voting systems where their electoral fate is entirely in the hands of their party, and when the national party leadership also strongly controls candidate selection, then MEPs find themselves more strongly influenced to follow their national party line.

Finally, I have myself (Scully, 2005) contributed one of the relatively few works that has explored rationalist ideas alongside alternative perspectives. An important part of many theoretical accounts of European integration, including some recent work that draws on broader social constructivist perspectives, is a theory of elite political socialization. Put simply, those most closely involved in EU politics, such as those serving in institutions like the European Parliament or the Commission, have often been posited as liable to 'go native' by becoming, as a result of their experiences in these institutions, progressively more pro-integration in their attitudes and behaviour. My work has explored this idea in the context of the European Parliament. A variety of empirical evidence about various aspects of MEPs' attitudes and behaviour is examined, but this yields no sign at all of substantial socialization processes in the hypothesized direction. Why do MEPs' not 'go native'? The most coherent explanation, I suggest, is one grounded in assumptions, common to much rationalist work on representation, that MEPs' behaviour will be shaped primarily by the objectives of 'Election', 'Policy', and 'Office'. Institutional socialization, I argue, operates most powerfully when helping actors to achieve their core goals; in the case of the European Parliament, I show that 'going native' would actually hinder this.

The works explored in this section do not by any means exhaust the body of rationalist literature on the European Parliament, still less that on other aspects of the EU beyond that which has already been reviewed here. But – in addition to being important contributions in themselves – they do illustrate the broader point that rationalist work on the EU is not a marginal part of the literature, but making important contributions to the mainstream of EU Studies, and informing the study of major political questions.

conclusion

This chapter has reviewed some of the major contributions of rationalist scholarship to studies of the EU. While the discussion has not been able to cover all areas of rationalist work – indeed, the very proliferation of rationalist work on the EU alluded to above makes this all but impossible[17] – it should by now be clear that rationalist scholarship has made some major contributions to learning and debate about European integration and the politics of the EU. The general argument advanced here has not been that all major contributions must be rationalist; but that a number of them have been, and will likely be in the future.

To reach this conclusion is not to suggest that rationalist assumptions provide an analytical 'magic bullet', inevitably penetrating to depths of understanding that other approaches cannot hope to reach; nor that rationalist scholarship in the social sciences has, in general, been without problems. Green and Shapiro (1994) have argued convincingly that much rationalist work has been characterized by a number of 'pathologies'. They further suggest that these problems have been the consequence of much rationalist work being 'method-led' rather than 'problem-led': that is, taking as a starting point 'how might rationalism explain X?' or 'how might a rationalist explanation of X be validated?', rather than searching for the best possible explanation of a phenomenon – which might or might not be grounded primarily in rationalist premises. While method-driven research is hardly unique to rationalism, and while it still may produce some good work, Green and Shapiro's general point is well-made. In the context of EU Studies, greater analytical benefits are likely to derive not from asking 'how might rationalist premises explain particular features of the EU?' but from posing more fundamental questions, such as: 'what are the most important questions about the EU that scholars can ask and should try to answer?' and 'how does rationality interact with other facets of human nature and organization to produce the politics that we seek to understand?' (Green and Shapiro, 1994, 204).

People who study the EU are seeking to understand one of the most remarkable political creations in human history. To the extent that rationalist ideas can continue to make a contribution to learning about the EU, they will thus be making a contribution of immense value.

notes

1. For an informative and entertaining collection that illustrates some of the controversies that rationalist work can generate see Friedman (1996).
2. Complaints about the undue prominence given to rationalist work, and contentions about its marginal contribution to the development of understanding, were a central element in the anonymous 'Perestroika' manifesto of 2000 that caused considerable controversy in American political science. The manifesto attracted public attention for its scathing critique of the American Political Science Association, and prompted sharp debates within many university departments and at several conferences.
3. Green and Shapiro mention, as examples, Thomas Hobbes' *Leviathan*, much of the work of Karl Marx, and Hans Morgenthau's *Politics Among Nations* (1994: 3); numerous other examples could easily be adduced.
4. Much rationalist work does seek to ground its explanations in individual-level analysis, but many do not or they analyse collective entities as if they were unitary actors.

5. For a summary of rational institutionalism, see Weingast (2002).

6. The implications of the highly technical nature of much rationalist work for much of the debate over the value of such approaches are nicely summarized by Green and Shapiro: '[P]rotagonists tend to speak past one another. Practitioners operate within the confines of an esoteric technical vocabulary that is seldom understood by anyone else. Critics tend to ignore or heap scorn on the rational choice approach without understanding it fully. They dismiss its assumptions or scientific aspirations, or they get it wrong in elementary ways. Not surprisingly, practitioners generally ignore them' (1994, ix).

7. A hugely important work in understanding the importance of the 'median voter' for modelling of collective choice was that of Duncan Black (1958). Black's work was in turn developed in a hugely important way by McKelvey (1976), who showed the very high probability of collective choice in multiple dimensions being 'chaotic'; and this work in turn has been a major stimulus to much of the rational-institutionalist research examining how institutional mechanisms can bring greater order to, and shape the outcomes of, political choice processes.

8. One important direction in which work on collective action has been taken is the examination of the use (and abuse) of public goods – an important landmark here was Hardin's essay on 'The Tragedy of the Commons' (1968).

9. Specifically, Moravcsik examines whether or not Preference Formation was shaped primarily by geopolitical interests rather than economic ones; that Negotiations were led by supranational factors rather than intergovernmental ones; and that the Institutionalization of Agreements followed 'federalist ideology' or 'technocratic management' imperatives rather than ones of 'credible commitment'.

10. Or, as Moravcsik himself puts it, 'Those who gained the most economically from integration compromised the most on the margin to realize it, whereas those who gained the least or for whom the costs of adaptation were highest imposed conditions' (1998a, 3).

11. As Moravcsik puts it, 'Each grand bargain ... set the agenda for a period of consolidation, helping to define the focus and pace of subsequent decision-making' (1998a, 1–2).

12. A strong argument could be developed that one of the most important contributions of the work of Pollack and others on 'integration as delegation' is the impetus it has given and continues to give for substantially more research to be conducted on comitology. While much of the subject matter of the individual committees concerned may be arcane, the political issues raised by the existence and functioning of these bodies are certainly not arcane.

13. Hosli (1997) also examines the voting power of groups in the European Parliament; for more general examples of the voting power literature applied to the Council see Hosli (1996), Raunio and Wiberg (1998).

14. Some of Tsebelis' work (for example, Tsebelis 1994) has gone beyond the simple one-dimensional model presented here, and used a more complex two-dimensional representation.

15. It is also worth noting that, just as much of the academic controversy of Tsebelis and Garrett's arguments was erupting in print, the codecision procedure itself was being amended in the 1997 Amsterdam Treaty in a manner that removed the major point of theoretical contention!

16. The data on roll-call votes in the European Parliament since 1979 is freely available from: <http://personal.lse.ac.uk/HIX/HixNouryRolandEPdata.HTM>.

17. The journal *European Union Politics* (established in 2000) has been a particularly prominent outlet for much recent rationalist work on the EU. One recent issue (December 2003) selected at random illustrates the increasing diversity of rationalist work, including as it does articles on judicial politics in the EU, bureaucratic and budgetary politics, agricultural politics and EU enlargement, and rationalist 'analytical narratives' on the historic development of the EU, as well as continued discussion about the utility of voting power analysis.

3

constructivism and sociological institutionalism

antje wiener

introduction

This chapter demonstrates the close interdisciplinary relationship between constructivist political science and organizational sociology. What is now commonly called the 'constructivist turn' in International Relations theory and, subsequently, in studies of European integration, builds on an interest in 'the social' among political scientists. This interest follows from the observation that many analyses of institutions tend to be 'undersocialised in the sense that they pay insufficient attention to the ways in which actors in world politics are socially constructed' (Wendt, 1999, 3–4). This has produced a new focus on the input of social facts (Ruggie, 1998) and the influence of social practices (Wendt, 1987; Koslowski and Kratochwil, 1994), and has facilitated an enhanced understanding of the social construction of European integration (Christiansen *et al.*, 2001). As I argue in this chapter, this focus on the social represents a conceptual innovation of paradigmatic reach in political science, and offers an important tool for analysis of European integration.

The chapter summarizes the theoretical background from which constructivist and sociological institutionalist approaches have emerged and points to some important examples of empirical research on the EU where they have proven particularly insightful. It begins by addressing the importance of institution-building beyond the state, a core research object for those who study the EU. It then goes on to identify key elements of constructivist and sociological institutionalist approaches. The final section illustrates the application of these approaches in empirical research on EU enlargement and European constitutionalism.

institutions as object of analysis in european integration research

Institutions can be defined as formal and informal procedures, routines, norms and conventions, embedded in the organizational structure of the polity or political economy (Hall and Taylor, 1996, 938). It is noteworthy that constructivists and sociological institutionalists tend to focus on soft institutions, such as ideas, social and cultural norms, rules and routinized practices. Institutions have become important objects of investigation for analysts of European integration, in part due to theoretical spillover from International Relations theory and sociology. Many working within these disciplines share an interest in understanding the expanding processes of governance beyond the nation-state (Jupille *et al.*, 2003). Another important explanation for the importance of institutions in this field follows from the fact that the Europolity's design fundamentally depends on supranationally-constructed and transnationally-evolving institutions. European integration challenges the realist assumption of an international society of independent states governed by the principle of anarchy (Bull, 1977). It raises questions about states' interest in formal institution-building and cooperation, and about the influence exerted by these new institutions on state behaviour (for an overview see Cram, 1996 or Cini, 2003).

It is possible to observe some other general trends in how those who do research on European integration have approached the study of institutions. At first sight, institution-building in the integration process appears to rely decisively on the founding treaties and their periodic revision at intergovernmental conferences. Yet, while the acts of treatymaking and revision are always submitted to a final decision within the institutional framework of the Council (which grants voice and vote to the signatories of the treaties), the actual substance of treaty revisions is usually discussed, conceptualized and prepared by other European political organs. Since the Maastricht treaty negotiations, groups and bodies, including the Commission (as guardian of the treaties), the Committee of Permanent Representatives and, increasingly, the European Parliament, lobby groups and interinstitutional groups,[1] have gained considerable influence over this process. As such, it has not only become important to produce factual accounts of institutional change relating to the four central organs of the EU – the Council, the Commission, the Court of Justice and the Parliament. It has also become important to explain which actors' interests were most decisive in the process; what motivated changes; what ends participating actors pursued; and what consequences institutional change entailed for power relations. In other words, analysis of the role of actors, processes and organizational structures has been an important theme in the field, particularly with a view to understanding processes of interest aggregation, identity-formation and the transfer of action potential.

approaches to institutional analysis

It is helpful to distinguish three main types of institutional analysis: agency-oriented rational actor models; structure-oriented approaches; and interactive approaches. The first of these was discussed fully in Chapter 2 of this volume and will, therefore only be briefly addressed here. I will elaborate on constructivism and sociological institutionalism in more detail. It is worth noting at this point that sociological institutionalism, or modern constructivism, is a structural approach, while what might be called reflexive constructivism, strives to address interactivity and hence belongs to the third type of institutional analysis. The importance of distinguishing between these approaches lies in the choice of dependent variable. Modern constructivists, drawing on organizational sociology, are interested in studying state behaviour that is guided by norms, with these norms as intervening variables. In contrast, reflexive constructivists are interested in understanding the *meaning* of norms. Thus, institutions are assigned different roles according to different underlying theoretical assumptions about political behaviour. They may be viewed as enabling, in that they entail an extension of behavioural options, such as providing standardized rules (March and Olsen, 1998; Checkel, 2001b). However, institutions may also be considered flexible and changing in relation to context and practice, a conception which stresses interactive reasoning instead of behaviourist rule-following. In sum, differing basic assumptions tend to produce differing analytical frameworks, research questions and research designs.

agency-oriented approaches: institutions as strategic context

Agency-oriented approaches work with the assumption that rational interests inform strategic behaviour, on the basis of exogenous preference formation, independent of societal or cultural factors (Thelen and Steinmo, 1992, 9). Those who share this view assume that an individual's interest in increasing, stabilizing or, at the very least, maintaining power, motivates behaviour. This is based on the law that actor '*A*' is motivated by her interest in wielding power over actor '*B*'. The central research question posed by this approach is therefore directed towards identifying the condition '*X*' under which that interest can be most effectively pursued.

Actor-oriented approaches (see, for example, Scharpf, 1999) rest on the 'individualism assumption' which 'treats individuals as the basic (elemental) units of social analysis. Both individual and collective actions and outcomes are explicable in terms of unit-level (individual) properties' (Jupille *et al.*, 2003, 12). Accordingly, it is assumed that institutions, such as international organizations, conventions, cooperation agreements, treaties or committees, are established in order to provide manageable information for political actors in decisionmaking processes. In other words, institutions are understood as providing a monitoring role. This view is based on the assumption that institution-building is initiated as a consequence of actors' interests, and that it is, therefore, potentially reversible (Alt and Shepsle, 1990; Garrett, 1992; Garrett and Weingast, 1993). Examples of this approach in political science, and, to some extent, in economics, include game theory and negotiation theory (see, for example, Axelrod, 1984; Zürn, 1999; and Scharpf, 1988). The actor-oriented approach has been challenged by work identifying the 'path dependent' impact of institutions on behaviour. Scholars have shown that the strategic pursuit of interests at one particular point in time may be constrained at another time through 'lock-in' effects. These effects are produced by institutions that were originally created to pursue the strategic interests of actors, whose interests were informed by material resources at time n (Pierson, 1996). A key problem emerges when the routinization of institutions beyond the time period in which they were considered appropriate and desirable ends up having a constraining impact on behaviour at time $n+1$ (North, 1990; Pierson, 1996). In other words, the reversibility of institution-building cannot be assumed. Research on European integration has documented instances of path dependence and lock-in effects, particularly during what I have described as the second and third phase of European integration (for further discussion see below; see also Wiener, 2003b; and Diez and Wiener, 2003, chapter 1).

structure-oriented approaches: institutions as guidelines for social behaviour

In contrast to agency-oriented rational actor models, structural approaches contend that actors are influenced by additional – structural – context conditions, which are created by social, institutional and/or cultural environments and/or mechanisms. Structures exert additional constitutive and/or regulative impacts on behaviour. Thus, while actors may behave in a power-oriented and rational way, it is also necessary to consider the influence of structure on interest and preference formation. These approaches seek to identify the structures that are relevant for action, recognizing both their stability and the critical junctures that may induce change. Rather than according primacy to the agency of individual and collective actors, they analyse the guiding and/or prescriptive impact of institutions on behaviour. From this point of view, 'institutions constrain and shape politics through the construction and elaboration of meaning' (March and Olsen, 1989, 39). Structure-oriented approaches are based on macro and organizational sociology (Powell and DiMaggio, 1991), which conceive of institutions as either aggregated 'rules' or as 'single standards of behaviour' (Finnemore and Sikkink, 1998, 89).

For these approaches, sociocultural factors matter for behaviour, even in the absence of legal or formal political organs. It is assumed that social norms guide behaviour, with social norms defined as 'collective expectations for the proper behaviour of actors with a given identity' (Katzenstein, 1996, 5; Finnemore and Sikkink, 1998; March and Olsen, 1998). Two types of institutions and their respective impact are often identified. On the one hand, international institutions, such as the EU, are assigned the role of creating interactive spaces for elites who then take an active role in diffusing norms, ideas and values through interactions back in their respective domestic contexts. On the other hand, norms, such as human rights norms, may also be assigned regulative and constitutive influence (Risse *et al.*, 1999; Williamson, 2000; Mueller, 2004; Schimmelfennig, 2001; Wiener, 2004).

For scholars who study institutional change in the context of European integration, questions about the role of supranational institutions in diffusing and stabilizing the emergence of norms and routinized practices are of particular interest. For example, studies on the 'Europeanization' of citizenship norms or environmental standards, have demonstrated that norms entailing prescriptive rules emerge through processes of learning and diffusion in supranational institutions. Moreover, these norms are often diffused with the additional pressure of advocacy groups (Checkel, 2001b; Keck and Sikkink 1998; Sikkink, 1993). In other words, norms exert policy-changing pressure in the domestic contexts of the EU member states (Cowles *et al.*, 2001; see also Chapter 4 in this volume).

interactive approaches

A key feature of interactive approaches is the assumption that the interrelation between structure and agency is key. These approaches emphasize the role of social interaction, caution against the valuation of structure over agency or vice versa, and focus on the concept of intersubjectivity. Additional considerations are changing identities and their influence on preference formation (see Chapter 8 in this volume) and the analytical challenge of conceptualizing the mutual constitution of institutions and actor identities through interaction.

intersubjective approaches: institutions constituted through practice

Intersubjective approaches to institution-building have been of particular interest to the constructivist turn. In contrast to the rational actor approach, which perceives institutions as exogenous factors mobilized to further actors' interests in decisionmaking, intersubjective approaches question the analytical separation of institutions, interests and identities. In other words, these approaches start with the assumption that political action, identities and institutions are mutually constitutive. Institutions are not only assigned a regulative role in relation to behaviour, they may also constitute actors' identities.

Institutions, interests and identities relate to each other through 'communicative action'. This concept is drawn, albeit selectively, from Habermas (1981), and particularly from his ideas about communication as strategic action. From this perspective, communication produces an impact on soft institutions, such as norms. It is assumed that negotiators are ready to be persuaded by the better argument, brought to the fore through controversial debate, that shared references are constructed by the process of arguing and bargaining in negotiating situations. Agreement on types of norms at the supranational level, then, follows the logic of arguing (Risse, 2000). However, according to this view, shared references are cut off from debate and from contestation about compliance conditions, standardized rules or general norms and principles that occur during processes of implementation. Insofar as these debates become crucial for successful norm compliance, this approach suffers from an 'analytical' gap, which separates analysis of interaction at the supranational level from the expectation of rule-following triggered by norm diffusion at the domestic level.

While this approach offers a helpful research platform for analysing supranational debates such as those on the Constitutional Treaty, it does tend to circumvent questions about the sociocultural origins of, or the generation of norms. The meaning of norms therefore remains undertheorized. It becomes disconnected from the very practices which, according to constructivists of all sorts, significantly influence norm construction and change. In other words, the social embeddedness of arguing about the level, validity and social facticity of norms is underanalysed. Yet, it is precisely this analytical appreciation of societal embeddedness – such as information about the 'customary' dimension of constitutional law – that brings crucial insights on the meaning of norms.

reflexive approaches: contested meanings of institutions

Reflexive constructivism borrows from the sociological argument about the dual quality of structures (Giddens, 1979). It adopts the idea developed by authors like Anthony Giddens, Pierre Bourdieu and Charles Taylor that structures are constituted by, and changed through, social practices. According to Taylor, for instance, 'the practice not only fulfils the rule, but also gives it concrete shape in particular situations. Practice is [...] a continual "interpretation" and reinterpretation of what the rule really means' (Taylor 1993: 57). From this perspective, it therefore becomes necessary for analysis to go back to practices that contributed to the creation of a rule if its meaning is to be fully understood. These practices also involve contestation by way of discursive intervention and imply an ongoing process of (re)construction.

International Relations scholars, in particular, have addressed the empirical problems posed by this type of research by focusing on discourse as the 'structure of meaning-in-use', and by conceptualizing discourse as 'the location of meaning' (Milliken, 1999, 231; Huelsse, 2003). Empirically, this focus involves studying social practices as discursive interventions, such as those in official/policy documents, political debates, and media contributions. Discursive interventions help establish a particular structure of meaning-in-use, which works as a cognitive roadmap and facilitates the interpretation of norms. This structure exerts pressure for institutional adaptation on all the actors involved. At the same time, discursive interventions referring to this structure affect its robustness. It is important to note that this assessment of norms leads beyond a neo-Durkheimian perception of norms as social facts exerting structural impact on behaviour. It requires analysis of norms conceived as embedded in sociocultural contexts that provide information about how to interpret a norm's meaning in context.

In sum, reflexive constructivism assumes that norms possess a dual quality: they are both constructed and structuring (Wiener 2003c, 2004). Hypothetically, the meaning of norms evolves through discursive interventions that establish a structure of meaning-in-use. Successful rule-following therefore depends on the overlap of norm setters and norm followers' structures of references. It follows that studying social practices in context allows analytical access to the interpretation of meaning, which produces sustained compliance with norms. Understanding contestation also sheds light on the different meanings of a norm, which may eventually increase the probability of a shared understanding of that norm emerging.

classifying constructivism and sociological institutionalism

In this section, I argue that constructivism is a theoretical position characterized, in metatheoretical terms, by a shared claim to theorizing the 'middle ground'. As Figure 3.1 shows, constructivist approaches mark a point above the baseline of a triangle connecting theoretically incommensurable 'rationalist' and 'reflexivist' standpoints.

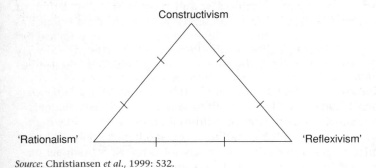

Source: Christiansen et al., 1999: 532.

Figure 3.1 Core theoretical positions

The 'constructivism' point of the triangle bundles approaches that are explicitly distinguished from the two corner baseline positions. As this section demonstrates, constructivists are, at least in principle, interested and able to communicate with either rationalists or reflexivists.

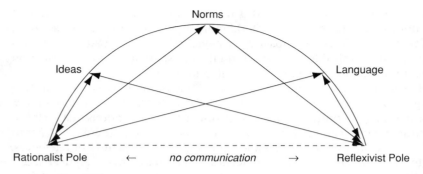

Source: Christiansen *et al.*, 1999: 536.

Figure 3.2 Establishing the middle ground

Constructivist approaches are distinguished from each of the two pole positions; establishing variation among constructivist stations. The semi-circle thus evolves according to the four following criteria: (1) Preference for ontology over epistemology; (2) Ontological preferences such as, for example, ideas, norms, language; (3) Distinction from pole positions; (4) Variation of methodological preferences.

One of the key features of the 'constructivist turn' is the development of research questions that seek to identify a communicative bridge between the two non-communicating rationalist and reflexivist poles. Different attempts to achieve this goal can be presented as 'stations on a bridge', as depicted in Figure 3.3. The stations represent the respective ontological *foci* of the various constructivist approaches: differing preferences for ontology over epistemology; degrees of differentiation from rationalist and reflexivist

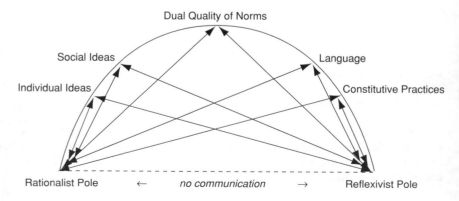

Figure 3.3 Stations on the bridge

positions; and variation in methodological preferences. (For more details on the 'station model' see Wiener, 2003c.) Nevertheless, all are characterized by a shared research interest in the influence and role of soft institutions, such as ideas, norms and rules, on the one hand, and/or sociocultural factors, such as identity, discourse, and language, on the other. These objects of study form the five stations represented in Figure 3.3, namely individual ideas, social ideas, constitutive practices, language, and (the dual quality of) norms. They are now discussed in turn.

individual ideas

The first cautious step away from the rationalist pole was taken by neoliberal institutionalists who defined ideas that were held to explain 'political outcomes' as 'beliefs held by individuals' (Goldstein and Keohane, 1993, 3). This approach, which has become important in foreign policy analysis (Goldstein and Keohane, 1993, 3), is based on the assumption that individual ideas or 'principled or causal beliefs' work as 'road maps'. While still working with the positivist assumption that interest formation is exogenous and based on material resources, reference to ideas is distinct from the research practice of the rationalist pole. According to Goldstein and Keohane (1993, 6), it is

a challenge to both rationalist and reflectivist approaches. Although we concede that the rationalist approach is often a valuable starting point for analysis, we challenge its explanatory power by suggesting the existence of empirical anomalies that can be resolved only when ideas are taken into account. We demonstrate this need to go beyond pure rationalist analysis by using its own premise to generate our null hypothesis: that variation in policy across countries, or over time, is entirely accounted for by changes in factors *other than* ideas. Like reflectivists, we explore the impact of ideas, or beliefs, on policy.

The concept of intersubjectivity, and especially its implications for change in supranational and transnational norms, remains underexplored in this approach, largely because researchers have mainly analysed formal institutional change (for example, Katzenstein, 1993, 268; Sikkink, 1993, 166). Ideas are theorized as individually appropriated, rather than being understood as socially constructed reference points which, in turn, have social impact.

social ideas

Research represented by the second, social ideas, station in Figure 3.3 appreciates the role of ideas, norms and rules forged within a social environment and thus takes a more definitive step towards the constructivist turn. Ideas are understood as socially embedded. They represent shared reference points that not only send the same message to different actors but which also cause the same behaviour among these actors. March and Olsen (1989, 26) have characterized this shared reaction to norms as the logic of appropriateness. That is, ideas are not exclusively situated in, or generated by, the brains of individual actors; they also involve a social structuring element. Thus, it becomes possible, for example, for researchers to analyse how different actors behave in different contexts (Thomas *et al.*, 1987; Boli and Thomas, 1999; Wobbe, 2000). This emphasis on ideas within a social environment brought with it a new emphasis on the constitutive and regulative dimensions of ideas, rules and norms. However, analysis represented by this station does not lose sight of the relationship between actors and social structures. As Thomas Risse notes, 'this means ... one can continue to study "beliefs" in terms of what is inside people's minds and simultaneously insist that these beliefs are representations and enactments of social and intersubjective culture' (Risse, 2000, 5).

This approach sees norms and social knowledge as constitutive for actors' identities. Yet while the principle of mutual constitution has had an impact on the perception of identities, interests and ideas at this station, the methodological and empirical focus is less on the emergence, than on the constitutive and regulative impact, of norms. Furthermore, the assumption that social norms are stable also tends to underlie this approach.

In line with these views, a growing research programme on the behaviour of actors in world politics has emerged which focuses on areas such as human rights, equal rights policy, education and the diffusion of administrative culture (Finnemore, 1996; Klotz, 2001). In addition, the new research focus on arguing and bargaining discussed above has had a considerable impact in consolidating a shift of analytical perspective. Above all, the logic of arguing focuses on the impact of agreement on the role of particular norms in international negotiating situations. It demonstrates that the contested validity of norms in negotiating situations and the implementation of norms in social contexts require mediating processes of socialization, learning and/or shaming by advocacy groups.

constitutive practices

Constructivist perspectives, located near the reflexivist pole in Figure 3.3, engage with reflexive sociology rather than organizational sociology and are thus more distant from the rationalist pole (Powell and DiMaggio, 1991). The core theoretical basis of this perspective is provided by Giddens' structurationist approach (Giddens, 1979). This approach has challenged traditional formulations of core concepts such as sovereignty, through a combination of de- and reconstructive analyses. Biersteker and Weber (1996), for instance, define sovereignty as a 'set of constitutive practices', and in so doing allow examination of the concept (and others like it) within the particular context where they emerged. As the authors explain, 'the modern state system is not based on some timeless principle of sovereignty, but on the production of a normative recognition in a unique way and in a particular place (the state)' (Biersteker and Weber, 1996, 3).

Research on the social world relates to the ontologies of identity and social practices. It thus offers the bases for systematic assessment of variation in the process of state-building and identity-formation. Adopting the intersubjectivity premise, the constitutive practices station places the ontology of interaction above that of both agency and structure. Assigning such a central weight to interaction emphasizes the possibility of change, in contrast to the social ideas station's conceptualization of social facts, which draws on organizational sociology.

language

The next, or the language, station shares a focus on speech acts with the social ideas station. However, while the former is, in principle, interested in persuasion by way of arguing, the latter refers to language as not only descriptive, but also as social action (Kratochwil, 1989; Fierke, 1998; Diez, 1999a). For example, Kratochwil notes:

> our conventional understanding of social action and of the norms governing them is defective because of a fundamental misunderstanding of the function of language in social interaction, and because of a positivist epistemology that treats norms as 'causes'. Communication is therefore reduced to issues of describing 'facts' properly, i.e. to the 'match' of concepts and objects, and to the ascertainment of nomological regularities. Important aspects of *social* action such as advising, demanding, apologizing, promising etc., cannot be adequately understood thereby. Although the philosophy of ordinary language has abandoned the 'mirror' image of language since the later Wittgenstein, the research programs developed within the confines of logical positivism are, nevertheless, still indebted to the old conception. (Kratochwil, 1989, 5–6)

While acknowledging the guiding role of norms, this station emphasizes the constitutive impact of interaction. It is thus almost diametrically opposed to that of the social ideas station, which assumes that ideas are constitutive for identities. In turn, the language station argues that speech acts or discourses are constitutive for rules and norms in particular contexts (Fierke, 1998; Diez, 1999a and 1999b; Doty, 1997; Milliken, 1999). The securitization literature presents a good example of the constitutive role of speech acts as it assumes that security problems are constructed on the basis of speech acts (Huysmans, 1998, 527; Buzan *et al.*, 1998).

This concept of language as social action – and thereby constitutive for the emergence of soft institutions such as rules and norms – helps to draw a clearer picture of the contradiction between the perceptions of the regulative role of ideas on the one hand, and constitutive role of ideas on the other.

dual quality of norms

The previous station moves on from the social ideas station, which represents scholarship more interested in norm stability and its impact on behaviour than on understanding the impact of norm flexibility. The final station on the bridge, the dual quality of norms station entails theoretical assumptions that have received comparatively less attention than those discussed in relation to the individual ideas, social ideas, constitutive practices and language stations.

Appreciating the dual quality of norms – that is their regulative and constitutive construction – continues to represent a conceptual challenge for scholars. In other words, full exploration of Ruggie's triad of the origin, role and function of norms (Ruggie, 1998) is still limited to the latter two aspects of role and function. In addition, the argumentative dimension of norm research demonstrates that apart from the problematic and complex issues of theorizing and applying the concept of intersubjectivity, the issue of contextual variation – that is, the multiple sociocultural contexts of norm emergence and implementation – also presents a conceptual challenge for work on norm resonance. This involves questions about the validity of norms across the boundaries of political arenas and about the role and assessment of life-worlds (Mueller, 2004) in the legitimation and contestation of norms.

Characterization of norm emergence as a *process* has contributed to the absence of analytical insights into the constructed quality of norms, such as the possibility that the meaning of norms changes and to conflicts that may result from different interpretations of norms in varying sociocultural environments. Empirically, this oversight affects research on long-term norm resonance in compliance processes, an area of particular importance for work on the EU given the salience of discussions about constitutionalization in transnational politics (Weiler, 1999b; Weiler and Wind, 2003) and the legalization of international politics.

The assumption of norm stability is problematic for research on norm resonance since norm change requires an understanding of the mutual constitution of practice and norms. In addition, it is necessary to mediate between international and/or transnational contexts on the one hand, and domestic contexts on the other. While current research on norm validity focuses on argumentation and bargaining during international negotiation processes, analysis of the arguing process is not pursued further into contested domestic contexts. It follows that norms entailing few prescriptive standards – such as so-called thin norms – will cause a broad range of possible norm interpretations. This enhanced range of norm interpretations may produce a large range of identifications with the norm, which in turn may create conflicts between norm expectation and norm substance.

Norm research, therefore, also needs to address the validity assumption of norms. In a given political context, the potential for norm legitimacy rises in proportion to the possibility for norm addressees to contest the meaning of norms. In other words, for a robust assessment of politics beyond the state, the stability assumption of norms as social facts, which entails standardized rules for behaviour cuts too short. After all, norms possess stable and flexible qualities; that is, they are constructed through social interaction on the one hand, and have a constitutive impact on behaviour, on the other. This dual quality of norms is documented in interdisciplinary work bringing together political science, law, sociology and cultural studies. In the next section, I offer two examples of how this approach may apply to analyses of the EU in the area of EU enlargement and European constitutionalism.

constructivist and sociological institutionalist perspectives on eu enlargement and eu constitutionalism

Before examining the insights of constructivist and sociological institutionalist approaches to these two crucial areas of EU development, it is necessary to identify different phases of European integration, phases which are distinguished by types of institution-building (Table 3.1), and to address associated research questions and theoretical approaches (Table 3.2).

Table 3.1   Three phases of institution-building

Phase	Type	Place	Dynamic	Institutions
I	Integration (more/less)	Supranational level	Bottom-up	Hard
II	Europeanization (more/less)	Domestic, regional level in member and candidate countries	Top-down	Hard/soft
III	Politicization (more/less)	Europolity; transnational spaces	Trickle-across, bottom-up, top-down	Hard/soft

Source: Adopted from Wiener (2003).

As Table 3.1 shows, it is possible to identify three types of institution-building in the process of European integration. The first type of institution-building is integration through supranational institution-building. The second involves Europeanization, or domestic institutional adaptation to European integration. The third type is associated with politicization, which involves a more complex process of sociocultural and legal institutional adaptation in vertical and horizontal dimensions.

As Table 3.2 shows, these types of institution-building roughly correspond to different chronological phases in the development of the EU and to the predominance of different research questions and theoretical approaches

Table 3.2   Leading research questions

Phases	Questions	Theoretical Approaches
I: *Integration*	**Why** institutions on supranational level?	liberal intergovernmentalism; neofunctionalism
II: *Europeanization*	**How** to adapt to institutions domestically?	multilevel governance; neoinstitutionalism
III: *Politicization*	**What** type of polity?	democratic theory; constructivism; critical approaches

(for more detail see Diez and Wiener, 2003, chapter 1). In the first phase, between the 1960s and mid-1980s political scientists, and in particular International Relations scholars, debated whether intergovernmentalist or neofunctionalist paradigms presented the best explanation of supranational institution-building. The second phase, between the mid-1980s and early 1990s, brought in scholars with a background in Comparative Politics, Public Administration and Public Policy. This research analysed divergence and convergence in policy implementation, as well as the diffusion of European regulations and standards. The third and current phase, beginning with negotiation of the Maastricht Treaty in the early 1990s, introduces a shift in institutional analysis. In particular, it has brought the normative question of legitimate integration once raised in the wake of the Treaty of Rome (see Haas, 1958) back onto the agenda.

Following the landmark treaty changes in the Maastricht, Amsterdam and Nice Treaties, and the nature of the post-Cold War and post-September 11 international environments, the central questions facing European integration scholars are:

- Which polity or which model of a political system to build?
- How far to go with enlargement, or where do the boundaries of Europe and its values lie?
- What type of constitutional framework is needed to regulate politics and in which particular arenas? Or, in other words, how to establish institutions with an input into subnational, transnational and global politics?

As the recent constitutional process testifies, many of those directly involved in EU politics are asking similar questions. According to one member of the European Parliament, for instance:

despite being agreed as international treaties, the treaties are something akin to the Constitution of the European Union. Therefore they accomplish the role of a constitution. For me the question is not, whether Europe has a constitution, but *whether Europe has the constitution it needs*. That is precisely the question. That's what this is all about. And ... the answer is clear: the European Union does not have the constitution it needs.[2]

Addressing these issues will depend on how the three questions identified above – questions about the type of polity, the boundaries of Europe, and the relevance for particular political arenas – are answered. Various attempts to do this, such as those offered by the European Commission's 2001 White Paper on Governance,[3] and numerous proposals regarding the reorganization of European political organs, demonstrate the scarcity of conceptually-convincing and politically-feasible approaches to constitutional change. To lawyers, projects that aim to achieve the constitutionalization of the treaties, come as a surprise after years of integration through law. After all, constitutionalization has been an ongoing process for decades.

After the shift in analytic focus from the *politics* of integration, to *policies* of institutional adaptation (such as Europeanization) (illustrated in Table 3.2), students of European integration have been pushed to face the *polity* dimension. Questions of identity, democracy and security, amongst others, have been brought to the fore with developments such as the introduction of EU citizenship and the 'communitarization' of the Schengen Agreement abolishing internal border controls. Foreign policy challenges such as the Kosovo crisis, the 2001 terrorist attack on the World Trade Center and political crisis in the Middle East, have increased the challenges confronting the EU on the world stage. In addition, there have also been new questions to explore regarding the process of enlargement, with the new accession criteria settled in Copenhagen in 1993, and with increased pressure for institutional adaptation in candidate countries, European political organs and in existing member states.

The current phase of late politicization presents a context of complex institutional change, characterized by multiple processes of institutional adaptation. In addition to the bottom-up and top-down perspectives on institutional change indicated in Table 3.1, future-oriented debate over fundamental issues of political responsibility and constitutional design have taken precedence over day-to-day policy issues. As a consequence, the EU is now increasingly analysed as a political system. Furthermore, underlying security and financial interests informing the choice and definition of the Copenhagen accession criteria in areas such as minority policy, agricultural policy, visa policy, and fundamental freedoms also raised questions about the political constitution, leading principles and the value system of the EU as a polity. In this phase, legal work on European integration has gained in increasing importance for political science approaches and *vice versa*. The largely hidden link between 'integration through law' as an approach that offered explanatory guidance for lawyers during the first phase of integration, on the one hand, and 'integration through policy', present in political science research during the second Europeanization phase on the other, should now be scrutinized with a new focus on 'integration through politics'. I now turn to a discussion of democratic theory dimensions of the EU's transnational constitutional setting. Following James Tully's work (2002), the principle of contestedness is conceptualized as a normative perspective on constitutionally regulated institutions. This principle also follows the constructivist assumption of the dual quality of norms discussed in the previous section. It can be illustrated through two examples of evolving norms and their respective contested meanings in Europe: namely, European citizenship and the constitutional debate. I discuss both of these more fully in the rest of the section.

However, before I do so it is important to point out that both the discussions on European citizenship and constitutional debates elucidate the evolving meaning of soft institutions, based on discussions about norms, and thereby provide new ways of assessing the evolution of a democratic and legitimate process of governance beyond the state. It begins with an institutionally established safeguard mechanism for ongoing deliberation about the meaning of norms and rules. In so doing, it establishes an institutional framework that allows for a flexible and equal assessment of the facticity–validity tension, based on public participation. In other words, it offers a constitutionally-entrenched link between 'institutionalized deliberation and public debate' which 'must, indeed, interact' (Joerges, 2002, 146). Indeed, it is here that the Europolity's best and worst outcome may well be decided. In this context, the key problem in academic assessments of the constitutional debate follow from analytical bracketing, essentially omitting analysis of interactive social practices as constitutive for normative meaning. The result is a lack of information on the role of – controversial – associative connotations about the meaning of constitutional substance. In the process, the influence of intangible factors such as cultural resources, for instance, which are essential for generating norm resonance, remains blurred. While academic debate focuses on the discussion of different constitutional models and their substantive aspects (which model is considered legitimate?), shared constitutional norms inevitably acquire varying interpretations through associative connotations that are developed within different sociocultural contexts (which meanings of a norm and which expectations?). It is ultimately the associative connotations within these contexts that constitute unintended consequences of institution-building.

citizenship

Formal institutionalization of EU citizenship in the Maastricht Treaty presents a classic example of institution-building with unintended consequences. This is due to the fact that as a legal norm, EU citizenship has little prescriptive force. If it has such a prescriptive force, EU citizenship might allow for the identification of guiding capabilities and behavioural performance, as constructivist proposals about the logic of appropriateness in compliance research lead one to expect (Checkel, 2001b, 200). What is puzzling about the latter is that EU citizenship has provoked political reaction, despite the absence of standardized rules of behaviour. Political actors, such as lobby groups, associations and interest groups, have made explicit reference to EU citizenship, even going so far as demanding treaty revisions.[4] This mobilization in reaction to a newly established institution was less puzzling for authors who analysed EU citizenship as *practice* – that is, those who analysed it as the politics institutionalizing the terms, and forging the meanings, of citizenship – than for those who analysed EU citizenship as a new legal norm. Practice-oriented work was able to demonstrate that the institution of EU citizenship – as in Maastricht Treaty – represented just *one* aspect of the multiple and fragmented meanings of European citizenship. The larger and more encompassing understanding of the meanings of citizenship has evolved in relation to European citizenship practice, to involve sociocultural spaces, or transnational, national or international interactions that remain theoretically (and therefore also empirically) hidden to structure-oriented behaviourist approaches.

It is in this way that more than 25 years of European citizenship practice have transformed national citizenship. While modern nationally-defined citizenship refers to identity and regulates rights and access based on membership within a centrally organized constitutional state (for an overview see Wiener, 2003a), the EU has forged a fragmented type of citizenship which is neither centrally-defined, nor centrally-practised.[5] Indeed, EU citizenship is unthinkable without reference to national citizenship, as the Amsterdam Treaty revision spelt out in Article 17 (1) EC. This fragmentation of citizenship rights within the Europolity has created a new meaning of citizenship, that is deduced from the universal norm of citizenship, and that challenges modern concepts of citizenship. However, this transformation of meaning is not readily visible in the citizenship articles (Arts 17–22) of the EC Treaty as a prescriptive force which guides behaviour. Instead, meaning must be empirically explained and *mediated* to facilitate understanding. Without successful mediation of meaning and an understanding of where to locate them, political reactions to EU citizenship must remain a puzzle for actor-oriented and structure-oriented approaches of institution-building. After all, in the absence of prescriptive force, behavioural change is not expected. However, if one accepts the premise of the dual quality of norms as structuring and constructed, it is possible to shed light on this puzzle. Once the principle of contestedness is taken as the starting point, norm implementation is always related to deliberation about the meaning of these norms. It is this perspective which eventually allows for an analytical approach which can get to grips with the fragmented meaning of diverse norms of citizenship.

constitutionalism and enlargement

The principle of contestedness has two implications for the constitutional process. The first refers to the evolving norms of constitutionalism generated by social practices in the enlargement process. While the constitutional debate which has been largely carried out in the old, western member states provides a framework for open and constructive thought, the enlargement process has, for more than a decade, been dictated by rule-following behaviour, which allowed for 'socialision into' the community. Constitutional debate in the old, western member states has been future-oriented in both style and dynamics, and, with respect to procedure and substance, can be evaluated according to democratic criteria. Following Habermas and Tully, the yardstick for legitimacy in a political community is the principle of equal access to participation in debate over the validity of norms by all those potentially influenced by the outcome of the process. Here the logic of arguing and the principle of contestedness are central to actors' behaviour.

The enlargement process, however, is largely guided by the expectation of rule-following consistent with behaviouralist assumptions about compliance behaviour (Chayes and Chayes, 1995; Schimmelfennig, 2003a; see, critically, Wiener and Schwellnus, 2004). Indeed, academic work on enlargement predominantly applies the assumption of strict rule-following and the implementation of the compliance criteria (Schimmelfennig and Sedelmeier, 2002). The behaviour of the candidate countries is determined by the guiding impact of the accession criteria, identified in 1993 in Copenhagen and the substance of these criteria is not renegotiable. Nonetheless, it was expected that the constitutional settlement agreed in 2004 would be acceptable to all signatories of the Constitutional Treaty, including both old and new member states. The accommodation of diversity, based on day-to-day experience in *all* social contexts, is therefore vital. Academic research on the Constitutional Treaty thus requires a critical understanding of the interrelation between both the constitutional debate about political finality of the EU on the one hand, and the political process of enlargement on the other (Wiener, 2003b). The link between the two offers an understanding of both processes as not only potentially conflictive, but also as producing additional hurdles for the acceptance of a revised common constitution in an enlarged EU.

The constitutional debate, and preparation for the massive enlargement in 2004, demonstrated the dual challenge of accommodating diversity in a modern constitution beyond the state. Beyond the analytical linking of the two processes, the challenge consists of establishing a constitutionally entrenched institutional body, offering the possibility for ongoing transnational democratic deliberation, recognition and constitutional revision in the long run. Even though there are grounds for some doubt, it may still be worthwhile assessing the potential of the Convention model and ability to provide fair and equal participatory conditions for both current and future member states.

After all, candidate countries are expected to act according to the compliance rationale and practise rule-following in line with the policy of conditionality governing enlargement. Yet, at the same time, they were called to participate constructively in the Convention and in wider public debate on the future of Europe. For example, the German Minister of Foreign Affairs, Joschka Fischer 'encouraged Poland and the other east and central European countries applying for membership of the European Union, to *participate in the debate over EU finality*' (*Frankfurter Allgemeine Zeitung*, 26 January 2002, 4 [emphasis added]). The then candidate countries were thus forced into a process of identity formation following the process of 'othering', which has been constitutive not only for fragmented identity formation, but also for considerable cleavages in the assessments of old and new members of the community. This raises four central questions. First, does restricted participation and opposing identity formation favour a successful outcome for constitutional processes?; second, what was the Convention's contribution to the resolution of this dilemma?; third, how might the situation be improved?; and fourth, what are the long-term consequences for establishing democratic legitimacy in the process of European integration?

With reference to the different logics of action, it is possible to conclude that, in principle, the following conditions are necessary for democratic governance: First, according to Habermas's ideal speech situation, all participants of a debate must be able to debate under equal conditions, including those of information, voice and vote, in order to generate, identify and accept shared norms. That is, all participants must, in principle, be ready to be persuaded by the better argument, and to revise their previously held position accordingly. The starting point for finality/compliance situations in the EU differs from this basic scenario, however. For example, the Copenhagen accession criteria have not been defined by the EU with sufficient precision to allow for uncontested implementation (for example, in the area of administration); nor have EU member states been scrutinized on the question of whether they meet the criteria themselves (for example, in the area of minority rights). In addition, the so-called transition rules, in the area of freedom of movement for workers, for instance, will create unequal conditions among future EU citizens. While perfectly legitimate from a political and legal position, these are examples of areas where the public perception of equality may not conform to agreements at the governmental level, and may therefore prompt political mobilization as an unintended consequence of institution-building. Furthermore, the then candidate countries worked with a considerable information deficit in all areas, including the Convention, a body in which they had the right to voice, but not to veto. They thus entered the EU with a clear structural disadvantage (Landfried, 2004).

In conclusion, establishing spaces for transnational deliberation remains a core issue on the agenda for constitutional revision. Indeed, given past experiences of constitutional change, the main issue appears to be less one of agreeing on a new constitutional model. More important is the issue of establishing transnational *fora* for deliberation in selected policy areas, fora in which elected representatives from political levels of governance and public associations would be entitled to participate as equals in ongoing debates as European citizens.

conclusion

The conceptual starting point for constructivist and sociological institutionalist approaches to European integration is the assumption of a link between the social construction of institutions and the successful implementation of rules, norms and legal principles. This sociological concept of constitutionalization is based on the cultural embeddedness of constitutional dynamics. It aims to recover the customary aspect of constitutional law, based on a reflexive approach to soft institutions, while favouring the thick concept of the *nomos* rather more closely than the lean concept of modern constitutional law (Craig, 2001). While the gradual and long-lasting process of constitutionalization in the EU entails both types, a sociological conception of constitutionalization understands the concept as involving two types of institutions. First, constitutions offer an institutional context for the political community as a whole; second, they themselves consist of an aggregation of institutions. The proposal to extend modern constitutionalism towards the customary, offers a shift of focus away from analysing the expanding formal *acquis communautaire*, towards understanding the *acquis* as a 'socially embedded' set of both hard and soft institutions (Wiener, 1998; Merlingen *et al.*, 2000), created through social practices. The substance of these institutions is thus culturally and historically contingent and depends on social interaction. Without that interaction, rules and norms do not exist. Legal and social institutions are interrelated insofar as the former require the latter if they are to be meaningfully implemented, or for that matter, in order to resonate with their respective context of implementation. This approach allows for the analytical inclusion of multiple sociocultural trajectories, which produce and transform the meaning of 'European' in analyses of constitutional issues, based on the Aristotelian understanding of a constitution as an 'institution of institutions' (Onuf, 1989, 222). Crucially, it allows a focus on constitutional norms as evolving through social practices, even before a constitutional text is identified as a constitution and labelled accordingly.

The late politicization phase and its focus on the finality debate follows a long period of constitutional politics carried on without any particularly defined political goal for the Europolity. As one of the many unintended consequences of institution-building in the process of European constitutionalization, the finality debate encapsulates the breathless constitutional process which is likely to generate even further unintended consequences. In the process, normative concerns are raised about a European Constitution that would lead beyond the simple reorganization of the treaties (Weiler, 1999b). In this context, understanding institution-building and its often path-dependent impact is crucial. In other words, the meaning of institutions and their constitutive and regulative influence on behaviour changes once it is transferred across the sociocultural boundaries which forge the meaning of core constitutional norms. That is, the facticity and validity of norms produce conflicting interpretations across national boundaries in the territory within which a European Constitution would apply. Historical institutional analyses have pointed out the significance of identifying institutional impacts over long time periods, with reference to changed resource constellations (such as, power constellations, market resources and interests). This so-called problem of 'snap-shot', as opposed to 'moving picture', analyses also applies to the impact of sociocultural resources that produce unintended consequences under the conditions of time and context change. 'Associative resources', such as expectations, interpretations, and meanings, are also subject to change, misinterpretation and contestation (Wiener, 2001). The example of EU citizenship substantiates this particular effect and the constitutional process is likely to repeat that experience.

notes

1. For example, the Reflection Group involved in preparation of the 1996 intergovernmental conference.
2. Interview with a member of the European Parliament, Brussels, 29 August 2001; on file with the author; emphasis added.
3. For further discussion on the Commission's 2001 White Paper on Governance see Joerges et al., 2001; Scharpf, 2001, 1.
4. Compare Articles 8a–e EC of the Maastricht Treaty and amended to become Articles 17–22 EC in the Amsterdam Treaty.
5. See the current constitutional stipulation of citizens' rights in Articles 17–22 EC, as well as in a number of EU Treaty Articles, for example Articles 13, 119 EU etc.

4
europeanization: solution or problem?

claudio m. radaelli

introduction

Some years ago, Simon Hix and Klaus Goetz (2001, 15) observed that 'Europeanisation has all the hallmarks of an emergent field of inquiry'. The field has now come of age. It is now time to take stock of what has been done so far.[1]

We may as well start from the radical question of whether the shift towards Europeanization, reflected by bibliometric exercises (see the data in Featherstone 2003, 5–6; Giuliani, 2004), is indicative of a new theoretical orientation or whether it is simply a reflection of the faddish popularity of the term. Almost twenty years ago, Kratochwil and Ruggie (1986) put a similar question to the then emergent field of 'international governance' by asking whether the shift represented a haphazard sequence of 'theoretical or topical fads'? To use their language, which draws on the terminology of Imre Lakatos (1978): Is Europeanization rooted in a core concern and 'set of puzzles' that provide some coherence to this field? Is Europeanization a progressive programme? Or does it produce degenerative problem shifts? For Lakatos, in degenerative programmes, theories are fabricated only to accommodate known facts. By contrast, progressive research programmes predict novel facts.[2]

These are difficult questions to operationalize, especially in a relatively new field of scientific inquiry. How can one pin down precisely what the 'set of puzzles' really is – if different approaches lead to different definitions of the 'set'? Furthermore, the answer will depend on how demanding the definition of a progressive programme is. My view is that it is too early to engage with 'yes-no' tests on the 'progressive programme' question. And of course Lakatos had in mind large fields of inquiry, whereas Europeanization is a relatively small sub-set of an interdisciplinary field of research (that is, EU Studies). However, we can use Lakatos' framework to ask whether some interesting puzzles are emerging (at least in embryonic form), and whether some novel facts have been uncovered by Europeanization.

In this chapter, I answer Lakatos' re-formulated question with a preliminary 'yes'. The most original work on Europeanization[3] has contributed to the emergence of new insights, original explanations and interesting questions on three important issues: understanding and analysis of the 'domestic impact' of international politics; the question of how to endogenize international governance into models of domestic politics (in terms of research design); and the relationship between agency and change. These three issues are prominent in the research agendas of International Relations, theoretical Policy Analysis, and Comparative Politics. Hence research on Europeanization has the merit of having brought EU Studies into mainstream political science (Hassenteufel and Surel, 2000).

One theme throughout the chapter is that, in order to develop a progressive agenda, Europeanization should be seen as a problem, not as a solution. Europeanization does not provide any simple fix to theoretical or empirical problems. Quite the opposite: it can only deliver if it is approached as a set of puzzles. Europeanization is a problem in search of an explanation – not the explanation itself. At this stage, its potential is greater if one turns to Europeanization as 'something to be explained', not 'something that explains'.[4]

The chapter begins by introducing the specific domain of Europeanization, followed, in the next section, by analysis of different (but not necessarily incompatible) perspectives on Europeanization. The third section forwards some suggestions on how to make sense of Europeanization research designs. This is followed by a section presenting the main mechanisms of Europeanization, and a section presenting the principal results of empirical research. The final section draws conclusions on what has been learnt so far and what we still need to learn.

A preliminary remark: this chapter concentrates primarily upon Europeanization in the context of European integration. It also focuses on the long-term dynamics of European integration, and does not, therefore, review studies of how European politics and policy affect the new member states. Some general propositions presented here may travel well, for example in work on enlargement (see Grabbe, 2003). However, practical limitations require a slightly narrower focus.

the specific domain of europeanization

Although there are many possible approaches to Europeanization, depending on the disciplines and specific questions of different research programmes (Featherstone 2003; Olsen 2002), one simple way to get to grips with definitions and their scope is to make a distinction between background concepts and systematized concepts (Adcock and Collier, 2001). As a background concept, Europeanization refers to all the possible meanings we may want to include in an encyclopaedia. Thus, the historian may well look at the evolution of Europeanization starting from the Renaissance, and link it to the rise of trade and individualism in Europe. It is the task of an encyclopaedia to report on all the major meanings associated with a concept. But in a dictionary used by a community of specialists, there is a need for a systematized concept. This chapter deals with the latter.

Let us start by demarcating the difference between Europeanization and the set of puzzles typical of classic European integration theories. Europeanization is a set of post-ontological puzzles. This means that we start from the notion that there is a process of European integration under way, and that the EU has developed its own institutions and policies over the last fifty years or so. Accordingly, the puzzles do not refer to the nature of the beast (to paraphrase Puchala, 1973). They do not address the question of why and how member states produce European integration, nor whether the EU is more intergovernmental or more supranational. Instead, the theoretical effort in Europeanization as a research agenda is all about bringing domestic politics back into our understanding of European integration, without assuming that the balance of power between the state and European institutions is being tilted in one direction or another. The question of the balance of power is more important for classic theories of European integration than for Europeanization. Although the final power outcome is not prejudged, ultimately Europeanization provides a theoretical lens on the effects of integration on domestic political structures. As shown by Corporaso (2006), it closes the loop between domestic politics, integration, and the domestic political systems responsible for integration in the first place.

Some theories of governance (see Rhodes, 1997) go even further than neofunctionalist arguments in addressing the balance of power between state and supranational institutions. They predict the hollowing out of the state from above and from below.[5] By contrast, Europeanization is more interested in adaptation to Europe, without making bold predictions. Domestic institutions are supposed to be malleable (to different degrees), but they are not withering away. A final element that distinguishes Europeanization from other conventional approaches to politics in Europe is the absence of assumptions about convergence.

Turning to definitions of Europeanization, there are various suggestions in the literature. Risse *et al.* (2001, 3) opt for the following definition: 'We define Europeanisation as the emergence and the development at the European level of distinct structures of governance.' Although the whole book from which this definition is drawn (Cowles *et al.*, 2001) is clearly dedicated to domestic policy adjustment, the definition seems to shed more light on the creation of European governance than on the domestic consequences of integration.

As such, it does not demarcate the specific territory of Europeanization as a field of inquiry.

Olsen (2002, 944) shows the limitations of definitional exercises by arguing that Europeanization is a set of model-building puzzles, not a set of definitional puzzles. He then goes on to illustrate the many faces of Europeanization. His approach covers a very broad spectrum, including Europeanization as political integration and political unification. This wide spectrum is almost without boundaries and is somewhat discouraging. Yet Olsen's approach has the advantage of redirecting scholars from unidirectional patterns of causation to mutual adaptation and coevolution between the domestic and the European level – a point well-illustrated by Gualini (2003, 6).

The definition I propose is Europeanization consists of processes of a) construction b) diffusion and c) institutionalization of formal and informal rules, procedures, policy paradigms, styles and 'ways of doing things'. It also consists of shared beliefs and norms that are first defined and consolidated in the EU policy process and then incorporated in the logic of domestic (national and subnational) discourse, political structures and public policies. This definition is grounded in an understanding of Europeanization as an interactive process, rather than as a simple process of unidirectional reaction to 'Europe' (Salgado and Woll, 2004, 4). This facilitates an approach to Europeanization that is well beyond a narrow, top-down notion of 'impact' (of the EU on domestic systems). The idea of impact is somewhat static and mechanistic, whilst real-world processes of Europeanization provide considerable opportunities for creative usage of Europe. Domestic actors often have discretion to use Europe in many different ways. They may discursively create impacts. They may draw on Europe as a resource without specific pressure from Brussels. They may become trapped in European discourses and socialization, processes that cannot be captured by a narrow notion of impact (Jacquot and Woll, 2003; Thatcher, 2004). Europeanization deals with how domestic change is processed, and patterns of adaptation can be more complex than simple reactions to 'Brussels'. Indeed, complex adaptation patterns and interactive logics are common terms in new studies on Europeanization (Megie and Ravinet, 2004).

This leads to the discussion of what is new in this field. Figure 4.1 contrasts the focus of classic European integration studies (first arrow) with two approaches to Europeanization (roughly speaking, top-down and bottom-up). The top-down approach to Europeanization (second arrow) is typical of work done in the 1970s and 1980s, a classic example being the series of volumes published by Pinder in the early 1990s assessing member states' membership of the European Community (see also Rometsch and Wessels, 1996). The top-down approach, which is still present in current research projects, tends to rely on the 'chain':

'pressure' from Europe on member states → intervening variables → reactions and change at the domestic level.

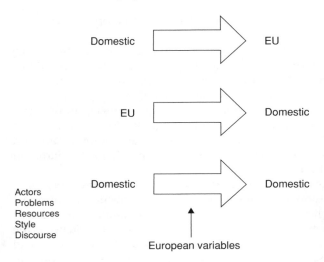

Figure 4.1   Three approaches – European integration, top-down Europeanization, and bottom-up Europeanization

Most of the analysis of top-down Europeanization conducted before the 1990s sought to track down the implementation of European policies. The objective was to understand how member states organized their European business. Both 'pressure' and 'intervening variables' received a rudimentary treatment. Recent projects informed by this approach are more theoretically robust. An outstanding example is found in the volume edited by Cowles *et al.*, (2001). Pressure is clarified in terms of 'goodness of fit' (this is not just the fit or lack of between EU and domestic policies, but covers structural-institutional fits as well). In addition, the intervening variables are made explicit and, instead of being generated by *ad hoc* explanations based on the peculiarity of the political systems of the Member States, are grounded in either social constructivism or rational choice institutionalist frameworks (Börzel and Risse 2003).

The bottom-up cluster (third arrow) has a completely different research design. Instead of starting from European policies (or politics) as independent variable and tracking down the consequences for domestic actors, policies and politics, it starts and finishes at the level of domestic actors. This may seem paradoxical, but actually the third arrow in Figure 4.1 simply exposes the limitations of the language of dependent and independent variables. As Gualini convincingly argues (2003), Europeanization is not the *explanans*, the phenomenon that explains the dependent variable, or the 'solution', to paraphrase the title of this chapter: It is the *explanandum*, the 'problem' that needs to be explained.[6]

The bottom-up research design starts from actors, problems, resources, style and discourses at the domestic level. Put differently, the starting point is a system of interaction at the domestic level. By using time and temporal causal sequences, a bottom-up approach checks if, when, and how the EU provides a change in any of the main components of the system of interaction. Finally, 'bottom-uppers' try to measure the consequences of all this in terms of change at the domestic level. Of course, one can see this as yet another mechanism of 'impact', but with the qualification that the notion of impact goes beyond the 'reaction' to Europe and includes creative usages.

Let us now illustrate the third arrow with an example (see also Bull and Baudner, 2004; Busch, 2004; Thatcher, 2004 and Zahariadis, 2004). In a study on alcohol monopoly in Finland, Norway and Sweden, Ugland (2003) shows that at the beginning of the 'policy story', domestic policy actors were coping with alcohol as a problem of health policy. The advent of EU competition policy produced a reformulation of policy problems. Alcohol policy is now subject to competition policy and to single market regulations. Countries like Finland can no longer maintain monopolies and at the same time export 'Finlandia' – a well-known vodka – throughout Europe on the basis of monopolistic protection at home. The very idea of an alcohol policy, at the end of Ugland's story, has been recategorized as competition policy (as opposed to the previous categorization of health policy). This change, he argues, cannot be ascribed to any other force than EU policy.

As mentioned, the story starts and finishes at the level of the domestic system of interaction. By doing so, Ugland avoids the pitfall of studies that start from European policies, directives and regulations, and track down their implementation at the domestic level. The pitfall is one of pre-judging the role of Europeanization (Dyson, 2002). How do we know that Europe is really affecting the logic of interaction at home? All in all, we observe change at the domestic level, but this may well be the result of other processes.[7] It may be that Europe is not important at all in terms of the logic of interaction, even if directives and policies coming from Brussels have been implemented. With a research design like that illustrated by the third arrow in Figure 4.1, one can see if and when Europe changes the logic. The analyst is also in a favourable position to observe when major alterations of the prevailing logic are produced endogenously at the domestic level or by more global pressures.

There are other interesting properties. To begin with, Europeanization is not approached as a new form of theorization with its own new vocabulary (such as 'goodness of fit' – see below). Rather, Europeanization is seen as 'orchestration' of existing concepts and theories, with major theoretical import from Comparative Politics and theoretical Policy Analysis (Featherstone and Radaelli, 2003, 340). Secondly, whereas previous research considered Europeanization an end state, recent research has embraced the notion of Europeanization as process (Goetz, 2002). The question is not one of assessing whether a country has become Europeanized or not. As *explanandum* or 'problem', Europeanization demands explanation of what goes on inside the process, not a simple black-box design in which one correlates the input, 'EU independent variables' to the output, 'domestic impact'. Thirdly,

Europeanization covers both vertical processes (from the EU to domestic politics) and horizontal dynamics. The EU may provide the context, the cognitive and normative 'frame', the terms of reference, or opportunities for the socialization of domestic actors, who then produce 'exchanges' (of ideas, power, policies, and so on).

Fourthly, although some authors still make the argument that a precise definition of Europeanization should cover the homogenizing impact of the EU on 'specific institutions and practices across a wide range of state activities' (Page, 2003, 163), the new approach makes a careful distinction between the definition of Europeanization and its possible impacts in terms of convergence or divergence. Indeed, as it will be shown later on, there is more empirical evidence pointing towards a differential impact of Europe than towards convergence. Thus, it is not surprising that Page has not found much support for Europeanization as homogeneity. His definition of Europeanization confuses the concept with its possible outcomes.

To conclude on the insights provided by bottom-up studies: Europeanization is not a new theory. It is an approach that enables us to orchestrate existing concepts and to contribute to cumulative social science research (by drawing systematically on concepts and models produced by Comparative Politics and Policy Analysis). It is a process, rather than end-state. It is an *explanandum*, rather than an *explanans*.

governance, institutionalization and discourse

There are three aims in this section. The number of studies on Europeanization is well in excess of what can possibly be reviewed here. However, they can be reduced to a limited number of 'deep interrogations' on the nature of the process. Accordingly, the first aim is to show how Europeanization can be seen as governance, as institutionalization and as discourse. While these are three ideal-types, and most authors find it useful to mix them in order to provide empirically rich accounts, this three-fold distinction sheds light on the nature of Europeanization. To clarify: the differences in the three approaches to the 'deep interrogations' should not be exaggerated; perhaps they simply show the most important sides of the prism. The second aim is to illustrate a two-track strategy of inquiry. On the one hand, logic suggests that we focus on change (or lack of it), and consider Europeanization, without pre-judging its role, in the context of other possible factors of change. On the other hand, the processual nature of Europeanization should be acknowledged up-front. The third aim is to discuss the implications of this approach.

Let us commence with Europeanization as governance. A number of authors treat Europeanization as a process of governance (Bache, 2003; Buller and Gamble, 2002; Goldsmith, 2003; Gualini, 2003; Kohler-Koch and Eising, 1999; Scharpf, 1999; Winn and Harris, 2003). Bache anchors his analysis to contemporary models of governance, such as the 'differentiated polity' model put forward by Rod Rhodes (1997). Goldsmith and, more explicitly, Gualini, draw systematically on multilevel governance. Kohler-Koch and Eising (1999) argue that Europeanization is a process by which understandings of governance in Europe are changed. They argue, for instance, that Europeanization has modified shared notions of governance in EU member states by establishing the principle of partnership between private and public actors and by inserting regions into a complex set of layers of governance.

This way of making sense of Europeanization has the advantage of contributing to cumulative social science research. Instead of assuming a *sui generis* 'nature' for Europeanization, one can relate the concept to our knowledge of governance. Future research, informed by 'Europeanization as governance', could tackle the thorny issue of whether Europeanization produces new governance, or hybrids of existing forms of governance. Another interesting question for this approach relates to its normative implications: is Europeanization producing good and legitimate governance in Europe? Or is it reducing social policymaking capabilities at the domestic level without compensating for this through a model of 'social Europe' delivered by EU institutions (Scharpf, 1999 and 2001; Mair, 2004, 47)?

Without denying that Europeanization is predominantly about governance, a second group of authors conceptualize Europeanization as institutionalization (Cowles *et al.*, 2001; Börzel, 2004; Kurzer, 2001; Olsen, 2002; Radaelli, 2003a). Indeed, the definition of Europeanization proposed above refers to Europeanization as a process through which formal rules and informal ways of doing things are first discovered and experienced in the EU context and then institutionalized by means of the behaviour of domestic actors. This is pretty close to the idea of European institutionalization proposed by Stone Sweet *et al.*, (2001). The difference is that the latter make a case for the growth of supranational governance along revised neofunctionalist lines, whereas the object of Europeanization is elsewhere, as illustrated above. Cowles *et al.*, (2001) conceptualize institutionalization as the emergence of distinctive structures of governance (for further discussion see Börzel and Risse, 2003), which in itself is an important illustration that different visions of Europeanization are often complementary rather than mutually exclusive. Nevertheless, their take on institutionalization is quite distinct in that it is based on the claim that the exclusive factor producing domestic change is the misfit between the domestic and the EU level. Put differently, in order to create domestic change, 'Europe' must be somewhat uncomfortable for domestic institutions.

As mentioned, the causal chain of institutionalization starts with adaptational pressure (created by misfit) and proceeds through two different possible pathways. The former is based on resource redistribution and the role of actors in an opportunity structure altered by EU variables. The latter has more in common with social constructivism and hinges on processes of socialization. Börzel and Risse (2003) account for specific intervening variables. When pressure operates as new opportunity structure, the intervening variables are the number of veto players and supporting formal institutions. Veto players and formal institutions convert new opportunities into concrete redistribution of resources, and thus contribute to differential empowerment. When pressure is instead channelled through collective understandings and norms, norm entrepreneurs and cooperative informal institutions can facilitate socialization and social learning. In turn, socialization and learning contribute to the institutionalization of norms and to the development of new identities. To conclude, this is a three-step framework based on adaptational pressure, mediating factors, and domestic change.

The major criticisms to Börzel and Risse boil down to the observation that this is not the only way things work. There are examples of Europeanization without major adaptational pressure. Domestic actors can use 'Europe' even in the absence of pressure. They can adapt domestic policy and produce change independently of pressures arising out of institutional misfit (Knill and Lehmkuhl, 1999 and 2002; Thatcher, 2004; Jacquot and Woll, 2003). Added to this is the observation that the degree of fit is discursively and socially constructed; it is not an objective measure. Much of the debate on welfare state reforms in Southern Europe, for example, is between those who argue that domestic policies are in line with European constraints (such as the stability and growth pact), and those who think that the fit between domestic policies and 'Europe' is poor, and hence that major reforms are needed. All in all, the 'goodness of fit' framework is somewhat excessively structural. There is not enough room for agency. True, actors are not completely neglected, but they act only in response to pressure. Instead, actors can also choose and learn from Europe outside adaptational pressures (Jacquot and Woll, 2003, 3). Thatcher (2004) shows how domestic reformers have been able to use European telecommunication policies to transform minimum pressure into major domestic change through a variety of discursive and bargaining strategies. Structural pressure would have predicted limited change. In order to understand the magnitude and the process of change, one has to include domestic actors and their creative usage of Europe.

The framework of institutionalization, however, cannot be reduced to goodness of fit propositions. Other authors have gone much further. Gualini, for example, blends multilevel governance with institutionalization to show how policy change can create major institutional transformation – a point that chimes with Giuliani's observation (2001) that Europeanized policies impact on polity. This makes the analysis of Europeanization much more dynamic. Instead of separating the domains of policy, politics, and polity (as Börzel and Risse, 2003, do), one can investigate the dynamic relations between policy change and macroinstitutional structures. Deep down, one can see the research agenda suggested by Theodor Lowi many years ago ('policies determine politics') rejuvenated by these recent developments.

Giuliani (2004) explicitly links new institutional theory (specifically, the organizational theory of institutionalization) and Europeanization. He argues that 'Europeanization as institutionalization' means essentially that (i) the EU is specialized and differentiated, (ii) there is self-validation of the EU, and that (iii) EU decisions cannot be derived from the utility functions of one member state or a stable group of member states. Self-validation is a classic feature of institutionalization processes in complex organizations. It means that an organization is valued (positively or negatively) *per se*, beyond the implications for individual members. By putting Europeanization on solid neo-institutional tracks, this suggestion sheds light on the 'deep nature' of Europeanization. It tells us that it is a process through which the EU gains its own autonomous meaning and self-validation within the logics, cognitive frames and behaviourial norms of domestic actors. I will turn to the implications of this point in a moment, but it is necessary to introduce the third framework first.

The third understanding is Europeanization as discourse, a claim made by Hay and Rosamond (2002) and Kallestrup (2002). Policymakers and stakeholders construct Europe through language and discourse. In turn, discourse is cast in different forms, from rhetoric (Schimmelfennig, 2001) to policy narratives (Radaelli, 1999). Hay and Rosamond note that Europeanization can be the vehicle through which discourses on globalization are institutionalized in domestic politics. Schmidt and Radaelli (2004; see also Schmidt, 2002) look at discourse in its institutional setting. They use the notion of discursive institutionalism. Discourse has a transformative power in EU policy and politics, but in order to understand if and when Europeanization produces change, one has to situate discourse in its institutional 'riverbeds'. Turning to Figure 4.1 one more time, discourse can change the preferences of actors, reformulate policy problems, make a style more confrontational or more cooperative and increase or decrease the value of resources (for example, by contesting the legitimacy of corporate actors).

Yet discourse is not just language. It is also an interactive process. Indeed, it is a set of ideas *and* an interactive process. The ideational dimension itself divides into two activities: a cognitive activity that enables actors to make sense of reality (drawing on knowledge, policy analysis, information about problems, actors and resources) and a more normative activity of assessing and judging reality, which refers to the world of norms, values and principles. The interactive dimension of discourse covers the relations between policymakers at the stage of policy formulation (how they convey meanings, in which institutional forums, through which acceptable norms of behaviour and expression) and how policies are communicated to the public.

making sense of europeanization

It is clear that the three different answers to the deep interrogation about the nature of Europeanization are not mutually exclusive, and that most authors use more than one framework. Let us try to take stock of these complementary frameworks then. One first element in common to the three approaches is the emphasis on domestic change. This is a convenient point of departure. Change or lack of change may be difficult to measure. Some aspects of change are subjectively (and often discursively) defined. Yet domestic change or lack of it provides a clear focus for the analysis of Europeanization as process. The question to address is how does one know that change is correlated or caused by Europeanization, and not by other variables. We have already mentioned the danger of pre-judging the impact of Europeanization. Other variables, like globalization and domestic politics, may matter more than Europeanization (on the 'globalization versus Europeanization' debate, see Verdier and Breen, 2001; Fligstein and Merand, 2001). The problem is compounded by the strategy of some political leaders to disguise globalization or domestic politics within a discourse of Europeanization – either by blame-shifting strategies or by using the appeal of Europe to add legitimacy to choices originating at home.

One can try to reduce the probability of making mistakes by using a number of simple devices. The first rule is that, in order to produce domestic change, Europeanization must precede change. This is not as simple as it seems. Europeanization often covers slow processes of socialization of domestic elites into European policy paradigms. These processes may co-evolve with national processes to redefine existing policy paradigms. The result is that it is not really clear whether Europeanization has overtaken domestic processes or just added to them. Take the case of Italian elite in EMU: Prior to Maastricht, the experience of the Exchange Rate Mechanism had certainly contributed to the socialization of Italian elites into a framework of sound finance and policy coordination. But during the same years a slow process of redefinition of monetary policy was under way at home, with the divorce between the Treasury and the Bank of Italy and the rise of monetarist ideas at the level of the elite (Dyson and Featherstone, 1999). In these circumstances, it is not easy to show whether Europeanization precedes domestic change or not.

In any case, the limitations of the *post-hoc, ergo propter hoc* prediction are well known. A process can take place before another without necessarily being correlated with it, let alone be its cause. This suggests a second control, based on mental counterfactuals. Would change have taken place anyway without Europeanization? Take the example of alcohol monopoly mentioned above. Would Finland and Sweden have redefined alcohol monopolies as a problem of competition policy without the activism of the European Commission and the treaty obligations on state aids and competition? Now take the example of Italy and EMU: Would Italy have moved to a sound finance paradigm and limited budget deficits without the role played by the European 'constraint'? Would this country have found its own way to macroeconomic stability without the fear of being left out of the eurozone?

Counterfactual analysis is a relatively common device in International Relations and Comparative Politics. Yet in order to perform it correctly one has to specify a number of 'alternative mechanisms'. This is where the third device to control hypotheses enters the scene. It refers to the explicit formulation of rival alternative hypotheses. All too often research on Europeanization is not clear enough on how globalization or domestic politics (to mention the classic rival alternative hypotheses) could have produced change. Research designs based on bottom-up approaches provide powerful controls for alternative hypotheses, but only if the alternatives are clearly formulated at the outset. Otherwise there is the risk of examining the evolution of policy and politics at the domestic level without awareness of what else (apart from Europeanization) could affect the system of interaction. Put bluntly, the risk is one of not 'seeing' rival mechanisms at work. The three views of Europeanization discussed in the previous section sit comfortably with these controls. Perhaps some 'Europeanization as discourse' advocates would reject the positivist bias of this methodology. But most people looking at Europeanization as discourse are outside the postmodernist camp and still operate using the logic of scientific inquiry and empirical analysis. Another possible exception comes from the 'goodness of fit' school. In this school, the issue of whether 'Europe' precedes 'domestic change' is not problematic: the study of Europeanization – they would argue – exists only insofar as there is a clear 'EU origin' (policy or politics). Starting from this origin, the analyst tracks down adaptational pressure and investigates the absence or presence of change. Nevertheless, most studies seem to point towards three important elements:

(1) There is Europeanization when the logic of domestic political actors changes. This happens when elements of EU policymaking become a cognitive and normative 'frame of reference' (Muller, 1995; Surel, 2000) and both the logic of action and the logic of meaning are guided by Europe. Think of Europe as the 'grammar' (Muller, 2000; Muller and Rouault, 1997) of domestic political action. (2) Europeanization is change both in the sense of responses to EU pressures and in the sense of other usages of Europe that do not presuppose pressure. (3) Europeanization is a process consisting of complex sequences and time patterns.

The reference to time and sequences is not trivial. One implication of getting the time dimension right is that it can avoid classic pitfalls in causal analysis. There are areas like justice and higher education where many initiatives of cooperation have not taken place in the context of EU processes (Megie and Ravinet, 2004). Yet there may be cases in which these initiatives have been facilitated by Commission white papers and socialization processes orchestrated by the Commission. One may find that once the Commission failed to create consensus on 'genuine EU measures', cooperation among certain countries then proceeded along non-EU tracks. But these tracks would not have been initiated had the Commission not contributed to agenda-setting and socialization.

The presence of fully-fledged European policies in a certain domain is not a pre-condition for Europeanization. Irondelle (2003) shows how French military policy has become Europeanized even though EU policies in this area have never taken off. Despite the absence of EU policies, the cognitive and normative policy frames of French policy have been gradually and increasingly redefined along European lines. Irondelle does not argue exclusively in terms of socialization. He demonstrates how pressure and rational calculations have also been part of the picture. His explanation is therefore compatible both with rational choice and social constructivism. Another implication is that Irondelle reaches his result only by getting the time dimension and the sequences right, as shown by his process-tracing design (Irondelle, 2003, 214).

To conclude, Europeanization does not require agreement on EU policies, but processes of socialization are not a sufficient condition for Europeanization. There may be considerable socialization without policy change at home. It is only when socialization is followed by domestic change than one can speak of Europeanization.

Socialization is not even necessary in processes of Europeanization where EU policies are absent. One might imagine, for example, a process of negotiation of EU directives for, say, liberalization, that remains stymied and controversial for several years. Decisions at the EU level do not materialize and beliefs remain polarized. Yet policymakers from countries adverse to liberalization may feel that they will lose the battle one day, and in order to suffer less later decide to launch a limited process of liberalization now. Controlled liberalization *ex ante* is better than imposed liberalization *ex post*. In this case, Europeanization is not the product of socialization, but of more rational mechanisms of anticipated reactions.

Another advantage of this approach is that it gets rid of the confusion between uploading and downloading. There has been some discussion on whether Europeanization refers only to the process of downloading policies, or whether it should also include the activities of uploading preferred policies in the context of EU policy formulation and EU decisions (see Börzel, 2002 on uploading and downloading). An understanding of Europeanization based on the three elements mentioned above (Europe as logic and frame, change, and time-sensitive analysis) does not need to postulate a simplistic life-cycle of policies. Failed uploading may nevertheless lead to some repercussions and reorientation at home. Downloading can make a marginal impact on domestic policies, but there may be more horizontal processes of benchmarking and cognitive reorientation in the same policy area eventually conducive to change. In this case again, what matters is change at home, of the type that can be captured by bottom-up research designs and careful process-tracing, although it should be observed that bottom-up research designs do not necessarily have anything to do with the uploading *versus* downloading discussion.

how europeanization produces domestic change

In order to analyse and measure the power of Europeanization, one has to think of mechanisms. We have already touched upon one of these mechanisms, the goodness of fit. But now it is useful to proceed more systematically. A number of building blocks for the analysis of mechanisms have already emerged. Europeanization is about governance and processes. It covers both cases where EU policies exist, and other cases where EU-level discussion does not end up with policies, yet domestic actors reorient their behaviour because 'Europe' has become the common grammar. This reorientation can be explained by preference change within socialization, but can also be the result of more rational calculation and anticipated reactions. Finally, Europeanization can be both 'vertical' (as shown by the discussion on uploading and downloading) and 'horizontal'.

Table 4.1 (adapted from Bulmer and Radaelli, 2005) introduces a number of different mechanisms of Europeanization and links them to various modes of governance. There are at least three different modes of governance in the EU policy process. They can be described as bargaining, hierarchy, and facilitated coordination. Bargaining and negotiations are not exclusive of policy formulation. There is a lot of bargaining at the level of domestic actors and between governments and the EU when directives are transposed into national legislation and implemented. Compliance can also be seen as negotiation. Actors can bargain over sanctions, but also in terms of interpretation of rules (Tallberg, 2002). When actors bargain, the main mechanism of Europeanization is adaptation as a result of anticipated reaction. Domestic actors formulate expectations of what the result of negotiation may be. They may calculate that it is better for them to change before the process of bargaining is concluded in order to gain some credit at home, or to limit the negative consequences of future decisions. Alternatively, one can see bargaining as a *sui generis* process of socialization, and hypothesize that preferences may gradually change in the context of long processes of negotiation. Although the default explanation of change at home relates to opportunity structure (last column in Table 4.1), there is some limited mileage for learning.

Table 4.1 Modes of governance, mechanisms, and explanations

Mode of governance	Type of policy	Analytical core	Mechanism	Default explanation
Bargaining	Positive or negative	Formulation of EU policies Implementation	Anticipated reactions	Structure of political opportunities
Hierarchy	Positive	Market-correcting rules, EU policy templates	Vertical	Goodness of fit
Hierarchy	Negative	Market-making rules, absence of EU policy templates	Horizontal	Regulatory competition
Facilitated coordination	Coordination	Benchmarking, soft-law, Open Method of Coordination, transfer, lesson-drawing	Horizontal	Learning

Source: Adapted from Bulmer and Radaelli (2005).

The second mode of governance is hierarchy. The EU governs hierarchically in two different ways. It can produce policies of positive integration that 'correct' the results of the market. Or it can engage in negative integration, by striking down the barriers to the market (Pinder, 1968; Scharpf, 1999). It is not relevant for our discussion, whether the EU does this via direct action by the Commission (competition policy), Council legislation, or the jurisprudence of the European Court of Justice. They are all forms of governance by hierarchy. The key difference between positive and negative integration is the presence or absence of EU models. In positive integration, the EU, more often than not, produces its own model of what policies should look like. As there is a model, there is some form of adaptational pressure, although not the same pressure for every member state. If pressure is very high, member states will not have the capability to change. The model is far too distant from their policies. One can think of the difficulty countries like France found in following EU templates for the liberalization of electricity. At the opposite pole, if adaptational pressure is very low, because EU and domestic models are compatible, there is no need to change things at home. The result is that major change is predicted in cases of manageable misfit. Overall, this is a vertical mechanism.

When the EU engages with negative integration, there is no major model or EU template. All the EU imposes hierarchically is the 'level playing field'. Rules against discrimination between residents and non-residents are a typical example. European Court of Justice jurisprudence striking down barriers to trade and freedom of establishment is another example. Negative integration is imposed hierarchically on member states, but the final outcome depends on the propensity and capacity of governments to engage in regulatory competition. As such, the mechanism is more horizontal than vertical. It is not at all a matter of fit or misfit. It is a matter of willingness and capability to change domestic policies in order to attract capital and highly-skilled labour.

The problem is that we still do not know much about regulatory competition (but see Vogel, 1995 and Murphy, 2004 on international regulatory competition). The idea of races (to the bottom or to the top) does not help much. Competition over policies and legal systems among states is not the same as competition between two companies over prices. For example, a state may well reduce a tax rate in order to attract corporations, but firms will change their location on the basis of a number of variables, including the quality of the labour force, the presence of major risks such as organized crime, and transport costs. A tax rate does not provide information on how taxes are enforced. A recent review of regulatory competition in Europe (Radaelli, 2004) did not find much evidence of this mechanism in Europe, probably because aggressive competition necessitates a transparent and fundamentally open market, and many EU markets are still somewhat opaque and protected.

The final mode of governance is facilitated coordination. When the EU uses this mode, it operates like a forum for discussion and a platform for policy transfer. Some forms of facilitated coordination have been around for a while, and not only in the EU, as shown by the literature on soft law (Schäfer, 2004; Snyder, 1994). However, facilitated coordination has been rediscovered and improved with the Lisbon agenda ambition to make the EU 'the most competitive knowledge-based society in the world' (Joao Rodrigues, 2004). Under facilitated cooperation, the EU organizes cooperation among member states, but does not produce European legislation. It produces opportunities for learning – the default explanation of Europeanization for this mode (Table 4.1, last column).

This mode of governance is typical of benchmarking exercises. For example, the directors of better regulation programmes in the EU meet routinely to discuss good practice in public management reforms and to assess the quality of regulation at the domestic and EU level. The aim is to facilitate mutual learning and diffusion of good practice. With the open method of coordination, governance by learning, socialization, and policy transfer have been codified and to some extent institutionalized. There is a lively debate on whether the open method of coordination can deliver or not (Borras and Greve, 2004; Ferrera et al., 2002; Radaelli, 2003b; Scharpf, 2002; Wincott, 2003). In terms of Europeanization, however, it is difficult to show that some domestic policy changes are a result of the open method of coordination rather than the consequences of domestic politics. It is not easy to measure the power of soft law, learning, and peer pressure. There is more research at the theoretical level than systematic empirical evidence. When available (Borras and Greve, 2004; De la Porte and Pochet, 2002; Bertozzi and Bonoli, 2002, Radaelli, 2003c), empirical research shows that in some policies Europeanization by facilitated coordination proceeds by ideational convergence, that is, changes of the cognitive and normative frames used by domestic policymakers. This does not mean convergence of domestic policies, of course. Indeed, one sceptical line in the debate is that the open method of coordination has created a community of discourse, but no real change in labour market, pensions, and social inclusion except where change is pushed by more concrete domestic processes of politics and policymaking.

Indeed, the literature on policy transfer tells us that effective transfer requires more than governance architectures like the open method of coordination. It also requires robust networks of stakeholders that facilitate the adoption of new policies at home, a strong civil society, and administrative-political capability to consciously modify, edit and adapt foreign experience to national circumstances (Jacoby, 2000; Rose, 2002). Although the open method of coordination has produced momentum for the discussion of politically sensitive reforms of the welfare state, its potential in terms of Europeanization is limited when the domestic coalitions for reforms are weak, or the stakeholders do not engage creatively with the imported institutional models.

what does the empirical evidence tell us?

Commenting on the empirical results of the literature is not an easy task. The results of major projects completed by teams of scholars are of course available (Cowles *et al.*, 2001; Héritier *et al.*, 2001; Featherstone and Radaelli, 2003; Hix and Goetz, 2001; Knill, 2001a; Dyson and Goetz, 2003). But they vary depending on frameworks employed by individual authors, including the above-mentioned distinction between Europeanization as governance, institutionalization and discourse. Furthermore, the notion of impact embraced by authors like Risse and Börzel refers to vertical mechanisms of adaptation, where evidence should point to change resulting from adaptational pressure. They approach Europeanization as *explanans* rather than *explanandum*. By contrast, authors interested in facilitated coordination and 'framing mechanisms' (Knill and Lehmkuhl, 2002) search for evidence that does not necessarily arise out of adaptational pressure. In more discursive approaches, Europeanization is investigated as a problem (that is, an *explanandum*). Mörth (2003) and Kallestrup (2002), for example, are interested in the process of editing and translating EU ideas and paradigms into national policy.

Five results stand out, however. Firstly, empirical evidence on the Europeanization of public policy is more robust than evidence on the Europeanization of political competition, state structures and the polity domain. Some policies are more impermeable to 'Europe' than others (Bulmer and Radaelli, 2005), as shown by the difference between competition and environmental policy, on the one hand, and higher education and justice, on the other.

One limitation of the current literature is that it works in a 'compartimental-ized' manner by considering only one dimension at a time. The most exciting projects, however, have shown that the three dimensions (politics, policy, and polity) interact, often in subtle and indirect ways (Giuliani, 2001; Gualini, 2003; Ladrech, 2002). This is the second result. Europeanized policies change state–society relations (see Cowles *et al.*, 2001 on pressure groups), empower technical bureaucracies, change the institutions of economic policy (Dyson, 2002), transform the cultural and organizational 'governance software' of departments (Jordan, 2003), transform the operating environment for party politics (Ladrech, 2002), and enable domestic actors to tilt the balance of power between regions and central government (Bull and Baudner, 2004). The adage that 'policies change but politics and polity do not' is obsolete. Europe-anization has, therefore, an important message for those who are interested in how governance is changing in Europe.

Thirdly, and (to some extent) consequently, the linkages between policies and the political-polity dimensions lead to an increasing stickiness of the national (and often regional) and European levels. There is no fusion of the various levels, but if Europe becomes the grammar of domestic political action and if the external environment becomes endogenous, the different levels may collapse in one dimension of Europeanized political action. However, Europeanization is not convergence. Even in such cases, the pattern is more one of clustered than of uniform convergence across Europe (Börzel, 2002; Goetz, 2002). The idea is that countries with the same structural characteristics respond with similar strategies to the opportunities and constraints provided by Europeanization. However, it is difficult to generalize across policy areas, as the same country often responds in dramatically different ways to Europeanization, depending on the constellation of actors and resources available in policy areas.

Convergence should be measured along a continuum. At a minimum, convergence means domestic policymakers share 'European' vocabularies. If Europeanization produces a convergence of paradigms and ideas of good practice, one can also speak of ideational convergence (Radaelli, 2003c). The next stage is convergence at the level of decisions. When similar decisions are implemented in a relatively uniform way, the degree of convergence increases. Finally, one can imagine the case of convergence in outcomes. Future research should explore, in a more systematic manner, types of convergence. More importantly still, it should expose the implicit theories of implementation contained in claims about convergence. For example, empirical studies routinely confirm that even hierarchical modes of governance in the EU do not produce policy convergence. But to imagine convergence of outcomes in the EU requires a theory of implementation close to the ideal-type of perfect, rational, chain-of-command administration. This is tantamount to ignoring the last thirty years of implementation research. Another example is provided by the discussion on limitations of facilitated coordination. If one argues that the open method of coordination is failing because it is not delivering convergence, one is neglecting the basic fact that facilitated coordination acknowledges diversity and different models of capitalism up-front. More generally, the whole issue of convergence in the EU should be framed in the context of the principle of subsidiarity.

To conclude this discussion of convergence, it is important to note that this is not a top-down process. In his analysis of competition policy in the UK and the EU, Zahariadis (2004) finds that even pace-setters like the UK may not be interested in uploading their model, or in other words, they may not be interested in contributing to the development of EU policy. The resulting incongruence between the EU and the domestic model does not necessarily 'produce change, much less convergence' at the domestic level (Zahariadis, 2004, 69). The EU and the UK models of competition policy have not converged for years. When they did converge, this was not the result of the pressure from above, but the outcome of domestic political processes. So, although the EU may provide an 'activating stimulus' for convergence (Zahariadis, 2004, 49), the actual process is driven by domestic politics.

Fifthly, empirical research has begun to examine the impact of Europeanization in the context of other possible pressures for convergence, such as globalization and international policy diffusion. Levi-Faur (2004) has argued that the impact of Europeanization in analyses of electricity and telecommunications sectors decreases when one performs controls such as comparing patterns of privatization in the EU with similar patterns in Latin America. However, although the overall direction of policy change may not be predicted by Europeanization, the latter may explain the scope of change and final outcomes – a point on which the discussion is fully open.

conclusions: where do we go from here?

I would like to conclude by going back to the question posed in the introduction about progressive problem shifts and the set of puzzles. Firstly, the question: What is the potential of Europeanization as a research agenda? The above discussion suggests Europeanization provides a valuable shift of focus by generating a set of questions for analysing the interplay between different levels of governance. Indeed, Europeanization may contribute to our understanding of the changing nature of governance and the state by endogenizing international governance in the models of domestic politics and policy. However, Europeanization is not a new theory. It is a way of organizing concepts. For political science in particular, it contributes to 'normalization' (Hassenteufel and Surel, 2000) in the sense that it systematically draws on Comparative Politics, International Relations, Policy Analysis and international political economy. Europeanization is compatible with different perspectives prevalent in politics and International Relations disciplines (Featherstone and Radaelli, 2003). Accordingly, it does not need to create its own *ad hoc* theoretical models. This is an advantage, as EU Studies are often accused of having abused *ad hoc* theory, rather than drawing on Comparative Politics (Hix, 1999).

Having clarified in what sense Europeanization is a research agenda, this chapter has also shown the set of research puzzles that characterize this field. Methodologically, the most promising puzzles revolve around the notion of impacts, how to control for rival alternative hypotheses, and how to integrate agency in the explanation of change. Preliminary responses in the literature point towards complex notions of causality (Elster, 1989a) and comprehensive sociology (Jacquot and Woll, 2003). In turn, these complex notions expose the limitations of research designs oriented towards tests of simple causal hypotheses. One challenge for future research is how to embrace these complex notions and be 'clear enough to be wrong' (Sabatier, 2000). It is necessary to ask, for example: If Europeanization is a frame of reference, what are the empirical indicators that show its existence or absence? This raises the further issue of operationalization. So far, the literature has produced more metaphors than systematic attempts to operationalize variables – and without operationalization 'large *n*' comparisons are impossible. (For recent work on operationalization see Falkner, 2003 and Giuliani, 2003.)

Turning to empirical results, most of the current focus is on the mechanisms of Europeanization and whether, where and how they are producing substantive change. Future research will have to get to grips with the limitations of each and every mechanism. The goodness of fit mechanism, for instance, has to account for agency and the transformative power of discourse to gain more precision. The mechanism of regulatory competition is still unexplored, and perhaps too obsessed with races and their direction, rather than being concerned with how to explain real-world processes of competition. More interdisciplinary research is needed in this field. Finally, mechanisms of facilitated coordination should clarify the conditions for learning and how the latter produces change. The emphasis on learning should not obfuscate the fact that learning can be conflictual and asymmetric. Additionally, more research is needed on how soft and hard mechanisms (for example, governance by hierarchy and facilitated coordination) interact in the same policy area. Convergence and compliance are still relatively unexplored concepts, although new research shows how problem-shifts induced by Europeanization may help (see Zahariadis, 2004 on bottom-up convergence and Tallberg, 2002 on compliance).

Finally, political scientists in particular need to bring politics back into the analysis of Europeanization – a point made by Peter Mair (2004). By focusing on cleavages, dimensions of conflict, and patterns of contestation, Europeanization can inform analysts about the nature of the EU and its member states as a political system, with its own processes of boundary building, representation and political structures. In this way, Europeanization may be able to penetrate the nature of EU politics much more effectively than the major theories of European integration.

With all its limitations, Europeanization provides a fascinating perspective on how governance is changing. As such, it is a valuable tool for research. It is not a 'solution' (this time in the sense of providing off-the-shelf explanations). It is a challenging, exciting 'problem'.

notes

1. Research for this chapter was carried out at the University of Exeter in the context of the Integrated Project "New Modes of Governance" <www.eu-newgov.org>, financially supported by the European Union under the 6th Framework programme (Contract No CIT1-CT-2004-506392).
2. For a simple introduction to these concepts see the famous talk on science and pseudo-science originally broadcast on 30 June 1973 (text accessible at <www.lse. ac.uk/collections/lakatos/scienceAndPseudoscienceTranscript.htm>). The text also appears in the introduction to Lakatos (1978).
3. I have come across sceptical readers arguing that Europeanization is just a waste of time. They point to some 'Europeanization' articles and papers which either re-brand honest empirical research on EU policies as 'Europeanization' or (worse) literally regurgitate classic concepts and ideas about political integration and implementation originally formulated by lawyers, policy analysts, and political scientists. In this chapter I look at the added value net of bandwagon effects. As shown by Mair (2004,

337) the number of articles on this topic is increasing. A consequence is that there are some bandwagon effects common to all topics when they gain popularity. Some articles rebrand well-known features of European integration as 'Europeanization'. It takes a decade or so for a new field of research to 'settle down' and clarify concepts and research agenda. Thus, although bandwagon effects exist, it would be unfair to argue that there is nothing new in Europeanization. At least *some* work in this area has produced challenging propositions and fresh ideas. Mair (2004, 346), who certainly cannot be accused of following the Europeanization bandwagon, contrasts the innovative work on Europeanization and European integration with his past experience of reading 'dull descriptive, and atheoretical' papers on European politics and policy.

4. Throughout the chapter, I will draw on Gualini's idea of Europeanization as *explanandum* (Gualini, 2003).

5. With the qualification that hollowing out can also be the result of processes of regionalization induced by European integration.

6. The identification of *explanans* and *explanandum* as 'solution' and 'problem' is quite common. See <www.iscid.org/encyclopedia>.

7. In this chapter I do not deal with the thorny issue of how to measure change. Change is often in the eye of the beholder, and what looks like inertia at time n may well become deep transformation at time $t+n$. My views on this topic are in Radaelli (2003a, 37–40).

5
conceptual combinations:
multilevel governance and policy networks
alex warleigh

introduction

In this chapter I consider two recent additions to the EU scholar's analytical toolkit: the concepts of multilevel governance and policy networks. I seek to explain the meaning of these concepts and to set out their respective uses for advancing our theoretical understanding of the EU. I argue that the two concepts are of greatest utility when they are used together rather than separately, hence reference in the chapter title to 'conceptual combinations'. I argue this because multilevel governance is a concept which helps us understand the kind of polity that the EU has become and how it is currently evolving, whereas policy network analysis helps us understand the complex processes of alliance construction, bargaining and deliberation through which EU public policy is actually produced. In other words, when taken together, the two concepts can give EU scholars a workable understanding of the nature of the EU system and how it works. We can thus go some way – but not all the way – towards filling the 'grand theory-shaped hole' (Warleigh, 2000a, 173) that has been present in recent EU theory, and combine insights from different approaches more successfully than in the past.

Multilevel governance and policy networks approaches are particularly useful because they help EU scholars address a recent shift in how public power is exercised. Across the Western world, and arguably beyond, hierarchical and heavily institutionalized ways of 'doing politics' are becoming less prevalent. Instead, power is wielded by actors and groups both in and around formal state institutions. Furthermore, state actors share power, at least to some extent, with actors from the private sector, civil society and non-state institutions or agencies. State power is being re-thought (but not removed!), as pointed out by Hajer and Wagenaar (2003, 5). Thus, new takes on EU theory have to address not only the problems that defeated their forebears. They must also address what appears to be a rather different world of policymaking, in which not only the range of actors involved, but also the very ways they produce policy, have changed.

This shift is often thought of as one from 'government' to 'governance', and it is particularly evident in the case of the EU. As a supranational institution, or set of institutions, the EU is a means by which member state governments seek to collaborate to achieve policy goals. Its development reflects the contemporary shift towards involving international actors and processes in what would previously have been national processes of policymaking. Furthermore, it is an incomplete and evolving polity, in which power is *shared*, rather than formally separated. This sharing of power occurs both horizontally (that is, between the EU institutions) and vertically (that is, between national, sub-state and EU levels). As a result, the EU relies on experimental forms of policymaking, involving many groups of actors and several different decision rules. These processes rely on coalition-building and informal politics to a very significant extent (Warleigh 2000b; Richardson, 2001; Christiansen and Piattoni, 2003). Thus, if scholars are attempting to understand and explain the process of EU policymaking and the nature of the EU polity, they will need to be alive to its evolutionary and explicitly political – or *contested* – nature.

The structure of the chapter is as follows. First, I explore the concept of multilevel governance, setting out its principal tenets, development to date and its application to EU Studies. Second, I perform a similar task for policy networks analysis, albeit more briefly. In the third section, I harness the two concepts together to constitute a working theory of EU governance, drawing on aspects of multilevel governance and policy network analysis to understand both the general nature of the Europolity and day-to-day policymaking therein. Finally, I evaluate the utility of this multilevel governance-policy networks analytical framework and set out what I consider to be its strengths and weaknesses.

multilevel governance

main tenets

Multilevel governance is an approach primarily associated with Gary Marks and Liesbet Hooghe. Their work (see especially Marks *et al.*, 1996; Hooghe and Marks, 2001a; Marks and Hooghe, 2000 and 2004) emphasizes the roles played by individual actors in the EU (Marks, 1996), and therefore develops a subtle and insightful understanding of the range of strategic, normative and ideational variables that can shape EU policy decisions. Multilevel governance scholars insist that neither member states nor the EU institutions are monolithic (Hooghe, 1996a) and that the development of the EU polity is shaped, in broad terms, by cross-institutional and cross-national alliances of actors who share the same objectives on a given issue.

Multilevel governance analysis originated in the study of EU cohesion policy, and in particular its 'partnership' principle. This latter principle stipulates that, in the formation and implementation of cohesion policy, actors from sub-state governments and regional-level civil society must play a meaningful role alongside actors from national governments and the EU itself.

Multilevel governance scholars found in this partnership principle evidence of an intertwining EU system that gave formal as well as informal roles and powers to a range of actors. This included both governmental and non-governmental actors at each level of the polity – EU, national, regional and local. This kind of intertwining system had not been rigorously conceptualized by earlier theoretical approaches, which focused on a two-level analysis, namely national and EU levels.

Multilevel governance paints a picture of an evolving EU polity in which powers are uneasily shared between actors at the local/regional, national and 'European' levels, and in which actors other than member state central governments are capable of autonomous and influential action. At the EU level, the longstanding powers of the Commission and the newer legislative powers of the European Parliament mean that national governments no longer control the legislative process, even as a collective. Multilevel governance thus detects a process whereby 'states in the European Union are being melded into a multilevel polity by their leaders and the actions of numerous subnational and supranational actors' (Hooghe and Marks, 2001a, 27).

This melding process is partly – perhaps mainly – the result of deliberate choices made by national elites to delegate powers 'upwards' (to the EU) and 'downwards' (to the regions/localities) in order better to achieve their policy objectives. However, as the authors go on to argue, the specificities of the EU system are not primarily the result of deliberate design. Rather they are the product of a disorganized series of choices and bargains made by member states over time, and the actions taken either by those states or by the EU institutions to deal with the often unintended or unanticipated consequences of those choices (Hooghe and Marks, 2001a, 75).

A member state decision to share power at the EU level can be taken for various reasons. A first reason why member states might choose to construct a multilevel governance system is ideological conviction. New ways of solving policy problems such as power-sharing with other partner governments may be seen as more efficient or simply a better way of doing things as a matter of principle (Kohler-Koch, 1996). There is clearly a normative element to both European integration and the decentralization of domestic governance, which can perhaps best be summarized as peace-keeping and security in the first instance and democracy in the second. However, such normative logics are complemented by a set of variations on a more hard-nosed theme: achieving policy goals that would otherwise be more difficult, or even impossible, to realize.

Marks and Hooghe's second explanation for the creation of a multilevel governance system is central governments' wish to reinforce their power in international negotiations. If a national government can plausibly claim to its peers that it needs concessions in order to 'sell' an agreement domestically, perhaps to a regional tier of governance or to other key players, it is more likely to receive such concessions and thereby obtain an outcome in line with its key preferences. In a related argument, the third explanation is that creating a multilevel governance system can empower national governments vis-à-vis powerful domestic actors and interest groups. It may allow national governments to escape blockages in the national policymaking system or help them to force troublesome domestic groups into complying with national governments preferences. A fourth reason for the creation of such a system is to bind the hands of successor administrations. Governments or individual politicians with deep convictions on a given issue, which their domestic opponents inside or outside their own political party do not share, may seek to ensure that conviction is translated into public policy in a way that their successors in power will find difficult to overturn. EU legislation, which can only be removed by a new agreement or decision at EU, rather than national, level, is one way politicians may be able to bind their successors. In essence, consensus can sometimes be found at EU level even if it cannot be found domestically, and relevant policy can thus become 'locked in'.

Two further factors that might lead governments to establish a multilevel governance system relate to strategic decisions of a slightly different kind. Choosing to govern via a multilevel governance system allows national governments to achieve their objectives while maintaining the option of blaming others for unpopular decisions, a sleight of hand which can be electorally convenient. Alternatively, national governments may agree to the creation or reinforcement of a multilevel governance system because it is a necessary precondition for the achievement of their real objective. This kind of reasoning might be advanced to explain why the then prime minister of the United Kingdom, Lady Thatcher, agreed to institutional deepening in the EU, notably the introduction of qualified majority voting and the beginnings of legislative power for the European Parliament: It was the unavoidable precondition set by other member states as the price to be paid for establishing the single market, the UK's key objective at the time.

The seventh reason given by Marks and Hooghe to explain the creation of a multilevel governance system in the EU is of an entirely different nature. The argument is that member states sometimes agree to the creation or deepening of multilevel governance because they have no choice: either through subtlety, or through the overt use of the powers given to them, EU institutions can present the member states with non-negotiable demands. At a day-to-day level, this might be seen in the European Parliament's successful use of its legislative powers to gain concessions from the Council of Ministers. At a macro level, it can be observed in the Commission's long-term strategies to create new competencies or even new institutions at the EU level (Tömmel, 1998). Multilevel governance analysts have even observed it in the politics of treaty change (Marks *et al.*, 1996, 352–3). The idea that member states might be compelled to 'agree' to the deepening of European integration is of course controversial (see below). However, the key point to note here is that multilevel governance scholars argue that national elites perceive gains in European integration, or may be unable to prevent it despite their own reservations. Thus, multilevel governance is an approach that recognizes state power but does not consider it the whole story.

critique, reformulation and the use of multilevel governance in eu studies

Multilevel governance has been subject to criticism on a number of grounds, which can be grouped into three main categories: the allegation that multilevel governance does not follow rules for the production of sound social science theory; the allegation that multilevel governance is internally confused; and the allegation that some of the key claims of multilevel governance scholars are exaggerated. I investigate each of these clusters of criticism in turn.

is multilevel governance sound social science theory?

Several scholars have been reserved in welcoming multilevel governance on the grounds that it does not conform to the requirements of 'good theory'. This reflects the fact that multilevel governance was elaborated at a time when reflection about not just EU theory, but about what makes good social science theory in general, was common. Some critiques refer to the requirements of orthodox social science, while others argue that in fact multilevel governance has not distanced itself sufficiently from the rather positivist approach of US social science prevalent during the last century.

The first camp of critics have argued that multilevel governance rests on an unsuitable foundation. Beginning as a case study of one policy area – cohesion policy – whose institutional arrangements (particularly the 'partnership principle') are not typical of those found in other policy areas, critics have asked: On what basis do multilevel governance scholars seek to generalize their insights to the rest of the EU policymaking system? To some extent, variation in the influence of substate actors in different policy areas can be accepted as part of the differing pattern of influence that multilevel governance scholars expect for all actors in the EU policymaking process. However, there are clear problems of generalizability at play here, particularly as multilevel governance scholars place such importance on the issue of *multilevel* policymaking processes involving actors from levels of power other than the national and the supranational (for further analysis on this point see Bache and Flinders, 2004). Liesbet Hooghe had the grace to concede as much in one of her earlier pieces (Hooghe, 1996c), but multilevel governance scholars have yet to develop a convincing reply to their critics on this issue. Instead, they have tended to rely on pointing out problems with other rival theories or other assets of multilevel governance, a tactic that is unsustainable in the long term.

Furthermore, it has been argued that multilevel governance is not sufficiently precise, and thus that its ability to predict events or explain phenomena must be applied only at a very general level (Adshead, 2002; Peters and Pierre, 2004). In particular, it has been alleged that multilevel governance is underspecified in two key respects that lie right at its heart. First, it does not supply the conceptual mechanisms for understanding exactly how changes at one level of the posited multilevel system are linked to changes at another level, or how these changes can impact on each other (Adshead, 2002). Second, its account of how and why substate actors mobilize is thin on three counts: its definition of 'mobilization'; the reasons why substate actors seek to mobilize in EU politics (particularly regarding intra-state causal factors); and regarding analysis of the various informal and formal channels of mobilization open to such actors (Longman, 2002; Jeffery, 1997 and 2000).

In the second camp, it has been claimed that multilevel governance does not reach its promise in terms of breaking with traditional understandings of either key concepts or good practice in theory-building. Of course, it has never been clear that such was the ambition of multilevel governance scholars, but it has been demonstrated that metatheoretical conservatism may reduce the value of multilevel governance in certain ways. For example, Aalberts (2004) argues that an explicitly constructivist reading of the concept of sovereignty would enable multilevel governance scholars to complete their (often implicit) wish to redefine the concepts of state power and even the state itself, and thus develop a more coherent theory. Elsewhere (Warleigh, 2003b) I have argued that a wish to engage with positivistically-cast theories on terms that their critics would recognize as valid has occasionally led multilevel governance scholars down blind alleys, such as the problematization (rather than simple acceptance as a given) of variation in substate authority engagement with the EU.

Marks and Hooghe's (2000) essay, 'Optimality and Authority: A Critique of Neoclassical Theory', shows why such criticisms could be made. It is a reflective piece in which the authors explicitly discuss (and anticipate further variants of) the allegation that their approach is too 'rationalistic'. In the essay, Hooghe and Marks emphasize the actor-centred and sociological institutionalist aspects of multilevel governance, particularly its stress on ideas and values in determining actor behaviour. However, despite this *démarche*, Hooghe and Marks remain firmly in the 'orthodox' camp regarding their approach to theory-building: Even in the essay mentioned directly above, Hooghe and Marks seek to generate causal, rather than constitutive, theory.[1] Of course, this only matters if we think orthodox approaches to key concepts and theory-building require revision. Analytically speaking, however, such criticisms of multilevel governance may mean, at the very least, that it has more in common at a metatheoretical level with its self-appointed 'Other' (liberal intergovernmentalism) than is often recognized by multilevel governance scholars themselves.

is multilevel governance internally coherent?

Allegations that multilevel governance is internally inconsistent may in part derive from the problems set out immediately above: Scholars have interpreted the same body of work rather differently. However, there are issues of both theoretical rigour and organizational clarity to be addressed here. On the first count, multilevel governance suffers from a Macbeth-like surfeit of ambition (Warleigh, 2000a) that threatens to undermine its real achievements. Multilevel governance is what might be called a middle-range theory. It originally set out to analyse and explain the present condition of the Europolity in a general way, providing a solid understanding of that system. This, in turn, allows other devices to be used to explain both how and why European integration was initiated, and how the micropolitics of the EU – that is, its day-to-day legislative process – functions. Multilevel governance scholars have tried to cast the approach as something rather more than that: as both a means of understanding the entire European integration project (Marks et al., 1996), and even an approach to understanding decisionmaking more generally – at international and local levels (Marks and Hooghe, 2004). This clear case of concept-stretching makes multilevel governance somewhat incoherent because it takes a set of analytical tools that are perfectly appropriate for a particular task (exploring the workings of EU cohesion policy and what they imply for the EU system in general) and misuses them. In so doing, it undermines both the clarity and the purpose of the original analysis.

Perhaps also as a result of the ambition surplus, multilevel governance writing is sometimes unclear on key issues. There is inevitably an element of subjective interpretation here; everyone reads through lenses of their own making. However, multilevel governance does require further clarity in some of its principal tenets, especially if its claims to be more than a middle-range theory of EU politics are to be taken seriously. A suitable example is the old issue of structure versus agency. As a self-consciously actor-centred approach, this problem is perhaps an unanticipated weakness in multilevel governance; and yet, Rosenau (2004) charges multilevel governance with paying too much attention to institutions, and therefore not enough attention to non-institutional actors and decisionmaking fora. Peters and Pierre (2004), making precisely the opposite allegation, charge it with paying insufficient attention to institutions.

does multilevel governance make exaggerated claims?

Scholars outside the multilevel governance school have argued that multilevel governance is no more than a metaphor encapsulating an understanding of the current Europolity, and that it rests on exaggerated understandings of the relative power of various actors in the system. First, one does not have to be a paid-up intergovernmentalist to question the assertion made by multilevel governance scholars (Marks *et al.*, 1996, 352–3) that in essential decisions shaping the EU system, such as treaty change, actors other than national governments may have meaningful power. True, it is plausible that non-state actors could feed ideas into national government preference-formation processes about what should go into the new Treaty, but even advocates of liberal intergovernmentalism would agree to that possibility. It is also plausible that actors from the Commission or even the European Parliament could act as brokers of compromise when national government representatives reach an impasse. What seems unlikely, however, is that when it comes to the actual decisions that shape the rules of the game – essentially deciding what goes into a new treaty – that any actor other than national governments has any influence. This was shown clearly in the negotiations that produced the Nice Treaty, and even more clearly in the refusal by the member states to accept the Draft Constitutional Treaty produced by the deliberative Convention on the Future of Europe without months of further bargaining and package deals.[2]

It has also been argued that multilevel governance scholars underestimate the capacity and will of EU member states to resist shifts towards the new forms of policymaking that such scholars assume are rolling-out across the EU. For example, in her study of regional development in three member states, Adshead (2002) argues that if national governments are not willing to be influenced by the EU in terms of how they develop their regional policies, they can and do resist such changes. Other forms of empirical work have brought different multilevel governance assumptions into question. Jeffery (2000) has questioned the very will of substate actors to engage with EU policymaking, and studies of how partnerships at regional level actually work have pointed out that participation in such partnerships by substate actors is far more common than their actual influence over policy outcomes (Bache, 1998). Similar conclusions have been drawn in studies of EU citizenship and civil society groups' lobbying in Brussels and Strasbourg, which multilevel governance scholars take as emblematic of a new kind of polity, but which empirical study often reveals as rather limited phenomena (Bellamy and Warleigh, 2001; Warleigh, 2001).

reformulation

Thus, multilevel governance has been widely criticized on several counts. As part of the process of creating new conceptual tools, this sort of critique is to be expected. Recent work by Marks and Hooghe (2004) seeks to reply to some of this criticism by elevating the normative aspects of multilevel governance to new salience and by producing a typology of multilevel governance systems that is then used to describe the condition of the Europolity.

That the normative aspect of multilevel governance should be emphasized more strongly in Marks and Hooghe's recent work is perhaps unsurprising. EU theory in general has undergone a 'normative turn' recently in order to address issues of the democratic deficit as well as reflect on metatheory (for an overview see Warleigh 2003a). Thus, Marks and Hooghe (2004, 16) claim that multilevel governance is normatively superior to the monopoly of power by national governments. This is so on the grounds of efficiency, that is an improved capacity to deliver public policy through collaboration with other actors, competition between different tiers, and a resultant capacity to be experimental or innovative. They also argue that multilevel governance is superior on democratic grounds, because multilevel systems can reflect the diverse range of citizens' preferences on a range of policy issues more effectively than individual nation-states. While not every scholar would share this view, those who defend the democratic value of international organizations on similar grounds are sufficiently numerous to suggest that this claim is not inherently controversial (see, for example, Zürn, 2000).

More likely to cause debate is Hooghe and Marks' new typology of multilevel governance, shown in Table 5.1.

Table 5.1   Marks and Hooghe's new typology of multilevel governance

Variable	Type I	Type II
Jurisdictional scope	General purpose	Function-specific
Membership	Non-intersecting	Intersecting
Number of levels of governance	Limited	Unlimited
Scope of institutions	System-wide	Varying – flexible range of institutional architectures
Sense of community among involved actors	High	Low
Privileged function	Voice	Exit
Policy issues addressed	Basic politics, including redistribution	Market-making problems

Source: Adapted from Marks and Hooghe (2004).

The typology is controversial because Hooghe and Marks appear to put forward a vision of the EU that is at variance with both their own previous work and observable trends in EU politics. As Table 5.1 shows, Marks and Hooghe argue that multilevel governance comes in two varieties, Types I and II. Type I relies on a hierarchical division of powers between various levels of power. Responsibilities and capacities to act are clearly spelled out, as in a federal state. The membership of Type I multilevel governance organizations is determined territorially or communally, meaning that it rests on a clear sense of identity and 'we-ness'. Such organizations have a limited number of levels, and their institutions enjoy powers that range over the whole set of policy issues in the system (albeit respecting the separation of powers mentioned above). The issues addressed by Type I multilevel governance organizations occupy an impressive span, and include the basic controversies of national politics, such as redistribution. Thus, the privileged function of this type of multilevel governance system is *voice* (that is, the ability to take part), as expressed 'in conventional liberal democratic institutions' (Marks and Hooghe, 2004, 28).

Type II variants of multilevel governance, however, are function-specific – that is, they focus on a narrow range of issues, with certain issues being placed explicitly outside their scope. In such multilevel governance entities, independent jurisdictions dedicated to particular policy issues overlap, as does the membership of each policy-based jurisdiction. This is seen as necessary for the production of relevant public goods or policies. The number of levels in Type II multilevel governance is potentially unlimited, with power being exercised not at discrete levels of governance in hierarchical order but rather by shifting patterns of actors who form issue-based coalitions. The sense of community required in Type II multilevel governance is much less intense, resting on shared interests that may change, rather than shared values or identity. As a result, actors involved seek to privilege *exit* mechanisms (that is, the ability to break alliances and/or form new ones) rather than the ability to deliberate and agree outcomes by consensus. Tending to focus on a narrow range of policy issues, Type II variants of multilevel governance may have primary responsibility for the creation and maintenance of a well-functioning free trade regime/common (single) market.

For Marks and Hooghe, Type I multilevel governance is to be found in every state in Europe, or at least in those that are already members of the EU. Type II multilevel governance is to be found at the global level of governance, in cross-border regional cooperation in North America and Western Europe, and at the local level in many Western states (Marks and Hooghe, 2004, 22–6). Where it is *not* to be found is in the EU system itself. The EU is classified as the major exception to the absence of Type I multilevel governance at the international level on the grounds that it has few, rather than many, tiers of governance and that it makes one single policy for the entire EU, rather than allowing competing policies to coexist in a given issue area (Marks and Hooghe, 2004, 23).

It is the location of the EU as an example of Type I multilevel governance category that excites criticism. The statement that the EU has few rather than many levels of governance seems reasonable. However, by definition, so do local governments and transborder regions, which Marks and Hooghe have no problem treating as Type II multilevel governance. Moreover, Marks and Hooghe admit that even a very narrow understanding of the use of flexibility in European integration – for example, opting-out of EU policy in the single currency and border control regimes – undermines the second ground on which they classify the EU variant as Type I multilevel governance. A more satisfactory reading of flexibility, which takes into account the long history of quasi-permanent national derogations from EU policy, the use of extra-EU mechanisms for cooperation by EU states (for example, NATO, or Anglo-French cooperation on defence matters), and the fact that member states increasingly opt out of EU policies through choice rather than technical incapacity to implement the new legislation, blows the idea that the EU has no competing policies in its areas of competence out of the water. Marks and Hooghe almost admit this alongside their concession that the EU's pillar structure (which will survive even if the present Constitutional Treaty is ratified) and varying decision rules undermine the credibility of any claim that the EU has a single institutional architecture (2004, 23). A further issue which they do not address is the recent tendency for new forms of EU policymaking that allow the co-existence of different national policy regimes, such as the Open Method of Coordination, benchmarking and 'best practice' exchange used, for example, in much recent EU social and employment policy.

Moreover, there are several other factors that would seem to classify the EU as Type II multilevel governance. In keeping with the typology's specifications, the EU has a limited range of competences, which tend to focus on the single market and whatever flanking policies can be squeezed out of it. It does have intersecting jurisdictions, because certain states opt out of various policies, but the range of such states is different in each policy case. For example, the United Kingdom, Denmark and Sweden sit outside the eurozone, but in the case of the Schengen legislation on border control, Sweden joins the mainstream, Denmark sits half-in and half-out, the UK's opt-out is shifting towards a degree of opting-in, and Ireland replaces Sweden as an 'outsider'. Furthermore, non-member states such as Norway and Switzerland take part in a large number of EU policy regimes, especially those regarding the single market. The sense of shared identity and solidarity in the EU, at elite and popular levels is notoriously (and disappointingly) low (Warleigh, 2003a).

Perhaps the only variable on which the EU can be assessed as Type I multilevel governance is the issue of 'privileged function'. This is because many states join the EU to have the power of 'voice' or to shape legislation that affects them whether they are members or not. However, even here it is not clear that Marks and Hooghe's definition of voice, or deliberation in liberal democratic-style institutions, applies to EU politics. The EU's resemblance to liberal democratic norms is almost universally challenged (Warleigh, 2003a) and its day-to-day policymaking privileges issue-based coalitions of actors who protect their capacity to 'exit' such alliances at any time (Warleigh, 2000b). Thus, the reformulation and new typology of multilevel governance raises more questions than it removes. Somewhat oddly, Marks and Hooghe appear to be seeking to apply the concept to the EU, and to both international and national politics too. Questions about the proper scope of multilevel governance remain, as do concerns about its capacity to be operationalized. I now turn to the concept of policy networks in order to trace its contribution to EU Studies, and subsequently to investigate whether and to what extent it can act as a helpful supplement to multilevel governance.

policy networks

The policy networks concept derives from efforts to understand how policy is made in national political systems under conditions of the shift from government to governance. Much early work in the field was done in the UK. Scholars such as Rod Rhodes (1997) sought to go beyond both formal procedural accounts of policymaking and those privileging market-based normative accounts of how public goods and policy could best be provided. Their research problem was to understand how actors from different institutions collaborated to achieve policy outcomes, and how central authorities dealt with (or managed) the representation and mobilization of actors from the periphery and/or sectoral interest groups. In order to understand these processes, which rely on the construction of alliances and the aggregation of interests, Rhodes developed the notion of the 'policy network', a 'set of resource-dependent organisations' (Rhodes *et al.*, 1996, 368), in which actors jostle for influence and position. Policy networks can thus be understood as 'hybrid means of coordination that (are) neither of the market nor embedded in a formal hierarchy' (Heinelt and Smith, 1996a, 2).

Taking its cue from institutional theories of politics (Rhodes, 1997), policy network analysis argues that an actor's influence over outcomes is dictated by whether she can gain membership of, and importance within, a privileged group of actors who control events in a given policy field. Actors seek to join the network because of this power, and because they do not have sufficient resources themselves to shape policy outcomes independently of other actors. Their relative standing and power within a policy network will be dependent on the quantity and quality of resources, such as the money, knowledge, skill and contacts that they have available (Peterson, 1995).

Policy networks thus serve several useful functions. They set limits on who can participate in policymaking; they define the roles that these actors can play; they screen out, and bring in, agenda issues; they shape actor behaviour through the elaboration of rules and norms; and they privilege certain interests and outcomes (Rhodes, 1997, 9–10). However, they also undermine transparency and accountability, because decisions that once might have been made publicly are now made behind closed doors by a privileged group of actors (Rhodes, 1997, 10).

Different kinds of policy network have been uncovered in public policymaking. However, although various categories of these networks have been established (Rhodes and Marsh, 1992), the principal distinction among types is that between 'policy communities' and 'issue networks' (summarized in Table 5.2).

Table 5.2   Rhodes' Typology of Policy Networks

Policy community	Issue network
Small membership	Large membership
All members have useful resources	Useful resources concentrated in hands of subsection of membership
Based on iterated exchange – can lead to further shared interests and values	Based on varying levels of contact
Win-win outcomes	Win-lose outcomes

Source: Adapted from Rhodes et al., 1996.

Policy communities are said to exist when a small number of actors, all of whom have resources that are useful to the others, cooperate over the medium to long term on a range of issues that concern them all. Such repeated cooperation can produce further shared interests, and even shared values (Rhodes *et al.*, 1996). Policy communities tend to achieve win-win outcomes, that is, results that all members of the community are happy with and results from which they all stand to gain. 'Issue networks', on the other hand, involve a large number of actors, who are in irregular contact with each other and not all of whom have significantly useful resources for all the other members of the network. Such networks can be successful in influencing policy decisions, but tend to produce outcomes that benefit their members differentially rather than equally. In EU Studies, this issue-network-versus-policy-community typology has been echoed in debates about how best to understand the alliances actors build when seeking to change or make EU policy. These alliances have respectively been categorized as 'policy coalitions' (Warleigh, 2000b) and 'advocacy coalitions' (Sabatier, 1998). (For a helpful set of essays on EU interest representation and the kind of networks and processes it involves, see the essays in Warleigh and Fairbrass, 2003.)

critique and utility in eu studies

Critiques of policy network analysis in EU Studies have been relatively few. They tend to rely on unfair accusations of concept-stretching, which can easily be countered by Rhodes' repeated and explicit statement (for example, Rhodes *et al.*, 1996, 369) that the approach is a 'meso-level concept' with clear limits to its scope. However, as a corollary, policy networks analysis is insufficient as a general theory of either EU politics or European integration – a point whose validity advocates of the approach also accept (Rhodes *et al.*, 1996, 378). A further general criticism of policy networks – namely that they are helpful metaphors but no more – can also be discounted (Adshead, 2002).

This is because the approach sets out the bases for research hypotheses and questions, and is thus operationalizable.

However, criticism of the applicability of the concept to EU Studies has been made on more substantial grounds, namely that as a conceptual tool derived from national (or comparative) politics it is unsuitable for use in a trans- or international organization such as the EU (Kassim, 1994). The debate over whether the EU should be analysed using tools from Comparative Politics or International Relations characterized EU theory in the mid to late 1990s, and still continues. It is however clear that International Relations theories have little if any value in explaining the day-to-day process of internal policymaking in the EU (Hix, 1994 and 1998; Peterson, 1995; Warleigh, 2000a). This is the case no matter how useful international relations theories have been in their accounts of why the EU was established, the foreign policies of the member states, or the EU's own ability to be an actor in world politics.

Nonetheless, Kassim's challenge that, as a 'fragmented' and 'changeable' system, the EU denies the continuity associated with the networks model gives pause for thought (Kassim, 1994, 16). It is true that in EU politics patterns of resource dependency can change fairly radically, and the scope for longstanding policy communities may thus be reduced. Such a hypothesis would be worth testing. However, it is equally plausible that in such a changeable system, with shared powers and variable decision rules, actors are compelled to create issue networks to generate any public policy at all. In other words, policy networks analysis helps us understand how the informal politics of the EU allows actors to agree a definition of a problem, select one or more from a range of possible solutions, and propose joint action to solve the problem (Heinelt and Smith, 1996b). It also helps explain how different, and sometimes rival, sets of actors can exist at the various levels of the EU system (Heinelt and Smith, 1996b) or within the same policy area (Rhodes and Marsh, 1992).

Thus, as a device to analyse the processes whereby EU public policy is made, and as long as the concept is applied to non-institutional as well as institutional actors, policy networks analysis is, *a priori*, applicable in EU Studies. In fact, Rhodes (1997, 138–9) argues that there have been three phases of policy networks analysis in EU Studies. The first, from the mid-1980s until approximately 1990, centred on empirical investigations of EU policymaking processes and found evidence of nascent networks. The second, in the early 1990s, used networks as a device to explain theoretically how EU decisionmaking works in terms of the EU institutions' internal politics, inter-institutional relations and interest representation. The third phase, in the early mid-1990s, focused on EU structural and cohesion policy, and the role of this policy as a creator of policy networks. As a result, it is clear that policy networks approaches can generate useful insights into EU politics and policymaking. (For further reading on policy networks approaches in EU Studies see Peterson, 2004.)

a working theory of eu governance: maximizing the utility of multilevel governance and policy networks?

why combine multilevel governance and policy networks?

At the start of this chapter I made the claim that multilevel governance and policy networks concepts give the greatest benefit to the scholar when they are used together. This is because they seek to accomplish different, but complementary, analytical tasks. In isolation, each approach can tell us only so much about the nature of the EU polity (multilevel governance) or the process of EU decisionmaking (policy networks). Taken together, however, they can allow the scholar to understand both issues. There are limits to the utility of the two concepts, even taken together: neither of them is capable of explaining the creation of the EU itself or predicting its evolutionary path, two of the main tasks of orthodox integration theory. However, in the current period of theoretical revision, in which scholars are attempting to rebuild EU theory from the bottom up, such reduced scope is no worse in the present case than in that of, say, the currently fashionable concept of Europeanization.[3]

Before attempting to harness these two approaches together, it is worth clarifying exactly those areas of EU governance (defined as system evolution and public policy making) that they can help analyse. I should also clarify here that I am proposing a combination of policy networks ideas and *Type II* multilevel governance in Hooghe and Marks' 2004 typology.

There are perhaps five main requirements of a workable EU theory that can be met by combining multilevel governance and policy networks approaches. These are summarized in Table 5.3.

Table 5.3   The theoretical value of combining multilevel governance and policy networks

Theoretical need	How it is met
Explaining the nature of the EU political system	Multilevel governance
Explaining how EU decisionmaking works	Policy networks analysis
Applicability to full range of actors involved	Multilevel governance, re sub-state governments and actors; policy networks re inter-institutional and non-state actors
Applicability to all policy areas/pillars	Policy networks
Capacity to generate testable hypotheses	Multilevel governance's assertions about how and why states choose multilevel governance systems; policy networks' claims about how and why actors cooperate

Source: Author.

First, and perhaps most importantly, multilevel governance can be used to explain the quixotic nature of the present Europolity, particularly its mixture of intergovernmental and supranational elements, its reach into domestic structures and policymaking processes, and also its limits. Policy networks can be used to understand how this system produces policy, using the idea of networks both horizontally (at EU level, to explain intra- and inter-institutional coalition-building) and vertically (to show how actors and networks link up at subnational, national and EU levels to achieve their objectives). Taken together, the two approaches generate the ability to theorize in a way that is applicable to the whole range of actors involved. Multilevel governance was the first approach to EU Studies that explicitly gave a role to actors from the substate level, thereby lending it potentially greater purchase than orthodox approaches. Policy networks approaches explicitly seek to understand the reality of policymaking processes, and therefore include the whole range of actors who take part in a given decisionmaking process.

As a further use, policy networks approaches can explain why certain actors are excluded from decisionmaking (on the ground that they lack useful resources), which helps to put flesh on the bones of multilevel governance's systemic-level understanding of decisionmaking processes in general. The approaches can be combined and applied to all policy areas and pillars of the EU; they expect the range of actors involved to change according to policy area if the decision rules set this out as a requirement, and can easily encompass varying levels of influence across policy issues and even time. Finally, and fundamentally, in combination, the two approaches can serve to generate testable hypotheses about the evolution of the EU system and its decisionmaking processes. Using multilevel governance's explanations of why states choose or agree to the development of the Europolity, it is easy enough to generate hypotheses about why they might agree to or oppose particular issues of system design (such as the Constitutional Treaty). Using policy networks analysis, decisionmaking in or between any of the EU institutions, and involving both institutional and non-institutional actors, can be examined to test the relative influence of particular institutions and groups of actors, and also the means by which that influence is exercised.

complementarity: can multilevel governance and policy networks be combined?

The principal question that needs to be addressed here is one of suitability: do multilevel governance and policy networks have complementary, but sufficiently different, purposes and focuses? The answer is positive: Peters and Pierre (2004) note that the two approaches have similar focuses on governance through networks, and Rhodes (1997, 382) lists four grounds on which multilevel governance and policy networks sit well together. These are the focus of policy network analysis on resource dependencies and understanding the role of all actors concerned with a particular issue; the ability of policy networks analysis to link domestic and inter- or transnational issues; the focus of policy networks analysis on resource distribution as a measure of power differentials; and the fact that both multilevel governance and policy network analysis can be seen as middle-range theories. Cooke (1996, 32–5) also points out that policy networks analysts explicitly permit its combination with other approaches to obtain greater intellectual purchase. Cooke also adds that with its focus lying primarily on explaining outcomes of a policymaking process, policy network analysis is in particular need of reinforcement by means of some device which might explain and characterize the system in which the policymaking takes place, a device such as multilevel governance. By combining the two approaches, scholars can thus harness insights that would otherwise be floating and un-linked (Peterson, 1995; Warleigh, 2000a).

However, it is necessary that the tasks and functions of each analytical device be strictly and explicitly demarcated, so that neither is overstretched. In the present case, multilevel governance is clearly intended as a means to analyse the nature and ongoing evolution of the Europolity, whereas policy networks analysis is intended as a means to understand how the policymaking process works at both a general level and in specific cases. Thus, policy networks can be used to flesh out some of the underspecified aspects of multilevel governance work. For example, Adshead (2002, 22–3) points out that multilevel governance scholars accept the notion that EU governance is network-based, but fail to explain sufficiently how these networks arise or impact upon the powers of central (national) governments. She goes on to argue that policy networks analysis can fill this gap, especially through its argument that networks form opportunistically as the state 'rolls back', a decision that can itself be made on ideological grounds or through (quasi) external pressures, such as the EU.

Finally, combining policy networks and multilevel governance forms of analysis helps with the revision and reorientation of both the combined device and its individual components. This is because each component of the combined analytical device is dependent on, but not completely conditioned by, the other. Explicit acknowledgement of the strengths and weaknesses of each approach justifies their use in tandem, and revisions to either approach may be carried out without necessarily impacting on the viability of the other. This is a clear advantage over orthodox integration theory, which makes claims to 'grand theory' status and thus has to be taken as an all-or-nothing proposition, and in which revisions of certain tenets (such as neofunctionalist revisions of 'spillover') have major consequences for the credibility of the entire theory.

evaluating multilevel governance / policy networks as a combined frame of analysis

There are further benefits to be obtained by EU scholars through the use of a combined multilevel governance–policy networks analytical device. First, by using the multilevel governance concept modestly, it corrects what may be a tendency in MLG to treat multilevel governance as a potential theory of everything. It also helps scholars measure (or at least understand) the extent to which rights of participation in EU policymaking equate to actual influence over that process. A further benefit is that policy networks analysis can be used to explore the extent to which multilevel governance really is present in policy areas other than structural or cohesion policy.

On the other hand, by linking analysis of how the policymaking system works to a clearer understanding of the nature of the EU polity, scholars are reminded of the bigger picture. They are more able to link isolated cases to the system in general and thereby facilitate the use of policy networks analysis as part of a range of more normative enquiries, such as: Who is excluded from the policymaking process, and why? What changes to the EU system would be necessary to rectify this? Should such changes be undertaken? What legitimacy-generating potential is there in network governance? And how far is the EU along the path from network governance to 'network democracy'? (Jachtenfuchs *et al.*, 1998).

However, it must be admitted that combining multilevel governance and policy networks analyses cannot solve every problem in EU theory. First, there is the obvious and already-admitted lacuna that neither of these approaches can explain the origin of the EU itself. Second, beyond a certain fleshing out of the relevant resource dependency factors, policy networks analysis cannot do much to help explain why certain substate actors seek to mobilize in EU politics, and others (which may have equally strong domestic powers and resources) do not. Furthermore, the constructivist trend in EU theory somewhat bypasses this joint analytical device, because part of the reason for the compatibility of multilevel governance and policy networks is their shared rationalistic basis and quasi-positivist orientation. Thus, while a combined multilevel governance–policy networks analytical device has clear advantages, it also has clear limits.

conclusion

In the last decade or so, scholars have turned increasingly to concepts of multilevel governance and policy networks in order to understand how the EU functions, and what kind of polity it is. This is because EU theory in general has undergone something of a restructuring, focusing on middle-range theory in an effort to understand how recent developments in the integration process, especially since the Single European Act, impact upon both the EU itself and how it can best be understood conceptually. The two concepts have varying foci, but are complementary in that they respectively shed light on the nature of the Europolity and how policy is actually made within it. They can thus be combined, and used as a two-level analytical device to understand how the multilevel EU system functions. In this chapter I have argued that by taking this step, scholars can generate a more robust understanding of the ongoing evolution of the EU and how particular policy outcomes are achieved. I have also demonstrated that, by linking the two conceptual devices together into a single analytical framework, they can be used to critique each other through an ongoing process of dialogue and conceptual honing, thereby contributing to the development of deeper and more rigorous EU theory.

notes

1. On the differences between causal and constitutive theory, see Wendt (1999, chapter 2).
2. It might be objected that citizens can have power in these types of decision when member states decide, or are obliged, to hold referenda to approve the treaties. So far in EU history (the Danish referendum on Maastricht, and the Irish referendum on Nice) it has been true that rejection of a treaty has led to concessions to the member state in question of a negative kind – for that particular member state only, certain provisions will not apply. However, this does not amount to the power to determine the content of the treaties positively. Nor is it the kind of non-national government influence anticipated by multilevel governance scholars, who stress the role of the Commission and substate actors of a governmental kind.
3. Moreover, as I argue elsewhere (Warleigh, 2000a), it is possible to add a further theory to the multilevel governance–policy networks device in order to get closer to the predictive/explanatory powers claimed by neofunctionalism and intergovernmentalism.

6

the study of eu enlargement:
theoretical approaches and empirical findings

frank schimmelfennig and ulrich sedelmeier

introduction

The political relevance of EU enlargement, both for the EU's internal development, and for international relations in Europe more broadly, is undisputed. Yet for a long time, enlargement has been a neglected subject in studies of European integration and in the theory of regional integration (see also Friis and Murphy, 1999; Wallace, 2000a). Classical approaches to the study of regional integration, such as neofunctionalism and transactionalism, mention the geographical growth of international communities only in passing (see Deutsch *et al.*, 1970, 4, 43–4; Haas, 1968, 313–17; Schmitter, 1969, 165). This neglect reflects the fact that enlargement only appeared on the EU's agenda after the heyday of regional integration theory and that for much of the EU's pre-Cold War history, it has been limited to sporadic instances: the United Kingdom, Denmark and Ireland joining in 1973; Greece in 1981; and Spain and Portugal in 1986.

With the end of the Cold War, however, enlargement has become a permanent item at the top of the EU's agenda. Three members of the European Free Trade Area (EFTA) joined in 1995 (Austria, Sweden and Finland). Eight Central and Eastern European countries (CEECs) – the Czech Republic, Estonia, Hungary, Poland, Latvia, Lithuania, Slovenia, Slovakia – plus Cyprus and Malta joined in May 2004. Bulgaria and Romania have concluded accession negotiations and are expected to join in January 2007. The European Council invited Turkey to start negotiations in October 2005, if Turkey recognizes

Cyprus. Croatia was scheduled to start accession negotiations in March 2005 (which were postponed due to the country's failure to extradite General Ante Gotovina to the UN war crimes tribunal) and the EU has also acknowledged membership prospects for the other countries of the western Balkans.

The increased salience of enlargement since the end of the Cold War has produced a sizeable body of literature. While much of this literature consists of descriptive studies of individual policy areas and country cases, the EFTA enlargement and eastern enlargement have also triggered some theory-oriented work. These analyses have started to address a number of weaknesses that have characterized the study of enlargement: Namely, the lack of comparative research designs; an underspecification of dependent variables and a neglect of important dimensions of enlargement; an underspecification of explanatory factors or independent variables and a subsequent reluctance to explore alternative explanations. More work is needed to address these weaknesses, to make the insights drawn from such studies more generalizable and thus to contribute to our cumulative understanding of enlargement.

This chapter makes three main contributions to the study of EU enlargement. First, we define EU enlargement as a process of gradual and formal horizontal institutionalization. We distinguish four main dimensions of enlargement, and draw out key research questions from each dimension. Second, we identify key explanatory approaches, namely realism, liberal intergovernmentalism, supranational institutionalism and constructivism and relate these to the four main dimensions of enlargement research discussed in the first section. We suggest that, rather than striving for some kind of 'enlargement theory', it is more fruitful to link the study of enlargement to the study of institutions in International Relations and EU Studies. Of course, this is not the only way to conceptualize enlargement. For example, the 'governance approach' to the EU can also provide important insights into enlargement (Friis and Murphy, 1999). However, to study enlargement as 'institutionalization', we present the key explanatory factors that three rationalist approaches (liberal intergovernmentalism, realism, and supranational institutionalism) and a constructivist approach propose and derive from them hypotheses about the main dimensions of enlargement. Finally, we present an overview of the state of research on EU enlargement in order to demonstrate the usefulness of these theoretical approaches for structuring the debate.

research focus and theoretical approaches

dependent variables in the study of enlargement

In order to delimit the study of EU enlargement, it is useful to clarify what we consider part of enlargement. Elsewhere, we have defined enlargement as 'a process of gradual and formal institutionalization of organizational rules and norms' (Schimmelfennig and Sedelmeier 2002, 503). While 'deepening' can be considered as vertical institutionalization, *horizontal institutionalization* concerns the geographical spread of institutions beyond the incumbent actors. The behaviour of a larger group of actors becomes governed by EU rules. Enlargement is thus not limited to the formal act of accession or formal agreement on the terms of enlargement in accession treaties. Rather, we suggest that the study of enlargement should also focus on all acts of *purposive alignment* with EU rules by non-members. Such processes of alignment might be directly motivated by accession in view of the EU's accession conditionality. Alignment might also result from EU rules embodied in formal agreements that create an institutional relationship short of full membership, such as the Europe Agreements with the CEECs or the Stabilization and Association Agreements with the western Balkans. Such agreements also include those leading to the participation of non-members in selected policy areas, such as the European Economic Area agreement, or Swiss treaties with the EU. Finally, alignment might be a response to the negative externalities of regional integration. Horizontal institutionalization is thus a matter of degree, and enlargement should be understood as a *gradual process* that begins before, and continues after, the formal accession of new members.

What are the consequences of such a definition of enlargement? First, by defining enlargement as horizontal institutionalization, we establish an explicit link to the study of institutions and open the analysis of enlargement to theories about the establishment and effects of institutions. Second, it widens the field of enlargement studies beyond the narrow focus on decisions about formal membership. Widening the research focus in this manner means that we can identify four main research areas or aspects of enlargement, which generate separate dependent variables for the study of enlargement. The literature on EU enlargement has focused primarily on three dimensions of the politics of enlargement that concern the process leading to formal acts of accession. These dimensions can be labelled as (1) applicants' enlargement politics; (2) member state enlargement politics; and (3) EU enlargement politics, for which we can further distinguish between (a) the macro or polity dimension and (b) the substantive or policy dimension. A further dimension concerns (4) the impact of enlargement; that is the effects of these formal acts, or the effects of their anticipation. For each of these main dimensions of enlargement, we can identify key research questions.

applicant enlargement politics

The basic question with regard to this dimension is why and under which conditions non-members seek accession to the EU. Since horizontal institutionalization does not only relate to full membership, the broader question is: Under what conditions do outsiders pursue institutional ties with the EU? And what kind of institutional relationships do outsiders prefer? Empirical studies of this dimension have primarily focused on the United Kingdom in the first enlargement (Lord, 1993), as well as on the EFTA enlargement (Bieler, 2000). Another important aspect of this dimension of enlargement is the study of countries that decided *not* to apply for membership, or countries where electorates did not endorse accession (Gstöhl, 2002). Mattli (1999) provides a comprehensive comparative study of the conditions under which states join regional organizations.

member state enlargement politics

The main question posed by research addressing the second dimension of EU enlargement research is: Under what conditions does a given EU member state favour or oppose enlargement to a particular applicant country. Studies in this dimension usually unpack a government's preferences and analyse internal conflicts about enlargement. The positions and preferences of the big member states have been a major focus of this research, especially governments that were crucial in a particular enlargement round, either as opponents of enlargement or as key advocates (Collins, 2002; Hyde-Price, 2000; Tewes, 1998 for German policies on eastern enlargement).

eu enlargement politics

The key question in the third dimension is: Under what conditions does the EU admit a new member, or modify its institutional relationship with outside states? There are two analytically separate aspects of this question, which relate respectively to the *macro dimension* and the *substantive dimension* of enlargement. The *macro dimension of EU enlargement politics* relates to the EU as a *polity* and concerns the question of candidate selection and patterns of EU membership. The main questions are: Why does the EU prefer to admit one state rather than another? And why does it offer membership, rather than some other form of institutional relationship, or no institutionalized relationship at all? (For eastern enlargement, see Fierke and Wiener, 1999; Schimmelfennig, 2001; Sedelmeier, 2000; Sjursen, 2002.) The *substantive or policy dimension of EU enlargement politics* concerns the concrete substance of the organizational rules that are horizontally institutionalized. Studies of this dimension seek to explain the specific content of EU policy towards candidates in distinctive policy areas. This might concern the outcomes of accession negotiations (see Preston, 1997 for a comparative analysis of successive enlargement rounds; Ruano, 2005 for the accession negotiations on agriculture with the United Kingdom, Spain, and the CEECs; Granell, 1995 for EFTA enlargement, or Avery, 2004 for eastern enlargement). It also includes the nature of pre-accession conditionality or association policies (for the Association Agreements leading to eastern enlargement, see Friis, 1998a; Papadimitriou, 2002; Phinnemore, 1999; Torreblanca, 2001a). The key analytical question is: To what extent do EU policies in particular issue areas reflect the preferences of certain actors, such as the applicants, member states, interest groups or institutional actors?

the impact of enlargement

Enlargement affects both the EU and the states to which its institutional rules are extended. With regard to the impact on the EU, it is most often asked how enlargement affects the internal distribution of power, both among the member states within institutions and between institutions. Analysts also frequently ask how enlargement influences the EU's identity, norms, and goals, the effectiveness and efficiency of EU institutions and decisionmaking, and the effect of widening membership on the prospects for deeper integration. However, most relevant for the study of horizontal institutionalization is the *impact of enlargement on new members and on candidate countries.*[1] Here, the main questions are: How does enlargement change the identity, the interests and the behaviour of governmental and societal actors? Under what conditions do non-members adopt EU rules? Research interest in this dimension of enlargement has increased recently, with growth in the study of 'Europeanization', particularly studies looking at the impact of the EU on (new) member states (see Chapter 4 in this volume). Empirical studies have therefore concentrated mainly on the more recent EFTA enlargement round (Falkner, 2000) and eastern enlargement (Schimmelfennig and Sedelmeier, 2005a), but have also traced the longer-term impact of earlier enlargement rounds (Börzel, 1999 on Spain).

theoretical approaches to the study of enlargement

Studies of enlargement, even many theoretically-informed contributions, are weakened by a tendency to rely on a single-case design and a failure to explore alternative explanations. To make their findings more comparable and to generate cumulative insights, we suggest linking the study of enlargement to broader theoretical debates in International Relations and EU Studies. Linking up with broader theoretical debates allows the researcher to draw on (mid-range) theories, concepts and explanatory factors that generate hypotheses about the conditions of institutionalization and about institutional effects. Given the potential to test such generalizable propositions, therefore, even qualitative, single-case studies can produce comparative insights.

In enlargement research, we identify two main attempts to link the study of enlargement to the study of international institutions. An edited volume by Keohane, Nye and Hoffmann (1993) focuses on the debate between approaches emphasizing domestic politics, state power and international institutions. Elsewhere, we also argued that the current International Relations debate between rationalist institutionalism and constructivist institutionalism provides a useful framework of analysis (Schimmelfennig and Sedelmeier, 2002 and 2005b). These two frameworks are compatible, in the sense that the approaches tested in Keohane *et al.* (1993) are all different versions of rationalist institutionalism. If we combine the two frameworks, we can thus derive from them four explanatory ideal types: realism, liberal intergovernmentalism, supranational institutionalism, and constructivism.

Not all of these approaches may be equally applicable to each of the four above-mentioned dimensions of EU enlargement research. Moreover, they may not necessarily offer mutually exclusive explanations (for possible syntheses between competing institutionalist schools, see Jupille *et al.*, 2003). Rather, we consider them partially competing and partially complementary sources of theoretical inspiration that can help to structure analyses of EU enlargement. The theoretical assumptions underpinning these approaches have been fully elaborated in other chapters in this volume (see Chapters 2 and 3) and elsewhere (Rosamond, 2000a and Wiener and Diez, 2003). We will therefore provide only a brief overview before going on to outline the factors that realism, liberal intergovernmentalism, supranational institutionalism and constructivism emphasize in relation to the four main sets of research questions, or dimensions of the study of enlargement.

At one level, we can draw a broad distinction between realism, liberal intergovernmentalism, supranational institutionalism on the one hand, and constructivism on the other, based on differing logics of action that underpin the approaches. Realism, liberal intergovernmentalism and supranational institutionalism are based on rationalist assumptions. They thus share an individualist and materialist ontology and assume that actors' behaviour follows a logic of consequences. By contrast, constructivism is based on a social and ideational ontology, assuming a 'logic of appropriateness' (March and Olsen, 1989, 160).

At another level, these approaches differ in their perspectives on the causal status and purposes of international institutions, such as the EU. At one extreme, realists consider international institutions as marginal phenomena in world politics. For liberal intergovernmentalism and supranational institutionalism, institutions do matter, but in a more limited way than for constructivism. For the former, welfare maximizing actors create international institutions in order to achieve absolute gains from cooperation. Institutions allow states to pursue their interests more efficiently by reducing the transaction costs of cooperation; that is by providing a stable forum for negotiations, or acting as a neutral provider of information and monitoring. Both liberal intergovernmentalism and supranational institutionalism thus share a rational institutionalist view on the causal status of institutions: institutions affect the behaviour of actors by providing constraints and incentives that alter cost-benefit calculations. Where the views of the two approaches differ, is the extent to which institutions can constrain states. While liberal intergovernmentalism considers international institutions as tools that states control, supranational institutionalism proposes that institutions can become purposive and autonomous actors in their own right and constrain states beyond what was intended when they created the institution and delegated powers to it. Still, in both approaches, institutions are generally secondary to individual, material interests. They remain intervening variables between the actors' material interests and their material environment, on the one hand, and collective outcomes, on the other.

By contrast, in the constructivist perspective, institutions have a fundamental impact on the behaviour of actors because institutions shape actors' underlying identities and interests. Actors do not simply confront institutions as external constraints and incentives which they need to factor into their calculations. Rather, institutions provide meaning to the rights and obligations entailed in their social roles. Actors conform to institutionally prescribed behaviour out of normative commitment or habit. International institutions are 'community representatives' (Abbott and Snidal, 1998, 24) as well as community-building agencies. For constructivists, the origins, goals, and procedures of international organizations are strongly determined by the standards of legitimacy and appropriateness of the international community, rather than by utilitarian demands for efficient problem-solving (Barnett and Finnemore, 1999, 703; Katzenstein, 1996, 12).

In turn, these different views on the role of international institutions lead to competing hypotheses about the rationale, the conditions, and the mechanisms of EU enlargement. In the following sections, we match these competing hypotheses up to the four dimensions of the study of enlargement outlined in the first section. Particular attention is paid to the factors that realism, liberal intergovernmentalism, supranational institutionalism and constructivism emphasize in their explanations of enlargement and, to the extent that they are applicable, their corresponding hypotheses. Table 6.1 summarizes these factors.

Table 6.1 Theoretical approaches and key explanatory factors for enlargement

	Realism	Liberal Intergovernmentalism	Supranational Institutionalism	Constructivism
Applicant/ Member state politics	Anticipated effect of enlargement on a state's: – autonomy – security – relative influence in EU	Anticipated effect of enlargement on a state's welfare (depending on domestic economic structure)	Anticipated effect of enlargement on: – the EU's collective interests – competences and budgets of individual institutions	Extent of applicant's identification with the EU and its constitutive norms
EU macropolitics	Preferences of most powerful member states	Relative bargaining power and side-payments	– agenda-setting and entrepreneurship by institutional actors (Commission) – presence and strength of transnational interest groups in favour of enlargement	Extent of shared collective identity and constitutive norms between EU and applicants
EU substantive politics	as above	– as above – formal decisionmaking rules	– as above – formal decisionmaking rules	Ideas and policy paradigms underpinning particular policy areas
Impact on new members	n.a.	Empowerment of domestic actors; domestic adoption costs	n.a.	Socialization and persuasion; legitimacy of EU rules and norms

theoretical hypotheses for the study of enlargement

enlargement politics of member states and applicant countries

The enlargement politics of both member states and applicant countries are about the enlargement preferences of individual states. At this level of analysis, each explanation thus respectively emphasizes, for the preference formation of both member states and applicant countries, the same factors, which then explain whether a member state favours the accession of a particular country, and whether a given country seeks to join the EU.

All three rationalist approaches assume that *expected individual costs and benefits determine the applicants' and the member states' enlargement preferences. States (or EU institutions) favour the degree of horizontal institutionalization that maximizes their net benefits.* More specifically, a member state favours the integration of an outsider state on condition that it will reap positive net benefits from enlargement, and that these benefits exceed the benefits it would secure from an alternative form of horizontal institutionalization. Conversely, a non-member state seeks accession to the EU if it benefits more from membership than from any other form of relations with the EU. This general hypothesis, however, begs the question of what the relevant costs and benefits are. In this respect, realist and rational choice institutionalist approaches (liberal intergovernmentalist and supranational institutionalist) focus on different factors and their hypotheses accordingly vary to a significant extent.

realist hypotheses

Realists assume that state actors are mainly concerned with *external autonomy* and power. In international cooperation, they worry about the distribution of benefits among the participating states, because the *relative* gains and losses vis-à-vis other states will affect their future international power position and security (for example, Walt, 1987; Waltz, 1979, 117–27). States' enlargement preferences, therefore, mainly depend on general systemic conditions, in particular (changes in) the security environment. Correspondingly, a member state favours enlargement, and a non-member state bids to join the EU, if this is a necessary and efficient means to balance the superior power or threat of a third state (or coalition of states), or to increase its own power.

More general *autonomy* costs arise from forgoing unilateral policy options that horizontal institutionalization implies both for the member states and the applicants. Since member states have already lost policymaking autonomy in issue areas regulated by the EU, autonomy costs mainly consist of according new members equal decisionmaking rights. In general, under the EU's qualified majority voting rule, the individual member states' degree of control over outcomes decreases with enlargement (Kerremans, 1998). Formal models, including voting power analyses and a spatial approach, have attempted to quantify the impact of enlargement on the internal power distribution (Steunenberg, 2002). In return for reduced control over the internal agenda, member states do, however, gain better control over external political developments in the applicant states. For applicant states, the greatest cost is the loss of policymaking autonomy as a result of membership. This loss, however, can be compensated by rights to participate in EU decisionmaking and through the protection of state autonomy that EU membership provides.

liberal intergovernmentalist hypotheses

Liberal intergovernmentalism assumes that a state must reap net *welfare benefits* in order to support (or seek) accession to the EU. Such welfare benefits derive from three main sources: policy costs/benefits, transaction (or management) costs/benefits, and domestic autonomy gains. While liberal intergovernmentalism considers *autonomy* benefits and costs to be secondary, gaining a particular type of autonomy might be a key consideration for applicant countries. However, this concerns not so much autonomy vis-à-vis other states, but rather their own societies (Vaubel, 1986; Wolf, 1999).

Applicant countries derive *policy benefits* from participation in the EU's 'club goods', such as access to a larger market or eligibility for EU budget receipts. Policy costs involve membership contributions and the adaptation of domestic policies. Conversely, incumbent members benefit from the contributions of new members to the club goods, while crowding costs arise from having to share collective goods with the new members. The factors that determine the size of policy benefits relate mainly to a state's domestic structure and patterns of (primarily economic) interdependence (Moravcsik, 1998b). For example, the more dependent a state is on the EU for its trade, the stronger is its demand for membership. Conversely, the more important, in terms of trade or investment, a non-member state is for a member state, the more likely it is that this member state will support its accession. Economic interdependence might also be affected by systemic conditions, such as geographic proximity, or changes in the world economy. For example, a denationalization of the economy creates incentives for joining the EU. Furthermore, the degree of integration in the EU itself affects economic dependence. The deepening of economic integration creates negative externalities for outsiders (diversion of trade and investment) and triggers demand for membership. Demand for integration is thus shaped by the domestic structure, such as the relative strength of certain sectors of the economy: The stronger the domestic capital and export-oriented sectors are, the greater the demand for integration will be.

Enlargement generally decreases the *transaction costs* for both incumbent and new members through, for example, the provision of organizational services by EU institutions and faster communication and coordination. However, certain transaction costs rise. Additional members require additional organizational infrastructure and make communication within the organization more cumbersome and costly. Additional members also usually increase the heterogeneity of the membership, and 'the costs of centralized decisions are likely to rise where more and more persons of differing tastes participate' (Sandler *et al.*, 1978, 69). Applicants have to establish delegations at the headquarters of the organization and incur costs of communication, coordination and supervision in the relations between these delegations and state capitals.

supranational institutionalist hypotheses

Supranational institutionalism is only applicable to the dimension of member state politics insofar as it considers EU institutions as actors in their own right, capable of forming preferences about the accession of certain countries. EU institutions should be generally in favour of enlargement, as it increases their budget and the geographical reach of institutional rules. Like the other rationalist approaches just mentioned, supranational institutionalism expects the specific enlargement preferences of EU institutional actors to depend on expected net gains, either for the EU as a whole, or for a particular institution.

constructivist hypotheses

According to constructivism, applicants and members 'construct' each other and their relationships on the basis of the ideas that define the community that the EU represents. Whether applicant and member states regard enlargement as desirable or not depends on the degree of 'community' or 'cultural match' they perceive they have with each other. In other words, demand for integration follows from the degree to which the actors inside and outside the EU share a collective identity and fundamental beliefs.[2] We can thus derive the following general constructivist hypotheses about applicant and member state politics: *The more an external state identifies with the international community that the EU represents and the more it shares the values and norms that define the purpose and the policies of the EU, the stronger the institutional ties it seeks with the EU and the more the member states are willing to pursue horizontal institutionalization with this state.*

Applicant and member state politics are thus about whether an applicant state is 'European', whether it subscribes to the integrationist project of an 'ever closer union', adheres to the liberal democratic political value foundations of the EU, or shares the norms underlying specific EU policies. Depending on the extent of domestic consensus on the applicant state's identity and policy norms, enlargement politics in applicant countries will be more or less controversial and the resulting preferences about accession will be more or less stable and strong.

In the constructivist perspective, we would generally expect greater conflict within applicant states on the enlargement issue than within the member states. First, for an applicant state, the decision to join a regional organization, and in particular the EU, constitutes a major political reorientation, while for the member states, the decision to enlarge their organization is more a matter of policy continuity. Second, we would assume that member states share the constitutive values and norms of their community organization and have been exposed to socialization within the organization for some time.

eu enlargement politics

Concerning EU enlargement politics, the various approaches again emphasize similar factors for both macropolitics and for the substantive politics. With regard to the rationalist approaches, club theory would suggest that *the EU expands its membership if the marginal benefits of enlargement exceed the marginal costs for both the member states and the applicant states*. In the club-theoretical perspective, enlargement will continue until marginal costs equal marginal benefits. This equilibrium indicates the optimal size of the organization (Buchanan, 1965, 5; Padoan, 1997, 118). However, the outcomes of EU enlargement politics also depend on constellations of bargaining power and formal decisionmaking rules. The different rationalist approaches diverge in their assumptions about how and to what extent these two factors matter.

liberal intergovernmentalist hypotheses

Liberal intergovernmentalism suggests decisions on enlargement and the substantive content of enlargement bargains result from the unequal *bargaining power* of the incumbents. Moravcsik defines a state's bargaining power as 'inversely proportional to the relative value that it places on an agreement compared to the outcome of its best alternative policy' (1998a, 62). Member states that expect net losses from enlargement will agree to enlargement if their bargaining power is sufficient to obtain full compensation through side-payments by the winners. This, in turn, requires that the necessary concessions do not exceed the winners' gains from enlargement. Otherwise, the losers will consent to enlargement if the winners are able to threaten them credibly with exclusion, and if the losses of exclusion for the losers exceed the losses of enlargement.

The *formal decisionmaking rules* of enlargement increase the bargaining power of the states which do not expect to benefit from enlargement and possibly of the applicant countries. Enlargement requires a consensus of all member states. Furthermore, accession (or association) treaties have to be ratified by national parliaments of all countries concerned. Especially in the applicant countries, accession treaties can be subject to a referendum.

realist hypotheses

In contrast, realism would emphasize that it is not necessary that enlargement *as such* is beneficial to *each* member for the EU to enlarge. Rather, both the decision to enlarge and substantive politics are a reflection of the preferences of the *most powerful member states*.

supranational institutionalist hypotheses

Conversely, supranational institutionalism would suggest that the EU's enlargement politics are significantly influenced by the preferences of

EU institutions, especially the Commission. Institutional rules relating to enlargement might strengthen their position. The Commission assesses the candidates' preparedness for membership and plays an important informal role as a broker in accession negotiations. Association and accession treaties also require the consent of the European Parliament under the assent procedure. However, the European Parliament is not usually seen as a major player in enlargement politics. Garrett and Tsebelis concede that under the assent procedure it is 'reasonable to conceive of decisionmaking in terms of the Luxembourg compromise period' (1996, 283). Bailer and Schneider (2000) add that the European Parliament is constrained in the use of its veto against accession agreements because of its integrationist stance.

constructivist hypotheses

As constructivism often assumes strong institutional and cultural effects ('socialization' or 'Europeanization') at the systemic level, it would generally expect that member states have largely homogeneous enlargement preferences, and thus that there would be little conflict over enlargement. If we relax this assumption, we might expect to see more variation in preferences.

For example, tension among community values and norms, such as over whether to prioritize EU deepening or widening, will prevent a single, unambiguous standard from shaping the enlargement preferences of the incumbents. Moreover, identification with, and internalization of, community values and norms may vary not only among the non-member states, but also among the incumbent community actors. While we would expect EU institutions, such as the Commission, to hold preferences strongly influenced by EU norms, member state governments may be subject to partly competing influences from national and international identities and cultural environments. Finally, the resonance of *particular* EU norms might vary across different groups of policymakers, depending on their functional and organizational positions. While more general organizational norms and constitutive values might have a stronger impact on the macropolitics of enlargement, distinctive substantive policies might be shaped to a larger extent by the particular norms (or policy paradigms) underpinning the policy area in question.

Even in the case of normative conflict within the EU, however, the decisionmaking process will not be a bargaining process, but a *process of arguing* (Risse, 2000). If there is disagreement over which community norm applies in a given situation of enlargement, actors should promote their positions with arguments based on the collective identity, or the constitutive beliefs and practices of the EU. More fundamentally, arguing and discourse have the potential to modify old, or construct new, identities and norms. Incumbents and outsiders continuously seek to define and redefine the boundaries of the community between 'us' and 'them', and to interpret and reinterpret EU norms. As a result, we might observe changes in the definition of the EU and its enlargement practices.

Eventually, the outcome of EU enlargement politics will once again depend on the degree of community and cultural or normative match. *The EU expands to outside states to the extent that these states share its collective identity, values and norms.* The higher the degree of community and the better the cultural or normative match, the faster and the deeper the process of enlargement. Enlargement will continue until the (cultural) borders of the international community and the (formal, institutional) borders of the EU match.

the impact of enlargement on new members and candidates

Under what conditions do candidate countries and new member states adopt EU rules? With regard to new members, analyses can draw on concepts developed in the Europeanization literature. In order to capture the impact of enlargement on non-members, analyses have to be complemented with insights from conceptual analyses of the impact of international organizations on domestic politics. Accordingly, in this area of enlargement research, it makes sense to distinguish more broadly between alternative explanations suggested by rationalist and constructivist approaches.

rationalist institutionalist hypotheses

In (new) members, rational institutionalism suggests that a *misfit between EU rules and domestic rules leads to domestic change, if the resulting adaptation pressures change the domestic distribution of power.* While 'misfit' changes the opportunity structure, the capacity of actors to exploit these opportunities depends on two mediating factors: Veto points in the domestic institutional structure facilitate resistance to adaptation, while formal institutions might empower actors that benefit from domestic change (Börzel and Risse, 2003, 63–5).

With regard to non-member states, we can distinguish two main rationalist explanations that suggest different hypotheses about the conditions under which non-members adopt EU rules (Schimmelfennig and Sedelmeier, 2004 and 2005a). The first explanation emphasizes the *external incentives* provided by the EU for rule adoption, such as membership or associate status. The most general proposition for this explanation is that a *non-member state adopts EU rules, if the benefits of the rewards exceed the domestic costs of rule adoption.* A range of factors affects the size of these costs and benefits. These include the determinacy of the EU's conditions, the credibility of its conditionality, the type and speed of EU rewards, as well as the number of domestic veto players who incur net costs through the adoption of EU rules.

The second rationalist explanation emphasizes *domestic lesson-drawing* processes that lead to the import of rules from abroad, because they are expected to work more effectively than existing national rules. The most general hypothesis that derives from these considerations is that a *non-member state adopts EU rules, if it expects these rules to provide efficient solutions to domestic policy failure.* Favourable conditions for this kind of learning from abroad include the threat of domestic sanctions to governments if the status quo is maintained; the presence of EU-centred epistemic communities; and the transferability of EU rules into the domestic context. The last condition depends, in turn, on factors such as the availability of institutional, administrative and financial resources required for implementation, as well as on domestic veto players.

constructivist hypotheses

In (new) member states, constructivist or sociological institutionalist perspectives suggest that *adaptation pressures emanating from the EU lead to domestic change, if socialization and collective learning processes result in norm internalization and the development of new identities.* Facilitating factors include the presence of domestic norm entrepreneurs and a political culture conducive to consensus-building and cost-sharing (Börzel and Risse, 2003, 65–8; Checkel, 1999b; Cortell and Davis, 2000).

Similarly, with regard to non-member states, a constructivist explanation considers external incentives or the domestic effectiveness of rules of secondary importance to questions of rule legitimacy and processes of persuasion (Schimmelfennig and Sedelmeier, 2004 and 2005a). The general constructivist hypothesis is that *a non-member state adopts EU rules, if it is persuaded of the legitimacy of EU rules.* Hypotheses about facilitating factors thus include the legitimacy of EU rules and the legitimacy of its conditionality, the degree of identification with the EU, as well as the domestic resonance of EU rules.

empirical findings and theoretical controversies in enlargement research

This final section reviews theoretically informed, empirical studies of enlargement. We aim to indicate the main tendencies and controversies in the literature instead of presenting a comprehensive overview of enlargement research. Theory-oriented research on enlargement has concentrated on the two major enlargement processes of the 1990s: the 1995 'EFTA enlargement' and the 2004 eastern enlargement. Even empirical studies of the earlier enlargement rounds are rather rare, not to mention theoretically informed analyses. A recent commentary on the study of enlargement noted the drawback that the scarcity of comparative insights from earlier rounds presents for the study of enlargement (Wallace, 2002, 660). However, some authors have started to re-examine earlier enlargement rounds in order to compare them with subsequent enlargements and to establish the impact of these precedents (Ruano, 2002 and 2005).

Analyses of the last two enlargement rounds differ in a number of ways. First, the dominant research focus has been on different dimensions of enlargement. While research on EFTA enlargement has concentrated on applicant politics, studies of eastern enlargement have predominantly analysed EU (macro)politics. Second, we observe the prevalence of different theoretical approaches in the two cases. In the case of EFTA enlargement, rationalist explanations dominate and the literature mainly emphasizes the factors that fit well with liberal intergovernmentalist arguments. By contrast, constructivist factors have figured more prominently in accounts of eastern enlargement. Finally, the broader pattern of the EU's impact on the central European candidate countries has been largely captured within a rationalist framework.

efta enlargement

Studies of the EFTA enlargement mainly focus on the applicants' enlargement politics (but see Friis, 1998b). The EU's decision to accept the applications from the EFTA countries conforms with predictions of both liberal intergovernmentalism and constructivism. The key puzzle that these studies address is why EFTA countries started to pursue the goal of EU membership at the beginning of the 1990s, after they had initially chosen to remain outside the European Community. Realism pinpoints a key geopolitical factor that most analyses emphasize. The Cold War was a key impediment for the neutral EFTA members preventing them from applying for EU membership. Otherwise, these studies largely confirm liberal intergovernmentalist hypotheses about the importance of socioeconomic welfare considerations and domestic economic structures.

Ingebritsen (1998) argues that the oil shock induced the Scandinavian countries to transform their economic model in ways that were much more compatible with EU policies than in the 1970s. In addition, when the European Community launched its internal market programme, the EFTA economies performed worse than the original six member states in terms of economic growth and experienced a dramatic increase in outward investment. Mattli (1999) claims that a continuing 'performance gap' with the EU led the governments of individual EFTA countries to pursue membership in order to improve their re-election chances. The EU's internal market therefore provided a strong pull, as it offered the prospect of increasing competitiveness. At the same time, the threat of a relocation of investment had a push effect (Mattli, 1999, 82 and 89; Fioretos, 1997, 312–16; Bieler, 2000, 41–3 and 73–4).

Most authors emphasize differences in domestic economic structures to explain variations in different governments' responses to these structural changes and their ability to obtain public approval for membership. Ingebritsen (1998) attributes the variation in outcomes to different leading sectors in the Scandinavian economies. The capital- and export-oriented manufacturing sectors that dominated in Sweden and Finland could threaten to relocate in order to gain access to the internal market. By contrast, the fishing industry in Iceland felt threatened by the EU's fisheries policy, while the Norwegian oil industry was independent from the internal market. Fioretos (1997) also argues that export-oriented Swedish firms pushed the Swedish government to pursue EU membership by threatening to relocate their investment. Bieler's (2000) neo-Gramscian analysis of Sweden and Austria observes partly cross-cutting anti- or pro-EU membership alliances between business and labour associations and certain state institutions, depending on whether these actors were oriented towards domestic or transnational production processes.

Deviating cases, such as Switzerland, lead Gstöhl (2002) to complement a material cost-benefit analysis with a constructivist approach, which allows her to understand how particular national identity constructions result in 'reluctance' towards EU membership. For example, Swiss identity forms an obstacle to integration, as it is based on traditions of direct democracy, decentralization and neutrality, as well as aversion to foreign rule. Experience of foreign occupation also accounts for differences in Norwegian and Swedish attitudes towards the EU. Gstöhl thus emphasizes the importance of geo-historical factors, sociopolitical institutions and societal cleavages in such identity constructions.

In sum, these theoretically informed studies of EFTA enlargement suggest that only a combination of factors suggested by realism, liberal intergovernmentalism and constructivism can explain variations in the desire of EFTA countries to join and their governments' ability to win accession referenda. The absence of geopolitical obstacles (realism) and of identity-related obstacles (constructivism) and the presence of economic incentives (liberal intergovernmentalism) are all necessary conditions for the accession of the EFTA countries. The salience of constructivist factors differs among domestic actors. For governmental elites, identity-related factors that may have been obstacles to EU membership appear to have mattered less. By contrast, for electorates voting in national referenda, presumed characteristics of national identity and political culture (corporatism, neutrality) appeared more important than material cost-benefit calculations.

eastern enlargement

In contrast to EFTA enlargement, theoretically informed studies of eastern enlargement have focused predominantly on EU politics. The CEECs' desire to join the EU appears largely uncontroversial, as it conforms to the expectations of the main approaches. Realism emphasizes the security guarantees that EU membership provides against possible attempts by Russia to reassert its influence. Accession also provides the CEECs with certain autonomy gains through participation in EU decisionmaking. Liberal intergovernmentalism stresses economic gains through market access and investment flows, as well as the budgetary receipts from the EU's common agricultural policy and structural funds. Constructivism, on the other hand, calls attention to identity changes in the CEECs producing a desire to 'return to Europe' and the EU's embodiment of the European community of liberal democratic states.

Theory-oriented analyses of the substantive politics of eastern enlargement are relatively rare. Such studies focus mainly on the early stages of EU policy towards the CEECs and generally confirm the hypotheses of liberal intergovernmentalism. For example, Haggard *et al.*'s (1993) comparison of various EU policies emphasizes patterns of domestic politics, rather than theories that focus on international institutions or state power (see also Guggenbuhl, 1995; Papadimitriou, 2002). However, Sedelmeier (2002) argues that the balance of interest group pressure does not always provide reliable predictions of the outcomes of EU decisionmaking. He suggests that to understand the conditions under which EU policy might accommodate the preferences of the candidate countries, additional factors have to be taken into account. These factors concern the structure of the policy process (see also Ruano, 2005), as well as sectoral policy paradigms. The emphasis on policy paradigms as the set of ideas underpinning specific policy areas moves the analysis in the direction of constructivist approaches.

The bulk of theoretically informed studies of EU enlargement politics focus on the question of why the EU decided to enlarge. Moravcsik and Vachudova (2003) suggest that both the EU's decision to enlarge and the outcome of accession negotiations can be explained well by factors emphasized in liberal intergovernmentalism. Member state preferences appear to reflect differences in domestic socioeconomic structures, differences that lead to an uneven distribution of economic opportunities or competition, as well as rivalry for receipts from the EU budget. While the uneven distribution of costs and benefits from enlargement led to opposition from some member states, Moravcsik and Vachudova argue that these costs were not sufficiently large for them to block enlargement (2003, 50). The strongly asymmetrical bargaining power favouring the incumbents over the CEECs allowed reluctant EU members to minimize expected costs to the detriment of the new members.

However, a liberal intergovernmentalist account of eastern enlargement still leaves certain questions open. First, why did the reluctant EU member states agree to enlargement before the outcome of negotiations on institutional reform or the EU budget were clear? Second, even if these governments correctly anticipated that their veto power would allow them to obtain an outcome that would accommodate their preferences in these negotiations, accession deals might be threatened once the new members participated in EU decisionmaking after accession. Why did these member states take such a risk?

In line with supranational institutionalism, Smith (1998) explains the EU's enlargement policy emphasizing the strong role played by the European Commission (see also Friis, 1998c; Torreblanca, 2001a; Sedelmeier, 2000). By contrast, Skålnes (2005) draws on insights from realism to explain the EU's decision to enlarge, emphasizing the long-term security interest of EU members. The wars following the break-up of Yugoslavia and the Kosovo conflict raised concerns about stability in their neighbourhood and thus led both to the decision to enlarge and to include all CEEC applicants in accession negotiations.

The difficulty in explaining the EU's decision to enlarge purely with reference to the distribution of egoistic, material preferences and bargaining power has generated a sizeable body of literature drawing on constructivist insights and emphasizing the importance of EU identity. Some of these studies stress more broadly the EU's pan-European identity (Friis, 1998c) or its identity as a community of liberal-democratic European states (Schimmelfennig, 2001). Other studies focus on more specific identity constructions in the EU's relationship with the CEECs, such as a 'special responsibility' for the integration of the CEECs (Sedelmeier, 2000), of a 'kinship-based moral duty' (Sjursen, 2002), or of 'promises' made during the Cold War (Fierke and Wiener, 1999).

A challenge for these identity-based arguments is to explain the initially strong reluctance of a majority of member states to proceed with enlargement. Sedelmeier (2000) argues that the effect of EU identity is uneven across different groups of actors inside the EU. Those actors who identified most closely with the idea of the EU's 'responsibility' towards the CEECs, primarily located in the Commission, acted as principled policy advocates. For other actors, however, collectively asserted 'responsibility' and the commitment that it entailed acted primarily as a constraint on open opposition to enlargement. This, in turn, enabled policy advocates to move policy incrementally towards enlargement. Schimmelfennig's (2001) argument about the impact of identity on eastern enlargement is fully compatible with a (non-materialist) rationalist analysis. The EU's normative institutional environment did not affect actors' underlying interests, but increased the bargaining power of actors that favoured enlargement for selfish reasons. This environment allowed pro-enlargement actors to use references to the EU's identity instrumentally. Such 'rhetorical action' shamed the more reluctant member states into acquiescing in enlargement, since they were concerned about their reputation as community members.

In sum, theoretically informed studies of eastern enlargement suggest that the broad patterns of enlargement politics, such as the enlargement preferences of member states and applicants, as well as of the substantive politics of enlargement, largely confirm the hypotheses of liberal intergovernmentalism. However, without taking account of the identity-related factors emphasized in constructivism, it is difficult to explain how divergent preferences could result in a decision in favour of enlargement. Among the analyses focusing on EU identity we identify a sometimes implicit debate about whether the normative structure created by EU identity had a constitutive effect on actors' underlying preferences, or whether it operated merely as a constraint on behaviour.

the impact of enlargement on candidate countries

The impact of enlargement on applicant countries has emerged only recently as the subject of theoretically informed analyses. In particular, the literature on 'Europeanization' has contributed to analysis of the EU's impact on new members in previous enlargement rounds (Börzel, 1999; Falkner, 2000). In the context of eastern enlargement, a rapidly growing body of literature has analysed the impact of enlargement during the accession process on those countries that joined the EU in 2004. Given the political and economic transformation processes in CEECs, the EU's pre-accession adjustment requirements were the most explicit and most onerous to date. The candidates in the EFTA enlargement experienced major pre-accession alignment through the European Economic Area, but this process coincided much more closely with their accession. Hence, the EU's adaptation pressure prior to accession is most noticeable in the case of the CEECs. Studies of the impact of the EU on the CEEC accession candidates suggest a distinction between two main dimensions: the basic principles of democracy and human rights, and the specific areas of the *acquis communautaire*.

Analyses in the first area suggest that the initial starting positions of the CEECs made a key difference (Vachudova, 2001; Schimmelfennig *et al.*, 2003). The EU's influence was most obvious in the consolidation of political change in the unstable and fragile democracies, while it was unnecessary in the democratic front-runners and ineffective in non-democratic countries. The key factor that explains differences in CEEC governments' compliance with the EU's democracy conditionality thus appears to be the domestic costs of compliance. Governments that fear that compliance will erode their domestic power base are unresponsive to EU incentives. However, while Schimmelfennig *et al.* (2003) suggest that the EU's impact was essentially restricted to the intergovernmental channel, Vachudova (2001) argues that the EU also successfully influenced domestic politics and brought about electoral victories for democratic opposition parties. In sum, a rationalist framework appears well suited to explaining the impact of the EU in this area. However, constructivist approaches might be necessary to explain why some CEECs initially emerged as democratic front-runners in the absence of EU pressure.

The impact of the EU on the adoption of the *acquis* can also be told by and large in rationalist terms. The key conditions in this area relate largely to the presence of a credible membership perspective and the inclusion of specific rules relating to the EU's accession conditionality. Under these conditions, external incentives connected to EU accession appear to have outweighed issue-specific domestic adjustment costs (Dimitrova, 2002; Jacoby, 2005; Schwellnus, 2005; Sissenich, 2005). Domestic adjustment costs and veto players merely appear to influence the timing of alignment, but not whether alignment takes place as such. By contrast, before EU conditionality set in and prior to the establishment of a credible membership perspective, we observe only selective and patchy alignment of the CEECs with the *acquis* (Brusis, 2002).

However, some studies suggest that processes of learning and persuasion, as emphasized in constructivism, played a dominant role in certain policy areas for certain CEECs, such as for clean air policies in the Czech Republic (Andonova, 2003) or for central banking in Poland (Epstein, 2002). Furthermore, in certain cases such socialization processes account for variation in the attitudes towards EU policies among different groups of CEEC civil servants. Grabbe (2005) argues that this explains why the attitudes towards the EU's Schengen *acquis* are much more favourable among officials from interior ministries than from the foreign ministries.

In sum, the broad patterns of EU impact on accession countries can be well explained by factors such as membership incentive, domestic adjustment costs and the credibility of EU conditionality. However, since external incentives often merely resulted in the formal transposition of EU rules, their continued implementation and enforcement after accession might be problematic. As EU rules that were adopted through processes of learning and persuasion are much less likely to remain domestically contested, we would expect these processes to facilitate effective implementation.

conclusion

In this chapter, we have suggested a new way to structure the study of EU enlargement, primarily by directing attention to common dependent and independent variables. Rather than aspire to some kind of 'grand theory' of enlargement, we have argued that concepts in the broader discipline of International Relations provide useful analytical tools that facilitate debate and cumulative findings. Our overview of the theoretically oriented enlargement literature suggests that debate between rationalist institutionalism and constructivism and, to some extent, more finely-grained differences between the various rationalist approaches, provide a useful framework for analysis. This chapter also demonstrates that these alternative approaches do not necessarily need to be conceived as mutually exclusive explanations. Many contributions combine rationalist and constructivist insights. At the same time, our overview also shows that debates on some aspects of separate rounds of enlargement can be plausibly conducted exclusively in either a rationalist or a constructivist framework.

Enlargement politics has been the predominant focus of theoretically informed studies of EFTA and eastern enlargement. Given that the queue of (would-be) candidates is still long, conceptual insights and debates generated by this enlargement research remain important even after the 'big bang' accession in 2004. A next step will be to consider the impact of the EU on the new members who joined the EU in May 2004. Much of the pre-accession adjustment has consisted of formal transposition, with implementation lagging behind. It is thus necessary to consider how implementation and domestic enforcement will develop now that the external incentives of accession and conditionality are no longer the dominant factors driving the process.

In sum, research on enlargement has developed into a major growth area in EU Studies. The growth of the literature is increasingly accompanied by attempts to link EU enlargement to the general study of international organizations, a move which helps address previous weaknesses by generating more generalizable findings. The potential contribution of enlargement research can be realized still more fully, however, if analysts invest more in comparative research designs and pay more attention to under-researched dimensions, such as substantive policies and the impact of enlargement on candidates and new members.

notes

1. We suggest that the (anticipated) impact of enlargement on the EU is part the analysis of actors' preferences in the enlargement politics of the EU and individual countries.
2. On 'cultural match' and 'resonance' in constructivist analysis, see, for example, Checkel (1999a) and Cortell and Davis (2000).

7
conceptualizing the european union's global role
ben tonra[1]

introduction

The end of the twentieth century witnessed yet another turning point in the development of the EU's global role. The longstanding gulf between Atlantic and Continental-centred models of European security was tentatively bridged. The United Kingdom, as the pre-eminent Atlanticist power in Europe, had long insisted that European and transatlantic security was a seamless whole that would be weakened by any self-conscious effort to define European security outside the context of the North Atlantic Treaty Organization. French policymakers, by contrast, insisted that while the Alliance was crucial, Europe had to provide for its own security and then establish a true Atlantic partnership with the United States, a partnership predicated upon equality.

The December 1998 Anglo-French summit at St Malo did not, perhaps, provide for a full reconciliation of these positions but it did converge upon at least one common point; that the EU needed to develop a military capacity to sustain a coherent, effective and credible European foreign and security policy (Howarth, 2000; M. Smith, 2001). This consensus led directly toward a series of EU summit agreements first outlining and then giving substance to the creation of a European Security and Defence Policy (ESDP) which included the operational mandate, institutional expression, and decisionmaking capacity for a European Rapid Reaction Force. Through the Cologne, Helsinki and finally Nice European Council summits, ESDP – as a subset to the EU's existing Common Foreign and Security Policy (CFSP) – took shape.

In a parallel but equally significant process, the relationship between the CFSP and the EU's broader external activities came under increasingly critical scrutiny. The Chinese wall that had traditionally separated the EU's external relations (trade, aid and development cooperation) from the system of foreign policy coordination constructed between the member states, had worn thin. Their contrasting legal base, differing decisionmaking models, varied policymaking structures, and distinct policy tools were increasingly seen as impediments to the creation of an effective, coherent and credible foreign policy for the EU and its member states as a whole.

Moreover, in crisis after crisis, throughout the 1990s and into the following decade, the EU's foreign policy post-mortems were harsh. Policy failures – in whole or in part – were recorded in the former Yugoslavia, in Kosovo, in Rwanda, in the Congo, in Afghanistan and in Iraq. Even more dangerously, such crises often cruelly illuminated and in some cases exacerbated serious transatlantic and intra-European policy fissures (Lieven, 2002; Kagan, 2003; M. Smith, 2003). Clearly, the simple sum of member state and EU capacities was poorly directed and too often worked at cross-purposes. Thus, through the Amsterdam and Nice Treaties, and in the deliberations of the European Convention and the subsequent intergovernmental conference preparing the Constitutional Treaty, the EU's 'foreign policy' came under ongoing and critical scrutiny. One key theme throughout these discussions was the desire to eliminate, to the greatest extent possible, the divisions and fissures that separated the EU's external relations from the CFSP and ESDP.

As a consequence of all this activity, it became possible in the first decade of the twenty-first century to begin to talk seriously about the creation and operation of an EU 'foreign policy' (White, 2001), even as doubts were raised about a dangerous gap between the political rhetoric sustaining that idea and the development of foreign and security capacity on the ground (M. Smith, 2003).

This chapter seeks to highlight the difficulties of conceptualizing the EU as an international actor. It challenges assumptions that would offer a box neatly labelled 'EU' within either European integration theory or traditional International Relations theory. Having done this, the chapter then offers a menu of different approaches that seek – from either a rationalist or post-positivist perspective – to 'rethink' the EU as an international actor. It also looks at approaches assessing the transformatory capacity of EU foreign policy vis-à-vis national foreign policies, the use of foreign policy analysis, the role of ideas and identity and the significant 'normative capacity' of the EU on the international stage. Throughout, reference is made to empirical examples, and while no conclusion is offered as to how 'best' to study the EU from this perspective, the chapter celebrates the variety of possibilities open to students of the EU and of its role in an increasingly globalized world.

what are we looking at?

While practitioners have wrestled with institutional and constitutional devices to bridge their political differences, academic analysts have had their own struggle to come to terms with what was developing before their very eyes. For many years, analysts considered it highly unlikely that the member states of the European Communities – and later the EU – would ever consent or conspire to create a truly common foreign policy. Efforts seemingly made in that direction were either criticized as representing merely empty declaratory policy or, where more substantial moves were made, simply the culmination of converging national interests, especially among the more powerful European states (Allen, 1998). Certainly, early European integration theory found it difficult to encompass the stubborn reality that foreign policy continued to challenge neofunctionalist orthodoxies.

For neofunctionalists, the development of a truly collective foreign policy would have represented an orthodox expression of how they thought the EU worked; with the pursuit of shared interests being assigned ultimately to a supranational authority which, over time, would further extend its policy reach (Deutsch, 1954; Deutsch *et al.*, 1957; Haas, 1958). A spillover from low politics into high politics would thus ultimately take the EU from a Common Commercial Policy into a Common Foreign and Security Policy.

Quite a substantial literature has analysed the use of Community mechanisms for the pursuit of political or other foreign policy goals. In other words, this literature analysed a sort of foreign policy before there was a foreign policy. The most obvious examples related to South Africa in the 1970s and 1980s (Holland, 1988 and 1995), the Middle East (Ifestos, 1987; Greilsammer and Weiler, 1987), the 1982 Falklands crisis (Stavridis and Hill, 1996) and the Cold War's Helsinki process (Nuttal, 2000). In each case the use of trade and other economic tools was linked – sometimes explicitly so – with political goals such as the end of Apartheid, a peaceful resolution of the Middle East conflict, or support for the process of Cold War détente.

In the search for a European foreign policy, a number of analysts have insisted that too much is made of tentative efforts to coordinate sometimes abstract diplomatic positions, and not enough attention is paid to the real substance of European power and its global projection – trade and economics. Michael Smith, for example, has written (1998) on the need to reassess ideas of power and international actorness. He argues, for example, that the EU's Common Commercial Policy and its impact upon global trade agreements, has far greater foreign policy significance than analysts properly credit. Similarly, of course, the EU's Common Agricultural Policy has far greater effect upon the developing world than the effect of all the political declarations issued through the CFSP. Other analysts have focused upon the EU's enlargement policy as a foreign policy strategy in itself, a strategy designed to promote security and stability in the EU's neighbourhood (K. Smith, 2004). Others have assessed the EU's approach to key strategic regions such as the Mediterranean (Gomez, 2003; Maresceau and Lannon, 2001) and the countries of the former Soviet Union (Barysch, 2004), most of which have been conducted through the mechanisms of the EU's trade, economic and development cooperation policies.

While these approaches offer a necessary corrective to an unhealthy preoccupation with 'high politics', they still underscore the reality that the EU's coherence and effectiveness as an international actor relies upon a balance between different policy tools and an effective decisionmaking structure. That structure, however, has not developed in a way that reflects neofunctionalist logic.

When under pressure to address the political issues arising from trade, aid and economic relations, member states cut supranational institutions out by developing their own intergovernmental policy structure outside the European Community. Even in the areas where orthodox Community rules applied, such as trade and economics, member states proved themselves surprisingly adept at resisting efforts to extend Community competence to associated issues, such as intellectual property rights and trade in certain service sectors. Moreover, intergovernmental areas of cooperation in the realm of 'high politics' did not prove themselves amenable to a process of communitarianization (Hoffmann, 1966). They continued to develop and, to a degree, prosper outside the Community realm.

In 1970 the member states of the European Community established a procedure for coordinating national foreign policy positions. European Political Cooperation (EPC), as this procedure was called, was created outside the ambit of the Community's institutions and was based upon an explicitly intergovernmental base. It was only over time, and in the face of considerable political hesitation on the part of the member states, that EPC developed and itself became institutionalized. Indeed, it was not until the 1986 Single European Act that the basic infrastructure of EPC was set out in a formal treaty text. In form and content therefore, EPC appeared to be precisely the kind of interest-driven, member state controlled procedure that intergovernmentalists would have ascribed to the realm of foreign policy cooperation (Pijpers, 1990).

Witnessing the apparent stagnation of the European project in the 1970s and into the 1980s, some analysts saw the stubborn strength of intergovernmental interests – best exemplified in EPC – as an illustration of the proposition that state interests were the true driving force behind the integrative project, which was itself the product of a 'convergence of national interests' (Moravcsik, 1991). The EU's institutional superstructure could then be seen as the matrix within which an especially complex system of interstate bargaining would take place and through which the cooperative benefits of such interstate bargaining would be distributed (Moravscik, 1994). Analysts could also point to empirical case studies where the dominance of state interests in the construction of a 'common' European position could be seen (Ifestos, 1987; Pijpers, 1991; Hoffmann, 2000).

Ironically however, the frustrations of neofunctionalist theorists were later to be matched by those of an intergovernmental orientation. EPC and its successor CFSP did not always seem to help prove the intergovernmentalist case (Wessels, 1982). As EPC was replaced by CFSP and as subsequent reforms took root within CFSP, it became increasingly evident that CFSP did not itself play by an intergovernmental rulebook. Member state interests within CFSP did not appear to be the immutable object of state ambition that they should have been. Policymaking within CFSP did not precisely follow the intergovernmental script. Instead, CFSP witnessed the Commission assuming an increasingly prominent role, the involvement of the European Parliament, the introduction of qualified majority voting and the application of Community measures in support of CFSP. CFSP also became a vehicle for member states' clear ambition that the EU act internationally in its own right, rather than as a vehicle for the interests of the larger states (Cameron, 2002). Interestingly, however, if European integration theorists found themselves struggling to understand and explain the EU's international persona, International Relations theorists were positively dumbfounded.

the european union in the world of international relations

For many years, the EU simply did not appear on the horizons of International Relations theorists – and for very good reason. The EU, as an international actor, simply could not be accommodated within a large section of orthodox theorizing about the interstate system. The European Community and later the EU challenged deeply instantiated and widely held assumptions. As a result, it could be argued that the EU was 'somehow beyond International Relations' (Long, 1997, 187). For its part, the international system was one largely seen to be composed of states whose inter-relations defined the system of which they were a part. The EU was not an actor in this drama and, at best, could only be accommodated as a vehicle of the post-imperial interests of the larger powers. Even with the arrival of liberal approaches to International Relations, the EU was sandwiched together with other 'new' actors such as multinational corporations and transnational interest groups. Moreover, it could still only be conceived as an institutional illustration of cooperative problem solving among enlightened state agents and actors, alongside the United Nations and the Organization for Economic Cooperation and Development and the General Agreement on Tariffs and Trade.

For both realists and liberals then, the EU posed a fundamental paradox – it was not a state, yet was 'state-like' in so much of its relations with states and the interstate system. Foreign policy could only be understood as a subset of state activity directed towards the outside world. If the theoretical drawbridge was lowered to accommodate the 'foreign policy' of the EU, would not the same also have to hold true for the United Nations, for the Organization for Economic Cooperation and Development, for the Association of Southeast Asian Nations – perhaps even for the Coca Cola company? And yet, if the theoretical rules were applied with rigour, how credible would it be to assess the impact and capacity of the foreign policies of more than 200 states in the international system and yet ignore the international impact of a political community that accounted for about one quarter of world trade and global wealth creation?

European integration has never fitted easily within a rationalist-dominated international theory. Neorealists and neoliberals have tried to explain the EU from the perspective of interstate cooperation. From that angle, a key issue that emerged has been debate about the relationship between relative gains and absolute gains. Realists insisted that cooperation would be limited, as states would be preoccupied with maximizing their absolute gains from any system of cooperation. Liberals, on the other hand, argued that a web of interstate cooperation might indeed develop based upon an acceptance of relative gains. A second point of contention is the extent to which institutions can ameliorate anarchy, with realists emphasizing the fundamental role of anarchy in defining the international system and liberals insisting that institutions offer the possibility of governance transcending anarchy.

Nevertheless, neorealists and neoliberals share much more analytical territory than they dispute. One key example here is the extent to which they both argue that power rests at the core of politics and that such power derives from the pursuit of individual material interest. Another is that the range of questions open to analysts is precise, centring upon how interests are bargained and the processes of strategic decisionmaking that lie behind public policy choices. The comparative power of the rationalist approach and a partial explanation of its dominance is that it offers to the holders of power a precise and sparse account of their reality without opening uncomfortable doors into realms which draw their own positions into question. It also seems to relate more directly to 'the facts' of international politics and because of the way in which it defines the world and interrelationships within it, the approach often looks just like common sense (Wagner, 2003).

When looking at the EU's performance, particularly at times of crisis, the explanatory power of rationalist accounts is tremendously persuasive. The collapse of the former Yugoslavia (Almond, 1994; Glenny, 1993) and the subsequent conflict in Kosovo (Ignatieff, 2000) are convincingly explained in terms of conflicting member state national interests, the EU's failure to reconcile those differences and a resulting psychosis in EU policy which weaved dangerously between hubris and humiliation. Similarly, when looking at the Middle East crisis, rationalist accounts privileging the role of national interests and competition with the United States, offer a parsimonious explanation of why the EU is an ineffectual regional actor (Aoun, 2003). They also offer a precise and concise explanation of how EU policies have failed to leave any substantive mark on the conflict (Dosenrode and Stubkjaer, 2002) and what is required if the EU is to engage successfully as a serious and effective actor (Roberson, 1998; Everts, 2003).

In contrast, constructivist accounts of European integration have had more to say about governance, identity, norms and belief structures than either of the two rationalist approaches. They open the door to a wider and perhaps significant set of questions when looking at the international persona of the EU, including questions about the creation of a transnational European identity, the impact of Europeanization on national foreign policies and the export of European values and norms through EU foreign policy. Such questions are of immediate relevance to an understanding of Europe's global role, but are outside the pale of analysis within rationalist worldviews. When looking at the Middle East, for example, constructivist analyses do not focus on the short-term 'realities' of the immediate crisis but upon the longer evolution of policy and regional capacity on the part of the EU and its member states (K. Smith, 1998b and Soetendorp, 2002). In the Yugoslav and subsequent Kosovo crises, constructivist analyses also focused upon the way the EU responded by trying to export and instantiate its own norms and values (Manners, 2002) and the way such values can prompt substantial policy action in the form of 'humanitarian intervention' (Wheeler, 2000).

rethinking the european union's global role

The EU's emerging foreign policy has not – as we have seen – lent itself to easy categorization and has successfully resisted being boxed into our existing understanding of European integration or international relations. It might even be argued that the EU is best viewed as a transitional entity, or one that generates international relations but which also remains itself a subsystem of those international relations (Filtenborg *et al.*, 2002). In recent years too, the development of the EU's international capacity has made the effort to understand it even more challenging.

This is rooted in EU foreign policy's capacity to transform the construction, content and expression of the national foreign policies of the EU member states. Regarding the construction of foreign policies, it is clear that institutionalized policy coordination – involving common EU-wide work practices and structures, a partially shared information base, a common substantive agenda and a unique policymaking structure – has established a truly collective context through which a significant proportion of 'national' foreign policy is now formulated and pursued. Whether characterized as 'Brusselsization' (Allen, 1998) or 'Brussels-based intergovernmentalism' (Howarth, 2000), it amounts to a fundamental shift in the way national foreign policies are being constructed. This does not eliminate the role of national perspectives or even of declared 'interests'. It does, however, underline the degree to which national foreign policies are translated and formulated through a European context even before they hit the avowedly intergovernmental negotiating table (Tonra, 2001).

Regarding the content of national foreign policies, there is also evidence of fundamental processes of change. These are illustrated by 'a consequent internalisation of norms and expectations arising from a complex, collective policymaking system' (Tonra, 2001). Hill and Wallace (1996) define this process as one in which rationality is seen differently as a result of intensive exchange between officials. Earlier, Nuttall (1992) identified this as a 'consultation reflex' in which officials sought out the views of colleagues before constructing their own analyses of the situation and possible policy responses. The impact of this internalization of beliefs and norms is that the content of national foreign policies has gradually shifted over time. While it is difficult to apply the *ceteris paribus* principle, analysts have identified such shifts for a range of states and over a range of issues (Pijpers, 1996; Aggestam, 2000a; Sjursen, 2000; Torreblanca, 2001a and Tonra, 2001).

In the case of foreign policy expression, it is also evident that much has changed in recent years. The cognitive reach of all but the largest and most sophisticated member state foreign policies has been broadened and many member states must involve themselves – even if only peripherally – in a much wider range of issues than heretofore. External actors expect the EU to have a response to international events and crises and EU member states frequently justify their own policies by virtue of collective foreign policy endeavour. This may, at times, be seen in very instrumental terms; that is, the EU is being used as an excuse to mask an uncomfortable national policy preference. However, it is more often the case that many member states have to generate and defend positions that even ten or fifteen years ago they would not be expected to have held (Tonra, 2001).

In response to all of these challenges a number of analysts have sought to 'rethink' the EU's foreign policy and to apply alternative approaches to the study of the EU's global role. Some such approaches have sought to deconstruct state-centric views of world politics by shifting analysis away from how state-like the EU's foreign policy is towards analysis of its international 'presence' (Sjøsted, 1977) and 'actorness' (Allen and Smith, 1991). These concepts are then used to link the internal workings of the EU across different functional policy areas with its overall impact on the external environment. The EU clearly acts internationally and even if it is not a fully-fledged actor (K. Smith, 1999) it is nonetheless necessary to consider its impact and how such action is politically derived within the EU (H. Smith, 1995; Ojanen, 2000; M. Smith, 2000). It is also important to try and avoid looking at the EU as if it were 'an incompetent state' (Bretherton and Vogler, 1999, 3) and instead to consider its real world capacity to shape events outside its borders, both by its own volition and in response to third party expectations and demands.

When the focus of analysis moves from what sort of actor the EU is to consideration of its attributes as an international actor, a range of analytical issues arise. One key issue identified is the 'Capabilities–Expectations Gap' first outlined by Chris Hill (1993). In this article Hill compared and contrasted public expectations of what the EU was supposed to accomplish in the world with the means and capacities that member states had actually bestowed upon it. The comparison was unfavourable and identified a 'gap' which implied that the EU 'was not an effective international actor both in terms of its capacity to produce collective decisions and its impact in events' (Hill, 1993). Furthermore, this approach is especially well-equipped to deal with the EU's evolution as an international actor, particularly as a collective foreign policy develops, because it is able to measure the ways in which 'actorness' increases (or decreases?) over time (Bretherton and Vogler, 1999, 1–45). The approach can be criticized, however, because it is still predicated upon a model of actorness similar to that of a state. Thus, if state foreign policy is the benchmark against which the EU's international actorness is assessed, two logically consistent, but fundamentally opposed, conclusions could be made. It could be argued that either the EU is on the road towards the construction of a state-like foreign policy, which is then a matter of time, of political will and/or of institutional design (Galtung, 1973). It could also be argued that since the EU cannot and will never be a state, it is condemned to Sisyphus-like existence, with its system of intensive diplomatic coordination measured against a set of criteria it is condemned never to fulfil (Eliassen, 1998; M Smith, 2003).

Another approach is to move further in our consideration of the EU as a unique system of external relations. Brian White (2001), for example, has applied a model of foreign policy analysis to what he identifies as a European foreign policy system composed of three distinct subsystems: EU external relations, CFSP and national foreign policies. Rejecting both actor-centred and institutionalist approaches, White argues that an EU foreign policy system can be identified and studied on its own terms. The disadvantage of such an approach is that while providing a well-ordered structure on which to pin considerable empirical material, the model finds it difficult to incorporate theoretical concepts rooted in the primary agency of ideas, norms and beliefs.

In somewhat similar vein, Mike Smith (1996, 1998 and 2000) argues that the EU can be viewed as having a part-formed foreign policy, the bulk of which is provided by its trade and economic capacity (M. Smith, 1998). Crucially, Smith points to the significance of the interplay between member states, EU institutions and the external environment in providing an explanation for the shape of EU foreign policy. The negotiated order that results, rests upon a rule-governed process that is also highly sensitive to external demands deriving from an increasingly globalized world. In a later development of this thesis, Smith offers a conceptual link between the de-territorialization of the state and the ways in which regional and perhaps even global governance might foresee an 'extra-national' or even 'post-modern' EU foreign policy (M. Smith, 2003).

These alternatives remain, however, essentially rooted in a rationalist understanding of foreign policy and a largely positivist approach to social science. Two further alternatives move beyond these essentialist conceptions and posit an understanding of EU foreign policy that is more centrally rooted in identity, beliefs and/or values.

considering identity and ideas

If the ideational foundations of foreign policy are to be taken seriously and the analyst is to move beyond seeing ideas either as 'hooks' in the hands of individual utility maximizers, or as another set of parsimonious variables, then our conceptual horizons might be significantly broadened. While arguments about the positivist nature of constructivism continue (S. Smith, 1999), another set of writers have argued that the foundations of EU foreign policy can best be excavated from the archaeology of identity, rather than that of interests (Tonra 1997, 2001 and 2003; Aggestam, 1999 and 2004; Bretherton and Vogler, 1999; Manners, 2002; Manners and Whitman, 2003).

A constructivist approach offers a norm-based account of institutions that overcomes many of the weaknesses of more instrumental, rationality-based models of a neoliberal/neorealist synthesis. The focus on beliefs, identity and norms opens new pathways for analysing the EU's international capacity. For example, it allows analysts to look at the growth and development of a 'European' identity in foreign policy (Joergensen, 1997; Manners and Whitman, 2003) and the role of public opinion and discourse in the creation of such an identity (Larsen, 1997; H. Smith, 1995). The analyst may also examine the implications of such a development for the creation of the EU as a normative actor driven by identity and values rather than interests (Manners, 2002; and Matlary, 2002).

The point of departure for constructivist approaches is consideration of actors as role players rather than as rational utility maximizers. James March and Johan Olsen (1989) offer a conceptual model in which actors work to a 'logic of appropriateness'. Within this logic, state actors (or agents) consider the context and expectations of the decisionmaking situations in which they find themselves and base their resulting decisions accordingly. That relationship, however, cannot presume any ontological primacy between agent and structure. While the actor's identity and options for choice are shaped by the institutional structures that she inhabits, these self-same institutional structures exist and evolve as a result of their constitutive actors' identities and choices.

Thus, the conception of the EU's foreign policy is not that of a forum within which state/actors' interests are bargained, but an environment from which foreign policy evolves and within which the interest/identity of actors/policymakers are transformed. The first point of reference for national policymakers becomes 'what will the European partners think' rather than 'what is our position on this'. This shift is crucial. What it suggests is that policymakers see themselves not as neomedieval emissaries of pre-defined national positions but as policy arbiters. They are, in effect, seeking to internalize the identity ambitions of colleagues, in order to see that their own positions are at least complementary. In recent years this has been augmented institutionally within CFSP by the development of the policy-planning cell, which was designed to engage in what might be seen as a process of anticipatory internalization.

The ambition to construct a coherent and credible European 'voice' in world affairs has been an important recurrent theme in the development of the EU's international capacity. Crucially, this European voice was designed to have a global rather than a local echo. Despite the limited nature of EPC and the Community's broader problems during the early 1970s, member states were quick to react when it was suggested that their collective activities might be delimited. Their 1974 'Declaration on European Identity' was a direct riposte to US Secretary of State Henry Kissinger's 1973 effort to define Europe's international ambitions in a regional rather than global context. The Declaration stated forcefully that: 'Europe must unite and increasingly speak with one voice if it wants to make itself heard and play its proper rôle in the world'. This identification of EU foreign policy with the expression of a single set of ideas or beliefs has also been evident in other EU measures. These include the establishment of the office of High Representative of CFSP through the Amsterdam Treaty and the Constitutional Treaty's provisions merging that office with External Relations Commissioner's office in order to create an EU Foreign Minister.

The original purpose behind the CFSP post was to engender greater identification with a European political voice, or to personify the EU's international identity. In the event, this has been only partially successful, since the voice lacked the added credibility of also commanding the external relations of the EU. European Convention proposals to merge the two posts into one were explicitly presented as a means whereby the EU's 'voice' would have greater clarity and credibility (Convention, 2003).

Constructivism also offers a framework that explains the centrality of 'values' in the development of EU foreign policy. If the ontology employed here 'emphasises the dependency of state identities and cognitions on international institutions and relates the formation and maintenance of particular regimes to these pre-established identities' we should witness a strong emphasis being placed upon the definition of collective values. The first formal delineation of EPC in the 1970 Davignon Report spoke of the member states' ambition to make an international contribution that was '... commensurate with its traditions ...'. These were later defined in the same text as including '... the common heritage of respect for the liberty and the rights of men ...'.

This normative orientation of EU foreign policy has since become a significant vehicle for theorizing the EU's global role. From its earliest inceptions, writers have been struck by the fact that the European Communities (and later the EU) were applying a new language to foreign policy and had the potential to make a very new contribution to understandings of international politics. Francois Duchêne (1972) argued that this new European polity was indeed a new construct in the international firmament. It was a political entity with a powerful trade and economic identity, but a comparatively weak political/security structure. Thus, it might best be characterized as a new 'civilian power' in international relations. His argument, however, was bigger than that, in as much as it also set out the thesis that this new 'civilian power' might supplant traditional military power as the preferred means by which influence might be exercised in the modern world (Duchêne, 1972 and 1973). The thesis was hotly contested and disputed in a now famous reply from Hedley Bull (1982). More recently, it has been taken up by scholars interested not so much in fact that the EU has an impact on the international system, but in the fact that the EU has a very unique impact and identity.

A number of writers have focused on the very strong normative orientation of the EU's international actions towards issues of international justice and human rights (Manners, 2002; Aggestam, 2000a and Sjursen, 2003). This, they argue, arises from the nature of the EU and the ways in which it acts as a normative exporter of values and beliefs. Manners and Whitman (2003) for example, move decisively away from analysis of the EU as an actor to that of the EU having an international identity that now allows the analyst to consider how the EU 'is constituted, constructed and represented internationally' (Manners and Whitman, 2003, 383). They insist that the EU's international identity can only be successfully read by employing *both* social and political theories, and conclude that it is necessary to move beyond essentialist, positivist and rationalist predispositions in order to look at the EU's international identity as an ongoing 'contestation of complex, multiple (and) relational identities' (Manners and Whitman, 2003, 397). They go on to characterize the EU as an open, pacific, principled, consensual, network characterized by an unconventional, contra-Westphalian nature.

By focusing so intensively on the nature of the EU's international identity, the path is also opened to considerations of how that identity may then impact upon the international system. In other words, if the EU is so different – indeed, according to Manners and Whitman (2003), it is a 'difference engine' – then what are the implications of this for the EU's foreign policy? Sjursen (2003) argues that there is a growing literature focusing on the nature of the EU's international impact. Citing Rosencrance (1998), Aggestam (2000a), Menéndez (2002) and Manners (2002), she argues that the EU does indeed represent something fundamentally different in the international arena and that this difference is rooted to normative considerations of justice and human rights. Despite entering several important caveats to this hypothesis (Sjursen, 2003, 49), she argues that cooperation based upon increasingly intensive communicative processes may offer a better understanding of why the EU has been constituted by, and then acts as such a significant exporter of, certain norms and values.

conclusion

Originally, the European 'project' was predicated upon delivering 'peace' in Europe by, at least in part, withdrawing the tools of modern war from the hands of nation-states. Vesting control of steel and coal into the supranational High Authority was a vindication, a declaration, that the relationship between two key state actors in Europe – France and Germany – would never be the same again. From these roots, explanations of European integration as pre-eminently a 'peace project' emerged. However, as Europe prospered, these roots seem to have been lost. Increasingly, European integration has been seen in materialist terms, as a means to serve the interests of states and/or transnational groups such as European political and social elites, the corporate sector, organized labour and sectoral groups of every caste and kind.

Meanwhile, visions of Europe's global role shifted. Early debates surrounding the 'peace' mission of the early EU – the civilian power thesis – were swiftly discarded and the EU was increasingly defined relative to the existing international power architecture. For their part, classical realists dismiss the EU as an irrelevance and delight in highlighting the absurd and sometimes dangerous pretensions of an entity that lacks even the basic prerequisites of a serious international actor. Other, perhaps more sophisticated realists share similar scepticism, but leave a door open to the remote possibility that the EU, over time and in a set of very particular circumstances, might itself adopt the appropriate manners and dress to join the ancient Westphalian dance of states.

Today, liberals are similarly divided. Perhaps the lesser number look at the EU internationally and see it as a vehicle through which the member states can pursue, just as at they do with domestic policies, their longstanding international interests in a more efficient and effective manner. Through the collective infrastructure of the EU, the old mercantilist ambitions of European adventurers are married to those of mobile international capital and so take full and early advantage of an emerging era of liberal globalization. Europe can then contest with the United States and Japan in a new field of combat: that of economic competitiveness, trade and innovation. Freed of Cold War restraint and the baggage of ideological conflict, the recent and ongoing battles over beef, bananas and Boeing offer a foretaste of this brave new era.

For perhaps a larger number of liberals, the EU is thus far unique, but something more properly seen as a vanguard. The EU can offer itself as a template for other international regions responding to the increasing pressures of globalization. The era of nation-states is passing or being transformed so that if the great global challenges are to be met, humanity needs to organize itself on a different level – through the EU, the African Union, through the North American Free Trade Agreement and the Association of Southeast Asian Nations and the Economic Community of West African States and, ultimately, the creation of new systems of global governance. These will serve to tame the international forces unleashed by globalization and to offer effective collective solutions to shared problems in a smaller and global community.

For another set of analysts, however, a rationalist conception of the EU as a problem solving, interstate institution of whatever variety is profoundly unsatisfactory. The European project was designed, as a means to transcend interests, to establish new yet synergistic identities, to sustain and acculturate new values and beliefs. It was not, in this view, conceived of in a framework of mutual or self-interest. In a sense, such analysts seek to return to the EU's original 'peace project' and to take up the challenge of its originator, Jean Monnet, who famously commented that if he had to do it all again he would have started with culture, the very realm of identity, values and beliefs, rather than coal and steel.

It is not inevitable that the EU will pursue, must pursue, or should pursue, its global role in the same manner as states or indeed as an international organization. One might indeed argue, that for the EU to replicate itself in the image of a state would be to recreate at a continental level the precise conditions of conflict that the EU was designed to overcome. The EU's relations with both the Russian Federation and the Islamic World are a case in point. The EU has tremendous potential as a global actor. The responsibility of all students of Europe is to open themselves to debates which broaden rather than narrow the range of the possible, which question rather than reify the subjectivities and identities that underpin this EU, and which admit that there are many routes to understanding the EU in a way that expands, rather than delimits, its future paths.

note

1. Thanks to colleagues of the EU Commission funded FORNET academic research network on EU foreign policy (www.fornet.info) for their incisive comments on an early draft of this chapter which was presented as a paper to their Working Group on Theories and Approaches to the CFSP at the London School of Economics and Political Science.

8
european identity: theory and empirics
paul gillespie and brigid laffan

introduction

When presenting his country's EU Presidency programme to the European Parliament in July 2003, the Italian prime minister, Silvio Berlusconi, suggested to a German member of the European Parliament that he could play the part of a 'capo' – concentration camp guard – in a forthcoming film. The German government demanded an apology and the German chancellor cancelled his planned holiday in Italy. The statements emanating from the Italian prime minister grated. The sentiments expressed were not representative of the civility that has become commonplace in relations between Europe's political leaders. The statement held echoes of a different Europe, a Europe of closed rather than liberal nationalism. Parallel to the launch of the 2003 Italian EU Presidency was the conclusion of the Convention on the Future of Europe. The Convention agreed the text of a draft Constitutional Treaty, which formed the basis of negotiations in a new intergovernmental conference. Member states eventually signed the new 'Treaty Establishing a Constitution for Europe' in October 2004. The preamble to the Constitutional Treaty claimed that:

... while remaining proud of their own national identities and history, the peoples of Europe are determined to transcend their former divisions, and, united ever more closely, to forge a common destiny.

The sentiments expressed in the Constitutional Treaty represent the Kantian dream for Europe, a Europe of 'perpetual peace', forged out of the shadow of the past and in anticipation of a better future. The juxtaposition of the

131

Berlusconi outburst and the Constitutional Treaty underlines the unsettled and unsettling dynamic of identity and the politics of identity in the evolution of European integration.

This chapter focuses on the relevance of the concept of identity to the study of European integration and the EU. It reviews theoretical and empirical debates about identity and identity politics in relation to the EU. It begins with analysis of why identity has become salient in both scholarly and political debates on integration. The chapter then proceeds to unbundle identity; exploring both theoretical and empirical dimensions. The second section addresses identity as a concept – like so many concepts in the social sciences a contested one – and provides an overview of theoretical debate about identity and European identity. The chapter then explores empirical evidence about identity by addressing two topics. First, is a treatment of the idea that the EU has been an identity builder since its inception. This is followed by analysis of identity and territorial politics in Europe, including opposition to the EU. The conclusion provides a summary of the main findings and a discussion of future research in this field.

why has identity become so salient?

In the old debates between intergovernmental and neofunctional accounts of European integration, little attention was paid to questions of identity. Neither the impact of the EU on state and substate identities, nor the possible emergence of a European identity was the subject of sustained scholarly interest. This changed in the 1990s with the appearance of a burgeoning literature on questions related to identity in Europe. Scholars at the European University Institute in Florence, for instance, established a Forum in 1993–94 to explore national and regional identities (Haupt *et al.*, 1998). This was followed by a second Forum on European identity and the European public space between 1999 and 2001. Furthermore, a major EU Fifth Framework project on *Europeanization, Collective Identities and Public Discourses (IDNET)* was completed in March 2003 (see Risse and Maier, 2003). As part of the project, an extended bibliography on identity was produced. The bibliography cites work in numerous disciplines, different methodologies, and from varying theoretical perspectives including postmodernism, social constructivism, systems theory, social identity theory, psychoanalysis, modernization theory, institutionalism, rational choice, critical theory and the theory of collective action. The bibliography has 900 items, which represents a major research resource for those interested in European identity. The study itself was exemplary in terms of its range, disciplinary reach and theoretical underpinnings.[1]

Interest in identity does not appear to have abated in the early years of the twenty-first century. Official Europe began to explore the question of European identity much earlier. In 1973 at the Copenhagen Summit, the then nine member states adopted a 'Declaration on European Identity'. The

Declaration, which coincided with the first enlargement, was made after the EU achieved the key objectives of the 1957 Rome Treaty and at a time when the EU was attempting to increase its role in the international system. This official attempt to foster a European identity reflected both the desire to strengthen political Europe and aspirations to promote Europe as a global force. The 'Declaration on European Identity' found little resonance among the wider public, however. Nor were its aspirations and rhetoric reflected in the then European Community, characterized at that time by considerable conflict and stagnation. The resurgence of integration in the mid-1980s and the sustained deepening and widening of the EU thereafter brought identity questions back onto the political and scholarly agenda, where they have remained.

The politics of identity came to the fore because of the interaction and intersection of a number of different forces. One of those was European integration. The resurgence of market integration enhanced the salience of integration for Europe's member states. The processes involved became more visible and more politicized, and the regulatory politics of the internal market and the launch of the single currency had an identity dimension. In addition to market integration, the EU embarked on a deepening of political integration in a manner that touched on political identities in Europe. The 1992 Treaty on European Union made provision for European citizenship, resting on national citizenship, but providing additional rights to those holding this status. Although the provisions on citizenship were limited and linked to citizenship of a member state, their inclusion in a European treaty served to underline the changing contours of belonging and rights in Europe.

The dynamic of political and economic integration in Europe has always been intrinsically linked to wider developments in the international system. The disintegration of communism in the eastern half of the continent, symbolized by the collapse of the Berlin Wall on 9 November 1989 had a profound impact on Europe's geopolitics. The EU, for long secure under a North Atlantic Treaty Organization nuclear umbrella, was faced with continent-wide responsibilities and demands from the former communist states for aid, recognition and ultimately membership. The states of central Europe effectively drew on their European credentials to ensure that full membership of western institutions symbolized their 'return to Europe'. In itself, the continent-wide enlargement highlighted questions about Europe's boundaries and the limits of membership. The collapse of communism also brought with it memories of a different Europe: the nightmare of history that Europe was trying to escape. The violent break-up of the former Yugoslavia, characterized by the re-emergence of ethnic conflict of an extreme variety, raised questions about Europe's responsibilities for stability on its own continent. The EU's relatively effective policies in relation to east central Europe were in stark contrast to political and human tragedies in the Balkans. As the EU's external actions in trade negotiations and foreign policy became more coherent in world politics, there was feedback in terms of political identities. The Iraq war in 2002–03 became a defining moment in transatlantic relations, leading to negotiation of new structures to express its external identity more effectively. The dynamic of integration, particularly the deepening of political integration, raised questions about national identities in Europe at the same time as the boundaries between inclusion and exclusion were being altered. Within many European states submerged or peripheral, nationalisms re-emerged seeking their space in the new Europe. As the integration process became more ambitious, discussion about political integration among practitioners and scholars resonated with debates about identity, citizenship and public space. To the politics of interest were added the politics of participation and belonging.

unbundling identity: the theoretical debate

It helps to think about conceptions of identity historically, since the changing use of such an ambitious term reveals much about its substantive meaning. In his semantic history of identity, Gleason noted:

> The historically minded enquirer who gains familiarity with the literature soon makes an arresting discovery – identity is a new term, as well as being an elusive and ubiquitous one. It came into use as a popular social-science term only in the 1950s. (1983, 910)

The proliferation of identity studies across the social sciences and humanities since then coincided with an explosion of 'identity talk' and identity politics in the societies these disciplines sought to understand.

Since 'identity' – the phenomenon if not the word – has a definite history, the categories used to understand and analyse it must begin with how identity became a major issue in Western societies around 1800 and how it changed over the following 200 years (Bendle, 2002). In the shadow of the decline of feudalism, the emergence of state sovereignty, the Enlightenment, the industrial and democratic revolutions, the erosion of religious authority and the rise of Romanticism, 'politics replaced liturgy as the recognised source of societal rules' (Green, 2000, 70). From then identity largely took the form of nationalisms and the creation of nation-states. As documented by a rich literature on theories of nationalism, identity became associated with the pursuit of bureaucratic homogeneity, economic standardization, linguistic uniformity, state sovereignty and cultural monomania (Özkirimli, 2000). The great changes washing over the contemporary world, which might be described as a transition from hard to soft identity, from modernity to post-, or at least late, modernity, a transition in which the EU's pooling of sovereignty is a prime example, must also be accommodated in use of the term.

Political identity implies 'a form of civic solidarity among strangers' (Habermas, 2001, 16). It concerns the circumstances in which 'I' should properly use the term 'we' to create a political community (McKenzie, 1978, 12). Its origins and development form a major part of the agenda of social and political theory as it has recently been defined. There are important differences of emphasis and continuing argument about how precisely this occurs, which are in turn reflected in political philosophies and programmes. National identity came to monopolize the field, given the depth and range of its impact on political practice and consciousness (Anderson, 1991, 7; Orchard, 2002, 420–1). This was reinforced by its coincidence with modern democracy through 'a circular process in the course of which democracy and the nation-state stabilised each other. Both have jointly produced the striking innovation of a civic solidarity that provides the cement of national societies' (Habermas, 2001, 16). It is only in the last fifteen to twenty years that serious efforts have been made, either analytically or politically, to disentangle political from national identity, an effort responding to changes in the international arena, including globalization, interdependence, regional integration and the end of the Cold War. This cross- and multidisciplinary endeavour has involved most of the human and social sciences. Four major insights have emerged in what has been a converging, if contested, field:

- identity is social and relational rather than solitary or atomized;
- it is not immutable or unchanging, but continually constructed and narrated;
- it is multiple, not singular;
- and in its national setting it is having to adapt to changing circumstances in which new transnational identities may emerge.

These four insights enable us to relate theories of identity to EU governance.

classifying identities

Contemporary accounts of European and other political identities may be classified according to two conceptual dimensions arising from various disciplinary literatures. These are illustrated in Figure 8.1.

It is commonly agreed that identity is concerned with the relationship between the 'self' and the 'other'. That is, how the individual relates to society in creating her personal identity. At the collective level a similar distinction is made, between 'us' and 'them'. That self and other are inherently connected has become a basic assumption of social theory (Berger and Luckmann, 1966; Castells, 1997; Giddens, 1991; Poole, 1999). This dimension of identity conceptions is represented on the horizontal axis of Figure 8.1.

The second dimension in the definition of identity relates the 'one' to the 'many'. It is represented in the vertical axis of Figure 8.1. Political identity,

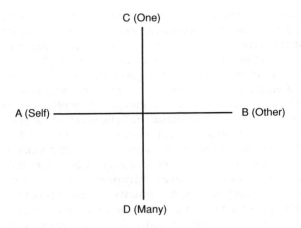

Figure 8.1   Dimensions of identification

manifested as nationalism, was commonly understood to be singular, uniform, homogeneous, concerned with a 'uni-identity' distinct from all others. On such foundations Gellner erected his well-known definition of nationalism as 'primarily a political principle, which holds that the political and the national unit should be congruous' (1983, 1). Recent changes in the infrastructure of national and international political life render such unitary assumptions more problematic, even redundant. Territorial bounding and affective national bonding between leaders and citizens no longer reinforce one another as they did for much of the modern European period, as territory, identity and function are reconfigured (Laffan *et al.*, 2000). The EU exemplifies such trends, which bring the neomedieval features of 'overlapping authority and multiple loyalty' (Bull, 1977, 254) back to international life. Thus we have a second dimension in the classification of political identity, which varies along a pole from the one to the many, the singular to the multiple, the monocultural to the multicultural, homogeneity to heterogeneity. Associated with this is the movement from closed to open boundaries.

As Table 8.1 shows, drawing the two dimensions together gives a fourfold typology of political identities and related theories. The horizontal line A–B is defined by the (qualitative) self–other/same–different/us–them/domestic–foreign/friend–enemy polarities while the vertical line C–D denotes the (quantitative) one–many/homogeneity–heterogeneity/closed–open/bounded–cosmopolitan ones.

Contemporary accounts of political identity within the EU may usefully be examined and summarized in terms of this classification. Many debates about the nature and future of European identity occur between the four boxes. Box I of Table 8.1 is defined by a combination of self-sameness and homogeneity, which approximates the classical nation-state defined by recent theorists of

Table 8.1   Political order, theory and identity

BOX I	BOX II
Classical Nation-State Ethnic or cultural nationalism Essentialism Communitarianism	*Post WWII West European State* Liberal nationalism Liberal intergovernmentalism Bounded integration
BOX III *Federal State* Pannationalism Communitarian federalism Multinational democracy	BOX IV *Multilevelled Polity* Multilevel governance Cosmopolitan democracy Postnationalism Neomedievalism

nationalism. Its continuing salience is asserted by political theories assuming that the shared cultural core of a nation – the demos – is necessary for social and system integration in liberal democracies, and that this shared cultural core may be directly read from their history. Writers such as Anthony Smith (1992 and 1998) and Walker Connor (1994), who are associated with the defence of primordial nationalism, have influenced those who argue that a political identity with the legitimacy to sustain disagreement and redistribution can only be established at the level of the national state. David Miller (1995), the theorist of liberal nationalism, made similar arguments, saying that the political trust needed to sustain democracy requires the common beliefs, language and affective sense of belonging provided by modern nationalism. As Abizadeh points out, 'this is a billiard-ball view of culture – one that anthropologists have fully discredited – which takes particular cultures to be (mutually exclusive) "entities" whose boundaries are neatly specifiable and overwhelmingly impenetrable' (2002, 502). It takes little account of the difference translation or multilingualism can make to political transparency in multinational democracies, or that there are in most contemporary democracies multiple, criss-crossing, overlapping, interwoven and entangled public spheres rather than culturally separated ones. Nevertheless, the argument that political identity can only be established at the nation-state level, an argument entailed by the assumptions built into Box I, remains surprisingly influential in these literatures as well as in political practice.

Analysis fitting with the assumptions of Box II, which move towards the 'other', reflects the realization that the growing interdependence of the contemporary world necessitates intergovernmental cooperation. Integration of policy is based on rational calculations of mutual interest, rather than on a merging of political identities or the creation of new transnational ones. Interstate elite bargaining better explains the pattern and course of European integration, notably at intergovernmental conferences, which set the parameters of routine EU policymaking. National preferences and domestic politics are crucial determinants of such grand bargains. The system's legitimacy is determined by these outputs rather than the need for further inputs from new sources, such as the legitimacy that political identities would provide. Such, in summary, is the theory of liberal intergovernmentalism elaborated most consistently by Moravcsik (1998a). He is sceptical of the need for a new discourse of European identity to sustain this level of integration, a view he says is confirmed by the outcome of the Convention on the Future of Europe (Moravcsik, 2003b). Regional integration has not, on this account, reached the point where it threatens the nation-state's future, but has functioned rather to save it (Milward, 1992).

Associated with these positions is the theory of 'bounded integration', which stresses the durability of nationalism in modern conditions. These are conditions in which the state has assumed a much more powerful position in the social life of citizens and where socialization occurs through educational institutions closely bound up with national culture, including languages. Road-building, legal unification and bureaucratic standardization create and recreate that culture, as do warfare, migration controls and the daily taken-for-granted, even routine and banal presentation of these realities and of international relations by governments and media (Mann, 1996; Cederman, 2001, 151–2; Billig, 1995). Cederman argues that 'an emphasis on integration's boundedness implies that the nation state represents a stable equilibrium capable of uniting large populations' and that bounded-integration thinking 'does not in principle exclude the possibility of democracy beyond the nation state; it just postulates more demanding and precise conditions for its success than do postnationalists' (2001, 157). Education, mass media and language are central in such an argument – and remain firmly under national control.

Within European integration theories, the liberal intergovernmental account may be contrasted with other approaches towards supranational governance, and particularly those that emphasize transnational exchange and social interaction across borders among governing elite on a continuum from intergovernmental to supranational politics, with varying degrees of institutionalization (Sandholtz and Stone Sweet, 1998). Such approaches represent a conceptual breakthrough, which departs from zero-sum assumptions about state sovereignty. They are further developed towards concerns with political identity in a new literature describing an 'extra-territorial constitutional system' in which 'political hierarchy and steering are replaced by segmented policymaking in multiple arenas characterised by negotiated governance', with citizens having additional rights and avenues for the pursuit of politics (Laffan *et al.*, 2000, 74 and 98). This literature does allow a role for identities, conceived as 'the introduction of political contests with a European dimension [and] a further deepening of European citizenship, which would allow for multiple identities and multiple citizenships, and an extension of associative democracy' (218). The developing literature on multilevel governance adds further substance to these new definitions of the

EU, allowing for a continuum linking national to local and regional tiers and to international and supranational ones (Hooghe and Marks, 2003).

These last theoretical developments mark a crucial transition on the vertical line of Figure 8.1 from homogeneity to heterogeneity, from the One to the Many. But which is the more appropriate typological box in Table 8.1 to place such an extraterritorial system? Box III would associate it with statist forms of federal government, which have been the traditional alternative to the nation-state in the period of democratic modernity; as the Austrian social democrats put it in the early 1900s, 'federalism is democracy's answer to empire'. This would shift the political hierarchy from the national to the supranational, reordering their relations of power, albeit within a negotiating framework in which nation-states remain predominant actors. A zero-sum assumption about political identification is built into such a transition. It is associated with the traditional rhetoric of European federalism, which foresees a state-like entity replacing distinctive nation-states.

Discourse theory has much to offer the student of such systems; but it would be foolhardy indeed to allow the rhetoric of European federalism to foretell political change without solid evidence that the nation-state is indeed being hollowed out and replaced by a new set of transnational interests (Diez, 2001). Such evidence is simply lacking, so far as transferred resources and competences are concerned, in the pattern of European integration established so far. Nor was it evident in the proposals of the Convention on the Future of Europe, the follow-up intergovernmental conference or the member state-approved Constitutional Treaty. Comparative figures for budgets and federal economic, military and redistributive powers show the EU does not have the capacity to become a federal superstate, even if it is endowed with postmodern or postnational modes of governing (Laffan *et al.*, 2000). Certain important actors in its developing political system continue to argue that it should have such a capacity – and they may be able to turn provisions for flexible cooperation to their advantage in coming years (Gillespie, 2001; Warleigh, 2002). But proponents and opponents of a federal Europe would be foolish to rely on teleologies linking political destiny to European civilizational identity as reliable evidence.

Pan-nationalism is one of the approaches that do just that, extrapolating political identification from the national to the putatively federal state, based on the history of nationalism itself and assumptions about an essential unity of European civilization, whether in its Christian or secular manifestations (Huntingdon, 1997; A. Smith, 1992). Within the political imaginary of modernism, which saw dramatic transitions from imperial to national forms of power, this may make sense. But it fails to take account of intervening changes in the nature of nationalism and the international and European systems. Efforts to cultivate a European identity are an increasingly prominent feature of official rhetoric in the EU, as discussed in the next section of this chapter. Nevertheless, official rhetoric is increasingly having to come to terms with the political realities and theoretical perspectives outlined in Box IV of Table 8.1, where recognition, difference and the other are central to the definition of identity (Fossum, 2001).

If political identity and democracy have gone together with nationalism in the creation of the modern nation-state, so too has much of the rest of the associated vocabulary of democratic theory, including legitimacy, representation and participation. It is predicated on homogeneity, whether ethnic or civic. How then can political identity and/or democracy be conceived in the multilevel, interdependent and heterogeneous reality that is the emerging EU, which could have up to 35 member states by 2020? This could only come about by a 'double conceptual disengagement: of citizenship from nationality and ethnicity and of democratic constituency from territory defined nationally, and in some cases from being defined in territorial terms at all' (Kuper, 2000, 164). Habermas notes that if the national form of collective identity was due to a 'highly abstractive leap from the local and dynastic to national and then to democratic consciousness, why shouldn't this learning process be able to continue' at the European or even the world level? (2001, 102). Weiler argues that the 'decoupling of nationality and citizenship opens the possibility of thinking of coexisting multiple *demoi*' based, critically, on different subjective factors of identification (1999b, 344–5). That conceptual disengagement is made more difficult by the very success of the nation-state models of political identity in capturing the field and defining the boundaries of domestic and foreign, us and them, self and other.

If states have provided the paradigm form of polity or political community in the tradition of Westphalian sovereignty set out in Boxes I and II, the EU is conceived in Box IV of Table 8.1 as a non-state or post-state political community defined by the degree of autonomous political authority it enjoys and in terms of the sense of belonging, identification or citizenship involved. Either way 'the idea of a "polity" must be seen in more-or-less terms rather than either-or terms. "Polity-ness" is a question of degree, of gradation along a continuum, rather than an absolute state' (Walker, 2001, 2–3). This extends the above-mentioned Sandholtz–Stone Sweet (1998) insight towards political identity, linking it with the points made by Laffan *et al.* (2000) and with the literature on multilevel governance about how those identities are expressed in this postnational setting, notably concerning multiple identities and citizenships and the nature of diversity (Gillespie, 1996; Mair and Zielonka, 2002).

The accounts of EU and European identity contained in Box IV therefore engage some of the most radical, critical and experimental contemporary social and political theories, including postnationalism, postmodernism, historical and social constructivism and institutionalism. They put in question essentialist assumptions, based on simple, homogeneous, categorical and unified identities, which continue to be widely, even if ill-advisedly, used in the definition of nation-states, spelt out in Box I (Abizadeh, 2002; Calhoun, 2001; Manners and Whitman, 2003, 396). They also open up methodological and empirical disputes, which can contribute to greater dialogue between different theoretical streams within International Relations and Political Science (for example, Checkel and Moravcsik, 2001). They also open up debate between International Relations and Political Science and disciplines such as history, anthropology, sociology, social psychology and political philosophy. Theoretical and political debates overlap, as is to be fully expected in a developing polity, since 'Europe remains an arena of contestation and integration is itself a contested project' (Laffan, 2001, 725). And further, 'it is wrong to try and avoid the politicisation of European affairs. Politicisation increases the salience of the EU in the perception of the citizens. Hence controversies about EU policy are not bad for European identity; they can actually increase the sense of community among Europeans' (Risse and Maier, 2003, 10). Among the controversies highlighted by the classification of political identities offered here are those between euroscepticism and federalism (Box I versus Boxes III and IV), based on zero-sum assumptions about sovereignty; between a unitary federalism and a multidimensional neomedievalism (Box III versus IV) or between liberal intergovernmentalism and a plurally identified European polity (Box II versus Box IV).

Many of these controversies were addressed both theoretically and empirically in the IDNET project cited above. This project brought together an interdisciplinary group of scholars to 'examine the processes by which, and the outcomes with which Europeanisation impacts upon and transforms collective identities relating to the nation state' (Risse and Maier, 2003, 1). The research project reported three major findings that helped to frame the theoretical and empirical research agenda on the politics of identity in Europe. First, most identifications with Europe take the form of 'country first, but Europe too' and that the real cleavage in mass opinion is between those who identify only with their nation and those who see themselves attached to both. Second, therefore, it is no longer controversial that individuals can hold multiple political identities. Rather what is important for analysis is how such identities are constructed and how they operate. They may be nested, as in a Russian doll; cross-cutting or 'marbled', a term taken from American federalism and adapted to the European experience. The term 'marbled' characterizes the various components of an individual's identity which cannot be neatly separated on different levels, as the nesting or cross-cutting examples imply, but influence, mesh and blend with one another. The third finding was that there is widespread evidence of a distinction between civic and cultural components of European identity (Risse and Maier, 2003, 15). Using the categories developed in the theoretical section and the insights of the IDNET project, we turn now to the empirical evidence that enables us to explore these controversies.

the empirics

the eu as an identity builder

From the 1980s onwards, there was renewed theoretical interest in the role of institutions in the structuring of political and social life. Authors such as March and Olsen (1989, and specifically 1998, 960) emphasized the co-evolution of identities and institutions and the deliberate creation of international identities. Institutionalist perspectives such as these underline the potential of the EU as an identity-builder in its own right (Laffan, 2004). The literature on the role of institutions is complemented by work of legal scholars theorizing European constitutionalism and the role of law in the dynamics of integration (Shaw, 1999; Weiler, 1999a).

The EU has engaged in the deliberate creation of supranational identities in three ways:

- The impact of the EU itself on political order and on its constituent parts
- The development of a normative frame for participation in integration
- The creation of symbols of belonging intended to alter cognitive frames in Europe.

The emergence of the EU, beginning with the 'inner six' and gradually spreading to 25 and more states, altered state identity in Europe. As the EU evolved into the most successful and robust forum for interstate integration, seeing off the rival European Free Trade Association, all states in Europe had to reach a *modus vivendi* with it, either as members, candidates or associated members. For all states wishing to join the EU, the decision to embark on accession was historic, a critical juncture in the history of each state. Even for those states, such as Norway, that did not join the EU, non-membership became a badge of state identity and the integration issue continued to be one of the most contentious and emotive political issues on or off the political agenda. No state in Europe or in its wider geographical neighbourhood could ignore the institutionalization of a new form of political order in Europe (Laffan, 2004). European integration has had a major impact on the classical nation-state, identified in Box I of Table 8.1 above.

The second dimension of the EU as an identity builder was the gradual development and consolidation of the EU as a normative order, a community of values. The founding value of the EU was peace, which resonated in the Schuman Declaration and in the original treaty texts. The EU's other values such as human rights and democracy were implicit rather than explicit at the outset. The process of constitutional change and enlargement has served to make the EU's values far more explicit over time. In the 1990s, the EU attached high levels of conditionality to the accession of former communist states. All candidate states had to be functioning democracies characterized by respect for human rights and the rule of law. The importance of these democratic norms for the process of enlargement demonstrated that the EU's normative frame is not merely symbolic but constitutive (Schimmelfennig, 2002, 598–626). The process of externalizing the EU's values was accompanied by efforts to make them more explicit in the EU's constitutional order.

The Convention on the Future of Europe, given the task of elaborating a Constitutional Treaty for the EU, devoted considerable time to a discussion of the EU's values and objectives. Titles one and two of the Convention's draft Constitutional Treaty and the member state-approved Constitutional Treaty define the EU's objectives and its underlying values. Article I-2 of the Constitutional Treaty reads as follows:

> The Union is founded on the values of respect for human dignity, freedom, democracy, equality, the rule of law and respect for human rights, including the rights of persons to belong to minorities. These values are common to the Member States in a society in which pluralism, non-discrimination, tolerance, justice, solidarity and equality between women and men prevail.

The values are again reiterated in relation to the EU's aims and objectives and its relations with the wider world. Part two of the Treaty incorporates the Charter of Fundamental Rights of the EU. The Constitutional Treaty marks a deepening of Europe's constitutional architecture and by definition of its normative framework given that constitutions represent a mixture of institutional provisions and the values underlying the polity (Shaw, 2003; Closa, 2003).

In conjunction with the deepening of the EU as a 'community of values', Europe's political leaders strove to mould EU-specific symbols. The symbols began to appear in the 1980s. They looked to the traditional symbols of state building, flags, anthems, a common passport, driving licence, the blue flag on beaches and car number plates. Throughout the EU individual citizens were given practical symbols of belonging and their visual universe was expanded to include EU-related symbols. Increasingly national politicians were happy to display both national and European symbols and Europe's communes identified themselves as part of a wider Europe.

The purpose of these symbols was to remind Europeans that their political and social world was changing. On the 1 January 2002, a very powerful and practical new symbol was added to Europe's rich forest of symbols when euro notes and coins began to circulate in the twelve member states that were part of the first wave of eurozone members. The continuation of two kinds of symbols on the coins is noteworthy; on one side we find the European symbol and on the other each member state has its own symbols. The differences on one side of the coins combined with the sameness on the other are in themselves a powerful reminder of the twin dynamics of unity and diversity in Europe. They are also a powerful reminder that the EU is not intent on transcending national markers of identity but on adding European symbols to the national.

Although empirical evidence points to the EU's power as an identity builder, this should not be overstated. The Commission was not particularly successful in the 1980s when it attempted to harness traditional state-building policies such as cultural policy and education as a means of fostering a European identity. Time and time again the Commission found its proactive policies in these areas diluted or prevented by reluctant member states (Theiler, 2004). Notwithstanding this, the EU, by its very existence, altered Europe's institutional landscape and in turn the institutional moorings of Europe's nation-states. To be a member state matters to state identity in contemporary Europe. State identity was not, however, the only target of top-down identity building in the EU. The inclusion of European citizenship in the Treaty on European Union, and deliberate attempts to foster EU-specific symbols to alter Europe's symbolic framework, were designed to alter individual identities and belonging in Europe. According to Surel, 'one of the principal "functions" of a cognitive and normative frame shared by a certain number of actors is effectively to develop a "collective consciousness" in them; in other words, a subjective sense of belonging, producing a specific identity' (Surel, 2000, 500). Citizens of the member states were invited to become part of a wider universe that included but extended beyond the national. How individual Europeans responded to this invitation, how top-down identity building interacted with bottom-up identity changes, are discussed in the following section.

bottom-up identity change

The EU's attempts to alter identities in Europe through top-down strategies have now been analysed; but what of individual Europeans? Where would individual Europeans find themselves in the boxes outlined above? Has there been bottom-up identity change so that individual Europeans identify with Europe? How does identification with Europe interact with national, regional and local identities? Are national identities in Europe becoming Europeanized? And are there differences between elite identities and those of the mass public? Does Europe resonate more strongly for some Europeans than for others?

The empirical evidence to answer these questions is patchy but it is relevant to begin with an elite/mass distinction (Risse and Maier, 2003). Since the 1950s, Europe's state elites have been drawn into intensive engagement in transnational and intergovernmental processes of governance. To govern in Europe at the beginning of the twenty-first century is to govern within the shelter of the EU's collective governance structures. To be a minister or civil servant in Europe today carries with it an obligation to participate in EU governance on a continuous basis. What do we know about elite attitudes and identities? In 1996, Eurobarometer conducted an elite survey known as the 'Top Decision Makers Survey' to elicit elite views on questions concerning the dynamics of integration. This survey did not ask direct questions that tapped into identity. However, it did ask the standard Eurobarometer questions on attitudes to EU membership and benefits from membership for their state. The most significant finding was that the

> ... [r]esponse to the finding as to whether membership of the European Union was a 'good' or a 'bad' thing showed 94% of top decision makers considered it a 'good' thing, 2% a 'bad' thing and 4% 'neither good nor bad'. This is in sharp contrast with the general public where the comparable figures were 48% 'good thing', 15% 'bad thing' and 28% 'neither good nor bad'. (Eurobarometer, 1996)

Furthermore, the perceived benefits from membership displayed a similar gap between elite and mass opinion. Ninety per cent of the top decisionmakers felt that their state had benefited from membership in contrast to the much lower 45 per cent of the general public. This does not tell us that the top decisionmakers identify with the European project but it does alert us to its salience for their way of governing.

There is a growing literature on the interaction between the national and European levels of policymaking, on the role of national civil servants in EU policymaking, and on the proliferation of committees in EU governance. This literature points to the intensive engagement of member state representatives in the EU and to the emergence of EU-specific roles within the EU institutions (Wessels, 1997; Beyers and Dierickx, 1998; Trondal, 2000; Laffan, 2004). However, the identity evoked in EU-level settings does not replace identities evoked in national institutions; rather it is complementary and secondary (Egeberg, 1999, 471). In this emerging literature, there is much emphasis on processes of norm development, socialization and learning, which in turn may create new or additional identities for the participants (Herrmann et al., 2004).

Empirical evidence of how individual Europeans respond to the identity potential of the EU depends largely on data from the Eurobarometer, although there are a number of smaller studies that offer important insights (Herrmann et al., 2004) Eurobarometer surveys have asked a number of questions over time that probe the degree of attachment of individual respondents to different territorial units (Citrin and Sides, 2004, 161–85). The respondents were offered the following levels of attachment – to town/village, region, country and at different times Europe or the European Community/EU. The most striking feature of responses to this question is the significant gap between attachment to the national territorial units and to Europe or the European Community/EU. Whereas between 88 per cent and 92 per cent of respondents expressed attachment to town, region and country, attachment to Europe, at its highest, was just over 60 per cent and attachment to the EU was 48 per cent. It is significant that attachment to Europe as a cultural/

geographical concept was higher than attachment to the EU as an evolving polity. This is in line with the finding in the IDNET project regarding the distinction between the civic and cultural components of European identity. The EU, as we noted above, hegemonizes civic identity, with the emphasis on democracy, human rights, market economy and cultural diversity, while a macrosociological-constructivist account of European civilization provides a persuasive anchor for a continent-wide identification (Giesen and Eisenstadt, 1995). If identification with Europe and/or the EU is part of a hierarchy of identities, it is far less salient to individual Europeans than attachment to town, region and country. This finding suggests that the outcome in Box III of Table 8.1, a federal state in Europe, is highly unlikely. It also lends support to those who underline the continuing salience of the national and the nation-state, as in Box II.

Eurobarometer reports go beyond questions of attachment, however, to probe the complementarity of different identities. For many years respondents have been asked if they identify with the following:

- Nationality;
- Nationality and European;
- European and nationality;
- European.

Analysis of responses to this question over time highlights the fact that for most Europeans the choice is between 'nationality' only or 'nationality and European'. The two other options, which give primacy to European identity, found favour with less than 10 per cent of respondents in the case of 'European and nationality' and less than 5 per cent for 'European' only. In Eurobarometer 37 (1992), over 50 per cent of respondents opted for the 'nationality' only category and 40 per cent for the 'nationality and European' category. Over time the percentage opting for 'nationality and Europe' increased and 'nationality' only decreased. Increasingly a significant proportion of Europeans are opting for 'nation first but Europe too' (Citrin and Sides, 2004). This suggests that for some Europeans there is no perceived trade off or incompatibility between national identity and a European identity. This group is open to the differences and multiplicity of identities implied in Box IV of Table 8.1.

That said, there remains a significant number of Europeans for whom an exclusive national identity is sufficient. This group could be associated with either Box I or II of Table 8.1. Some of this group not only fail to identify with Europe and the EU, but also oppose its creation and development. They remain wedded to conceptions of political order found in Box I. Given the elite consensus on engagement with the EU in most, albeit not all, member states, opposing Europe did not have a major impact on the dynamic of integration until the 1990s. The Danish 'no' to the Treaty on European Union in June 1992 sent shock waves through national governments and EU institutions as public opinion emerged as a salient factor in integration. The exploration of opposition to the EU was not the subject of serious scholarly concern until then.

The Eurobarometer series offers some indication of the degree of opposition or disenchantment with the EU among the public at large. A series of questions asked on a regular basis enables us to discern the proportion of the public who might be open to sceptical arguments about the EU. In questions about the image of the EU, the majority of respondents either had a positive or neutral image of the EU. However, 18 per cent of respondents held negative images. In relation to a question that probes how the respondents would feel if the EU were scrapped, Eurobarometer data demonstrate that 14 per cent of respondents would feel relieved and 45 per cent indifferent. On the question of support for EU membership, 13 per cent saw membership of their country as a bad thing (Eurobarometer 55, <http://europa.eu.int/comm/pubic_opinion/archives/eb/eb55/eb55_en.pdf>, pages 12, 31, 33). Responses to this group of questions suggest that between 15 and 20 per cent of member state citizens have deep reservations about European unification, the image of the EU and whether membership has been a good thing for their country. Citizens holding these views are likely to be far more open to eurosceptical arguments and ideas.

Opposition to the EU is not just a matter for individual citizens. It also finds expression in political parties and in anti-EU groups. Such groups are found in all member states and become particularly active during referendum campaigns. There are also a growing number of transnational groups such as the European Parliament group 'Europe of Democracies and Differences' established after the 1999 European Parliament elections as a successor to the *L'Europe des Nations* group. In 1992, a non-parliamentary group known as TEAM was established to bring together over forty anti-EU groups in a transnational network (www.teameurope.info/index.html). Opposition to Europe is, according to one in-depth analysis, found 'at both elite and the popular level' and is 'pandemic as a phenomenon in present-day Europe' (Usherwood, 2003, 13).

Analysis of euroscepticism distinguishes between 'hard' and 'soft' euroscepticism, with a further breakdown of the latter category into 'policy' euroscepticism and 'national interest' euroscepticism (Szczerbiak and Taggart, 2000). 'Hard' euroscepticism connotes a rejection of the integration project in its entirety, whereas 'soft' euroscepticism is more muted and related to how the EU functions and its policy range.

Euroscepticism both in its rhetoric and practice reifies the classical nation-state identified in Box I of Table 8.1. Moreover, eurosceptics tend to portray the EU in terms of Box III of Table 8.1, a pan-European superstate, a dangerous Leviathan that would subsume Europe's nation-states. The arguments of eurosceptical parties and groups present themselves as the defenders of the national. Left-wing opposition to the development of the EU tends to be based on an economic state/market critique whereas right-wing opposition focuses on issues with a strong identity component, immigration, EU citizenship rights, EU directives with an identity dimension and national sovereignty.

conclusions

This chapter has argued that political identity is a salient and necessary lens through which to analyse contemporary European integration. There has indeed been a 'veritable discursive explosion' in recent years about identity. At the same time, it has been subjected to a searching critique (Hall, 1996, 3), a critique that has included the argument that it is too broad and ill-defined for analytical, as distinct from popular, usage (Brubaker and Cooper, 2000; Handler, 1994). We agree, however, that it is 'an idea which cannot be thought in the old way, but without which certain key questions cannot be thought at all', notably those concerning agency and politics in contemporary society (Hall, 1996, 4). We have set out to show the relevance of identity to the process of European integration, one of the great experiments in modern (or late-, or post-modern) political agency. This makes the subject compelling, a meeting ground for both political and interdisciplinary debates about the changing nature of political order. Multiple and shifting identifications, growing pluralization of domestic and international politics, de-essentialization of political identity, increased celebration of diversity and more instrumental personal relationships all contribute to a softening of previously harder political identities (Green, 2000). Identities must therefore be taken fully into account when integration is theorized. Furthermore, the identification required to underpin European integration will not necessarily be the same, or as intense, as that associated with state and nation-building. As one writer puts it:

> [I]f the Union has no need to spill the blood of its population, to dig deep into the taxpayer's pocket, to function as the final rule-making body in all areas of policy or even to impose a uniform set of rules in all matters, it will obviously make far lighter demands than the traditional nation-state on the loyalties and cooperation of citizens. (Lord, 1998, 108)

As a result of the theoretical and empirical research reported in this chapter, it is clear that we now know a good deal more about how these identifications are constructed, how they operate and their possible future dynamics; cross-disciplinary work has been indispensable in reaching this point. Future research needs to deepen understanding of the boundaries between the four types of political order we have identified, of the ties and tensions between them and of the likely direction of their development. Since the EU 'is a complex entity with supranational, transnational and intergovernmental traits ... it may be conducive to a wide range of identities and forms of belonging', in which the politics of recognition and difference are highly relevant (Fossum, 2001, 3). We have seen how these vary between elite and popular levels, between different member states subject to many distinct historical and cultural influences, and between the different collective and individual political identities highlighted by the typology. There is real scope for research on political identity as the EU develops, enlarges and takes on a more well-defined international role. The former French foreign minister, Hubert Vedrine, makes the point that the positions of the Bush administration encourage the emergence of a European identity:

> Europeans today are building European power. Even those who don't want it, even those who if you ask them say no, it's dangerous. But in practice that's what they're doing. (Marlowe, 2001)

This confirms the point we made earlier, that identity is constructed vis-à-vis an other, in this case an other increasingly identified as the United States. We have stressed the close connection between contemporary political contests, polity-building and political identity, relating institutionalist literatures to cognitive and normative ones, historical and contemporary empirical work to theoretical concerns. Identity provides a frame of reference to relate these various levels.

The typology presented in this chapter relates self and other, the one and the many together in mutually constitutive or dialectical fashion, with an endless capacity for diversity. The theoretical and empirical ramifications of defining the EU as a 'pluriform social organisation' (Calhoun, 2001: 54) requires much more investigation. Thus while it is true that multiple political identities are no longer controversial, and that they may be organized within the EU in nested, cross-cutting or marbled fashion (Risse and Maier, 2003), this insight does not in itself resolve or exhaust the question of how they are constructed and operate. To describe multiple identities is not to explain them. There is no guarantee they will be harmoniously rather than conflictually nested, as is too often assumed in the EU's official discourse of multiple identity (Sassatelli, 2002, 440–1; Shore, 2000).

Research must specify the scope conditions and domain applications that can test such assumptions. It must bear in mind that these are politically and theoretically contested issues, as we see in arguments about whether there is a European demos or a European public sphere between those representing Boxes I and II against those representing Boxes III and IV of the typology. One set of researchers, for example, used discourse theory and methods to examine controversies about the emergence of a European public sphere. They were able to demonstrate that newspapers in five EU states used similar frames of reference in covering the 2000 Haider controversy in Austria. This showed that people do not talk about Europe that often, but if and when they do, they establish a 'community of communication' across borders in which similar issues are communicated at the same time with the same salience, speakers are treated as legitimate voices within a transnational community and similar reference points and meaning structures apply (Risse and Maier, 2003, 60).

In future research on multiple identities, it is necessary to go further towards 'the recognition of the heterogeneity of the in-group as well as the out-group' (Guerrina, 2002, 151). This 'allows us to deconstruct stereotypes and understand the fluidity' of both individual and collective identities and recognize that there are multiple selves as well as multiple others. Both in theory and political practice this would contribute to creating more open and inclusive boundaries within the EU and between it and the rest of the world. The extent to which these are open or closed is likely to remain at the heart of debates on European integration. Hedley Bull pointed this out when he introduced the notion of neomedievalism to explain emerging patterns of international politics in the 1970s, which have now become much more firmly entrenched. He argued that 'our view of possible alternatives to the states system should take into account the limitation of our own imagination and our own inability to transcend past experience' (1977, 256).

notes

1. This can be consulted in a database on European Identity, available to download at <www.uie.it/RSCAS/Research/EURONAT/Literature.shtml>, the Opposing Europe website at <www.susx.ac.uk/Units/SEI/areas/Opposingeurope.html>; a dedicated website providing a directory of anti-EU websites at <www.simonusherwood.fsnet. co.uk/weblinks.htm> (this website was developed by Dr Simon Usherwood as part of his doctoral research on euroscepticism in the UK and France).

9

eu legitimacy and normative political theory

andreas føllesdal

introduction

The aim of this chapter is to present some of the central research topics found in normative political theory relating to the EU.[1] Normative political theory uses methods of normative reasoning to address concepts, arguments and theories about the substantive normative standards necessary for legitimate political orders, institutions and policies. Topics covered might include 'democracy', 'fairness', 'equality', 'justice', 'citizenship', and 'virtue'.

The 'normative turn in EU studies' (Bellamy and Castiglione, 2003) has largely focused on how European-level institutions should be governed. This subject was placed on the public and political agenda largely as a result of the perceived legitimacy crises wrought by the Maastricht Treaty (and sketched in the first section below). Popular and legal conflicts during the ratification process strengthened the argument presented by politicians and scholars that the EU was suffering from a 'legitimacy deficit'. The second section dissolves this apparent consensus by exploring the various symptoms, diagnoses and medication proposed by experts in this field. The next section provides a taxonomy of conceptions, mechanisms and objects of legitimacy. The fourth section presents a unifying perspective based on the need for trust and trustworthiness, so as to explore how perceived normative legitimacy affects both compliance *and* long-term popular support for the EU. The chapter concludes by reviewing several central areas of normative research which serve to address – and perhaps alleviate – such legitimacy deficits.

the maastricht treaty: the end of popular and legal consensus

Widespread concern about the legitimacy of European integration can be traced to the Treaty on European Union, agreed by the member states in Maastricht in 1991. European governments had long based their involvement in European integration on an understanding that the public provided them with a 'permissive consensus' in support of deeper cooperation. The events of 1991–93 challenged this assumption.

Referendums on the Maastricht Treaty in Denmark, France and Ireland caused wide-ranging public debates about and elite dissent over the proper ends and institutions of the European integration process. The Treaty was rejected in a Danish referendum in 1992 by a vote of 51 per cent to 49 per cent only to be accepted a year later when the Treaty was changed to allow Denmark the right to opt out of the single currency. In France, the Treaty created serious cleavages within political parties, and only just won the support of a majority of the electorate in a referendum in September 1992, by a vote of 51 per cent to 49 per cent. In the UK, meanwhile, the House of Commons succeeded in approving the Treaty in 1993, but only with greatest of difficulty. These reactions served to politicize the European integration process, making it clear to national governments that they must henceforth pay much closer attention to public opinion and opposition elite. Falling support for European integration and falling turnout in European Parliament elections were taken as signs of a 'legitimacy deficit'.

In Germany and Denmark, the ratification of the Treaty was also challenged on legal grounds, though the German Constitutional Court and the Danish Supreme Court found the Treaty compatible with their national constitutions. However, the German Constitutional Court insisted on its right to protect fundamental rights, and to review decisions of the European institutions if it were felt that they might be acting beyond the limits of the Treaty. These requirements ran counter to the European Court of Justice's claim that it had sole competence to ascertain the legality of legislation made by the European institutions. The German Constitutional Court also insisted that the powers of the *Bundestag* could not be transferred without limits being placed on any such transfer; and nor could it be left to the EU to decide whether such transfers were necessary for it to fulfil its aims, as Article 235 (now Article 308) allowed. Moreover, transfers of powers must not reduce the democratic influence of citizens over state authority. The influence of individuals within the member states must continue to be secured, either via national parliaments or by increasing the European Parliament's influence over European policies.[2]

By contrast, the Danish Supreme Court found the Maastricht Treaty compatible with the Danish Constitution insofar as the transfer of sovereign powers happened only to a pre-determined and limited extent. Any expansion of authority deemed necessary in pursuit of the objectives of the EU would require the unanimous consent of the Council, and could therefore be vetoed by the Danish government. In 1998, the Danish Supreme Court also insisted that domestic courts had retained the final authority to determine the constitutionality and hence applicability of EC laws within Denmark, regardless of the decision of the European Court of Justice.

legitimacy deficit: symptoms, diagnoses and cures

Public opinion polls demonstrated falling support for European integration in the 1990s. Yet it is doubtful whether public opinion in general, and the referendums in particular, indicate popular discontent with the EU. Relatively low and falling turnout in European Parliament elections should not come as a surprise. Low levels of attention within political parties and by the media, in part due to institutional factors, generally reduce the popularity of what are often called 'second-order elections'. Scholars point out that public opinion is still highly supportive of European integration, even though that support is falling. Moreover, politicians are losing political support right across advanced industrial democracies (Dalton, 1999). Therefore, this is not a trend exclusive to the EU.

Such disagreements notwithstanding, many governments and EU officials have interpreted these events to mean that the legitimacy of the EU is at stake. Politicians have come to fear that Europeans might refuse to accept future steps towards deeper European integration, which might hamper the governability of the EU. To pre-empt such a scenario, it was felt that something had to be done to secure future popular support. The recent Convention on the Future of Europe offered a response to such concerns.

There were many influential contributions to normative political theory prior to the Maastricht Treaty (Scharpf, 1988; Majone, 1990; Mancini, 1991; Weiler, 1991). Scholarly attention began to increase however, as normative theorists claimed that the negative popular responses and legal challenges to the Maastricht Treaty were symptomatic of a legitimacy deficit, raising challenges for future integration and enlargement. This is not to say that this diagnosis went uncontested: some prominent scholars begged to differ, arguing that the EU was not suffering from a legitimacy deficit, democratic or otherwise. Others denied that there was a legitimacy crisis at all, but acknowledged that the perception of such a crisis does indeed exist (Banchoff and Smith, 1999, 3).

Even those who believe that there is a legitimacy crisis diverge when it comes to explaining the symptoms, diagnoses and cures. Symptoms have been explained using a variety of sources and evidence, including Eurobarometer data on support for the EU, and for one's own country's membership of it; World Values Survey data, showing mistrust amongst Europeans; reported data on mistrust of EU institutions by citizens;[3] data on the 'variable implementation of, or non-compliance with, EU Directives; Top Decision-Makers Survey findings on disparities between elite and public support for EU membership;

arguments about declining voter turnout in European Parliament elections; the absence of parliamentary control of executive bodies at the EU level; and, the fact that, increasingly, since the 1986 Single European Act, government representatives could be outvoted by a qualified majority in the Council of Ministers. Symptoms such as these led to a diagnosis of a 'legitimacy deficiency' specified as a lack of procedural 'input' legitimacy granted by citizens; as a lack of 'output' legitimacy, due to mismatches between citizens' preferences and what politicians were able to deliver; or as an absence of accountability. Yet others hold that one of the main problems is that European integration creates a democratic deficit *within* the member states, as the latter are no longer permitted or able to achieve popular demands (Scharpf, 1999).

Some analysts are optimistic about the prognosis, finding hope in 'deliberative comitology' (Joerges, 1999), or recommending safeguards through the setting up of independent agencies. Others hold that pessimists ignore the important role of domestic support for many national governments, which would tend to foster compliance even with legislation that emerges from the EU. Some warn against fixing something that 'ain't broke' (Weiler, 2001), while others recommend *keeping* the democratic deficit (Gustavsson, 1997). Yet some fear that the absence of a common language, media or public discussion, and the lack of functioning European-level political parties is problematic, though they disagree on the prospects for a speedy improvement of the situation (Grimm, 1995; Abromeit, 1998; Habermas, 1998).

It is no wonder that reflective scholars – not to mention politicians and civil servants – disagree about the medicine to prescribe. There are disputes over whether this should involve additional arenas for normatively salient deliberation and a simplification of the structures of decisionmaking; a strengthened legal standing for the Charter on Fundamental Rights; more member state discretion through the Open Method of Coordination; or a more efficient Commission, securing the European interest over conflicting national interests. Some have supported a constitution, whereas others suggest strengthening the European Parliament – or, instead, national parliaments (Neunreither, 1994). What makes this a complex question is that different conceptions of legitimacy lead to different prescriptions and proscriptions.

conceptions, mechanisms and objects of legitimacy

The label 'legitimacy deficit' covers a broad range of issues, giving rise to different taxonomies.[4] It is possible to identify four fundamental *conceptions* of what legitimacy is about, at least four *mechanisms* for achieving legitimacy, while focusing on at least six different *objects* of legitimacy. We begin with the four conceptions: legitimacy as *legality*, as *compliance*, as *problem-solving* and as *justifiability*.

First, until recently, questions about the legitimacy of the EU could be answered quickly by pointing to the EU's pedigree. Thus, states created the

Table 9.1a   Conceptions, mechanisms and objects of legitimacy (I)

Conceptions			Legality			
		Problem solving				
	Normative					
			Compliance and general support			
Mechanisms		Democracy, participation				
			Consent, output			
Objects	Political Community	Regime principles: objectives and ideals	Regime: the political order, including procedural norms	Institution or office	Political actor	Policy or decision

Table 9.1b   Conceptions, mechanisms and objects of legitimacy (II)

Conceptions			Mechanisms	Objects
	Normative			Political community
		Problem solving	Democracy, participation	Regime principles: objectives and ideals
		Legality		Regime: the political order, including procedural norms
				Institution or office
Compliance and general support				Political actor
			Consent, output	Policy or decision

EU to act in accordance with legal requirements that they themselves set down (see Weiler, 1991; Wallace, 1993; Weiler, 1995b; Lenaerts and Desomer, 2002). Moreover, democratic member states transferred limited parts of their sovereignty by treaty, forming a *de facto* European constitutional order, in order better to achieve their goals by means of coordinated action. The ruling of the German Constitutional Court on the legality of the Maastricht Treaty explored and accepted this account – within limits. Thus the EU's authority is only illegal when such limits are surpassed.

Second, much of the concern about the alleged 'legitimacy deficit' stems from fears authorities have over its likely impact on levels of compliance and implementation. However, while the 'permissive consensus' may be a thing of the past, current compliance may not be affected by the legitimacy deficit, as compliance, in the form of acquiescence, may stem from apathy or cynicism rather than from support for the system (Abromeit, 1998). Such fears may seem overdrawn, then, especially given the broad social acceptance of European integration and the EU political system. But this acceptance varies and seems to be decreasing over time, reflecting changing circumstances and events (Karlsson, 2001). Even so, active disobedience is unlikely to occur unless politically relevant groups mobilize. Nevertheless, politicians may want to reduce the risk of their citizens rejecting treaties, or refusing to comply with EU laws.

Third, the EU's legitimacy is sometimes seen as having been enhanced when it identifies and implements solutions, securing goals that would otherwise be unattainable. This can only happen where joint outcomes are delivered through the problem-solving capacity of the EU. Such objectives may include economic growth, peace in Europe, human rights compliance, or a sustainable environment. By way of an example, it is often said that the technocratic aspects of EU decisionmaking allow diffuse constituents, such as consumers, to pursue their interests in ways that would otherwise be extremely difficult (Majone, 1998b, 22–3). Similarly, the EU's common currency serves to prevent unilateral exchange rate adjustments, while the independent European Central Bank bolsters the credibility of the member states' commitment to sound monetary policies. Thus, the EU suffers from a lack of legitimacy when it fails to find and implement solutions to common problems.

Fourth, some are concerned about the *normative* legitimacy of the EU, often expressed in terms of *justifiability among political equals*, for instance by appealing to hypothetical notions of acceptance or consent. They 'ask whether the coercive exercise of political power could be reasonably accepted by citizens considered free and equal and who possess both a capacity for and a desire to enter into fair terms of cooperation' (Choudhry, 2001, 383). This form of legitimacy of a political order such as the EU, is seen to rest on whether affected parties *would* or *could* accept it, under appropriate choice conditions (Michelman, 2000; Waldron, 1987; Habermas, 1995; Rawls, 1993; and see also Føllesdal, 1998a; Lehning, 1997).

We may say, therefore, that laws (or authorities) are *legally legitimate* insofar as they are enacted and exercised in accordance with constitutional rules and appropriate procedures. Laws (or authorities) are *socially legitimate* if the subjects abide by them. Finally, laws (or authorities) are *normatively legitimate* insofar as they can be justified to the people living under them, and impose a moral duty on them to comply. Normative theorists often judge *normative legitimacy* to be fundamental. Yet the other conceptions of legitimacy are also normatively relevant. They are interrelated, often compatible, and can be mutually re-enforcing. For instance, simple rules and procedures may make it easier to determine legality and compliance, as well as justifiability – or its absence (Magnette, 2001). *Legal legitimacy*, in the form of constitutionalism and the rule of law, is often regarded as a necessary condition for the justifiability of a political order. Legal legitimacy may be regarded as a special case of social legitimacy where the rulers actually abide by the laws regulating their authority (Beetham, 1991). On its own, *general compliance* is insufficient for normative legitimacy, since people may comply with an unjust rule solely from fear of sanction, lack of alternatives or unreflective habit. Yet for compliance to be assured, it is often deemed necessary that the population believe the relevant institutions to be normatively legitimate

(Beetham and Lord, 1998, 10). Perceived normative legitimacy may also bolster the *problem-solving capacity* of governments. Thus Renaud Dehousse recently noted that 'Comitology's legitimacy is not merely a normative issue: it is likely to become a political problem' (Dehousse, 1999). Legality, compliance and general belief in normative legitimacy may all be necessary but insufficient when considering whether laws, authorities, institutions or the regime is actually normatively legitimate. Compliance and beliefs may simply be due to an ill-founded and mistaken ideology, in the pejorative sense, and not on premises that all have good reason to accept.

These four conceptions of legitimacy can be promoted through a variety of institutional *mechanisms*. These are: legitimacy through *participation*, *democratic rule*, *actual consent*, and through *output*.

First, the legitimacy of the EU is said to increase by including citizens and other parties in the decision process: 'Interest group and expert democracy may be regarded as direct participation, hence legitimate' (Andersen and Burns, 1996, 245; see also Banchoff and Smith, 1999, 11). Citizens may be drawn into political decisions at various stages, and may participate directly in referendums (Abromeit, 1998). Participation may boost compliance, especially if the parties consulted are able to bind their members into systems of network governance (Kohler-Koch and Eising, 1999).

Second, representative democracy is a special and important case of participation. The democratic character of domestic political rule is regarded as central to legitimacy across Europe – and indeed globally (Norris, 1999a). Citizens hold their rulers accountable for their use of public power by selecting among competing political parties on the basis of and informed by discussion of their relative merits and the objectives to be pursued. A prominent criticism of the EU has held that these measures are underdeveloped in European politics, preventing member state governments and parliaments from guaranteeing democratic control. The increased power of the European Parliament granted in the Constitutional Treaty may enhance this kind of legitimacy. Democratic arrangements may also generate compliance, partly because citizens see 'that their interests have been explicitly consulted, and that there are opportunities for re-opening the debate in the future' (Bellamy, 1995, 167; Mill, [1861] 1958; Manin, 1987, 352).

Third, some regard democratic legitimacy as a matter of voters conferring legitimacy by giving their actual consent (Beetham and Lord, 1998). Others stress the need to secure actual consent in the form of an uncoerced and informed consensus reached, on the basis of actual deliberation among all affected parties. Or institutions and a public sphere should be implemented that would come close to yielding agreement on principles that 'meet with uncoerced intersubjective recognition under conditions of rational discourse' (Habermas, 1995, 127; Habermas, 1998). In this vein, some argue that institutional forms such as comitology are embryonic arenas for 'deliberative politics' (Joerges, 1999, 311).

Finally, the problem-solving or 'output' legitimacy of the EU requires that organizations and member states explore, identify and finally agree on options that benefit them all (Jachtenfuchs, 1995; Karlsson, 2001, 273). The EU must then secure these options, achieving objectives that were hitherto out of reach (Banchoff and Smith, 1999). Central mechanisms for doing this are the ability to create *de facto* binding and sanctioned law, as well as the forging of credible commitments through regulatory agencies (Majone, 1998b). These arrangements bind member states and enforce compliance, preventing the free-riding that often threatens cooperative arrangements (Beetham and Lord, 1998; Scharpf, 1999).

Such considerations about legitimacy form part of alternative 'frames' for further integration (Kohler-Koch, 2000). Unfortunately, the different conceptions of and mechanisms for legitimacy can conflict, and may require resolution insofar as prescriptions for institutional reforms strengthen some forms of legitimacy at the expense of others. Efficiency, democracy and constitutionalism conflict, even in principle (Elster and Slagstad, 1988). Mechanisms of veto and rights that require actual consent may hinder efficient problem-solving (Tsebelis, 1990; Scharpf, 1999). Accountability may stifle the creative search for solutions (Scharpf, 1999). If the EU gets authority to tax and redistribute funds, this might increase its ability to solve problems at the expense of participation levels and democratic accountability (Börzel and Hosli, 2002). And the increased democratization and politicization of the EU Commission may threaten its problem-solving capacity and its credibility as a neutral guardian of the treaties (Lindberg and Scheingold, 1970, 269; Banchoff and Smith, 1999; Majone, 2001, 261–2; Craig, 2003, 3).

Normative theorists pursue different strategies of reconciliation. One approach is to question or deny some of these elements of legitimacy; to question, for instance, whether efficient problem-solving has anything to do with 'legitimacy' (Beetham and Lord, 1998). It has been argued that such strategies could proceed by checking support for various conceptions – among political parties, for instance (Jachtenfuchs *et al.*, 1998). However, it remains unclear why the popularity of an approach should be decisive, rather than the reasons offered for accepting some conceptions over others. Others suggest sector-specific resolutions, such as handling the legitimacy of a Common Foreign and Security Policy (CFSP) differently from that of monetary policy (Lord and Magnette, 2004, 190). These suggestions seem sensible, yet prompt questions of *why* different sectors should be legitimated in different ways. After all, disagreement over issues of scope may be as profound as that over the substantive criteria of legitimacy.

Some claim that the EU is *sui generis* as a political order, and that this has profound implications for its legitimacy. For instance, one might question whether the standards of legitimacy that apply to liberal democratic states should be applied in the case of the EU: standards such as voter account-ability and human rights (Lord and Beetham, 2001). Should, perhaps, other standards be used, such as non-majoritarian and post-parliamentary standards and models of accountability (Majone, 1994; Andersen and Burns, 1996; Héritier, 1999)?

A unified account of legitimacy may serve to guide discussions about trade-offs, scope and institutional design. Discussions about legitimacy and the EU have focused on at least six different objects of legitimacy. The preceding sketch of conceptions and mechanisms helps us see how these discussions fit together.[5] Legitimacy discussions may concern:

- a particular political *decision*, that is, a policy or piece of legislation, which may be legitimated both by being enacted *legally* by authorized officials, and through the *participation* and *actual consent* of affected parties;
- the *authorities*, that is, political actors or officeholders; a particular government or set of representatives legitimated through *democratic* elections and other modes of participation, for example;
- particular *public institutions* such as the European Central Bank. Their perceived legitimacy may come in the form of compliance (see, for example, Schmitt and Thomassen, 1999, chapter 4);
- the *regime*, that is, the political order as a whole. Such studies include an assessment of the procedural norms and authority structures that constitute the formal and informal rules of the game. Such legitimacy may be addressed by asking whether it *can be justified* to those subject to it. A related central issue is the *problem-solving* ability of the system, where empirical evidence must be used to demonstrate whether the EU is able to obtain the objectives stated in the Treaties, and whether it actually does so reasonably well;
- the regime *principles*, including the objectives and ideals pursued, such as general welfare, participation and the rule of law, the scope of decisions and division of powers (see Schmitt and Thomassen, 1999, chapter 3). Should, for instance, the aims of the EU include a social dimension?
- the *political community*, that is, a group of individuals participating in and maintaining common decisionmaking processes. Discussions of whether there is a European 'demos' are raised at this point. Are there problems that require a certain community to be in place if they are to be resolved? Kaiser (2001b) addresses this object of legitimacy when noting that there were national and transnational ideological preferences for continued integration *in some form*, even after the failure of the European Defence Community (EDC) in 1954.

The various conceptions of legitimacy address these six objects differently. *Legality* plays a strong and obvious role in linking the first four objects. The legality of the EU regime as a whole was challenged by the German and Danish Constitutional Court decisions. Regarding *social legitimacy*, or political support,

Easton notes the importance of 'diffuse' regime and community support to ensure compliance with authorities.[6] Citizens may provide *specific support* for particular decisions and authorities based on this more diffuse support for the institutions (Norris, 1999b, 264). Citizens may maintain *diffuse support* for the regime for a while, even if dissatisfied with present policy outputs, as long as these policies generally remain consistent with the regime values and objectives, including procedural justice and a sense of fair treatment (Inglehart, 1999a, 98; Miller and Listhaug, 1999).

The *normative legitimacy* of a particular institution or policy area can often only be assessed on the basis of an evaluation of the performance of the policy decisions emerging from the regime as a whole. Some note that diffuse support for the regime in the form of an affective orientation to it (Almond and Verba, 1963), as normatively legitimate, may arise either from above or below: from acceptance of particular incumbents, or from the legitimating ideologies of the regime when it is seen to regularly yield output consistent with the regime objectives (Easton, 1965, 290).

Against this backdrop, it appears that European integration and enlargement may involve drastic shifts in all four conceptions of legitimacy, across all six objects, including the political community. These shifts appear to threaten diffuse support for the entire political order in Europe, and require a reconsideration of the mechanisms by which legitimacy is induced. One reason why politicians and academics may be right to worry about the long-term consequences of a legitimacy deficit is that *current* levels of compliance are insufficient. Long-term support for the EU requires not only present compliance and support, but also long-term trust in the general compliance of others, both citizens and officials, and a shared acceptance of the legality and the normative legitimacy of the regime.

legitimacy and trustworthiness

An institutionalist normative political theory takes as its central subject matter institutions, defined in a broad sense as 'social practices', for example. In comparison, an interactionist or individual-based theory may also address institutions, but primarily sees them as facilitating and safeguarding the normative claims individuals make towards each other, independent of their institutional relationships. This difference in emphasis has implications for the approach and substantive content of normative principles.[7]

All the conceptions and mechanisms of legitimacy identified in the sections above can enhance political trust and trustworthiness in the EU. The need for trust and trustworthiness arises under circumstances of complex mutual dependence. Cooperation depends on the conscious or habitual expectation of the cooperation of others, with trust being 'confidence of the future regularity of their conduct' (Hume, 1960, 490). Such trust in future compliance by others is central for the long-term stability of a just political order. The truster must believe that it is in the interest of the trusted to act according to shared expectations, where such interests may vary. The trusted may act out of self-interest, within institutions that sanction misbehaviour. The trusted may act from a sense of appropriateness, such that only certain actions seem open to choice for her. Or the trusted person may be other-regarding, concerned for the truster's well-being. One version of the latter is where the trusted is known to be a 'contingent complier'. Such persons are prepared to comply with common, fair rules as long as they believe that others will do so as well.

Thus contingent compliance occurs[8] when a citizen decides to comply or otherwise cooperate with government demands either because she perceives government as trustworthy in making and enforcing normatively legitimate policies; and/or she has confidence that other citizens will play their part, out of what John Rawls calls a 'duty of justice' (Rawls, 1971, 336 and see Scanlon, 1998, 339):

> that they will comply with fair practices that exist and apply to them when they believe that the relevant others likewise do their part; and to further just arrangements not yet established, at least when this can be done without too much cost to ourselves. (Rawls, 1971, 336)

To ensure long-term support, it is important for institutions to develop and maintain a sufficiently large group of citizens and politicians who are contingent compliers. Trust in the compliance of others is not only a problem among individuals who prefer to free ride on others, but it is also problematic for 'contingent compliers'. The assurance problems among contingent compliers have long been recognized by political theorists, and were addressed by Rousseau (Rousseau, [1762] 1978, 2.4.5; Madison, [1787] 1967). Recent contributions, informed by game theory, have contributed to an enhanced understanding of the importance of institutions in providing sufficient assurance by mixing positive laws, transparency, shared practices, and socialization.[9] The literature on social capital provides further insights into how expectations concerning the actions of others – facilitated by institutions – affect the complex assurance problems faced in daily life.

Trust is particularly precarious when it comes to institutions that are not obviously in everybody's self-interest all the time. Trust can be engendered by institutions that facilitate generalized trustworthiness among strangers, both through mechanisms that reduce the risks or suspicion that others will defect, and through public mechanisms which socialize certain preferences. Trust and trustworthiness have become increasingly important for Europeans in the context of the EU. Consider, for instance, how changes from unanimity to qualified majority voting increase the need for trust and trustworthiness among individuals and among their representatives, requiring them to adjust or sacrifice their own interests and those of their voters for the sake of other Europeans.

Many social institutions can promote this kind of trust. Contract law, for example, can promote trustworthiness. It may do so both by reducing the risks of failed trust for example, by restricting the scope of valid majority rule by enforcing human rights law, and by shifting the trusted's incentives to make it in her interest to do what the truster expects. The three various forms of legitimacy – legal, social and normative – are all important in securing such expectations, and hence for the existence of institutions – or so I suggest.

Several requirements must be satisfied if 'contingent compliers' are to comply. As a 'contingent complier' I will comply with rules, institutions and officials' decisions *if*

(a) *I believe they are normatively legitimate.*

This may require, in cases of doubt, public knowledge that:

i) there is a plausible *public political theory* regarding, for example, democracy in and solidarity towards the political order. This largely appears to be lacking for the European political order. The following section sketches some contributions made by normative political theorists on this subject. Some of the heated debates in the Convention on the Future of Europe also concerned these issues (Olsen 2004);

ii) the institutions are *simple and transparent* enough for citizens to comprehend and assess. Assisted by the media, citizens and authorities must be able to determine whether institutions and decisions roughly match normative requirements;

iii) there is a general assurance that the institutions are effective and efficient, in the sense of producing the normatively desired effects without too much loss – at least when generally complied with.

(b) *I believe that most other actors will comply.*

Reassurance among 'contingent compliers' requires *more than* actual compliance by a large number of individuals. Each must also have reason to believe that many others will continue to comply in the future, since compliance by each is conditional on the expected compliance of others. Each must regard the compliance of many others as highly probable. Institutions can socialize individuals to this duty of justice.[10] When this socialization happens in public institutions, it provides public assurance and reminders that all, or most, citizens, including politicians, share these norms which tell us what justice requires. Expectations of others' future compliance are boosted when rules secure a fair output, and cannot easily be abused. Thus it is important for trustworthiness that the institutions deliver according to their stated aims, providing 'output legitimacy' (Scharpf, 1999). Such trust is at stake if some states or citizens are thought to be unable or unwilling to comply with EU rules due to lack of political will or resources for domestic implementation.

Institutions can also provide sanctions that modify citizens' incentives, reassuring 'contingent compliers' that they will not be 'suckers'. 'To the extent government coercive capacity assures potentially supportive citizens that there will, in fact, be relative equality of sacrifice, governmental institutions contribute to contingent consent' (Levi, 1998a, 26). EU arrangements that aim to harmonize national legislation may serve this role. Institutions provide important reassurance by facilitating the monitoring of compliance, even without formal sanctioning mechanisms. If government authorities believe that their trustworthiness is challenged, thereby reducing governance capacity, they may provide institutionalized sanctions to bolster their claims. Measures of this kind might include monitoring and efforts to simplify and democratize the EU institutions. Transparency, including access to information, may also be crucial for this end (Dehousse, 1999: Héritier, 1999).

Legal legitimacy assures citizens that authorities make decisions within a range that is expected, reducing the risks for those who comply, and ensuring, if the decisionmaking rules are normatively accepted, that the long-term, general result of these decisions will be in accordance with normative standards. Thus trust in the authorities is bolstered by diffuse support for the regime, which secures the authorities' trustworthiness, at least insofar as the regime itself is trustworthy.

'Contingent compliers' will comply with what they regard as normatively legitimate rules if they have good reason to believe that others will comply. Thus monitoring arrangements that confirm past general compliance and assess future compliance may be necessary to support such beliefs. Opinion polls that indicate low support for institutions, however, serve as warning signs to citizens and authorities that compliance might not be secure.

This is one reason why reports of low support for the EU are important, regardless of whether such reports are sound – and even if the EU is normatively legitimate. If it is not normatively legitimate, politicians should heed calls for making the institutions more just. If compliance is still not forthcoming other measures are also required to provide assurance. Thus, the role of the media is crucial in both encouraging and deterring general support.

The publicly shared beliefs about normative legitimacy held by citizens and public authorities are central in several ways to ensure trust. 'Contingent compliers', as defined here, can be expected to comply when they are assured of the compliance of others *and* when they regard the regime, its institutions, procedures, authorities and their decisions as normatively legitimate. If they doubt the latter, they may not comply. To reduce such doubts, the authorities seek to provide assurances that they govern fairly. Measures may include the extension of democratic controls and visible human rights constraints on decisionmaking. There are other mechanisms that provide transparency and control over authorities, such as the treaty requirement that administrators must give reasons for their decisions. Media freedom and vigorous opposition parties are other elements that are likely to enhance the trustworthiness of political authorities.

Diffuse support rests, then, on a sufficient match between the normative legitimacy of the political community. This consists of participants who accept the need for common decisions for certain ends, that is, the normative legitimacy of the regime. Moreover, it also includes the institutions' performance in specifying and securing outputs, as well as the normative legitimacy of the authorities, including their legal legitimacy.

How can the EU secure and maintain general trustworthiness among 'contingent compliers', especially during the regime changes wrought by treaty modifications? It is clear that a lack of channels for protest *within* a regime, in the appointment of officials, or the voicing of concerns, may lead to reduced support (Hirschman, 1970). Thus there must be visible, effective channels for replacing authorities, including at the European level. Moreover, diffuse support for the regime is enhanced if it appears to be working. Thus, while the Commission resignation of 1999 might be regarded as an illustration of deservedly low specific support for the Commission, presenting this as a way for the European Parliament to enhance the EU's accountability may increase diffuse support for the regime. Likewise, diffuse support for the regime may also increase insofar as the ongoing processes of institutional reforms are perceived as responses to popular pressure. This can be interpreted as illustrating the regime's responsiveness, bolstering trustworthiness in the form of diffuse support.

Three additional points may be made at this juncture:

- The general decline in support for governing institutions may partly be due to a perception of diminishing performance (Dalton, 1999). Insofar as this is the general perception, regime changes must show that the EU is not part of the problem, but part of the solution.
- Some scholars suggest that declining support is due to postmaterialist individuals, who generally express less support for existing hierarchical institutions, yet support democratic principles (Inglehart, 1999b; Dalton, 1999). These are 'critical citizens', who demand evidence that regime changes match their principles, and are likely to provide improved outputs. This group seems particularly interested in participatory mechanisms, which may itself be a reason to explore these kinds of institutions.
- Scholars who study the extent of support for the 'political community' note that disagreements about its membership, borders and purposes may deprive the regime of diffuse support. This suggests that we must take very seriously any lack of certainty over the commitment of citizens in the new (post-2004) EU member states, as well as deep disagreements over the objectives of European arrangements for common decisionmaking.

current normative research on the eu

This account of the relationships that exist among different forms of legitimacy serves as a backdrop to this section, which reviews some of the topics dealt with in normative political theory relating to the 2004 Constitutional Treaty.

One central topic concerns the basic constitutional form of the European political order. Should the regime or 'polity' have largely confederal or federal features, a network structure, or should it be regarded as a political order *sui generis*? There are numerous models of this kind, which reflect, for example, different historical trends (Jachtenfuchs *et al.*, 1998). Neil MacCormick, for example, has explored the distinctions between statehood and sovereignty, arguing that neither the member states nor the EU is fully sovereign in the traditional sense of enjoying legal or political power unlimited by other, higher legal or political powers. Yet the EU is a distinct community of law with a distinct legal order. He suggests that both the EU and the member states are 'commonwealths' in Hume's sense, securing different common goods for citizens (MacCormick, 1999; Hume, [1739] 1960).

The Constitutional Treaty increases transparency with regard to the sites of legal authority in the EU. It does so by identifying certain competences which are constitutionally exercised by member states, others that are exclusive to the EU institutions, and a third category that are shared, thus moving the EU toward a federal order by some accounts (Føllesdal, 2003). This kind of constitutional allocation of competences worries some theorists, because it may be a somewhat premature step for the EU. Such lists may also hinder multilevel cooperation and flexibility. On the other hand, a list of competences of this kind is often thought to prevent the dual risks facing federal orders: namely, creeping centralization and fragmentation (Dehousse, 1994; Abromeit, 1998; Moravcsik, 1998b; Swenden, 2004).

A central topic of concern, therefore, relates to the values and objectives of the EU. In Article 2, the Constitutional Treaty identifies the central values of the EU, including 'respect for human dignity, liberty, democracy, equality, the rule of law and respect for human rights. These values are common to the Member States in a society of pluralism, tolerance, justice, solidarity and non-discrimination.' Article 3 goes on to identify the objectives of the EU, including the promotion of peace, its values and 'the well-being of its peoples'. It shall also 'promote social justice and protection', 'economic, social and territorial cohesion, and solidarity among Member States' – at the same time respecting Europe's 'rich cultural and linguistic diversity'. There is a great deal of recent work by normative theorists discussing these values. Some of the objectives are old yet contested. For instance, the 1952 European Coal and Steel Community sought to provide assurances that former enemies would henceforth share the ends of mutual prosperity and peace (Schuman, 1950). While European integration has no doubt promoted economic growth, some suggest that the EU was not necessary for peace in Europe, since it is often said that democracies do not go to war with each other. Nevertheless, European integration may have served to hasten and stabilize democratization and human rights compliance in Europe. Other important objectives are more controversial. Some suggest that Europeans must cooperate to provide a counterforce to US military hegemony, or to secure the welfare systems characteristic of European states (Habermas and Derrida, 2003). Yet the efficacy of common decisionmaking among Europeans seems insufficient for the former, and may be unnecessary for the latter. Fritz Scharpf argues that while the mode of current decisionmaking in the EU may have increased the troubles of domestic welfare systems, the solution may actually be to allow greater member state independence (Scharpf, 1999, 27).

One reason for the scholarly attention that has been given to these values and objectives is the perception that they must be shared by citizens. Many note that citizens of multinational federal orders need a shared 'overarching loyalty' if the multilevel order is to remain stable. (Simeon and Conway, 2001; Stepan, 1999, 33). The content of such a shared loyalty remains contested, as seen in recent discussions over Turkey's membership application. Who should members of this political community be? Who are the Europeans? And what normative commitments should unite them? Much of the normative discussion in the literature concerns how European institutions should distribute benefits and obligations among Europeans, and how such decisions should be made (Bellamy, 1999). Several contributions to this literature have addressed whether Europeans must share some commitment towards the establishment of European-level welfare arrangements in order to maintain trust across the EU. David Miller, for example, argues that welfare arrangements can only be maintained among individuals who share a nationality and a culture, thereby denying the prospect of such a development in Europe (Miller, 1995; see Føllesdal, 2000). Others hold that a shared 'thin' political culture, based on commitment to the values of the constitution, may suffice (Habermas, 1992). Continued support for common arrangements only requires a 'civic demos', created by carefully crafted institutions, argues Fritz Scharpf (1997, 20). Such views raise crucial issues of institutional design: how to create self-sustaining institutions that will work both in the short run, with low levels of trust, and that will also promote trust in the longer term (Zürn, 2000).

Federal political orders often exhibit a conflict between the ideals of equality, on the one hand, and political autonomy, on the other. Individuals in different sub-units often enjoy systematically different standards of living, partly as result of the political powers enjoyed by these sub-units. Yet one of the objectives of the EU is social justice; another is the promotion of economic cohesion and solidarity among member states. Thus the present commitment to regional funds and agricultural subsidies, 'demonstrating consistency and solidarity ... between the Member States and between their peoples' (Treaty on European Union, 1997, Article 1) is challenged by the enlargement process. A commitment to equalize living standards would entail politically unacceptable costs, since the GNP per capita of the new member states is well below the EU average. Can such degrees of economic inequality be defended, as consistent with respect for the equal dignity of all European citizens? Much recent political philosophy has focused on distributive principles which apply to unitary states with a central sovereign (symptomatically see Rawls, 1993, xxii). While normative political theories of federal justice are scarce, they have, all the same, a long and distinguished pedigree (see Althusius, [1603–14] 1995; Hamilton *et al.*, [1787–88] 1961; Elazar, 1987; Norman, 1994; Kymlicka, 1995; Choudhry, 2001; Føllesdal, 1997 and 2001).

An important normative challenge relates to the pluralism of values, institutions and political cultures in Europe. Firstly, there are multiple conceptions of value and many different views about the good life among the European citizenry. Acceptance of such pluralism, within limits, seems highly appropriate for a 'European' theory of normative legitimacy (Rawls, 1993). Secondly, member states have diverse institutions providing different solutions to somewhat similar problems, shaping individuals' expectations and life plans in ways that cause conflict when seeking European-wide consolidation (Scharpf, 1997).

Partly to accommodate such diversity, the allocation and use of competences is to be guided by the subsidiarity principle, which implies that the burden of argument is on those seeking to centralize decisions. In the current Treaty, subsidiarity requires that:

> the Union shall act only if and insofar as the objectives of the intended action cannot be sufficiently achieved by the member states, either at central level or at regional and local level, but can rather, by reason of the scale or effects of the proposed action, be better achieved at Union level. (Article 9)

Unfortunately, the concept is fairly vague and contested (Streeck, 1996). There remain many unanswered questions. For example: Should subsidiarity also be used to allocate competences between the EU and the member states, and among regions and municipalities? Who should judge when common action is required? And how is this presumption against centralization best justified?

Another safeguard of diversity is human rights, as included in the Charter on Fundamental Rights in the 2004 Constitutional Treaty. Some scholars hold constitutionalized human rights to be a necessary condition for an acceptable political order (MacCormick, 1999). Others are wary of substantive constitutional constraints on 'unconstrained political debates' concerning norms and requirements (Dryzek, 1990). Democratic attempts at reaching compromises should only be secured by procedural constraints that 'allow individuals to fight for their rights themselves' (Bellamy, 1995 and 1999). In addition to this classical discussion, other normative issues are peculiar to the EU and other multilevel political orders. Human rights do not only constrain governments vis-à-vis their own citizens and toward other sovereign states: some human rights norms also regulate relations among the member states, holding them in some cases to higher standards. The need to enhance trustworthiness may necessitate human rights constraints of this kind.

Some clarification as to which democratic institutions in the EU are normatively acceptable is required, if for no other reason than such vague and contested terms as 'democracy' may otherwise be misapplied and lend support to reforms on false grounds (Schmitter, 2000). Schmitter thus recommends reforms, rather than revolutions, in seeking to enhance democratic control over EU-level decisions. Some authors hold that individual autonomy should be secured, based on the assumption that self-determination is a fundamental human good. This implies that the EU must be a freedom-enabling order, providing citizens with opportunities for active participation in shaping and sustaining their institutions (MacCormick, 1999, 164). Others hold that self-determination is a contested ideal, hence unsuited to use as a common normative basis. Several authors focus on the interest of individuals in ensuring security against interference and being subject to the arbitrary will of others (Pettit, 1997; Bellamy, 1999; Abromeit, 1998). Others argue that institutions should foster political involvement, both because it is required if the political order is to remain just, and to foster an appropriate human nature (Bellamy, 1999).

The Constitutional Treaty secures a variety of liberties that are considered to be worth protecting and promoting. Lynn Dobson (2004) identifies at least three conceptions: non-interference, non-domination, and enhanced capability sets. The Constitutional Treaty may secure autonomy, in the sense of non-interference through the use of human rights constraints, widely dispersed veto points and low thresholds for blocking coalitions, and the application of the subsidiarity principle. Non-domination, in the sense of freedom from potentially arbitrary interference, is achieved through the separation, checking and mixing of institutional powers, such as through the watchdog function of national parliaments. EU action promotes the capabilities of individuals by developing shared objectives on the basis of qualified majority decisionmaking and effective parliamentary majoritarianism. Discrepancies between citizens' liberties and those of their governments require further analysis, as does the question of immunity for the 'internal affairs' of member states. Difficult trade-offs also remain between various kinds of liberty.

One topic that has received a great deal of attention is the place of deliberation in the European political order. One controversial issue is how public political deliberation affects citizens' basic preferences, as compared to other inputs on character formation, such as the civilizing impact of hypocrisy (see Femia, 1996; Przeworski, 1998; Elster, 1998). Further methodological challenges arise in trying to disentangle processes that occur while parties are talking: when are they *arguing*, and when are they *bargaining*? Arguing is 'intrinsically connected to reason, in the sense that anyone who engages in argument must appeal to impartial values' (Elster, 1998, 6). By contrast, bargaining involves, in pure cases, processes where '[t]he outcome is determined by the bargaining mechanism and the bargaining power of the parties – that is, the resources that enable them to make credible threats and promises' (Elster, 1998, 6). Yet Elster goes on to acknowledge that arguing may also involve matters of fact (Elster, 1998, 7). Moreover, preference changes that arise from arguments may be changes in ultimate ends or changes in policy choices, with the latter being based on better information. In other words, some value deliberations affect individuals' ultimate ends, whereas others allow individuals to get a better understanding of possible alternatives and coalitions, resulting in more accurate probabilities and value estimates of outcomes (Przeworski, 1998). Many contributors to negotiation theory use 'bargaining' to cover the latter of these two, in the sense of the 'integrative bargaining' of 'Getting to Yes' (Fisher and Ury, 1987). How do we tell the difference between these processes? It is certainly difficult to infer from observed changes to policy preferences whether what has occurred is a modification of ultimate objectives – which is the main claim of some deliberative democrats – or a consequence of bargaining in the broadest sense. In either case it remains to be seen whether such shifts are normatively better, or simply contribute to the advantage of the group.

Another important concern is whether this kind of preference-transforming discussion should primarily take place within institutions that possess authority, or within 'civil society' (for the former, see Nino, 1996; and Weithman, 1995; on the latter, see Dryzek, 1996). It would seem that the impact of deliberation on interest formation rests on assumptions that are less plausible at the European level than at the national. The opacity of European institutions, the lack of a well-developed European public space, and the absence of European political parties, reduce the opportunities for character formation, and limit the informational bases and range of political choice. However, there is little reason to believe that these features are permanent: such pessimism would seem premature.

Note, however, that these considerations do not provide strong arguments that decisions in general should be taken in deliberating bodies, or that more deliberation among a greater number of individuals is always better, since a group may collude against others in what may appear to be deliberation. Nor does the need for preference modification require that we rank deliberation over preference aggregation: in other words, preference formation and other tasks of deliberation do not replace or compete against voting. We can be concerned with deliberation and at the same time be aware of the need for 'post-deliberative democracy'.

Many authors have argued that EU bodies should be democratized. The slow increase of powers to the European Parliament has served to reduce the democratic deficit, especially insofar as it allows directly elected representatives to codetermine legislation and to hold the Commission accountable (see recommendations in Lodge 1994; Wessels and Diedrichs, 1999; Lodge, 1996). However, these measures are contested. Some authors argue that the democratization of the EU must empower local democratic governance (Landy and Teles, 2001). Others even argue that the EU should maintain its democratic deficit (Gustavsson, 1997).

It is not obvious that majoritarian decisionmaking is appropriate, when segments of the population risk finding themselves in a permanent minority, especially if the majority cannot be trusted to consider the impact of decisions on minorities. The principle of one-person-one-vote may not be appropriate under such circumstances. Hence, the appropriate modes of securing responsive and accountable rule within federal and other multilevel orders for 'plural' societies, have received some scrutiny (Lijphart, 1999; Barry, 1991; Føllesdal, 1997). The heated discussions on the construction of the qualified majority vote in the Constitutional Treaty underscores the importance of voting rules both in allowing for effective decisionmaking and in protecting minorities against being overruled on a regular basis.

Some have argued that the EU must go beyond democratic institutions and instead rely to a greater extent on informal, non-hierarchical networks or independent bodies. There are many good reasons for including affected parties in deliberations or decisions, including the need to prevent domination. Considerations of autonomy and socialization are also relevant here. Yet there remain important and interesting differences among scholars about which arenas are best suited for participation. Some claim that comitology and networks, suitably modified, would enhance the legitimacy of EU decisionmaking. Christian Joerges, for example, argues that comitology can be a forum for 'deliberative politics' (Joerges, 1999, 311), and that this perspective might diminish concerns that comitology is illegitimate (Vos, 1999; Abromeit, 1998).

It remains to be determined under what circumstances observed preference modifications can be explained by shifts in expected payoffs, or, indeed, in ultimate objectives. It is also important to determine the risk of collusion. Such risks may be greatly reduced by constraining comitology. This can be achieved by involving other institutions, such as the European Parliament, to a greater extent.

Others hold that institutionalized networks provide good opportunities for participation, and that this enhances legitimacy (Héritier, 1999). These may be among the many sites where private and public bodies are able to meet to deliberate over solutions to conflicts (Bellamy, 1999). However, institutionalist issues relating to trustworthiness reappear at this point: how realistic is it that such networks will remain open, and not be skewed against emerging new points of view, preventing equal access to the agenda?

Some commentators hold that associations in civil society play an important role in correcting skewed representation, by providing information and socializing citizens (Cohen and Rogers, 1995; Hirst, 1994). It seems that many of these kinds of arguments are best seen as supplements or corrections to representative democratic channels however – not least because they appear to require the mediation of public power in order to correct what would otherwise be the skewed composition of associations.

Some authors criticize the hierarchical form of structure that 'inevitably fosters distorted communication and communicative rationality' (Dryzek, 1990, 141). Instead of focusing on traditional democratic institutions, these authors favour civil society arrangements stretching beyond public power, to involve informal mass movements, so as to avoid political influence and cooptation (Dryzek, 1990, 1996). To some extent these efforts at democratization within civil society and beyond the state are thought of as alternatives to representative democracy, whose current instantiations hardly merit the use of the word 'democratic'.

There is good reason to promote a civil society where policies and preferences can be openly debated and modified, contributing to fair solutions, consonant with the common good and minimizing the skewing effects of formal power. Such reasons include preference formation, autonomy, learning, and the fostering of a sense of inclusion, as is argued by a large number of democratic theorists, none of whom have been solely concerned with democracy as interest aggregation (Mill, [1861] 1958; Schattschneider, 1960; Schumpeter, [1943] 1976; Key Jr., 1961, 449; Riker, 2003, 172). These innovators hold that democratic arrangements should be replaced (Dryzek, 1990; Eriksen, 2000, 44). Other more cautious commentators explore how these networks may supplement competitive elections and other traditional institutional staples of democracy, and how these arenas may be maintained, undistorted, over time (Femia, 1996; Goodin, 1993).

Other authors have insisted on the need for political decisions, but have doubted the necessity of democratic accountability. Thus, Majone has defended the role of independent agencies, such as central banks, as non-majoritarian, non-democratic mechanisms for trust-building (Majone, 1994). Such mechanisms are legitimate on grounds of effectiveness, and because they are more responsive to diffuse interests (Majone, 1998b; see Magnette, 2000). Majone is correct that some decisions should be insulated from majoritarian political bodies, for reasons of trustworthiness. Yet citizens may also need evidence that these institutions reliably pursue the general interest, diffuse or otherwise. On closer scrutiny, it is also clear that Majone defends such agencies only when they are subject to various checks (Majone, 1998a). Thus, again, the suggestion is that representative democracy should not be replaced, but that bodies can be included in the system as long as they, in turn, are controlled by democratic bodies.

conclusion

The diagnosis of an EU 'legitimacy deficit' covers a broad range of symptoms and prescriptions. While both pessimism and optimism are premature, there seem to be good reasons for scrutinizing alternative strategies for enhancing the transparency, responsiveness and fairness of EU institutions, with an eye to how they can be justified before all citizens. The Constitutional Treaty of 2004 provides much in the way of constructive suggestions in this regard (Dobson and Føllesdal, 2004).

Legitimacy deficits are not, however, merely a matter of public opinion polls registering low levels of political support for institutions, policies and authorities. Legitimacy is about whether citizens have trust in the future compliance of other citizens and authorities with institutions they believe to be normatively deserving of obedience. Indeed, trustworthiness seems crucial for the long-term support of the EU's multilevel political order, and for the authorities' ability to govern. Normative political theory may thus contribute decisively in promoting the long-term stability of the system. '[I]n so far as political philosophy does seek to persuade members of a system of the existence of a verifiable objective common good, it does serve with respect to its possible political consequences, as a response that may aid in the growth of diffuse support' (Easton, 1965, 319, fn 3).

However, normative political theory is double-edged. If theorists were to find that there is no common good for Europe, or that the present regime or particular institutions fail to secure these objectives and values to a reasonable extent, what diffuse support there was may corrode even further. The regime may then lack the moral right to obedience. Normative political theory may bring that out into the open, adding pressure to the need for regime reform, rather than ensuring popular acquiescence to a political order that fails to respect all as equals.

notes

1. The aim of this chapter is to present some of the central research topics found in normative political theory relating to the EU. I draw in part on Føllesdal (2005).
2. German Constitutional Court, 1993, 'Brunner v European Union Treaty' *BVerfGE*, 89: 155.
3. Such findings must consider that reduced confidence in parliaments, parties and the legal systems seems to be a general trend across established democracies – see (Norris 1999a).
4. For other typologies, see Jachtenfuchs *et al.*, (1998), Beetham (1991), Beetham and Lord (1998), Lord and Magnette (2004), Höreth (1999), and, of course, Easton (1965).
5. I draw in part on the helpful tripartite distinction of Easton (1965), fruitfully expanded by Norris (1999b) and Dalton (1999) who use it for the concept of political support, which is close to but different from the notion of 'social legitimacy'.
6. See Easton (1965) for this discussion. See Luhman (1969) for similar approach: legitimacy as generalised willingness to obey.
7. For such distinctions and their consequences. See, for example Weale (1999, 20) and Pogge (2002).

8. I here modify Margaret Levi's model of contingent consent (Levi 1998a, chapter 2).

9. See Sen (1967), Taylor (1987), Elster (1989b, 187), Ostrom (1991), Scharpf (1997), Rothstein (1998), (Levi 1998b). Recent normative contributions addressing the standards of normative legitimacy on the explicit assumption of such contingent compliance include Rawls (1971), Thompson and Gutmann (1996, 72–3), Miller (2000).

10. Margaret Levi calls this 'ethical reciprocity', 'a norm requiring that individuals in a given population cooperate with government demands but only as long as others are also contributing' (1998b, 24–5).

10
political economy and european integration

amy verdun

introduction

European integration theory has seen a considerable resurgence since the signing of the Maastricht Treaty in 1992. Intrigued by the sudden progress in European integration that the Treaty on European Union symbolized, scholars developed theoretical insights into this process. Their theories typically built on the classic integration theories of intergovernmentalism and neofunctionalism, though others were also derived from general political science topics, such as institutionalism. The bulk of these new approaches, which were developed in the 1990s, were often considered as either metaphors (for example, 'two-level games') or mid-range theories; none was sufficiently well-developed to be considered a fully-fledged 'grand' theory. (One such example is the 'governance approach', see Jachtenfuchs, 2001; Pollack, 2001.)

One of the debates of the 1990s dealt with the question of whether European integration should be examined through the lens of International Relations theories or Comparative Politics (Hix, 1994). International Relations theories focus on explaining interstate behaviour, particularly government behaviour. They examine the relative power position of governments and what motivates them to collaborate. Comparative Politics typically examines differences among member states by looking at domestic structures and actors in order to gain a better understanding of national governments and their policies. In one sense, the issue of whether EU Studies should be dominated by International Relations or Comparative Politics was settled when consensus emerged among scholars that, even though the field originated in International Relations (with the work of scholars such as Deutsch, Haas and Hoffmann), it had meanwhile matured, and thus benefited directly from Comparative Politics insights. Nevertheless, theories developed in both International Relations and Comparative Politics often speak about different aspects of the EU, and thus do not always fully engage with one another. It is fair to say that EU Studies still needs to draw on both.

Political economy has traditionally been found at the intersection of International Relations and Comparative Politics. It takes on board insights from major International Relations debates, whilst being sensitive to economic structures, institutions and actors – not only international, but also national and transnational ones. This particular characteristic gives it an edge over both mainstream International Relations and general Comparative Politics approaches. Given that characteristic alone, political economy has something important to offer EU Studies.

Another advantage of political economy is its interdisciplinary nature. The study of European integration and the EU is an interdisciplinary field. Merely examining the *politics* of policy development might imply losing sight of the important economic factors that influence outcomes. Hence any serious analysis of European integration should be sensitive to influences from factors outside a particular disciplinary perspective. Political economy holds an advantage in that it includes at least two disciplines, economics and political science, and many would agree that it (at times) adopts insights from anthropology, business, geography, history, law and sociology. Moreover, a mix of economics and political science provides a useful combination because so much of the integration process is firmly embedded in economic principles and deals with economic issues such as competition, free trade in the internal market, macroeconomic policy coordination, and monetary unification – even if the procedures that generate outcomes are political.

Finally, EU Studies has been struggling to develop appropriate methodologies to examine the broad variety of issues facing the EU since its institutional maturation in 1993. Scholars have borrowed many different types of methodology, ranging from thick description to quantitative analyses and abstract game theoretic models (see Chapter 12 in this volume). The field has developed so much in recent years that it is important to have analyses that cover a wide variety of methods if the EU is to be fully comprehended. Once again, the political economy literature is home to a full range of methodological approaches. Employing these theories and methodologies, research findings generated by political economists contribute to a wider literature that moves beyond the *sui generis* perspective sometimes adopted in EU Studies. Using a political economy approach makes it easier to generalize from one's study to broader phenomena outside the realm of the EU.

This chapter examines political economy approaches in EU Studies. It looks at the role of theories and methods in this field, the value of drawing on the disciplines of economics and political science, and the types of studies that have adopted a political economy approach. Finally, the chapter reflects upon the role political economy could play in the future research agenda of EU Studies.

theories and methods

In the field of political economy one frequently comes across the distinction between *international* and *comparative* political economy. This division is not very helpful for EU Studies because, as was stated already, the field raises issues that are both comparative (among nations) and comparative internationally (above nations). Nevertheless, the term international political economy is more commonly used by the International Relations community to signify work that includes both economics and politics and that treats not only state actors and the international system, but also domestic structures, as important in analysis (see Lawton *et al.*, 2000). On the other hand, the term comparative political economy has been used by comparativists to signal their focus on analysis of differences among nations, in which economic and political factors play an important role. In other words, these terms find their origin in the theoretical approaches from which they derive, as well as the types of questions typically addressed within the literature. In light of the overlap between the two it would be difficult to say that there are clear boundaries; they are partly overlapping, partly complementary (see Jones, 2003; Jones and Verdun, 2005; Walzenbach, 2000). In what follows, I concentrate mainly on the international political economy literature but also briefly address comparative political economy approaches.

international political economy approaches

Although scholars of international political economy have traditionally been subdivided into three approaches – liberalism, mercantilism and Marxism (Woods, 2001) – this section focuses on the schools of thought (and divisions amongst them) that have become more dominant in the past decade.[1] Based on debates in international political economy journals, such as *International Organization*, one could say that it is fairly common to subdivide these approaches into four categories: neorealism, neoliberal institutionalism, social constructivism and critical approaches.

Neorealist approaches are among those in the field of international political economy that see the state as the dominant actor in determining outcomes in international politics. The seminal work in this field was written by Kenneth Waltz (1979), who argued that the international system can only be understood by looking at the actions of states acting in their own self-interest. They try to maximize these interests based on fixed *ex ante* preferences. The outside world is perceived as being in a state of chaos where anarchy prevails. While a major player can at times impose order on this chaos, such a state will only take action when it is in its own interest.

Waltz's original work did not identify any role for domestic politics or international organizations. Replying to critics (such as Keohane, 1986), neorealism opened itself to the possibility that domestic forces might affect state preferences and perceived interests, even if the state remained the focus of attention for explaining the outcomes of international bargaining and cooperation. Realist approaches have found their way into EU Studies, especially in explanations of the behaviour of states in interstate bargaining (Garrett, 1992; Grieco, 1995).

Neoliberal institutionalist approaches accept that states are the primary actors in world politics and, thus, that neorealism 'provides a good starting point for the analysis of cooperation and discord [in the international system]' (Keohane, 1984, 245). They argue, however, that institutions, defined by authors such as Keohane as 'sets of practices and expectations', can have their own effect. They can facilitate interstate agreements and enable states to pursue their own interests through cooperation (Keohane, 1984, 246). More recent institutionalist approaches have emphasized a larger role for institutions. They have stressed the importance of path dependence, socialization and policy learning (Hall and Taylor, 1996). Institutions, in this more recent work, set the path for development of policies, rules and procedures. Thus, historic precedents and standard operating procedures influence the policymaking process. Sometimes emphasis is placed on the fact that international institutions improve the effectiveness of outcomes by imposing rules and regulations. From this perspective, nation-states will be inclined to follow those rules and regulations more frequently, more consistently (and without direct reference to self-interest) than realist accounts would lead us to believe. In recent years institutionalism has been frequently adopted in EU Studies (for example, Bulmer, 1994a, 1994b; Pierson, 1996 and see Chapters 2 and 3 in this volume).

Since the second half of the 1990s social constructivism has often been identified as a 'new' school of thought. However, as often occurs with so-called 'novelties', this approach has been around for quite some time. Already in the 1960s Berger and Luckmann (1966) outlined their social constructivist perspective. They identified three core assumptions. The first concerns the nature of the individual. He/she is taken to be a social creature that creates and institutionalizes new knowledge about 'reality', and finds his/her personal identity based on social processes. The second assumption is that our observation of 'reality' may be an artefact, as it is coloured by whoever observes or interprets it. The third concerns how social scientists study social action. They are actively involved in the process, and hence their actions and earlier socialization colours their findings. Social constructivism became more prominent in the international political economy literature with publication of work by Ruggie (1975 and 1998) and others such as Checkel (1998 and 1999b), Finnemore (1996) and Risse (2000). More recently, a number of EU scholars have adopted social constructivism (Christiansen et al., 1999; Diez, 1997; Marcussen, 2000 and see Chapter 3 in this volume). There is no one uniform school of thought encompassing the so-called 'critical approaches'. Reference is often made to various forms of Marxism, the English critical school (Palan, 1992; see also Diez and Whitman, 2002), the Amsterdam school (Van der Pijl, 1998), the neo-Gramscians (Cox, 1981, 1983, 1995), and various forms of post-materialists, such as reflectivists (Jørgensen, 1997) and post-structuralists (Walker, 1989). What these approaches all have in common is that they criticize traditional approaches of international political economy and International Relations. They argue that the traditional schools focus too much attention on the state and fail to understand how underlying structure divides power and wealth. They are critical in that they see the status quo as benefiting the rich. Moreover, they argue that the international structure widens the gap between the 'haves' and the 'have-nots'. Critical approaches do not only criticize the traditional approaches for their normative biases and their choice of objects of study, they also criticize rationalistic academic methods and causal models based on hypothesis-testing. With social constructivists, they share the assumption that there is no clear 'reality out there' but that the world is to be interpreted and that the researcher plays an important role in that process. In recent years some studies of the EU have been inspired by these more critical approaches. The work of European scholars in particular has been open to the application of these perspectives (see, for example, Van Apeldoorn, 2002; Cafruny and Ryner, 2003).

The four approaches reviewed above have in common their focus on questions about the role of the state and interaction between the state and the international system. Neorealists place most emphasis on the state. Neoliberal institutionalists add to that the importance of institutions, as either rules and regimes or more formal organizations. Social constructivists add to these factors that actors (states, policymakers, social scientists) are all influenced by their culture, education, socialization and identity, and that these factors influence their role in the interplay between states, institutions and the system. The critical schools emphasize that those interactions are not value-free, and that the outcome ought to be taken into consideration when politics are practised and studied.

comparative political economy approaches

Comparative political economy is more difficult to categorize than international political economy, in part because there is some overlap between them. However, comparative political economy is distinguished by its focus on the comparison of systems, such as welfare states (Scharpf and Schmidt, 2000), different models of capitalism, socialism or communism (Hall and Soskice, 2001), or the transition of nations from socialism to democracy. It may also involve analysis of how specific countries respond to EU developments. A collective study edited by Kenneth Dyson (2002) is a good example of this; it examined how various countries prepared themselves for membership of EMU and what effects this has had on their macroeconomic policies. The principal focus of these kinds of studies is comparison of a system in one country or region with that of another. The theoretical approaches used to accomplish this objective often include those reviewed in the discussion of international political economy approaches above. They may also include others that look in more detail at the domestic historic path producing a country or a region's pattern of development.

Within the discipline of economics one could also find scholars who fit this category, such as those who examine the relationship between political and economic cycles. These scholars explore how governments and political parties reach out to the 'median', or the 'swing' voter (that is, those voters who can make a crucial difference in elections), and how policies and politics are made to accommodate these voters (Alesina, *et al.*, 1997). Whereas other economists might conclude that supply and demand ultimately produce an outcome that will be good for all (in economics terminology 'efficient'), these scholars examine how the political business cycle, which is generated by the mechanisms used to attract the median or swing voter, affects the economy. Another subfield within the economics discipline falling under the rubric of political economy is the study of fiscal policy and public finance. Scholars in this field focus on issues such as the choices of taxation regime, sizes of budgetary deficits and public debts (Persson *et al.*, 2000).

As mentioned above, methods employed in political economy research are varied. Spanning the full range of qualitative and quantitative methods, they range from the discursive-analytical, thick description type of analyses, to those that test a theory using hypotheses, and that develop models and test them with large amounts of quantitative data. Thus, political science (with many methods borrowed from economics) is clearly present in this subfield.

economics and politics

Analyses of many important EU issues require a basic understanding of both economics and political science. Many will have heard complaints from university students who found economics classes unhelpful because they were too abstract, 'assuming away' or 'keeping constant' the interesting political factors. Likewise many will have heard from disappointed students in political science classes, who only looked at major economic developments (why to adopt a single currency, for example) with reference to the role of ideas and regimes. The point here is that there are numerous areas that would benefit from proper cross-fertilization from both disciplines.

economics

Four insights in particular illustrate why the study of economics is important. The first, and most obvious, is that, *economic topics are at the heart of the*

European Union and European integration. As is well known, the EEC set out to create a customs union and eventually an internal market. It aimed at common policies, such as the Common Agricultural Policy (CAP), and the single market or '1992' project, aimed to complete this work. Other economic steps had a huge impact on the European integration process, such as the creation of the European Monetary System, with its exchange rate mechanism and the move to create an EMU by 1999. Economic topics such as these are central to the study of the EU.

Second, *economic principles are the very basis of the EU.* The decisions to move from the EEC, with its customs union, to the single market and then to EMU by 1999, were based on fundamental economic insights. These were first envisaged by economists such as Mundell (1961), Balassa (1961) and Tinbergen (1965) and eventually became both politically desirable and the subject of a large economics literature. These early scholars described major steps in the process of unification – from free trade area, customs union, single market, through EMU towards full economic or even political union. Robert Mundell (1961) spelled out his theory of optimal currency areas, indicating under what circumstances an EMU might be desirable. These early economists also produced other insights, such as the distinction between 'positive' and 'negative' integration (Tinbergen, 1965) and examined the conditions under which regional currency unions should be established (see also Heipertz and Verdun, 2004). These insights have subsequently been influential in broader political science debates (see for example the work of Scharpf, 1996).

Third, *economic mechanisms are the foundations of the EU.* The mechanisms of supply and demand, the business cycle, the unholy trinity[2] and the belief that dependent central banks are more vulnerable to political manipulation than independent central banks, are all economic mechanisms and concepts at the heart of the EU. The role of these economic mechanisms and concepts may not have been as important when the EU was first conceptualized back in the early 1950s, even though the founding fathers, Robert Schuman and Jean Monnet, were fully aware that small functional steps in the area of coal and steel could bring Europeans together. In the late 1970s and early 1980s, European integration went through a period in which elite sought direction on the question of whether integration should be based on 'dirigisme' or 'laissez-faire' principles. The fall of the Soviet Union and collapse of communism in Central and Eastern Europe did provide the EU with ammunition in favour of the argument that market principles were crucial and needed to be catered to (even if it remains unclear how large the role for governments and regulation needs to be). Thus, even though today's European Model of Society (Martin and Ross, 2004) is not fully regulated, nor based only on free market principles, it goes without saying that the current EU is based on market principles and that respecting these principles is crucial for the development of EU rules and regulations.

Fourth, *there are specific economic insights into core EU policies*. There are, of course, many of these insights, but let us look at a few in the area of CAP and EMU. CAP protects agricultural production in EU member states through one of three types of intervention: support prices, protection of the internal market through tariffs on products from outside the EU, or flat-rate aid to farmers (income supplement) (Neal and Barbezat, 1998). Economists show us how the CAP distorts competition, provides a cost to the consumer and the taxpayer, and causes overproduction which, among other things, leads to environmental damage. EMU is another important area of European integration to which the discipline of economics makes important contributions. The theory of Optimal Currency Areas (Mundell, 1961, 1973) explains the circumstances under which countries should fix exchange rates (or adopt a single currency). For example, the theory looks at the openness of the economy, the degree of interaction one state may have with other countries who might adopt a single currency, the convergence of interest rates among those countries, the synchronicity of business cycles, the stability of exchange rates and so on. When a significant number of these factors are in place, it is considered economically beneficial to join a currency area. However, this theory also spells out the risks of joining EMU if the conditions are not right. In such cases, countries will need to adjust to imbalances without having the exchange rate to turn to (see de Grauwe, 2003, 58–9). In other words, economics provides us with insights that are sufficiently general to enable us to examine more closely the costs and benefits of EMU.

political science

The discipline of political science also brings important insights to the study of European integration. Again, let us look at four particular insights. First, *politics is at the heart of European integration*. The EU is all about governing, building institutions and dividing powers of decision. The creation of the EU involved a major transfer of power from the national governments to EU-level institutions. Even the transfer of power from the national central banks to the European Central Bank was fundamentally about transferring sovereignty. The relationships among EU institutions, and that between EU institutions and national governments, are fundamentally political.

Second, *political science principles are at the heart of the EU*. The EU was set up as an organization that would produce peace in the region, first through collaboration in the area of coal and steel, and later through more general economic collaboration. The base principle was that cooperation and integration would diminish, indeed eliminate, the possibility of war. Joint governance (pooling sovereignty) would rule out warmongering. Other political principles that were to be prioritized in the EU were accountability, democracy, legitimacy and representation. The functionalist principles upon which the ECSC, Euratom and the EEC were established, did not require too much thought about democratic principles. However, as the integration process deepened, and especially after the difficulties ratifying the Maastricht Treaty, more and more citizens and politicians started to worry that these political principles were not properly dealt with in the context of EU governance (Verdun, 1998). Efficiency (or output legitimacy) was not the same as democratic principles (input legitimacy) (Verdun and Christiansen, 2000; cf. Scharpf 1999; see also Chapter 9 in this volume). This trend has since continued, culminating in strong votes against the Constitutional Treaty in the French and the Dutch national referenda.

Third, *political science mechanisms are at the core of the EU*. There are many mechanisms that political scientists refer to when explaining the dynamics of European integration. One such dynamic relates to who has power in the EU. Large member states are typically more powerful than small member states. Yet what determines the relative power of a member state? A member state is strong if it is large in terms of population, more still if it has a strong economy. By contrast it is weak if it is small, and more so if it has a weak economy. But there are more mechanisms that can give rise to increased power. A member state that has been member of the EU for a long time is typically more influential (relatively) than a member state that has just joined. A member state is more influential if it can set the agenda (for example when it holds the EU Presidency). It is weaker if it is merely reactive or has only a consultation status. Finally, one could also examine the mechanisms of negotiation. Maes and Verdun (2005), for instance, found that smaller member states do well in brokering deals or mediating.

Fourth, *there are important political insights into specific EU topics*. Turning to the examples raised above, the CAP was taken as an important policy area in the early days of European integration because of the importance of the 'politics of food' and the 'politics of farming'. In the postwar period, the idea of supporting farmers and securing agricultural production made sense to many politicians and citizens. The bitter winter of 1944–45 gave securing food on European soil special meaning in some cases (such as the Netherlands). Belgium, the Netherlands and Luxembourg had explored agricultural cooperation in the context of Benelux collaboration, and found it difficult to do successfully without other countries joining in (Maes and Verdun, 2005). In the case of France, farmers have been a politically important 'interest group' (albeit not always formally organized). For their part, the Germans had the lowest supply of agricultural products, which all other things being equal, would normally have meant having the highest prices (El-Agraa, 1990, 201). Furthermore, farmers were still an important constituency in member states. In this context, it is not surprising that a special policy was created at the EU level to support them. CAP was put in place so that the EU would be able produce plenty of food and the consumer would be able to buy it at a relatively low price (though the latter was not achieved). The original CAP was protective and planned and that insulated agricultural policy from both domestic demands and from US pressure for trade liberalization (Rieger, 2000).

Likewise, EMU represents a policy that essentially institutionalized choices made throughout the 1980s in light of experience with the exchange rate mechanism. When the Federal Republic of Germany successfully pursued low inflation rates, neighbouring states pursued policies that sought to avoid devaluation against the Deutschmark. As a result they effectively followed Bundesbank policies. Thus, an important explanation of the EMU regime (institutions, rules and geographical location of the European Central Bank) can be traced back to the dominance of German monetary authorities in the pre-EMU period (Verdun, 2000). In examining this in detail, Dyson and Featherstone (1999) stress the importance of policy learning and the role of shared sound monetary policy norms underlying the EMU project.

political economy

Many topics are found at the interface of economics and politics, and hence benefit from analysis incorporating insights from both economics and political science disciplines. When outcomes can no longer be explained merely by economic or political science explanations a political economy analysis becomes particularly handy. A political economist would argue that all economic topics related to the EU have an immediate political dimension. Indeed, the political economist would also argue that one is likely to miss all the interesting bits if one excludes political factors. Likewise the political economist, reading only the 'politics' of an EU topic that has an important economic dimension, would argue that without understanding the economics behind the EU one could never get the full picture. This is even true for the phenomenon of voting in the Council where the issues at stake include influence over the distribution of material gains or influence over the decisionmaking process. In this sense *political economy topics are at the heart of European Integration*.

A second, and related, point is that *political economy principles are at the core of the EU*. Political economy principles posit that these two fields intersect; this is the basic premise that there can be no economics without politics, and that most politics can be traced back to economic interaction. Other principles include the idea that member states operate in an 'interrelated' world. One country's policies and decisions are likely to affect another's. Differences among countries will remain, but the effects from outside cannot be neglected. Furthermore, as International Relations scholarship shows, the international system also has an effect on national policies.

Third, *political economy mechanisms play an important role in the EU*. For example, political economy theories stress the dynamics of realism (power struggle and interest protection) and institutionalism (institutions change slowly and have their own inherent logic). They emphasize that ideas, ideology and beliefs influence the policymaking process and demonstrate that policy decisions are not value neutral. In addition, there are various methodological tools in the field of political economy. To take again the example of voting in the Council, a range of game theoretic models can be used to calculate the likelihood of blocking minorities, the use of the population ratio and so on. Fourth and finally, if we turn again to the CAP and EMU, we can provide some illustrative examples of what political economy analysis looks like, demonstrating that there are specific political economy insights into core EU policies. The CAP was created to support farmers who represented an important political group in core countries such as France and the Federal Republic of Germany. Its success meant that European integration was able to produce policies that enabled redistribution from the EU to member state farmers, thereby producing 'positive integration', or a new EU-level policy. However its side-effects were many, including overproduction and a large percentage of agricultural spending consuming the common budget. It also frustrated international attempts to remove state intervention in this sector, which would have increased free trade in this sector to the benefit of both the consumer and developing countries. Furthermore, the reasons the CAP is so difficult to reform can be traced to a number of factors: the resistance of the farmers (particularly in France), corporatist structures that empower particular interest groups, and fear that loss of the agricultural sector would change landscapes and population composition (Grant, 2005). Eastern enlargement posed another challenge for the CAP, as it could not continue as it had been in an EU of 25 member states. Nowadays, the policy is one in which Europeanization and globalization go hand-in-hand (Hennis, 2001). Both pressures have an effect on the capacity of policymakers to reform the policy.

The second case, EMU, can also be best explained by combining economics and politics. The economics of European integration emphasizes the logic behind achieving various stages of integration (de Grauwe, 2003). But economics cannot explain how the member states make minor adjustments to the process, nor can it explain timing. Economists also have difficulty explaining why member states such as Denmark decided not to take part in EMU when their economic characteristics permitted membership, whereas others such as Greece, whose economic conditions are not particularly in line with those of the core of EMU states, have already joined. One needs to emphasize a combination of factors and to appreciate political economy motivations in order to understand such outcomes (see Verdun, 2000). I now turn to review how political economy approaches have been used in EU Studies.

political economy approaches in european union studies

Careful analysis of articles in three major EU Studies journals illustrates key themes, methods and research strategies employed in political economists' work on the EU.[3] In recent issues of the journal, *International Organization*, for instance, one finds studies that adopt a variety of political economy approaches and methodologies. A recent special issue on European monetary integration analyses why national governments choose the monetary institutions they do (Bernhard *et al.*, 2002; Frieden, 2002; see also Hallerberg, 2002). Bernhard *et al.* (2002) focus in particular on the relationship between central bank independence and fixed exchange rates. They argue that the political context influences the desire to aim for goals such as price stabilization. According to the authors, governments choose institutions that fit their preferences best but electoral, partisan and sectoral pressures also play a role in determining which monetary institutions are chosen. At the same time, the EU institutional context disciplines member states into accepting the rigorous framework of the independent European Central Bank (the most independent central bank in the world). The authors also distinguish between 'first generation' work on these issues, which focused on the choice of monetary institutions and exchange rate regimes in isolation from one another, and 'second generation' work. The latter differs from the former in that it studies the choice of exchange rate regime and the choice of monetary policy independence together. The special issue focuses on both economic and political factors and, importantly, the interaction between the two. The conclusions the authors draw relate to political economy factors, draw on political economy methodologies, and are formulated so that the conclusions could be applied to other cases.

In the same journal, Eising (2002) studies electricity liberalization in the EU. He aims to explain why the EU agreed to liberalize EU electricity markets when the outcome differed considerably from the member states' initial positions on this issue. The findings show that an intergovernmentalist approach is unable to explain the outcome, nor does any other approach emphasizing the power of larger member states. Instead, one needs to accept that member states are willing to change their policy preferences. The important variable is the EU institutional setting which is able to shape strategic action. In other words, institutional mechanisms are responsible for the policy outcome. In this case, French and German sectoral interests were overruled by macropolitical considerations (Eising, 2002, 116). Again, we see a mix of economic and political factors and a tendency to formulate conclusions so that they might be applicable to cases beyond those studied here.

A further study, by Ballmann, Epstein and O'Halloran (2002), looks at interinstitutional struggles between the Commission and the Council within 'comitology'. It examines the well-known assumption that comitology generally restricts the Commission's executive powers and enhances those of the Council. Using a game-theoretic approach, the study analyses how the three committee procedures (management, regulatory and advisory) operate, and how committees tend to favour the Commission's position, if it affects the policymaking process at all. This study examines power relations and interests of various actors and adopts a methodology more typically used in economics, but also increasingly employed in political economy work.

In an indication of the variety of theoretical approaches employed, Jeffrey Checkel (2001b) uses a constructivist approach to understand why agents comply with norms. In his study of European identity change in Germany and the Ukraine he finds that a constructivist account is better able to explain the outcome than a rationalist explanation. He finds that institutions influence the compliance process in three ways: through institutional legacies, the structure of domestic institutions, and through pre-existing norms present in institutions. As such, analysis incorporates some elements of both rational instrumental choice *and* social learning in the explanation of norm compliance. Of particular interest is Checkel's careful analysis of the role of argumentative persuasion and social learning as a way to explaining compliance. Checkel stays within constructivist reasoning yet uses the same hypothesis-testing methodology often used by rationalists to point out which factors best explain the outcome of international institutions. In so doing, he bridges the 'gap' between rational and constructivist approaches and clarifies which parts of the process constructivist approaches are better able to elucidate than rationalist approaches.

Recent issues of the *Journal of Common Market Studies* also contain numerous articles on EMU, though most of them are written by economists in the 'economics' political economy tradition (Buti and Giudice, 2002; Crowley, 2001; De Haan *et al.*, 2002; Tamborini, 2001; but see also Kaltenthaler, 2002). This 'economics' political economy tradition assumes that voters, interest groups and other stakeholders have needs that are taken seriously in government decisionmaking and often refer to the 'median voter'. Governments take into consideration the power distribution of voters. The articles in the *Journal of Common Market Studies* assess, respectively, the design and rationale of the fiscal rules of EMU, post-EMU scenarios based on Optimal Currency Area theory, the synchronicity of business cycles, and the future of balance-of-payments problems in the eurozone. Kaltenthaler (2002) examines the German origins of EMU (the role of interests and domestic actors) to explain EMU outcomes, explores the likely future behaviour of Germany and makes a strong case that the relationship between German reunification and EMU is causal. (For a contrasting constructivist analysis of Germany and EMU see Merlingen, 2001, and on Germany and the EU more generally see Hyde-Price and Jeffery, 2001.) These studies focus on the various political and economic factors that play a role in the development and governance of EMU. They focus on interest, preferences, institutions, rules, power relations and mechanisms of policymaking. These articles highlight how policy outcomes are related to the choice of institutional structures and rules, which in turn is determined by interests, preferences and power relations. Political economy approaches weave together these political and economic factors and draw on the methodologies common to the economists' profession and the political economy literature.[4]

Articles in the *Journal of European Public Policy* are generally more policy-orientated, but there are still a number of pieces in most issues that can easily be categorized as 'political economy'. Again for roughly the same time period

(2001 to 2002) we find articles on theories of European integration that fit with political economy as applied to policy sectors. The topics are wide-ranging.[5] As it is not possible to do justice to the nuances of all the arguments made in these articles, I will focus on just a few. Weber and Hallerberg (2001) seek to explain why firms may prefer European solutions. Looking at the cases of aerospace, pharmaceuticals and automobiles, their theoretical framework suggests that firms are willing to accept more cooperative structures as they are confronted with threats from abroad and high transaction costs. In order to explain why cooperation was a logical outcome, the authors examine preferences of firms, the options firms have available to them and the possible outcomes. Again we see a mix of economic and political factors used to explain the behaviour of firms. Vivien Schmidt (2001) examines the role of discourse in the adjustment of economic policy in selected West European countries. She examines the degree, and way, in which discourse makes a difference. Her argument is that the power of discourse differs from country to country. In the United Kingdom it was able to transform policies whereas in France the effectiveness of policy change lagged behind in part due to unsuccessful accompanying discourse. Again we see how interests, preferences and policy change are examined and factors such as discourse are analysed for their influence on the process.

In sum, this review of recent political economy research shows the types of policies that are studied and gives an indication of the diversity of methods and theoretical approaches adopted. This research represents the broad scope of perspectives mentioned above, with analyses ranging from a constructivist analysis – emphasizing learning, culture, persuasion – to the role of preferences and interests tested through various hypotheses and analysed through formal models. This multitude of studies offers a rich spectrum, which aims to provide generalizable findings that could be applied outside the realm of EU Studies, including Comparative Politics, International Relations, political science or economics more generally. It is this feature of political economy that makes it a particularly attractive subfield of study. Criticism of 'Area Studies' (European Studies, Latin American Studies and so on) has focused on the fact that scholars sometimes get too involved in their particular area of study and fail to draw out the parallels between their studies and those of other fields. If one were to adopt its theories and methods, political economy would prove itself general enough to allow EU Studies to relate more easily to general literatures that do not focus on the particular case of the EU. At the same time, because it draws on two fields of study, the nuances of a political economy approach may be empirically rewarding. Again, some studies of the EU focus too narrowly on only one aspect of integration and may, paradoxically, miss the empirical subtlety of the EU itself. Political economy offers the student of European integration a wealth of approaches and methodologies to choose from and in so doing helps to avoid being too narrowly focused on the specificities of the EU. Instead the researcher, using the political economy toolkit, should be able to frame his/her study terms that are broad enough to allow findings to be of interest well beyond the realm of EU Studies.

conclusion

This chapter has examined the role of political economy in EU Studies. It has reviewed the role of theories and methods in this field, covering insights from both economics and political science. The chapter has indicated how a political economy approach incorporates elements from both of these disciplines and examines how different principles, mechanisms and analyses of various areas of EU integration (particularly the CAP and EMU) might be studied through a political economy approach. The penultimate section offered a review of selected journal articles in order to illustrate the nature of current political economy research on the EU. Political economy offers theoretical approaches and a variety of methods that will enable EU Studies scholars to deal with the criticism that its focus on the EU as a *sui generis* phenomenon is too narrow and does not produce good social science. Political economy offers a more general framework.

Another criticism that is often heard regarding EU Studies is that it lacks methodological rigour and innovation. Again, political economy offers a variety of methodologies from which to choose. Furthermore, it is an area that nicely integrates two interconnected disciplines that more often than not are treated in isolation, but which in the case of the EU, are often found in tandem. Hence it offers interdisciplinarity, and thus insights from these two disciplines. Along with the resurgence of political economy in graduate programmes across the world, these advantages suggest that the political economy of European integration will become even more prominent in the research agenda of EU Studies scholars in the years to come.

notes

1. This review of the literature draws on Verdun (2003).
2. 'Unholy trinity' refers to the impossibility of having fixed exchange rates and liberalized capital markets and then assuming that a national government can have the freedom to set an independent monetary policy.
3. This section examines journal articles published in 2001 and 2002.
4. Other political economy research in the *Journal of Common Market Studies* includes, for example, the redistributive effects of the EU budget (de la Fuente and Doménech, 2001; Hodson and Maher, 2001); work on the 'Open Method' as a new form of governance; various articles on voting in the EU Council after Nice (Moberg, 2002 and Tsebelis and Yataganas, 2002); a study of EU border controls for the imposition of value added tax and how this works like a barrier to trade (Verwaal and Cnossen, 2002); the role of Christian democrats (a transnational coalition with a shared ideological identity) in the creation of the Maastricht Treaty (arguing against an intergovernmentalist approach); a welfare approach to explain UK accession, based on a formal model of Computable

General Equilibrium (Gasiorek *et al.*, 2002); and finally a critical assessment of the principal-agent model in the study of the EU (Bauer, 2002).

5. Including a special issue on historical institutionalism (Lavenex, 2001; Trondal, 2001; Zito, 2001); articles on firms and on private governance (Weber and Hallerberg, 2001 and Knill, 2001b respectively); studies of welfare adjustment and partisan politics in a country such as France, an analysis of the third way and welfare policies in Denmark and the Netherlands (Green-Pedersen *et al.*, 2001); a discourse analysis of economic policies in Britain and France (Schmidt, 2001); a discourse analysis of globalization and European integration (Hay and Rosamond, 2002); an examination of liberalization within Europe's single market and of the role of governments within this process (M.P. Smith, 2001); an analysis of non-compliance in the EU (Börzel, 2001); the question of why market integration might lead to support public interest-goals (Héritier, 2001, 848); various studies on EMU (for example Elgie, 2002; Heisenberg and Richmond, 2002; Hodson and Maher, 2002); only one study on the CAP (Coleman and Chiasson, 2002); and a special issue on regulatory reform (Héritier and Thatcher, 2002). Furthermore, there are numerous studies that have a focus on Central and Eastern European countries and how they differ from the other EU member states in one or more ways (a special issue can be found in Goetz, 2001). Finally, there is a recent special part-issue of *Journal of European Public Policy* (Jones and Verdun, 2003) that specifically examines political economy and European integration and which offers four theoretical approaches to EU Studies. An enlarged and expanded version of that project also addresses various empirical studies and represents the richness in methodologies that one finds in political economy studies of European integration (Jones and Verdun, 2005).

11
from state to society?
the historiography of european integration
wolfram kaiser

introduction

The historiography of European integration has expanded rapidly over the last two decades. This trend is partly due to the pervasive influence of the EU in contemporary Europe, resulting in a greater interest in its origins and development since the Second World War. Up to a point, this new interest in historiography has also resulted from incentives in other disciplines, such as political science, economics and law, which had been subject to a much earlier growth in EU research. Moreover, archival sources on the EU are now abundant and are becoming more easily accessible. The opening of most government archives in line with the predominant thirty-year rule has recently allowed research on the history of interstate relations and bargaining in the EEC/EC/EU and the European Free Trade Association (EFTA) to move into the 1960s and early 1970s. Although contemporary historians generally use other sources too, the government archives had been inaccessible to researchers in the social sciences. Thus, their opening promises important new results. Finally, the European-level coordination of research on European integration history has also been politically encouraged and subsidized. This policy aimed to overcome the national fragmentation of the historiography of modern Europe, which, since the nineteenth century, has been dominated by the nation-state paradigm, and (at least in the initial stages) was also expected to help legitimize the integration process.

Research on the history of European integration was first institutionalized with the creation of a specialized Chair (first held by Walter Lipgens from 1976 to 1979) at the time of the foundation of the European University Institute in Florence. The European Commission subsequently supported the formation of the European Community Liaison Committee of Historians in 1982 (legally constituted in 1989) to organize a first conference on the origins of the Schuman Plan in Strasbourg in 1984 (Poidevin, 1986). Since then, this body has held a number of conferences, which have – in their thematic coverage – largely followed the opening of government archives, and that have led to the publication of several multi-language edited books (Schwabe, 1988; Serra, 1989; Trausch, 1993; Dumoulin, 1995; Deighton and Milward, 1999; Loth, 2001a). Since 1995 the Liaison Group has also edited the bi-annual *Journal of European Integration History*. Despite its growth in recent years, European integration history is still a relatively small research field which does not yet play a major role in contemporary history more generally and is not particularly well connected to social science research on the EU. With very few exceptions (Gillingham, 1991, 2003) and very much unlike the situation in political science, historians face practically no competition from the United States. As a result, the Liaison Group still exercises an important influence in promoting research on the history of the EU and in defining research themes, even though there are now an increasing number of transnationally constituted initiatives outside this institutionalized framework. In contrast, the Jean Monnet network, which actually comprises many historians who are not really specialists in EU history, has had few significant effects (if any) on this kind of research.

Against this background, this chapter will first give an overview of the history of the historiography of European integration as it has developed since the 1970s, and will assess the achievements and shortcomings of the state of the art. It will then discuss the relationship between historiography and social science theory and research, making some suggestions as to how the historiography of integration could in future relate more coherently and contribute more effectively to the agendas of other disciplines. Finally, the chapter will outline new emerging research which draws upon recent historiographical and social science trends, and in particular the cultural history of politics and transnational relations and socialization, which has as its aim a redressing of the existing bias towards the analysis of intergovernmental bargaining and supranational policymaking.

a history of eu historiography

Historical research on the integration process started in earnest with Lipgens' publications on plans for the future of Europe advanced by resistance movements during the Second World War (Lipgens, 1968), and on the origins of European integration in the first few years after 1945 (Lipgens, 1982 [1977]).

Working with Wilfried Loth, who has presided over the Liaison Group since 2000, Lipgens (who died in 1984) also edited a comprehensive work in English, and published in four volumes on the European integration project and the role of pressure groups between 1945 and 1950 (Lipgens, 1984–91). In essence, he argued that European integration after 1945 marked a decisive break with the recent European past of national conflict and war, which it was designed to overcome. Although they were, to some extent, present in the interwar period, ideas about European integration mainly originated in the resistance movements and amongst those in exile during the Second World War. During and after the war of 1939–45, the concept of supranational integration was refined on the basis of the transnational relations which existed and persisted amongst resistance fighters and European pressure groups, culminating in the Hague Congress in May 1948. The common experience of fascism, national socialism and German occupation, as well as the fear of a Communist take-over assisted by the Soviet Union, legitimized supranational integration as the only promising institutional framework for postwar Western Europe, eventually leading to the formation of the first 'core Europe' organization, the European Coal and Steel Community (ECSC), founded in 1951–52.

In many ways, Lipgens' personal and academic background, as well as the general approach and substance of his publications, are quite typical of early integration history (Kaiser, 2002). To begin with, Lipgens actually started out as a historian of early modern Europe before he began to write critically about Bismarck's role in German unification. Despite his familiarity with neofunctionalist integration theory and rhetoric in the 1950s and 1960s, he was not particularly interested in social science research on European integration, especially in its theoretical conceptualization. His focus on the role of transnational social and political actors bears little resemblance to the neofunctionalist ideas in circulation at the time. Whereas Lipgens interpreted European integration as a broad societal movement, informed by common ideas and norms and led by political elites, the early neofunctionalists like Ernst Haas (1958) emphasized the influence of economic actors and technocratic supranational elites. In fact, Lipgens' approach was more informed by the older history of ideas in evidence in his previous publications, which concentrated on the intellectual origins of these ideas, rather than their social and political impact. However, his research failed to establish links between ideas and policy. Combined with the descriptive character of his works, this failure to demonstrate that the institutionalization of European integration in the form of the ECSC/EEC actually resulted from the ideas he found so intriguing led many later historians to reject not only Lipgens' somewhat old-fashioned approach, but also the argument that ideas of that kind mattered. Even so, a small group of historians most of whom have close links with the European Movement and are based largely in Italy, have continued to pursue Lipgens' research agenda on European ideas and pro-integration movements (Pistone, 1992 and 1996; Landuyt and Preda, 2000).

Lipgens' work was also representative of early integration history in its almost exclusive focus on the 'core Europe' of the six founding member states of the ECSC/EEC, that is, France, West Germany, Italy and the Benelux countries. As a result of the quite dogmatic analytical differentiation between supranational integration, which was innovative and worthy of study, and intergovernmental cooperation, which merely continued the disastrous interwar tradition of interstate relations and bargaining, the first integration historians like Lipgens and Raymond Poidevin, for example, concentrated exclusively on the pre-history and the origins of the ECSC/EEC. Geographically larger frameworks for market integration, such as the Organization for European Economic Cooperation (OEEC) and the European Payments Union (EPU), received scant attention, as did plans for a Nordic customs union or the formation of EFTA. The narrow focus on 'core Europe', which has favoured a teleological interpretation of the integration process reminiscent of the modernization theories applied to nineteenth-century Europe, is still prevalent in today's introductory texts on the history of European integration (Dinan, 2004; Urwin 2002; Bitsch, 2001; Loth, 1996). It was also (and up to a point, still is) reflected in the composition of the Liaison Group, which initially included only one historian (Alan Milward) from outside the six founding states.

The exclusive focus on 'core Europe' also resulted from the normative assumptions inherent in early integration history research, which treated the ECSC/EEC as a morally superior political framework. Lipgens, himself a member of the European Movement, was a radical supporter of supranational integration. For example, in an article for the didactics journal *Geschichte in Wissenschaft und Unterricht* (Lipgens, 1983), he demanded that teaching in European schools should explain European integration as 'the most successful peace movement ever' and that criticisms of 'Brussels bureaucrats' largely came from national bureaucracies intent on preventing the creation of a federal Europe. Lipgens was a Catholic and had been heavily influenced during the War by the preachings of the bishop of Münster, Clemens August Graf von Galen, who opposed National Socialism. Politically, he supported the Christian Democrats who were the main protagonists of integration within 'core Europe' and of a more federal institutional structure in the 1950s and beyond. Several other early integration historians had similar backgrounds – like Gilbert Trausch, the long-time director of the Robert Schuman Centre in Luxembourg, Professor of history at the University of Liège and second president (after Réné Girault 1982–88) of the Liaison Group (1988–2000). Trausch has also acted as an adviser on European affairs to a number of Christian Democrat prime ministers from Luxembourg as well as to former Commission President, Jacques Santer.

From the mid-1980s, the historiography of European integration began to expand to overcome these intellectual, geographical and normative limitations (Wurm, 1995), though new assumptions stifled innovative research in other ways. Starting with the revisionist account of European integration by Alan

Milward (1984), who focused on its economic dimension, many researchers with access to newly available government sources in state archives began to doubt the influence of ideas and societal pro-integration movements in postwar European integration. They reconceptualised policy developments as the result of the pursuit of national interests by governments in interstate bargains.

Integration history was largely hijacked by traditional diplomatic historians holding (implicit) 'realist' assumptions, but who had very little, if any, knowledge of International Relations theory. Conceptually and methodologically, many historical studies in this mode were less sophisticated than the 'dissident realism' of International Relations scholars like Stanley Hoffmann who had also emphasized (Hoffmann, 1966) the pre-eminence of the member states in European integration after the 'empty chair' crisis of 1965–66, but whose work was informed by a more differentiated understanding of domestic politics. Many diplomatic historians took interests as given or as quite freely defined by governments, without any systematic reference to domestic politics. The underlying assumptions are reflected, for example, in the habitual use of phrases such as: 'the British thought ...'. Diplomatic history of this kind has also usually resorted to the national approach to understand the policy of particular countries 'towards' European integration, often without any real multilateral contextualization. This has also been the dominant approach to analysing US policy on early European integration, using works largely or even exclusively based on American sources (Neuss, 2000; Lundestad, 1998; Hogan, 1987), which tend to overemphasize US influence. Archive-based studies of US policy on 'Europe' have now moved beyond the creation of the EEC (Winand, 1993) and are beginning to address EU–US relations from a bilateral perspective, focusing, for example, on trade relations in the 1960s.

The traditional diplomatic history approach shares underlying assumptions about the controlling influence of national governments on the integration process with Milward's revisionist account. Both analytical frameworks focus on the intergovernmental bargaining of nationally defined interests, explaining this within an (implicit) rational choice framework, and are almost exclusively based on state sources. Up to a point, their rise can be explained by the contemporary experience of many historians (and other EU scholars) from the mid-1960s to the mid-1980s, an experience of weak Commissions and little progress in European integration, as well as of the legally (and in terms of conducting the actual negotiations) dominant role of governments in major treaty revisions. Arguably, the same is true for the revival of the state-centred rational choice International Relations analysis of integration in the form of liberal intergovernmentalism (Moravcsik, 1998a).

At the same time, Milward, and other economic historians who have followed in his footsteps (Guirao, 1998), have largely rejected geopolitical explanations of governmental policy towards 'Europe' as designed, for example, to retain French great power status or to keep the Germans 'down'. Instead, Milward has interpreted European integration as a new, state-controlled regulatory framework for 'the European rescue of the nation-state' (Milward, 1992) and the resolution of the 'German problem' through market integration and a partially Europeanized welfare state. In this interpretation the creation of the ECSC amounted to an economic 'peace treaty'. Interestingly, Loth has recently argued (2001b, 91–6) that by taking the functional deficiencies of European nation-states after 1945 as his starting point, Milward actually shares one of the main basic assumptions of Lipgens' earlier work, even though he emphasizes the nation-states' inability to provide social welfare for their citizens rather than their ineffectiveness in guaranteeing security. Unlike most traditional diplomatic historians, Milward has put forward an overarching explanatory thesis applied to the European integration project as a whole, which, in many ways, is similar to liberal intergovernmentalism. Although it did create controversy among contemporary historians and was at least noted by some social scientists, economic history as a whole has remained marginal to the historiography of integration.

During the 1990s, the historiography of European integration has also significantly expanded its geographical scope. Quite comprehensive source-based historical studies of national European policies for the entire postwar period or covering specific time-spans have recently been published for such 'newcomers' as Austria (Gehler, 2002) and Sweden (Malmborg, 1995). Comparative research has also started in earnest, with the aim of determining motivating factors and domestic forces (Kaiser and Elvert, 2004). The historiography of national European policy is now more developed for some 'newcomers' than it is for founding states like France and (West) Germany. Rather bizarrely, thus far, the older member states' European policies have not been examined in monographs covering longer time spans or even the entire postwar period, although bilateral governmental relations have been researched in some detail.

As of 2004, British policy towards 'core Europe' is probably the best researched, not least because of its continuing divisive character in domestic British politics. Some normatively informed studies (Lamb, 1995), including one on Britain and the Schuman Plan by the former Labour politician Edmund Dell (1995), have roundly condemned British policy for missing various 'buses' at different stages in the postwar European integration process. Others have concentrated on the motives behind British policy, especially in the context of the first British application to join the EEC in 1961. Controversially, in my own work, I have suggested that the first bid for entry was mainly, although not exclusively, designed to 'appease' the new Kennedy administration into continuing the 'special relationship', and that it served useful external and domestic purposes, regardless of the actual outcome of the negotiations (Kaiser, 1999). On the other hand, Milward (2002a) has recently argued (in line with his overall approach to integration history) that British policy towards

'Europe' was based throughout on a 'national strategy' which rested on a broad consensus and was intended to effect Britain's transition from great power to that of a middle-ranking power. Lacking in an overarching thesis, several other archive-based collective volumes and monographs (Daddow, 2003; Broad and Preston, 2001; Ellison, 2000) have dealt with specific aspects of British European policy up until the late 1960s.

Finally, European integration history has largely overcome its normative beginnings and has experienced a substantial professionalization. This is clearly a precondition for its being taken more seriously within the discipline of history and by social scientists working on the EU. Most of the younger historians of the EU no longer aim to contribute to the legitimization of the integration process, so that the European Commission has also become less interested in fostering and subsidizing the historiography of European integration. Professional historians are conscious of the danger that they and their work might be abused in the interest of some kind of European nation-building project, in much the same way that national historians played a crucial legitimizing role in the process of nation-state formation and national integration in the second half of the nineteenth century, often fostering ethnic exclusivity, aggressive nationalism and ultimately, bloody interstate conflict.

By the start of the twenty-first century, the historiography of European integration had thus expanded and matured. In particular, it had overcome the methodological simplicity of the earlier history of ideas and of European movements, and the underlying normative assumptions of much of early integration history. In the process, however, it has become limited in other ways. Most importantly, the traditional diplomatic history approach has failed to reconstruct the *Community* dimension of integration, which extends beyond the sum of national European policies. At the same time, the economic history of integration has mainly concentrated on the role of national political and bureaucratic elite in governmental policy formulation. As a general rule, this approach lacks a sophisticated understanding of domestic politics, which might include the role of influential political actors like political parties and pressure groups, as well as the importance of the media and public opinion. Thus, it often fails to relate to larger, non-economic questions about the European politics of integration. In conclusion, most research has not only been very nationally introspective, but has also been state-centred. This is an overreaction to early integration history that has gone too far. As a result, most integration history has ignored the importance of supranational institutions and transnational actors both in EU politics, and in the slow formation of a European society.

integration historiography and social science research

Contemporary historians might have developed a more sophisticated conceptual and methodological approach to studying the history of the EU through closer collaboration with the social sciences. Yet few historians have related to theoretical and (although less so) empirical research in the social sciences in a systematic way. There are a number of reasons for this which help to explain the generally dismal state of interdisciplinary cooperation between history and the social sciences in EU research. In the main, these are related to the educational background of many leading EU historians, certain deeply ingrained characteristics of the discipline compared to the social sciences, as well as to the contemporary experience of profound disillusionment with over-theorizing.

Across Europe, many of the leading older integration historians had an education grounded in the humanities, without any significant social science training. Before concerning themselves with post-1945 integration history, most of them had been specialists in pre-1918 or pre-1945 national or European history, which had only been researched by the emerging social sciences to a very limited extent. In postwar Europe, however, this situation was fundamentally different. Nowadays, as a general rule, many social science studies are published before archival sources become accessible, although historians are able to discover new themes for research or ask a different set of questions based on their contemporary experience of integration. As a result of their educational and prior research background and of the ever increasing tendency to become specialized in one discipline and, within that discipline, of precisely circumscribed geographical spaces and shorter time-spans, much of the historiography of integration only relates to social science theory and empirical research in the most general of ways, if at all.

As a discipline, moreover, modern history (with the exception of the by now marginal orthodox historical materialism) tends to favour an eclectic approach to theory, selecting and assimilating available theoretical concepts and approaches, but without applying them rigidly to sources. In the 1960s and 1970s, some social historians (especially in continental Europe) attempted to transform history as a discipline into what they called 'historical social science', emphasizing the importance *inter alia* of structural forces and of using 'scientific' methodological precision in ascertaining their role in determining historical developments and in influencing the everyday lives of ordinary people. However, this historiography either focused on micro social history or on the social history of national integration, especially in the nineteenth century, and showed no interest in analysing international relations or the contemporary history of supranational integration. Indeed, these historians were basically opposed to the history of international relations, which they wanted to replace with *Gesellschaftsgeschichte*, or 'societal history', which, at the most, had a comparative, but not an international or transnational dimension. In response to this challenge, many diplomatic historians became very defensive and were reluctant to modify their approach in a way that could have been more fruitfully applied to the study of the integration process. The modernization of international relations history did make greater progress in American historiography under the pressure of more 'politically correct' and fashionable sub-disciplines, but it never became seriously interested in explaining European integration.

Meanwhile, structuralist social history, especially 'Germanic' historiography, has been severely criticized for its inability to capture and describe the life conditions of decisionmakers and ordinary people and for largely ignoring the cross-border dimensions of modern European history. This has led to a renewed emphasis in European historiography on agency rather than structure; and this is reflected in several archive-based biographies of leading European politicians like Robert Schuman (Poidevin, 1986), Konrad Adenauer (Schwarz, 1986 and 1991) and Jean Monnet (Duchêne, 1994). Although most integration historians will not deny the relevance of structural (socioeconomic) factors in explaining long-term transformations (as emphasized by Alan Milward and John Gillingham, for example), they tend as a general rule to be more interested in explaining the specificities of *particular* political, economic or institutional developments in integration and of *concrete* decisions at a given point in time. There is no doubt, for example, that general economic trends and pressures mitigated in favour of British EEC membership, but this alone does not explain why the British government first applied for full membership in 1961 and not in 1958 or 1966 or, indeed, why Britain did not seek a free trade area association with the EC to safeguard its core economic interests in 1972, as Sweden and Switzerland did. The same is true of other 'newcomers' in the integration process (Angerer, 1998; Kaiser and Elvert, 2004).

As a result of their focus on particular phenomena and decisions in time-specific circumstances moreover, historians of the integration process are also wary of theoretical over-generalizations which are often unsupported by the diverse original sources available to them, especially for research on postwar Europe. Such over-generalizations are structurally inherent in the social sciences. Indeed, they are in some ways one of their main strengths, as they allow social scientists to determine a clear hierarchy of different factors, such as material incentives or norms, in accounting for policy outcomes – something historians often find difficult to assess. At the same time, however, over-generalizations involve the methodological danger of re-interpreting the available evidence to fit a particular theory. Historians and political scientists have demonstrated, for example (Lieshout *et al.*, 2004; Trachtenberg, 2000; Merkel, 1999), that Moravcsik's use (Moravcsik, 1998a) of historical literature and sources to support his liberal intergovernmentalist theory is highly selective and in many ways misleading.

Historians are not only critical of the abuse of historical evidence and literature to support over-generalizations and integration theories, they also find it difficult to relate to Americanized political science research on the EU, with its tendency to debate at length quite minor variations in theoretical approaches, all of which appear to be characterized by the same sterile 'in-group' language, making them almost as inaccessible to researchers from other disciplines as to lay readers. While British political science has long been characterized by a dominant empirical approach, the growing theory orientation in other academic traditions has widened the gulf between history and the social sciences. Also contributing to the disciplinary divide is, finally, the limited predictive value of social science theory. In the field of EU research, disillusionment with the predictive claims of theories started in the 1960s with the initial failure of the neofunctionalists to allow for the possibility of regression, as in the context of the 'empty chair' crisis of 1965–66, which they only rationalized *ex post*. Since then (and also as a result of the dismal failure of the social sciences to foresee the breakdown of the Soviet bloc), political scientists have become somewhat more modest about the predictive value of their theories, although they have not given up on it altogether.

In these circumstances, it is perhaps surprising that a small number of contemporary historians have attempted to utilize and discuss theoretical concepts on the basis of historical evidence and even (although to a much more limited extent) to contribute to ongoing debates in the social sciences. Milward's view of interdependence or integration as a 'national choice' resulting from particular domestic socioeconomic strategies of governments (Milward/Sørensen, 1993) was directed as much against neofunctionalism as against what he has repeatedly criticized as the normative 'historical teleologies' (Milward, 2002b, 18) that appear to interpret the integration process in an almost Hegelian way as a historical forward movement towards a better Europe. Up to a point, Milward and other 'revisionists' have built up neofunctionalism, and the works of early integration historians, such as Lipgens, as useful bogeymen. In many ways, their criticism is reminiscent of Hoffmann's very much earlier dissident realist attack on neofunctionalism. In reality, neofunctionalism and integration theory more generally have evolved and become more sophisticated since then, as has the historiography of the integration process. As Gillingham – another critic of neofunctionalism – has pointed out, moreover (Gillingham, 2003, 488), liberal intergovernmentalism, which shares many basic assumptions with the 'national choice' approach, also has a very limited explanatory value, especially (although not exclusively) for everyday integration outside the context of 'big bargains'.

In fact, the longstanding controversy between different variants of neofunctionalism, on the one hand, and dissident realism and liberal intergovernmentalism, on the other, drawn from the two main International Relations theories and used to explain the integration process, has long since become very sterile. It was massively disrupted by the claim of Comparative Politics scholars (Hix, 1994) that the EU has developed so many state-like features that International Relations theory can no longer adequately explain its everyday politics. For the time being, however, historians will probably find it difficult to connect with more recent trends in EU theory, for example the understanding of EU politics as 'multilevel governance', because the state-like features were still so much more limited before the Single European Act and the Maastricht Treaty brought about profound constitutional change. Nevertheless, they clearly need to be aware of these theoretical debates as they move forward in time in their archive-based research, and especially if they want to address issues spanning the entire postwar period up to the present. In contrast, historians should find it easier to relate to other recent theoretical developments, especially historical institutionalist and constructivist approaches to the EU, as these have an explicit historical dimension in their explanation of the growth of institutional forms, practices and preferences and the evolution and longevity of ideational factors such as ideas and norms, and their influence on policy outcomes. Kaiser (2001a) has applied such a framework to the comparative outline of the European policies of six EFTA 'newcomers', for example, rejecting a one-dimensional interpretation of fundamental integration decisions said to result from the rational choice of governments based on their material interests and domestic socioeconomic strategies. Interestingly, Sieglinde Gstöhl (2002), in her study of the long-term evolution of the European policies of Norway, Sweden and Switzerland, has recently come to similar conclusions from a political science perspective, although still within a rational choice framework.

Instead of contenting himself with the destruction (in his view) of neofunctionalist assumptions about European integration, replacing them with a 'national choice' analysis, Milward has in fact gone much further, by relating to EU research in the social sciences. In an extremely ambitious programmatic statement in the first issue of the *Journal of European Integration History* (Milward, 1995, 7), he predicted that integration history would in future develop 'its own theories and a research agenda which derives from them', and that it would even reverse 'the theoretical flow ... from historical research to the social sciences'. It seems that Milward believes that he himself has developed such a theory with his 'national choice' interpretation of European integration 'as twentieth-century allegiance' (Milward, 2002b, 16). Yet, Milward's interpretation includes no testable hypotheses, nor does it attempt to model the integration process or systematically deduce predictions about its future. It is certainly not a theory by the standards of the social sciences. In one of his recent contributions to the debate (2002b, 19), he has admitted that 'history is not a good predictor. It cannot reduce the world to a sufficiently small number of variables to turn theory into predictive models.' In the same chapter, however, he proceeds (Milward, 2002b, 23) to speculate about the formation of *institutionalized* regional 'blocs' in the EU and to predict that 'it seems highly unlikely that the role and powers of the European Parliament will be strengthened' in future treaty revisions. While the former was never on the agenda of institutional reform, the Constitutional Convention of 2002–03 swiftly refuted Milward's prediction by opting for the near-universalization of codecision making.

Against the background of such sobering experiences, most integration historians will continue to refuse to meet the social sciences on their own terms of theory formation and predictions of the future. Instead, they will concentrate on generating empirical evidence, which may not only be useful for the historical study of European integration after 1945, but also for testing theoretical hypotheses. In fact, many social scientists have become just as disillusioned with over-generalizing abstract theories and their predictive value as historians. They are again turning to the study of European transformations over time, in historical perspective, something that was strongly discouraged for a long time during the 'scientific' phase of the social sciences from the 1960s through to the 1980s. Despite the single-minded attempt to 'prove' his theory, and the resulting methodological problems that arise as a consequence, Moravcsik's study of 'big bargains' since the 1950s (Moravcsik, 1998b) is an encouraging example of the renewed interest of political scientists in the history of the EU.

Social scientists working in other EU-related fields have also expressed a strong interest in the historical evolution of current phenomena of European integration and greater interdisciplinary collaboration with contemporary historians. To give but two examples, David Marsh (1998, 192) has criticized network analysis (whether at the national or European level) for being too static and for not understanding long-term change well, which it can only manage with a more developed historical perspective. Similarly, Frank Schimmelfennig (2003a) has drawn attention to the short time horizon of recent socialization research that fails to establish the durability of norm internationalization. More generally, historical institutionalism and constructivism have developed a particularly keen interest in change over time, in dealing, for example, with institutional practices and the formation and possible Europeanization of norms. Analyses from these perspectives clearly necessitate a sophisticated understanding of historical change and more effective interdisciplinary collaboration. They also need what Milward (1992, 20) once called 'solid scraps of nutriment' in the form of actual empirical evidence – not least from historical sources and literature.

For contemporary historians, therefore, the challenge is not only to relate more closely to contemporary social science (theory) debates about the EU, in order to have an impact that goes beyond their growing but still very specialized historical subdiscipline. It is also to encourage the rediscovery of the importance of history and historical sources in the social sciences generally, and more specifically in EU research. There are signs in recent historical research on postwar Europe generally, and not just on national governmental policymaking and the supranational institutions, that the resulting intellectual cross-fertilization is already contributing to a greater openness, not only in relation to social science research, but also in supporting exciting trends in history as a discipline. These new advances could assist researchers in the specialized subdiscipline of integration history to break out of the intellectual and disciplinary ghetto, in which the traditional diplomatic history and economic history of the EU have manoeuvred themselves with their extremely state-centred agenda of 'national interest' formation and intergovernmental bargaining.

new historiographical trends

Within the intergovernmental framework, a strictly multilateral and multiarchival approach to studying major bargaining incidences, such as the negotiation of new treaties and crises in the integration process, would already mark a major step forward in the historiography of the EU. Crucially, it would help to overcome the narrow limits of the predominantly national approach to analysing government policy 'towards' Europe, facilitating the source-based historical reconstruction of the negotiation process, with its multiple interactions, possible changes in preferences, issue linkages and bargaining outcomes. For the study of European integration in the 1950s and 1960s, this kind of multilateral research has been feasible for some time because only very few sources (such as sections of Charles de Gaulle's presidential archives) still remain closed to historians. Archive-based multilateral research is very time-consuming, however, and also requires a reasonable reading knowledge of several Community languages and not just French, which was the language of most internal sources until the British accession.

The first multilateral study in this mode was by Hanns Jürgen Küsters (1982) on the formation of the EEC and Euratom from 1955 to 1957. This was mainly based on the private archives of Hans von der Groeben, one of two German EEC Commissioners from 1958 (the other being the Commission President, Walter Hallstein), who played a key role as a senior German official in the Economics Ministry during the preparation of the Spaak Report in the spring of 1956. Yet, Küsters did not have access to any government archives at the time, as these were only opened for the mid-1950s in the late 1980s and in the first half of the 1990s. Consequently the source base for his research was only marginally larger than in the older political science research. Despite a plethora of publications on national policymaking, interest group pressures and other aspects of the negotiation of the Rome Treaties, there is still no multiarchival study of the negotiations based on the available governmental sources.

Nevertheless, some important interpretative outlines have already emerged. Most historians now agree, for example, that the widely used term *rélance européenne* (European 'relaunch'), which suggests that the integration process was re-started with radical new ideas after the failure of the European Defence Community (EDC) in 1954, is inappropriate for the creation of the EEC. This is because many of the EEC's economic integration aspects had been discussed on and off for a long time and were only superseded by the politically much more controversial debate on the EDC (Milward, 1992); and also because the overriding national and transnational ideological preferences for the continuation of integration *in some form* not only survived EDC failure, but were even strengthened by it in some important ways (Kaiser, 2001b).

Historians have also demonstrated how political leaders managed to overcome even relatively cohesive interest group opposition, for example from the French Patronat, to the creation of a customs union without massive safeguards, or how they were able to use interest group divisions to their political advantage – for example in the case of the West German *Bundesverband der Deutschen Industrie (BDI)*, where many sectors of second generation industrialization were very keen on the British proposal for a free trade area, as a roof over the EEC or even as an alternative to the customs union plan. On the other hand, Thomas Rhenisch (1999, chapter 5) has shown in some detail how German industrialists exercised great influence on the national negotiating position on the setting of the future external tariffs at the micro level of policymaking. Once the EEC was established, moreover, domestically and transnationally organized agricultural interest groups exercised an enormous influence (through their links with Christian Democrat and Liberal parties and national governments) on the formation of the Common Agricultural Policy (CAP) in the 1960s (Knudsen, 2001a and 2001b).

It is not only the negotiation and subsequent revision of major treaties, which, compared to the everyday politics of the EU, get excessive attention in intergovernmentalist accounts of integration, but it is also the actual operation of the supranational institutions that have of late caught the attention of historians. Thus, Dirk Spierenburg and Raymond Poidevin (1994) have studied in some depth the formation of the ECSC and, more importantly, the operation of its High Authority in the first few years of its existence. Piers Ludlow (1997) has analysed the internal coordination within the EEC of policy towards the first British (and Danish, Irish and Norwegian) application for membership. Controversially, he has concluded that the British government might have negotiated its way into the EEC at that time, had it been prepared to make greater concessions *before* de Gaulle's domestic political position was strengthened by the parliamentary elections of November 1962. This runs against the conventional wisdom that de Gaulle was opposed in principle to any enlargement (at least before the finalization of the CAP) and would have rejected the British application anyway. It also conflicts with other accounts of the Franco-British relationship during 1961–63 (Clark, 1994; Kaiser, 1995), which suggest that no understanding was possible on a number of issues, and especially on the nuclear question.

Ludlow has also begun to study the 'empty chair' crisis of 1965–66 from a multilateral and multiarchival perspective. Thus far, most studies have either emphasized that de Gaulle wanted to prevent the transition to majority voting at the beginning of 1966 because it was incompatible with his vision of intergovernmental European cooperation, or that he was keen to extract more concessions from his partners, and especially West Germany, on the CAP before France might be outvoted by the other member states with the political support of the supranational Hallstein Commission. Ludlow (2001 and 1999) has shown this to be a largely artificial explanatory dichotomy.

The two issues were in reality very closely linked. He thus refutes the long-standing view that de Gaulle's policy was motivated by clear strategic political and foreign policy goals as well as Moravcsik's provocative claim (Moravcsik, 2000a and 2000b) that institutional and geopolitical preferences were entirely secondary to economic interests in French European policy in this period. In a similar vein, research has begun on the formation of EFTA (Malmborg and Laursen, 1995) and its own major crisis, the 'surcharge crisis' of 1964–65 (Kaiser, 2001c) which the British government started with its decision to impose a tariff surcharge (illegal under the EFTA Convention) in order to protect sterling from devaluation.

While multilateral and multiarchival studies of intergovernmental bargaining and the early operation of the European institutions has made significant progress – even outside the core field of EU integration (Varsori, 1988) – the historiography of the EU in a wider sense has also expanded into other areas that are not directly concerned with institutions and policymaking. One important initiative originated in France where, under the influence of the Annales School, the historiography of international relations has for some time been much less narrowly focused on interstate relations, moving beyond the study of the foreign policy formulation of strategic interests and the political and military relations of the great powers (Soutou, 2000). Several decades ago, in their perspective on international relations history, Pierre Renouvin and Jean-Baptiste Duroselle introduced the concept of *forces profondes*. These are the geographical conditions, economic performance, constitutional arrangements, and also collective perceptions of oneself and others that influence cross-border relations between states and peoples. Bridging the divide in EU historiography between a 'political' and an 'economic' paradigm, the French tradition has tried to combine various structural forces and the agency of individuals in studying cross-border relations.

French scholars working with René Girault and Robert Frank initiated a major long-term collaborative European (although French-financed and -dominated) research network on 'European identity' in the mid-1990s. Organized in subgroups, this network has produced a substantial number of edited volumes that contain interesting empirical research. Few of these volumes are coherent in themselves, however. Nor do they amount to a major collective statement on the importance of 'identity' for national policymaking, pressure groups, European institutions or the growth of European allegiance. The network has favoured a somewhat 'constructivist' approach, although many historians contributing to it are probably more influenced (if at all, and often in an unreflected manner) by the side-effects of the cultural and linguistic 'turns' in history as a discipline, not by contemporary International Relations debates. The network has looked at issues such as the collective memory of the two world wars and the importance of the 1956 Hungarian Revolution, the 1968 Prague Spring and the 1981 suppression of the Polish Solidarity movement for ethnic, regional, national and other part-identities, as well as the collective identity of Europeans as a whole. Some of the research has been EU-specific, such as the work of a subgroup on European institutions and identity. In a useful edited book, for example (Bitsch *et al.*, 1998), Ludlow analyses the identity policy of the Hallstein Commission in the 1960s, whose interest in European identity formation was institutional in that it sought to legitimize its own role by enlarging the scope of the integration process; Kaiser looks at the not very successful attempts by EFTA and its secretariat to foster a separate EFTA identity; and Bruno Riondel discusses the role of the European Parliament in identity formation.

Regarding research on identity, historians face similar theoretical and methodological problems as social scientists. However, they often have different conceptual understandings of what constitutes individual and collective identity and face difficulties establishing clear links between identities, policymaking and policy outcomes. Contemporary historians can probably make the greatest contribution through their research on public discourses on 'Europe' and on political strategies to construct and strengthen a European identity. Regarding the former, Mikael af Malmborg and Bo Stråth (2002) have coordinated a *longue durée* historical study of the different meanings of 'Europe' in national political discourses, which have in the past influenced national integration, imaginations of Europe and, as some contributors argue, policy choices of political actors in relation to European integration. While 'Europe' has in some cases appeared as a welcome solution to domestic (identity) problems, as in the case of transition Spain in the 1970s, for others it has served as a counterimage, as in Britain and Scandinavia, who have developed understandings of themselves and their identities in contrast to continental 'core Europe'. On the other hand, historical research on strategies for the 'construction' of European identity and social integration is only just beginning. Historians are well equipped for this kind of research drawing on their in-depth analysis of national integration strategies in the second half of the nineteenth century.

Identity research is part of an emerging and larger trend in historical research on postwar Europe which, often implicitly, aims at understanding the integration process as the slow, but noticeable formation of a European (political) society in which European institutions and policymaking are embedded. Another dimension of this larger trend is attempts to adapt the notion of 'public sphere' for the study of integration history (Kaelble, 2002), as well as a growing interest in its transnational dimension (Kaiser, 2005). The latter research relates to recent trends in the social sciences that favour the study of the evolving societal aspects of integration, for example in the form of transnational (elite) networks and cross-border socialization processes – with Europeanization as one possible outcome of such transnational contacts.

Contemporary history is able to generate empirical evidence on the historical growth of transnational relations. It can also develop new perspectives on transnationalism on the basis of a wider range of sources and by addressing a different set of questions on the past, derived from the social sciences and contemporary experience. Thus, recent research has established (Berghahn, 2001) how pervasive the financial support of the American Central Intelligence Agency and American philantropic institutions like the Ford Foundation was for almost all non-Communist 'pro-European' transnational organizations after 1945, including the *Ligue Européenne de Coopération Économique* (Dumoulin and Dutrieue, 1993) and the *Council of European Municipalities* (Gaspari, 2002). While such external support helped to strengthen the anti-Communist Left and the democratic Right in Western Europe after 1945, contemporary historians have also demonstrated that it did not lead in a straightforward way to the adoption of American ideas about integration, which remained fundamentally embedded in European traditions and values.

Through the analysis of networks of networks, historical research can also help to explain policy outcomes as a result of compromises reached by different advocacy coalitions. By the early 1950s, for example, Christian Democracy, heavy industry and some trade unions were largely united behind the aim of 'core Europe' integration. They were not strong enough politically to impose their vision, however, and had to agree to the suppression of cartels and a relatively liberal policy on external trade in order to reduce the opposition, or gain the support, of neoliberals, Socialist parties and trade unions, who were critical of an economically protectionist and/or Catholic-dominated continental Europe without Britain and Scandinavia. Historical research can also demonstrate the importance of transnational networks for making ideas and policy concepts hegemonic. To explain preference formation in a purely national context, as Craig Parsons does in his ideational (political science) interpretation of the origins of the ECSC in France (Parsons, 2002 and 2003), can be very misleading. Scope for 'entrepreneurial leadership' in domestic politics has often resulted from transnational coalition building and concertation, for example in the context of the close formal and informal cooperation of Christian Democrats before and after the creation of 'core Europe' (Gehler and Kaiser, 2004), providing a fascinating parallel with Christian Democrat policy coordination at the highest level with the aim of influencing the outcome of the Maastricht Treaty negotiations in the early 1990s (Johansson, 2002).

As in other areas, historical research can also make a major contribution to explaining change over time in and through the 'transnationalization' of (Western) Europe. Historians have shown, for example, that more formalized transnationalization preceded European institutionalization, as in the case of the interwar cooperation of trade unions (Pasture, 2001), cautioning against ascribing too much importance to the EU framework for inducing transnationalization without carefully assessing other possible motivating factors. Transnationalization is also characterized by long-term continuities even over what appear as major historical 'breaks', such as the Second World War, as the example of the very close collaboration of French and German steel producers from the 1930s to the 1950s shows (Berger, 1997; Bührer, 1999). On the other hand, European institutionalization has had an important influence on the formation of transnational communities and socialization processes through incentives to influence supranational policymaking, strengthening cross-border contacts below the EU level and intensifying communication flows. In the future, historical research might fruitfully analyse the extent to which competitive institutionalization in the EEC and EFTA influenced transnationalization processes and perhaps strengthened diverging ideas and preferences in European integration in the 1960s and beyond. In relating closely to social science research on transnationalization and Europeanization, such research will hopefully link ideas to transnational social actors and their political and other activities and, where appropriate, demonstrate their impact on policymaking at the EU and sub-EU levels in historical perspective, thereby avoiding the pitfalls of early integration history.

conclusion

In the past decade the historiography of European integration has expanded significantly. It is now almost as large, diverse and fragmented as political science research on the EU. In the 1970s, the historiography of integration started out as a history of the European 'idea'. Due to its methodological deficiencies and also as a result of the opening up of and subsequent concentration on government archives, it was quickly superseded by a traditional diplomatic history of interstate relations and bargaining in the 'realist' mode and (although to a much smaller degree) the economic history of integration. Research in this vein has demonstrated the continuing resilience of nation-states and attempts by governments to retain overall control of the integration process. Resulting from their interest in long-term change, most historians now doubt that the European 'project' was designed as an extremely radical departure to 'overcome' the nation-state. They also doubt that it succeeded in doing so, whether intended or otherwise, or that globalization has been destroying the nation-state since the 1960s (although it may well have undermined it very much).

The reaction to early integration history and its normative assumptions about the inherent goodness of (supranational) integration went too far, however. The belief in the moral superiority of supranational integration and institutions was replaced with an equally questionable belief in the internal coherence, external strength and natural legitimacy of national governments and rationally formulated 'national interests'. Only because they were documented in archives, every thought of even very minor officials in marginal ministries suddenly seemed very important, even though the officials concerned were most likely convinced that they were only state-employed slaves executing higher orders. In this way, much of the state-centred diplomatic and economic history of integration became (and still is, up to a point) a caricature of national and European politics. In reality, national governments have been fragmented in their European policies, as a result of coalition demands or regional interests. They have often been weak in devising coherent policies and in exerting strategic control over negotiating processes, so that transnational and other influences have also shaped their behaviour. Their policymaking has in many cases reflected pressure group interests more than some supposedly general 'national interest', and when they have defined 'interests', these have reflected cultural assumptions, historical experiences and ideological preferences as much as rationally defined material interests.

The more exciting historical research on European integration has therefore begun to refine the intergovernmental perspective through a more sophisticated understanding of the domestic politics of governmental policymaking on 'Europe', as well as through the multilateral and multiarchival reconstruction of interstate bargaining processes. At the same time, historical research has gone beyond what was in many ways a narrow and sterile intergovernmental perspective, to discuss, *inter alia*, questions of national and European identity and allegiance, and the historical growth of transnational political and societal structures in the EU. In this vein, contemporary historical research is moving from a narrow focus on nation-states, interstate bargaining, supranational institutions and policymaking towards a larger conception of integration as the (slow) formation of a (highly fragmented) European (political) society. It is on this basis, that the contemporary history of European integration may meet the more exciting recent social science research on the EU in the future.

12
knowing europe: metatheory and methodology in european union studies

joseph jupille

introduction[1]

While hardly the stuff of headlines, metatheory and methodology play crucial roles in any area of scholarly endeavour. Representing the architectural scaffolding upon and operational directives according to which inquiry unfolds, metatheory and methodology do much to guide and implement individual studies, to structure a literature as a whole, and to define and evaluate its contribution to our knowledge of the subject at hand. Arguably, this intrinsic importance is elevated in the field of EU Studies, characterized as it is by an institutionally-unique object of study, an interdisciplinary tradition and inclination, and a substantially transnational research community. In such a setting, the challenges of knowledge production are substantial and the stakes in reconciling work along other dimensions higher. Metatheory and methodology in EU Studies thus play a substantial part in determining the extent to which these characteristics of our research endeavour to serve as obstacles or as opportunities, sources of stress that will muddle our efforts or sources of richness that can be opportunistically leveraged better to know the EU.

This chapter considers the role played by metatheory and methodology in EU Studies, with an eye to the assessment of the current state of, and future prospects for, knowledge about this unique political system. It begins with some general comments on the nature of metatheory and methodology and their interrelationships. The subsequent section empirically outlines the metatheoretical and methodological contours of the field. The final section reflects on the implications of this examination for our present and future knowledge of the EU, and thereby of the state of EU Studies as a field of scholarly inquiry. I conclude that, while EU Studies does involve a considerable and possibly increasing amount of specialization or fragmentation, with appropriate care the field can nonetheless help us better to know Europe and its ongoing integration process.

metatheory and methodology: conceptual, logical and practical issues

Since metatheory and, traditionally to a lesser extent, methodology are not always transparently discussed in single studies or even in assessments of the field, it makes sense to begin by describing them in a basic way and to trace through some of their interrelationships. I begin with the sometimes thorny and abstract question of metatheory, proceeding to consider methodology (to which less space is devoted), and then move to the more synthetic question of their interrelations and roles. While some allusion is made to research practices in EU Studies, this section intends only to set the stage for the fuller empirical assessment that follows in the third section.

metatheory

Despite the amount of attention it receives, metatheory remains a muddled concept. The issues involved in discussions of metatheory are big and complex, and this chapter is not the place to try to iron them out. For definitional purposes, I will simply embrace Overton's relatively straightforward characterization of metatheory as 'a set of interlocking rules, principles, or a story (narrative), that both describes and prescribes what is acceptable and unacceptable as theory – the means of conceptual exploration – in a scientific discipline' (Overton, 1998). Viewed in this way, metatheory sets forth the basic architecture and requirements of scientific research, both guiding it and providing standards by which it can be assessed by members of the scholarly community.

We can imagine many, possibly an infinite number, of cuts at metatheory. Tipping my hat to prevailing practice (though perhaps not to prevailing definitions), I identify five metatheoretical dimensions along which much work in EU Studies can be organized. The first involves the question of ontology, the philosophical theory of being or existence. Does the world exist independently of agents' perception or experience of it (objectively), or does it only exist in virtue of these factors (subjectively)? Turning things around, are agents constituted by their natural environments or composition (materially), or only by virtue of their location within humanly created structures of experience and meaning (socially)? These questions are fundamental, and it seems clear that one's position on these issues goes some way toward guiding, in very basic ways, how one goes about doing scholarly work.

The second dimension involves the question of epistemology, the philosophical theory of knowing or knowledge. Can we attain independent knowledge of the world (for example, through empirical observation) that helps us validly to adjudicate truth-claims about it? Or is all observation 'theory-laden', such that claims are not subject to independent empirical verification? Stretching the philosophical meanings usually attached to these terms, those who believe the former commonly go under the label of 'positivists', while those assenting to the alternative view are known as 'post-positivists'. Here again, and in obvious ways, our perspectives on these issues, while quite possibly adopted uncritically, do much to structure the way we go about our business, including framing the questions we (can) ask and how we seek to answer them.

A third cut at metatheory is social theoretic and is embodied in the ongoing debate and discussion between rationalists and constructivists. This dimension is rather hard to characterize, often (though not necessarily always) tracking the ontological and epistemological distinctions drawn above, and I will be deliberately vague here. Characteristic questions include whether actors' identities and interests are endogenous to the phenomena we seek to explain, and whether logics of appropriateness or logics of consequences (March and Olsen, 1989) drive human action. Work positing endogenous identities and interests or examining actor constitution tends to receive the label 'constructivist', as does work emphasizing logics of appropriateness over logics of consequences (see Chapter 2 in this volume). Alternative answers tend to be labelled 'rationalist' (see Chapter 1 in this volume). These distinctions are far from clear, these choices often far from dichotomous, and there has been considerable confusion in the rationalist–constructivist debate in EU Studies (as elsewhere). I discuss some of this below. For now, it suffices to suggest that rational choice and constructivism are, indeed, metatheories following the definition given above, and that they matter in the ways already identified.

A fourth cut at metatheory is disciplinary. Different disciplines (for example, sociology, economics, political science) and subdisciplines (for example, Comparative Politics and International Relations within political science) often entail different architectures of inquiry. They provide different sets of received wisdoms (and empirical puzzles), leading questions and suggested answers. In that sense, while they are not usually recognized as such, disciplines and subfields, arguably, are metatheoretical. Given my own disciplinary background and the recent centrality of these specific issues, in considering how disciplinarity plays itself out in EU Studies I will focus primarily on the putative separation within political science of approaches drawing primarily from Comparative Politics and those drawing from International Relations.

A fifth cut at metatheory, rather vaguer and perhaps something of a catch-all, might be labelled 'scholarly style'.[2] Do we seek to examine general theories, or, spatially, temporally or otherwise, particular instances? As ever, our position on these issues will considerably shape our research, defining its scope, shaping the questions we ask and the answers that we seek (or feel able) to give, and so forth. I consider these questions in terms of 'grand' versus particularizing theory in the EU, also casting an eye toward a longstanding and recently reiterated claim to the effect that these map nicely onto a transatlantic (US–European) scholarly divide.

Given these various permutations of metatheory and their various levels of abstraction (some being more 'meta' than others), what can be said about how they relate to one another? Table 12.1 gives a sense of possibilities here, indicating whether, on the basis of a casual analysis, it seems logically possible to combine different metatheoretical elements, here sometimes construed rather specifically (for example, as Comparative Politics and International Relations, rather than as different disciplines), both to reflect my own areas of expertise and to make the assessment more concrete.

Table 12.1 Possibilities for metatheoretical combination

		Epistemological		Ontological		Social Theoretic		Sub-Disciplinary	Stylistic	
		Positivism	Post Positivism	Social	Material	RC	C	IR	General	Particular
Epistemological	Positivism Post-Positivism	No								
Ontological	Social	Yes	Yes							
	Material	Yes	Yes	No						
Social Theoretic	Rational Choice	Yes	No	No	Yes					
	Constructivism	Yes	Yes	Yes	No	Yes				
Sub-Disciplinary	IR	Yes	Yes	Yes	Yes	Yes	Yes			
	CP	Yes	Yes	Yes	Yes	Yes	Yes	Yes		
Stylistic	Generalizing	Yes	No	Yes	Yes	Yes	Yes	Yes	Yes	
	Particularizing	Yes	Yes	Yes	Yes	Yes	Yes	Yes	Yes	Yes

RC: Rational Choice; C: Constructivism; IR: International Relations; CP: Comparative Politics

The upshot of this presentation is that there are many permissible combinations of these different metatheoretical elements. The exceptions primarily involve the philosophical dimensions of epistemology and ontology, which is perhaps why so much heat is generated (and ink spilled) in discussions involving them. Briefly, it seems pretty straightforward to argue that positivism and post-positivism cannot be combined. The question of combining material and social ontologies frequently arises, and while there is considerable disagreement on this point (Keohane, 2000; Krasner, 2000; S. Smith, 2000; Wendt, 2000), I take the view that these are foundational claims which are, therefore, unalloyable. Turning to combinations among epistemology and ontology, rather than within each, I follow Wendt and others (Wendt, 1998b, 1999; Dessler, 1999) in arguing that no such combination is logically excluded (see Kratochwil and Ruggie, 1986, 764–6), including the most controversial combinations, social–positivist (as in Wendt's constructivism) and material–postpositivist (as in some Marxist and other critical theory). The other strikingly implausible combinations would marry constructivist social theory with a materialist ontology (seemingly impossible given the fact that constructivism is in part defined by a social ontology) and post-positivist epistemology with a generalizing scholarly style.

For the rest, I take the view that combination is logically possible, if sometimes seemingly unlikely (or, at least, not often attempted). Most controversially, this implies denying any fundamental incompatibility among any of the following putative alternatives: rational choice and constructivism; Comparative Politics and International Relations; and generalizing and particularizing styles. As to the first, I am on record as arguing that there is nothing fundamentally incompatible between rational choice theory and mainstream constructivism; indeed, with Caporaso and Checkel, I have proposed a number of concrete ways in which they might fruitfully be brought together (Jupille *et al.*, 2003; see also Aspinwall and Schneider, 2000; Wendt and Fearon, 2001). Similarly, considerable evidence exists to suggest that Comparative Politics and International Relations can be combined in ways that are often extremely fruitful, for example by bringing domestic political factors into explanations of international relations. Hix's (1994) claim that these fields approach EU Studies in different ways has been overtaken by convergence (Jupille and Caporaso, 1999) and by increasing scholarly promiscuity regarding the legitimate sources for ideas, models, and methods. Finally, much scholarly research combines both generalizing and particularizing goals: many of us seek both to understand the details of our empirical cases and to generalize beyond them to other times and other places. While there are sometimes depth-and-breadth trade-offs, these tend to involve resource scarcity (time, energy and money) rather than logical incompatibility.

Summarizing, metatheories are the general architectural principles guiding the conduct and assessment of scholarly inquiry. Seen as such, there are many, and perhaps an infinite number, of metatheories. I have chosen to focus on five of these, to present their basic contours and to assess their interrelations. While the story here is far from 'anything goes', it seems quite plausible to suggest that many metatheoretical combinations are logically permissible, with some quite misunderstood and a good number grossly underexploited. In practice, of course, much of this only plays itself out in specific studies and literatures, which are also substantially shaped by methodological factors. I consider these next.

methodology

The concept of methodology, while itself problematic and contested, seems relatively easier to grasp, and hence demands less space here. Overton (1998) defines methodology as a set of interlocking rules, principles, or a story, that describes and prescribes the means of observational exploration in a scientific discipline. I will employ 'methodology' and 'methods' interchangeably, and use them to refer to a class of phenomena falling somewhere between metatheory (for example, positivist epistemology) and the hands-on 'tools' (for example, OLS regression[3]) with which inquiry is conducted. Viewed in this way, there are many different methodologies. Drawing from recent surveys in American political science (Pion-Berlin and Cleary, forthcoming 2005; Bennett *et al*., 2003), I focus on three types: qualitative, statistical, and formal, presented here in no particular order. While relatively pure applications are straightforward to identify, borderline and mixed approaches pose some challenges in practice, which I will discuss in the third section below. The overall goal here is to provide a workable framework, rather than a perfect one, so for now I place greater emphasis on clear definitions and 'ideal types'.[4]

Qualitative methodology describes work that relies on verbal (as opposed to symbolic or mathematical) presentation and primarily (though not exclusively) on non-numerical data, with numerical data used descriptively rather than inferentially. This definition unifies some very different tools with very different metatheoretical underpinnings, ranging from ethnomethodology, semiotic analysis, dramaturgical analysis, deconstruction, discourse and narrative analysis, and related methods (usually associated with post-positivism) to case study methods and small-N analysis (usually associated with positivism).

Statistical methodology differs from qualitative primarily in the greater emphasis on numbers and on the different uses to which they are put. I consider as statistical all works that employ inferential statistics, that is, quantitative use of sample data allowing generalizations to populations. This category 'begins' with correlational analysis (a borderline case) and anything reporting statistical significance levels, continues through widely used techniques, such as regression analysis, and extends to the many more sophisticated econometric tools finding use in the literature.

Formal methodology involves the use of symbolic logic or, in practice, mathematical models. Deductive character does not, in my view, define formal methods, since other methodologies can also operate by reasoning logically from first principles to entailed consequences. The key criterion is the language (symbolic/mathematical as opposed to verbal) in which arguments are presented.

Familiar tools associated with formal methods include the many forms of game theory, decision theory, computational models, spatial analysis, voting power analysis, and so forth.

Combining methodologies poses few of the problems encountered in potentially combining metatheories. There are no logical incompatibilities involved, though here too resource constraints, such as our willingness to invest time in learning new methods, come into play. But all such combinations, including a combination of all three, seem possible. What is more, given their different foci and the benefits of 'triangulation', multimethodological work often proves particularly informative. To be sure, EU Studies involves many debates over method. But these usually operate *within* metatheoretical (especially epistemological) frameworks, rather than *among* them, which takes some of the heat out of methodological discussions.

relating metatheory and methodology

Metatheory and methodology do not map cleanly onto each other, in the sense that there exist determinative correspondences between the former and the latter. There do seem to exist some elective affinities and aversions, however. Table 12.2 provides one view of how metatheory and methodology have tended to be combined in EU Studies.

Table 12.2   Practical Metatheoretical-Methodological Combinations

			Methodological Dimension		
			Qualitative	Statistical	Formal
Metatheoretical Dimension	Epistemological	Positivist	Many	Many	Many
		Post-Positivist	Many	None	None
	Ontological	Social	Many	Few	Few
		Material	Many	Many	Many
	Social Theoretic	Rational Choice	Many	Many	Many
		Constructivism	Many	Few	Few
	Subdisciplinary	Comparative	Many	Many	Many
		International	Many	Many	Many
	Scholarly Stylistic	Generalizing	Many	Many	Many
		Particularizing	Many	None	Few

In Table 12.2 individual cell values should be read as answers to the question 'how many works in EU Studies have undertaken this combination?' The story told here, like the one told above about intra-metatheoretical combinations, is that metatheoretical stances tend not to preclude any particular methodological approach. The exceptions are unsurprising: it is hard to conceive of work done within a post-positivist epistemology using statistical methods, since these latter rest squarely on the contested notion that observation and testing produce knowledge. Similarly, a particularizing style and statistical methods seem incompatible, since the very definition of statistics employed here involves inference, the generalization from samples to populations. The dearth of post-positivist formal modelling does not seem logically entailed; formal modelling, taken on its own, has little to say about our ability to learn from empirical examination, and so does not necessarily run afoul of post-positivist denials of that possibility. But that doesn't make this lacuna surprising. They likely resist each other because post-positivist epistemology tends, in practice (though not of logical necessity), to go hand-in-hand with an anti-deterministic subjectivist ontology, while formal modelling tends, in practice (though not of necessity), to employ deductive (closed and deterministic) reasoning about the world, itself presumed to operate in a lawlike way.

Based on this analysis, some counter-intuitive combinations have been employed. Consider the observation that some work exists that combines a social ontology (or constructivist social theory) with statistical and formal methods. Within EU Studies, Beyers and Dierickx (1998), Egeberg (1999), and Trondal (2002) provide the closest examples in terms of statistics, though they do not self-consciously identify as constructivists.[5] Regarding formal constructivism, Cederman's (1997) computational simulation approach to national identity formation, while not applied to the EU *per se*, suggests the fruitfulness of work marrying constructivist social theory with formal methods. Finally, the *a priori* implausible combination of particularizing style with formal methods finds expression in 'analytic narratives', which McLean (2003) has argued have come to be employed (if neither self-consciously nor formally) in EU Studies.

Based on the foregoing, numerous metatheories and methodologies, as well as numerous combinations of each and both, seem logically permissible and workable in practice. EU Studies, then, operates within a metatheoretically and methodologically permissive environment within which a thousand flowers might bloom. While allusions to past and current practice have been made in passing, it now seems appropriate to consider metatheory and methodology in the actual research practices of EU Studies. The next section undertakes this empirical examination.

metatheory, methodology and the conduct of eu studies

If generic discussion of metatheory and methodology raises abstract and thorny conceptual problems, empirical assessment introduces additional difficulties that should be addressed from the outset. To begin with, what follows reflects my own background, constraints and biases. Thus, I focus on English-language scholarship, especially published in journals, with at least some content currently available electronically, and mainly those with a substantial political science, often, mainstream American political science, component. My own positivism and soft rationalism also surely colour my knowledge and judgements of different approaches. My intent is not in any way to slight excluded work, for example, work published in non-English language journals, in journals aimed at other disciplines (for example, sociology, law and economics) or national audiences, or operating under different metatheoretical auspices. I will simply try to cover what strike me as some of the major sources that fall somewhere within my frame of reference. As possible I will try to blend narrative accounts and more narrowly-cast quantitative evidence, beginning with metatheory and moving on to methodology. The goal throughout is not to provide a complete account, but an illustrative one, with an eye not on testing claims, but on documenting areas and dynamics of metatheoretical and methodological divergence and convergence.

metatheoretical practices in eu studies

Beginning with metatheory, it seems safe to say that for a very long time conscious invocations of this concept as currently used – primarily in International Relations, and usually surrounding philosophical questions of epistemology and ontology and/or social theoretic questions of rational choice and constructivism – scarcely arose within the main EU Studies journal outlets (*International Organization* and *Journal of Common Market Studies*). Other outlets might well have been preoccupied with these questions; I doubt that this was the case at least through the 1970s, but I cannot be sure. But the longstanding paucity of explicit metatheory-qua-philosophy and metatheory-qua-social theory does not mean that other metatheoretical dimensions were not in play.

scholarly style

Scholarly-stylistic questions have long played a significant role in EU Studies. In the EU Studies context, 'scholarly style' refers primarily to the question of 'grand' (generalizing) theory versus concrete/grounded/particularizing theory, which is sometimes assimilated to American and European stylistic differences.[6] The 1950s and 1960s represented a first heyday of 'grand theory' in EU Studies. Karl Deutsch *et al.*'s (1957) transactionalism, Ernst Haas's (1958, 1961) neofunctionalism, and Stanley Hoffmann's (1966) intergovernmentalism all represented general attempts at classifying and explaining European integration.[7]

Deutsch offered a sweeping historical perspective, assimilating integration to general theories of national and supranational community formation. Haas provided a set of broad scale claims about elite activation, supranational entrepreneurship, and institutional and attitudinal integration as symptoms of life in advanced capitalist societies. Hoffmann assimilated the European project to the venerable tradition of International Relations realism, which traces its roots back to Thucydides and through the intervening centuries. To be sure, and to say the least, each 'knew his brief' in its historic and contemporary detail, showing acute perceptiveness about the specifics of the European case. But each invoked particulars within general, even grandiose frameworks, and, with varying degrees of explicitness, generalizable explanation was clearly the style of choice.

For various reasons, internal and external to each theory (see, for example, Caporaso, 1998), each of these grand theories passed more or less into desuetude in the 1970s. Paralleling the post-Luxembourg Compromise 'europessimism' and the post-oil shock 'eurosclerosis' on the ground in Europe, came the so-called 'Dark Ages' for integration theory in the academy, with relatively less (in the US at least) and seemingly less ambitious approaches to EU Studies holding sway (Keohane and Hoffmann, 1991, 8; cited in Caporaso and Keeler, 1995, 37, fn 16). As Smith and Ray (1993) and Caporaso and Keeler (1995) have argued, though, much excellent work was being done during this 'doldrums era'. With some exceptions (for example, surrounding the application of confederalist and federalist ideas (Taylor, 1975), applications of Marxist theory (Cocks, 1980), this work was simply less grandiose, often even less self-consciously theoretical. The pendulum had swung from generalizing to relatively particularizing styles.

The *relance* of the Community from the mid-1980s generated a new wave of grand theoretical work from the late 1980s. Sandholtz and Zysman (1989), Tranholm-Mikkelsen (1991) and others revived neofunctionalism in order to explain the Single European Act (SEA), while Burley and Mattli (1993) re-oriented the framework to explain the striking and ongoing process of legal integration in Europe. Moravcsik updated and partly reformulated intergovernmental theory, first giving it a modern political economy grounding in a liberal account of state preference formation and a negotiation theoretic account of bargaining (Moravcsik 1991, 1993), and ultimately adding a sophisticated theory of institutional choice (Moravcsik, 1998a), all with an eye on the EU's 'grand bargains' and their status as theoretically generic instances of rational international cooperation. Even transactionalism, long out of style, was updated, fused with neofunctionalist themes, and developed in Stone Sweet's expansive account of constitutionalization (Stone Sweet and Brunell, 1998). Grand theory was back.

This seems as good a place as any to address directly the longstanding impression that 'grand theory' has been the primary stomping grounds of American (or US-based) theorists, with Europeans focusing on more grounded and concrete applications. Most recently, Verdun (2003) has articulated this view and explored ways of bridging the putative gap between theoretically-minded and generalizing Americans and case-study-oriented and particularizing Europeans. Her purpose there is avowedly provocative, but it gives expression to a longstanding sense among many on both sides of the Atlantic (see Keeler, 2005). To what extent is this dichotomy a valid one?

To get at this question, I draw a distinction between working on the substance of the EU and invoking 'grand theoretical' language. The development of a general theory of regional integration has long served as the lodestar of grand theory in EU Studies. And while, by definition for empirical works considered here, this often went hand-in-hand with a focus on Europe, these two enterprises also moved in partly separate orbits. It seems possible that we can get at the putative regional difference by looking for differences in the propensity to focus on theory, relative to the propensity to focus on regional empirics. With this in mind, I conducted a JSTOR search of selected leading political science journals for references to the EU in article titles[8] that yielded 102 articles from 1949 to 2000. I then conducted a second search on the same sample of journals, across the same time period, on the term 'regional integration theory' within full article text.

The result is striking. Articles in US-based journals accounted for 59 per cent of the substantive EU focus, those in European journals for 41 per cent. But US-based journals contributed 58 out of 59 references to 'regional integration theory', 98 per cent, as compared to one reference (2 per cent) from the European journals. The substantive coverage provides the baseline here, and controlling for it eliminates any bias that might exist due to the fact that US journals are overrepresented within JSTOR. We will have occasion to revisit this question briefly in the next section on methodology, but for now it seems sensible to proceed as if scholarly styles do differ on opposite sides of the Atlantic.

Returning to the narrative, the reverberations of the EU's *relance* and its ongoing development continue to incite generalizing, if slightly less grand, theoretical work. This is so voluminous that only a flavour can be given here. Marks has articulated and subsequently developed a theory of 'multi-level governance', aimed at explaining political and institutional dynamics in compound polities (Marks *et al.*, 1996; Marks and Hooghe, 2001, see Chapter 5 in this volume). The rise of the 'new institutionalism' has generated a spate of work, including rationalist, rationalist-historical, sociological-historical and sociological accounts (Garrett and Tsebelis, 2001; Pierson, 1996; Armstrong and Bulmer, 1998; March and Olsen, 1998, see Chapters 2 and 3 in this volume), some of it quite synthetic and 'grand' in aspiration. Ongoing work on federalism (Sbragia, 1993; Kelemen, 2004), consociationalism (Taylor, 1991; Chryssochoou, 1995), and vast bodies of newer work on Europeanization (Cowles *et al.*, 2001, see Chapter 4 in this volume), governance (Hix, 1998; Jachtenfuchs, 2001), and democracy, give the sense that, while grand theory may no longer be the order of the day, generalizing theory remains a central metatheoretical commitment in EU Studies, peacefully coexisting with huge amounts of more particularizing work.

philosophy/social theory

The same cannot necessarily be said of the often related epistemological (positivist–postpositivist), ontological (social–materialist), and social-theoretic (rationalist–constructivist) dimensions of metatheory. Two problems arise in trying to narrate developments in these areas. First, scholars are not always explicit about these metatheoretical commitments, which makes it hard to identify what is on offer, what is being rejected, and what is at stake. Second, because of this, and because these metatheoretical categories are correlated with each other, the debates are often confusing and multi-stranded, with the role played by different metatheoretical elements difficult to disentangle. Indeed, if there were to be a thesis for this part of the chapter, it would be precisely that metatheoretical confusion in these areas has been rampant in EU Studies, and that we need to disentangle the various elements before we can identify where agreement can and cannot be reached and how the existence of alternative viewpoints impacts the collective literature. I will illustrate these points with reference to the rationalist–constructivist distinction, where I think considerable progress has been made.[9]

As noted above, both rationalism (rational choice) and constructivism are metatheories, in that they provide broad architectures for social inquiry. Each framework reduces to a few pretty simple propositions. Rational choice 'theory' assumes that actors, whose identities and interests tend to be given rather than theorized, operate according to a consequentialist logic, whereby they seek to get as much of what they want as they can, given the constraints within which they must operate. Constructivism evinces a more thoroughgoing concern for the origins of actors' identities and interests, as these are caused or constituted, and tends to postulate an appropriateness logic, whereby actors follow normative scripts regarding situationally-legitimate behaviour. In rational choice, actors ask themselves 'what do I want, and how can I get it?', while in constructivism they ask themselves 'who am I, and what should I do?' These alternative viewpoints obviously go some way toward structuring how scholars approach their work.

In much of the early discussion of these issues, these alternatives were posed in stark opposition to each other, and little was done to disentangle the other metatheoretical dimensions often unwittingly smuggled in. In my view this is changing. We see a clear development in EU Studies from 'dining at separate tables' (Aspinwall and Schneider, 2000) to dialogue, not in the 'pie in the sky' sense but, rightly and importantly, in the sense of identifying limits. I doubt that we will ever reconcile rival epistemological commitments, for example, and recognizing this clears the way for more informative and fruitful discussion where epistemology is not at stake. Post-positivists can have their discussions and positivists can have theirs, the latter taking place both within social theoretic traditions (for example, Jørgensen, 1997; Christiansen *et al.*, 2001; Moser *et al.*, 2000) and among them (for example, Schneider and Aspinwall, 2001; Checkel and Moravcsik, 2001; Jupille *et al.*, 2003).

subdisciplinary

Potentially weaving in and out of all of this is the question of disciplines and fields – here, Comparative Politics and International Relations – as metatheories. While not thinking in terms of metatheory, Hix (1994) famously argued that Comparative Politics and International Relations pursued separate projects, the first, (less privileged, perhaps because less grand-theoretical in practice) focusing on synchronic (everyday) 'politics' and the second, hegemonic, focusing on diachronic (over-time) 'integration'. They should, his argument implied, be considered 'separate but equal' approaches to knowing the EU and its development (see also Hix, 1996; Hurrell and Menon, 1996; Risse-Kappen, 1996).

My own view, already articulated elsewhere (Jupille and Caporaso, 1999), is that Hix's call for separate but equal fields was misguided, insofar as a series of trends promising to bridge the 'great divide' between domestic and international politics (Caporaso, 1997) was already well underway. It would be perverse if the erosion of such disciplinary boundaries were to be resisted in EU Studies, the object of study of which seems precisely to fall in the interstices of the two subfields! The question remains, though, of how this metatheoretical dimension has played itself out in EU Studies. In order to assess this, I compiled data on EU articles published in a sample of US-based journals whose field identities are relatively well-established: *International Organization* and *International Studies Quarterly* on the International Relations side; and *Comparative Politics* and *Comparative Political Studies* on the Comparative Politics side.[10] Figure 12.1 displays publication trends from 1968 (when both *Comparative Politics* and *Comparative Political Studies* began publication) through to mid-2003.

These trends support three observations. First, International Relations did indeed dominate US-published scholarship on the EU, at least into the 1980s. Second, relatively little EU work of any sort was being published in the US throughout the 1980s. Third, Comparative Politics and International Relations did, apparently, become more or less equal partners in the US-based EU Studies enterprise around the mid-1990s. This might reflect the catalysing effect of Hix's comparativist call-to-arms, or, observationally equivalently, it might reflect trends in the fields themselves and on-the-ground in the EU. Whether they continue to work in separate domains cannot really be addressed here, though I suspect that much cross-field reading and research is being done. What does seem clear is that the subdisciplinary balance of the field has equalized considerably.

What emerges from this portrayal of metatheoretical practice in EU Studies?

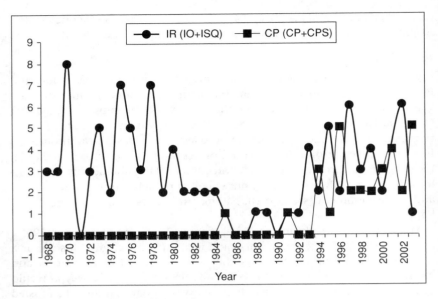

Figure 12.1   EU articles in selected US subfield journals, 1968–2003

The facile answer is that metatheoretical coherence coexists with metatheoretical diversity. But I think we can say slightly more than that. Starting from the top and summarizing briefly, I see neither the need nor the prospect for epistemological convergence, and view continuing inter-epistemological debate as a fruitless waste of time. Ontology seems to provide more fertile dialogical ground, with much terrain to till in terms of the balance between material and social factors as constitutive factors and causal forces in the EU. For the rest, the landscape is, as implied in the second section above, substantially open, with exciting possibilities for bridging work within and across the stylistic, social-theoretic, and disciplinary dimensions. Of course, how this work plays itself out will more visibly reflect methodological practices in EU Studies, to the consideration of which I now turn.

methodological practices in eu studies

EU Studies has always been a multi-methodological enterprise, as the empirics will shortly show. But presenting this aspect of the field raises its own problems, primarily of an operational nature. Above I defined three commonly used categories of methods: qualitative, statistical, and formal. However widely used they may be, these definitions are not without their weaknesses, and these weaknesses cascade down from concept to operationalization, that is, how one goes about measuring methodological practices. It thus makes sense to be as clear as possible from the start about how these will be assessed.

preliminaries

Let me begin by discussing the coding of methodologies. Work will be categorized as 'qualitative' when it relies on verbal (as opposed to symbolic) argumentation and when evidence takes primarily a verbal form. Work that includes quantitative (numerical) evidence will be classified as 'qualitative' so long as the quantities are used primarily descriptively rather than inferentially. Thus, I code as qualitative all of those articles that include neither formal models nor inferential statistics. Marginal cases here involve works that include extensive but descriptive use of numerical data such as frequencies, time-trends, and descriptive indices, all of which I retain within the qualitative category. Use of inferential statistics (roughly, anything reporting significance levels) triggers categorization as 'quantitative', even if the bulk of the evidence takes verbal form. Similarly, use of symbolic logic/mathematical models, including economic tools such as production functions and partial equilibrium models, will trigger categorization as 'formal', regardless of other methodological content.

The key problems arise where individual pieces of scholarship employ multiple methods, as so many seem increasingly to do. The 'trigger' coding rule solves this dilemma operationally, but only at the price of two sorts of problems.

First, this approach can easily miss the methodological 'thrust' of a given piece of research. A single p-value or a single spatial model, even coming on the heels of many pages of case study material, for example, would, by this approach, respectively trigger the 'statistical' and 'formal' codings. Second, this approach implies a methodological hierarchy, from qualitative to statistical to formal, that seems seductive (and is doubtless held by some), but that I forcefully reject. Learning of a foreign language, often a precondition to good qualitative work, strikes me as no less demanding than learning statistical techniques; statistical methods seem no less demanding than formal ones. The 'rigour' of scholarly work, in my view, does not depend upon the language in which arguments are expressed or the use to which numbers may or may not be put. All methodological categories can include both rigorous and sloppy applications.

The obvious alternative would be to code all of the possible combinations. This would seem to solve the 'implied hierarchy' problem, but it leaves the 'thrust' problem intact, and in any case the only meaningfully new category (qualitative + statistical + formal) occurs extremely rarely in EU Studies practice (9 of 1,223 articles coded for methods, 0.7 per cent, of that total).[11] In short, given the ubiquity of verbal presentation, attempting thoroughly to eliminate the 'thrust' problem, by judging what the 'principal method' used is, would substitute coder discretion, at great additional cost and possible risk, with minimal benefits, for the implication of a hierarchy of methods. Given these tradeoffs, and given an aspiration for workability and indicativeness rather than (illusive) perfection, I adopt the trigger coding strategy.

Turning briefly to content, I had to decide whether articles did or did not fall within the ambit of EU Studies. In making this (necessarily subjective) determination, I first inspected article titles, turning to abstracts and main bodies if there were questions. I also included general articles on regional integration theory in the 'EU Studies' category, though not those that preponderantly examined integration schemes in other parts of the world. A handful of borderline cases arose, but they did so infrequently and randomly enough that I do not suspect systematic bias.

With all of this said, a few words about the actual data. I rely on articles published in journals with substantial EU content. Three obvious inclusions are what I consider to be the main EU Studies journals for political scientists: *Journal of Common Market Studies*, *Journal of European Public Policy* and *European Union Politics*. The other obvious choice was *International Organization*, since it has a long history of publishing EU-relevant articles, and since I thought it important, given some of my descriptive aims, to include a US-based journal. The final journal, chosen primarily because it represents the European analogue to *International Organization* (as an International Relations rather than EU journal) is *European Journal of International Relations*. I provide some general information about each source in Table 12.3.

Table 12.3 Journals surveyed

Journal	Acronym	Location	Years	N articles	N EU articles	EU content
European Journal of International Relations	EJIR	Europe	1995–2003	148	22	14.9%
European Union Politics	EUP	Europe	2000–2003	70	53	75.7%
International Organization[a]	IO	US	1947–2003	1398	102	7.3%
Journal of Common Market Studies[b]	JCMS	Europe	1962–2003	880	752	85.5%
Journal of European Public Policy	JEPP	Europe	1994–2003	357	302	84.6%
Totals[c]				2853	1231	43.1%

Notes: [a] missing v.57 n.3 ; *IO* activities excluded; [b] missing v.20 n.4 ; annuals excluded; [c] 8 of 1231 not coded for methods

patterns of methodological practices in eu studies

Each of the three coded methods has found longstanding (if sometimes uneven) application in EU Studies. Qualitative methods dominate this sample, characterizing 85 per cent of all articles surveyed versus 10 per cent for statistical methods and 5 per cent for formal. While I have not carefully scrutinized specific tools used, it seems clear that, in the qualitative category, a wide range, including many of those listed in the second section above, have been employed, cutting across all of the major metatheoretical dimensions identified. Statistical and formal methodologists have used similarly broad ranges of tools. EU Studies demonstrates broad methodological openness along just about any axis – theoretical, substantive, historical, for example – that one might wish to identify. Each method demonstrates wide applicability across theoretical, substantive, and other concerns. Given space constraints, I cannot even begin to attempt a survey, even of the less widely used statistical and formal methods. Suffice it to say that just about every aspect of the EU that one might imagine has probably been approached using all three of the methodologies on which I focus. To focus the analysis, let me concentrate on two cuts at methodological practice in the EU, looking at distributions across the main journals (and the parts of the world in which they are published) and over time.

Figure 12.2 illustrates the distribution of different methodologies within EU work published in the five journals that I have surveyed.

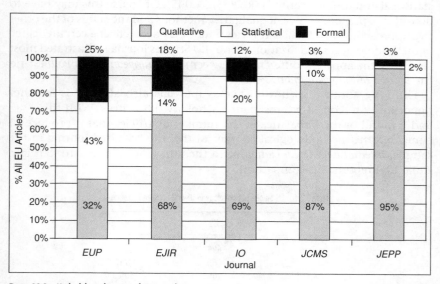

Figure 12.2   Methodological content of EU journals

A number of sometimes surprising observations suggest themselves. First, unsurprisingly, qualitative methodologies dominate overall and characterize sizeable majorities of the work published in all but *European Union Politics*. Second, though, a surprising picture of methodological pluralism emerges from this distribution. If by 'pluralism' one intends 'balance', *European Union Politics* comes out as the most pluralistic of the sampled journals, with roughly similar proportions of work done using qualitative, statistical, and formal methods. (It should be noted that most of the qualitative work appears in the journal's 'forum section', rather than in stand-alone articles.)

At the other extreme, the *Journal of European Public Policy* has been almost mono-methodological, with 95 per cent of its articles employing qualitative methods, though my sense in surveying the journal is that this tendency has softened somewhat in the last few years. Third, perhaps the most surprising result for me was the relatively high frequency of formal models in *European Journal of International Relations*, widely viewed as a bastion of post-positivist epistemology and constructivist social theory. Fourth, while not illustrated in the figure or elsewhere, my impression is that methodological content varies over time within many of the specific journals, possibly as a function of editorial priorities. Future work testing this conjecture might prove interesting. Fifth, and possibly unsurprisingly, correlating the proportions of each journal devoted to each of the three methods reveals strong negative and statistically significant relationships between both qualitative and statistical (R=–.983, p=.003) and qualitative and formal (R=–.934, p=.02) methods, but not between statistical and formal methods (R=.855, p=.065). Of course this may have to do with the preponderance of qualitative methods and the status of the other two approaches as residual categories. But it may also reflect a certain degree of methodological specialization within EU Studies journals, illustrated most clearly by the apparent differences between, say, *European Union Politics* and the *Journal of European Public Policy*.

Thinking about distribution across journals also affords us another opportunity to consider transatlantic scholarly differences. With this goal, and mindful of the imbalance in the number of articles that it produces, I compared the methodological content of the one US-based journal in the sample, *International Organization*, with the other four (European) journals. Table 12.4 reports this comparison.

Table 12.4   EU Studies methodology in US and European journals

	US	European
Qualitative	69%	86%
	(70)	(975)
Statistical	20%	10%
	(20)	(108)
Formal	12%	4%
	(12)	(46)

There are at least two ways of interpreting these figures. On one reading, US and European journals do indeed publish different kinds of work: *International Organization* publishes twice as many statistical articles as its European counterparts, in terms of the proportion of all work appearing in its pages, and three times as many formal articles. On a second reading, quite the contrary, what stands out is just how similar these profiles are, with the preponderance of work in EU Studies employing qualitative methods, regardless of the side of the Atlantic on which it is published. Indeed, knowing whether an article appeared in US-based *International Organization* or one of the European journals would not help us better to predict what methodology it uses, since our best guess would be 'qualitative' in either case (Goodman and Kruskal's $\lambda = 0$).

A couple of conclusions emerge from all of this. First, if it seems true that articles appearing in American journals are more preoccupied with general theory than are those appearing in European journals, this metatheoretical 'scholarly style' does not filter down to the level of methodology. Combining the two tables suggests that both more generalizing and more particularizing work can employ the full range of available methodologies. Second, in terms of methodology, the very concept of a 'European approach' seems overdrawn. One would be hard pressed to construct a narrative assimilating *European Union Politics* and the *Journal of European Public Policy* to a coherent 'European' approach to EU Studies.

Let me turn, finally, to the larger historical picture. How have the methodological practices of EU Studies changed over the five-plus decades of the field's existence? Figure 12. 3 illustrates these trends.

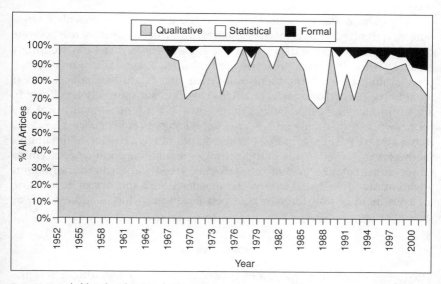

Figure 12.3   Methodological trends in EU Studies, 1952–2002

Let me again make just a few points about this 'big picture' perspective. First, until the mid-1960s, EU Studies exclusively employed qualitative methods.

Whether the change has to do with the rise of behavioural approaches to political science, the emergence of *Journal of Common Market Studies* (which published a certain number of econometric and formal articles from very early on), or a combination of the two, the methodological uniformity of these early years is striking. Second, and somewhat ironically, substantial inflections of statistical methods characterized both the initial serious troubles with the Community and with integration theory (late 1960s–early 1970s) and the relaunch of both from about the mid-1980s into the first part of the 1990s.

Third, the relative preponderance of qualitative methods during the period from around 1973 to around 1985 may go some way toward explaining why American observers, perhaps unimpressed with the 'scientific' merits of qualitative methods, have viewed this period as dark times for EU Studies. Fourth, it is worth noting that, while formal methods long represented occasional economist-driven blips on the EU Studies radar, trends over the last decade-and-a-half seem to suggest that that methodology is here to stay. Finally, correlating methodological content across time gives additional insight into the relationships among alternative approaches. Statistical and formal work give even less hint of a relationship from this perspective (R=.117, p=.412), and while statistical and qualitative methods maintain a strong negative relationship (R=−.961, p<.000), the rivalry between qualitative and formal methods, while still substantial, seems rather less acute (R=−.389, p=.005).

Briefly summarizing the foregoing, EU Studies seems to provide a large, but not unlimitedly large, methodological tent. True, qualitative methods are overwhelmingly preponderant. But the rise of new journals has seemingly created a situation wherein some methodological specialization is taking place around a core component of journals that might be characterized as 'qualitative plus'. Concretely, qualitative work is substantially less likely to appear in *European Union Politics* than in the other journals, statistical and formal work substantially more so; *Journal of European Public Policy* is far closer to the average in these respects, but also stands out as a bastion of qualitative methodology. Whether any of these things – qualitative dominance, seeming entrenchment of non-qualitative approaches, growing specialization and some apparent methodological rivalry – is considered desirable or not depends on an assessment of how knowledge is best produced, which I address by way of conclusion.

conclusion

The foregoing empirics paint a picture of considerable metatheoretical and methodological diversity in EU Studies. I have suggested that both metatheory and methodology represent compound categories that can be, and in practice are, combined in many different ways to produce a collective product – the field under consideration – capable of addressing a huge number of important questions in a variety of ways. It seems entirely fitting that a polity as diverse and complex as the EU should give rise to a scholarly product to match it. Generalities aside, though, this picture of metatheoretical and methodological diversity coexisting with aspects of rivalry and contestation should give us pause, and lead us to consider how the ways in which we organize our work enable us and others better to know its object of study. In short, what should our endeavour look like if we are individually and collectively to know Europe?

Let me frame this reflection by asking the following: what level of scholarly consensus (metatheoretical, theoretical, methodological, etc.) is optimal for the production of knowledge? This is a difficult question that raises a number of huge and complicated issues. The generic answer seems to be something along the lines of 'enough so that we can understand each other, but not so much that criticism withers and groupthink emerges'. That is, we require both certain shared foundations, vocabularies and standards of assessment, à la Kuhnian normal scientists, and the ability to think critically along Popperian lines. But these are platitudinous responses to serious questions, and we need to think more seriously, in ways that some American political scientists[12] and a transnational community of International Relations theorists are thinking, for example, about how these goals can be achieved. Something must generate the fruitful parabolic function linking excessively low and excessively high levels of scholarly consensus with low levels of knowledge production, and interim ranges of consensus, yielding higher knowledge payoffs.

My own preferred solution would be to encourage individual scholarly specialization of the sort Donald Campbell envisioned in his 'fish scale model of omniscience', with the field achieving 'collective comprehensiveness through overlapping patterns of unique narrowness' (Campbell, 1969, 328). Consider the conceptualization in Figure 12.4, appropriated directly from Campbell.

The top panel represents the danger that EU Studies should seek to avoid. In it, difference and consensus coexist in the worst possible way for knowledge production. Different schools of thought (or approaches, or disciplines, or whatever) represent substantially overlapping congeries of narrow specialties internally, and disconnected islands externally. Patterns of redundant narrowness limit knowledge production within schools, and the sheer impossibility of attaining expertise in multiple schools – Campbell's 'Leonardesque Aspiration' – prohibit any but the most superficial communication across schools. This particular mixture of diversity and commonality arises frequently, for example in the ways that universities and other academic institutions (such as journals) organize intellectual life along disciplinary lines, and it is lethal for knowledge production.

The alternative, the 'fish-scale model of omniscience' in the bottom panel, optimizes knowledge production. In the ideal-typical case, each individual becomes specialized in an area of knowledge unique to her, unbounded by, say, disciplinary strictures, but also unconcerned at the inevitable incompleteness of her individual knowledge (and hence unmoved by the 'Leonardesque Aspiration'). With enough people orienting themselves in this way, the result

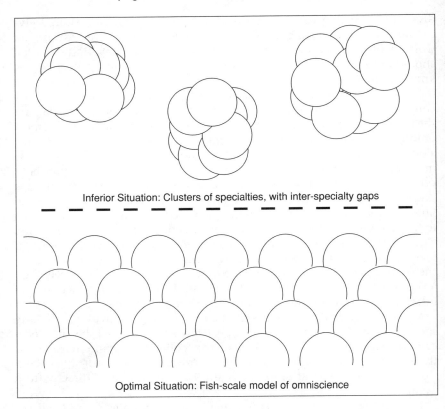

Inferior Situation: Clusters of specialties, with inter-specialty gaps

Optimal Situation: Fish-scale model of omniscience

Figure 12.4   The fish-scale model of omniscience

(Adapted from Campbell, 1969, 329.)

is a 'continuous texture of narrow specialties which overlap with other narrow specialties' (Campbell, 1969, 328). The continuity over the knowledge space is key, because it prevents unbridgeable knowledge gaps from emerging. In addition, it eliminates the requirement that every given pair of scholars consciously share an identifiable set of common standards. As long as coverage is continuous, and as long as scholars share standards with those closest to them, the collective scholarly endeavour can proceed, secure that every link in the chain connecting each to the others is governed by locally acceptable (but, ultimately, mutually recognized) standards.

The fish-scale image is, of course, somewhat fanciful, and confronts innumerable institutional obstacles. But it contains within it a number of ideals, such as individual specialization, irrespective of received institutionalized boundaries, that point the way toward leveraging the wide metatheoretical and methodological opportunities that exist in EU Studies, availing ourselves of the currently unique and historically unprecedented community of scholars engaged in the field, and paying symbolic tribute to the polity that forms the object of our inquiries.

notes

1. Initial reflections on the topic of this chapter were presented at the 44th Annual International Studies Association (ISA) Conference, Portland, Oregon, 25 February–1 March 2003. I would like to thank Scott Gates for his helpful comments on that occasion. The paper was also presented at the Sage/EU luncheon at the 9th Biennial European Union Studies Association Conference, Austin, Texas, 31 March 2005. I am grateful to Simon Hix for his helpful comments at that time.

2. 'Explanatory' style seems to fit better, but presupposes a goal (explanation) that is not universally shared, so I adopt the more neutral formulation here.

3. OLS stands for 'ordinary least squares'. Also known as the 'classical linear regression model'.

4. For some straightforward advice on how these methods can be implemented in the practice of EU Studies research, see Nyikos and Pollack (2003).

5. Jeffrey Chwieroth (2003) offers a non-EU example of the promise of quantitative constructivism.

6. I will focus on the ebb and flow of grand-theorizing, recognizing that particularizing work has continued unabated through the five-plus decades of EU Studies.

7. The fact that all three of these pioneers were European émigrés working in the US makes it harder to disentangle putatively 'European' from putatively 'American' styles, though I address this question more concretely below.

8. JSTOR is an electronic archive of scholarly journals. JSTOR title search 'European Community' OR 'European Communities' OR 'European Union' OR 'European integration', articles only, for the following journals: *American Journal of Political Science* (AJPS), *American Political Science Review* (APSR), *British Journal of Political Science* (BJPS), *Comparative Politics* (CP), *International Affairs* (IA), *International Organization* (IO), *International Studies Quarterly* (ISQ), *Journal of Conflict Resolution* (JCR), *Journal of Peace Research* (JPR), *Journal of Politics* (JOP), *Legislative Studies Quarterly* (LSQ), *Political Research Quarterly* (PRQ), *Political Science Quarterly* (PSQ) and *World Politics* (WP).

9. What follows draws substantially from Jupille, Caporaso, and Checkel, 2003. My co-authors deserve some of the credit but probably none of the blame for the presentation here.

10. For all of the journals except *CPS*, these figures primarily report references returned by a JSTOR search (conducted 18 December 2003) on 'European Union' OR 'European Community' OR 'European Communities' OR 'European Economic Community' OR 'European integration' in the title or the abstract (articles only). Issues outside of JSTOR's coverage window were hand-coded from the following sources: *IO*: Swetswise database, 1998–2003; *ISQ*: Ingenta database, 1998–2003; *CP*: October 2000 (vol. 33, no. 1). 2003 from journal's web page <http://web.gc.cuny.edu/jcp/issues.htm>. *CPS* is not archived at JSTOR, and the reported figures derive from keyword searches on 'European Community' and 'European Union' conducted by staff at Sage Publications. I would like to thank Jim Caporaso for help in obtaining these latter data.

11. It is simply shown that the tri-methodological category would be the only new addition. There are seven theoretical combinations of the three categories: 1) qualitative only; 2) statistical only; 3) formal only; 4) qualitative + statistical; 5) qualitative + formal; 6) statistical + formal; 7) qualitative + statistical + formal. But, given the ubiquity of verbal presentation – has anyone ever seen a *purely* statistical or a *purely* formal piece of work, in EU Studies or elsewhere? – categories 2, 3, and 6 must be eliminated. This leaves categories 1, 4 (identical to my 'statistical' category), 5 (identical to my 'formal' category) and 7 (the only new category, and the costs and benefits of which I discuss in the text).

12. *PS: Political Science and Politics* 36, 3 (July 2003) offers a variety of perspectives on the tradeoffs involved in considering methodological pluralism.

13
cleavages, controversies and convergence in european union studies

wolfgang wessels

introduction

When embarking on an examination of the literature on the European Union, whether for research or teaching purposes, one is confronted by a curious set of sensations and impressions. The 'state of the art' – or what might be called, in Eurospeak or Community jargon, the *acquis académique* – is a strange mixture of theoretical trends, empirical analyses, thick descriptions, political narratives, ideological visions, *Leitbilder* (world visions), constitutional ideas and norms and political strategies. Supplementing these variations, there is a broad range of methods that have been used to explore, explain, evaluate and extrapolate insights into the EU system and its environment. However, many of the classic contributions in the field cannot easily be pigeonholed into one of the categories above, as they often combine several cross-cutting characteristics. Moreover, the borders of what is considered the 'state of the art' are ambiguous and not clearly defined. In contrast to the *acquis communautaire*, there is no court to make definitive and authoritative judgements about what does and does not belong to the 'patrimony'. While academics have often tried to define what is appropriate research and what is not, the market for academic ideas is not clearly demarcated, and entry to it is relatively open. As a consequence, disputes about the *acquis académique* are lively, and riven by many cleavages.

The various approaches used by academics to explain the EU reflect theoretical traditions that are characterized by an impressive vitality, frequent academic 'turns' and a diversity, which generates a considerable degree of confusion and fragmentation.[1] It is fascinating to observe an evolving research area such as this, characterized as it is by stimulating and thought-provoking academic contributions, which compete for attention. Examining this *acquis* can be frustrating, however, if one is looking for an easy path through the maze. Some traditions vanish, while others remain, and real life developments in the EU offer new objects of research. Efforts at identifying schools and phases of theoretical development (see for example, Schmitter, 2004, 8; Cowles and Curtis, 2004, 298) may be helpful in opening the gates to an initial survey of the literature, but it is difficult to make use of them as a roadmap through the ever-growing multi-faceted and divergent approaches that exist.

the dynamics and constraints of an evolving field

All the standard indicators used to chart the development of maturing fields of social science have experienced growth and differentiation in the case of EU Studies. The number of research facilities and academic publications, including relevant journals,[2] has grown, as have the thematic, theoretical and methodological approaches used within both research activities and academic networks.[3] Perspectives on the development of the study of European integration and the EU were, and still are, significantly influenced by working conditions on the ground, and thus, not insignificantly, by funded research projects and programmes. These may be nationally resourced, as in the case of the Deutsche Forschungsgemeinschaft's 'Governance in the European Union' programme; the British Economic and Social Research Council (ESRC)'s 'One Europe or Several' programme; or the Oslo programme on 'European Systems of Governance'. At the European level, the EU research framework programmes have also encouraged many new initiatives and have led to a considerable body of research output. For example, the EU's Sixth Framework Programme is currently funding networks and research teams examining 'forms of governance' (CONNEX) and changed security dimensions (Challenge), whilst also including 'integrated projects', such as on 'new modes of Governance' (NewGOV). We can expect further novel and possibly innovative research stemming from these programmes. Other chapters in the Framework Programme that are devoted to the social sciences[4] promise results in more basic research which are likely to generate reformulated questions, as in the case of projects that deal with developments in the enlarged Union (see Wider Europe, Deeper Integration – Constructing Europe (EU-CONSENT)). Plans for the Seventh Framework Programme have already indicated the core themes of EU funding for 2006 to 2010.[5]

In some member states, other organizations, such as the Volkswagen Foundation[6] in Germany, also grant support to EU-related projects; and others have created their own research centres.[7] In all funded projects, the decisions of actors outside academia have influenced core aims and issues. However, representatives from the academic world do play central roles as advisers and evaluators, establishing the main direction of the research to be conducted and assessing individual applications. Consequently, it is, at least in part, down to the discipline itself to determine to which fields and projects financial support will be allocated.

Another indicator for the growth of the discipline is the supply of teaching, which has expanded noticeably over the last few decades. 'European Studies', comprising a wide spectrum of subjects and content, has become a permanent fixture. The Europe-wide introduction of Masters courses, in line with the Bologna process, will complement these developments. The teaching of postgraduate studies has been established and extended at the College of Europe in Bruges and Natolin and in other specialized courses, such as in Basle, Berlin, Tübingen, Hamburg, Nice and Vienna. The European University Institute in Florence, as well as scholarship programmes funded by the EU itself, provides opportunities for doctoral and post-doctoral studies on EU-related subjects. EU Studies is now a widely taught subject in various forms and at different levels of university education.

A growing number of academic institutions across Europe and beyond[8] have been instrumental in producing a new generation of professional academics working in the field of EU Studies. For them, entry into the academic market is relatively open. This situation has been promoted through the opening up of transnational opportunities, which suggests that the wider academic discursive realm has come to be shaped by a process of Europeanization, and even by globalization. With English as the lingua franca and using modern technology, networks have been both deepened and widened. The market for academics with EU-related specialisms has grown considerably as a consequence.

Depending on one's view, the state of the discourse on the EU can be described as open and pluralistic or as anarchical and fragmented. What seems clear is that the preliminary or partial results of single studies are rarely referred back to and subsequently integrated into a clearly defined body of work. As a consequence, revealing insights and inspiring perspectives on the EU are simply lost. For example, the works of C.J. Friedrich and K.W. Deutsch are mentioned from time to time, but are generally not taken as serious starting points for research. Moreover, contributions from the 'dark ages' of integration in the 1970s (see for this assessment Keohane and Hoffmann, 1991) and the early 1980s (Hrbek and Schneider, 1980), as well as those of critical theory, are all too often forgotten, and contributions in languages other than English are hardly ever integrated into the *acquis* (Hallstein, 1969; Dahrendorf, 1973; Schneider, 1977; Quermonne, 2001). Even so, conventional approaches often re-emerge after some time in a 'reinvented' form, with only slightly modified premises, while other seminal works within the literature on the EU remain influential, and continue to direct our efforts in different ways, based on new interpretations. Classic founding theories – such as (neo)realist, (neo)federalist and (neo)functionalist approaches – are repeatedly revived and sometimes offer considerable gains in insight as a consequence.[9] The attempt to establish 'neo-neofunctionalism' (Schmitter, 2004), and modern takes on federalist thinking (see for example Burgess, 2004) give testimony to the recurring renaissance of traditional theories, dating from an earlier generation of political scientists. Thus, it appears that trends in the 'state of the art' are defined less by paradigm change (Kuhn, 1988) than by differentiation and pluralistic coexistence.

Research networks have repeatedly sought to promote publications of single authors as key works in the field. While this may be necessary, and even stimulating, it bears the real risk of artificially perpetuating controversies between different schools (Loth and Wessels, 2001). Differences in theory or methodology can be cultivated beyond their inherent boundaries, and the potential for securing the benefits of mutual insight may be lost in the process. A didactic review of the literature might reveal valuable traditions and helpful lines of development. This kind of chronological ordering of academic phases must not, however, lead to an unproductive limitation of perspective, as in the form of 'footnote cartels'. Such categorizations can serve to direct the new researcher: but if understood as hard doctrine they might end up concealing valuable academic insights.

Thus, notwithstanding the self-stylizing of some authors and schools, no single theoretical direction can currently be asserted as the 'dominant school'. This makes the task of summarizing and categorizing the abundance of literature on the EU extremely difficult.[10] Attempts at definitively drawing up the boundaries of single periods on the basis of theoretical approaches are usually short-lived, as new understandings are eventually established, changing previously held convictions or mental maps. Similarly, one should be careful not to overrate statistical evaluations. The Social Science Citation Index (SSCI)[11] can help identify key individuals and projects enjoying great respect in the field. But at the same time, they might also be perceived as the product of battles between individuals who hold certain positions of academic dominance.

push and pull factors

There is yet another major factor driving diversity in the field of EU Studies. Over the last fifty years, the integration process or, more specifically, the EU system, has become considerably more politically relevant as an object of research and teaching, and, at the same time, has developed many unexpected features. Even more than in the past, we are confronted with the task of describing, analysing and assessing trends in the widening and deepening of the Union, and of trying to understand and explain precisely what impact these developments have on the member states. Examining the EU as we would with a political system allows the observation of very noticeable trends of growth and differentiation, namely: the evolution of the legal constitution; the increase in the quantity and scope of legal output; the growth in the complexity of the EU's institutional architecture; the application of new procedures to the 'living constitution' of the EU; the increase in the number of member states, EU citizens, national, regional and local administrations involved in European affairs; an inflow of interest groups, non-governmental organizations (NGOs) and other representatives of civil society; more media attention; and the initiation of a diplomatic role for the EU. As a consequence, there is now more research on what might be considered the 'conventional objects' of political science, with the integration process offering new and worthwhile areas of specialization for researchers in this field.

The process of constructing the EU through Intergovernmental Conferences (IGCs) creates another set of challenges for the academic world. Political scientists play a role in shaping the field of their study, creating an optimal problem-solving area for themselves. Increasingly, academics are faced with demands for normative contributions, suggesting that academic reflections will often be subject to a particular *Zeitgeist*. Major events in EU history can serve as points of departure for both research and, moreover, for teaching on the EU. The Treaty establishing a Constitution for Europe, and the 2004 enlargement round offer challenging opportunities for academics to revisit conventional approaches and to test novel ones, as well.[12] The teaching of EU Studies can make good use of these historic milestones to confront diverging theoretical explanations and political strategies.

While we witness an evolution in the concerns and interests of academics working on the EU, it is also possible, however, to observe the growth and differentiation of the field at large. In the case of disciplines such as political science, colleagues from the newer member states now participate in EU-wide projects. With this growth in numbers, scholars are increasingly looking for additional areas of specialization. The 'pull' (from the EU) and the 'push' (from the discipline) thus contribute to a growth in a range of diverse activities that are characterized by controversies and cleavages.

cleavages and controversies

seeking positive approaches

Given the abundance of EU-oriented research, it remains to be seen which approaches and methods will be understood in the future as the most relevant contributions to theory-building. This means that research standards must continue to be subjected to discussion. The methodological purity, often reflected in the teaching of EU Studies, must not be permitted to constitute an obstacle to more comprehensive insights drawn from a range of other approaches and methods. Moreover, inspiration can also be drawn from sources other than theoretical works, such as the Commission White Papers (see for example European Commission, 2001).

A central task for all disciplines is the constant reidentification of the research object, and the pursuit of issues that follow from that. This insight raises questions, if only implicitly, about the basic ontology underpinning theoretical approaches, as well as about the appropriate means of capturing and analysing European realities. Major cleavages are likely to emerge around the object of and approaches to such studies. Major lines of inquiry must involve looking at fundamental questions: for example, how the five decades of European integration might be explained and evaluated. This is likely to be controversial, as well as productive.

In our reflections on the reason and purpose of EU Studies, we are frequently confronted by the need to label the EU system. There are many different labels describing the EU: 'state-like' (Oppermann, 1993, 109); 'analogous to the state' (Lübbe 1994, 146); 'post modern state' (Caporaso, 1996); 'quasi state' (Wallace, 1996); 'para state' (Wessels and Diedrichs, 1997); 'international state' (Wendt, 1998a); 'fused federal state' (Wessels, 2000 122); and 'fédération des Etats-nations' (Jospin, 2001; Delors, 2000). Given the paramount importance of the state in modern political thought (Morris, 2004, 195), reference to the EU in this way is understandable. Yet, how we might deal with the ever recurring tension between the *sui generis* nature of the EU system and the urge to compare it to existing state concepts remains controversial. One way out of this dilemma is to employ notions of 'governance', indicating that there exists in the EU a mode of governing without a state-like government. This label is used quite extensively, for example in the terms 'network governance' (Kohler-Koch, 1999, 15); 'polycratic governance' (Landfried, 1999, 173); 'committee governance (Christiansen and Kirchner, 2000, 15); 'collective governance' (Wallace, 2000); and 'multilevel governance' (Jachtenfuchs and Kohler-Koch, 2003; Hooghe and Marks, 2001a). These labels still manage to deal with the state-like functions of the EU, but avoid employing conventional categories. Finally, as a consequence of the constitutionalization process, it is possible that labels drawing on the notion of 'federation' will re-emerge. Federalism has had and will continue to have periods of renaissance, though its explanatory power might be low. Many perceive it as little more than a political ideology, and as such, not particularly useful for theoretical work.

With most of these terms, however imaginatively they are used, there is a basic methodological problem. This relates to their static nature. Snapshots of the EU preclude the possibility of grasping evolutionary dynamics (Hay, 2002, 135). It is desirable to identify underlying 'laws of motion', and to try to identify a general theory of integration that might enable us to explain the forms and forces of integration dynamics beyond a mid-range approach, which is bound to a specific space and time.

The first step towards operationalizing research on the origins of integration, is the identification of indicators. In identifying the determinants of integration, we should exploit the full range of approaches, drawing on different contexts and traditions that are often overlooked, for example, historical studies which focus on underlying currents in economic and societal developments in Europe (see Chapter 11 in this volume). While a general theory should be the ultimate aim, such an outcome is not likely to come easily. A more pressing task, however, lies in combining and delimiting theoretical stances in ingenious ways, so that research on European integration might be undertaken on various levels of analysis (see Peterson and Bomberg, 1999), thereby optimizing the explanatory potential of existing approaches.

In discussing the prospects for a general theory of integration, the question of the guiding research perspective is frequently raised. One major cleavage recurs: should the evolution of the EU system over the last fifty years be examined as a whole, or should researchers adopt a microcomparative perspective and concentrate on single phenomena? Would the latter mean that the EU could be treated as a 'normal' political system, in which, for example, the European Parliament is compared to national parliaments (Maurer and Wessels, 2003; Hix et al., 2002; Hix, 2001)? This kind of approach does not resolve the debate about the *sui generis* character of the EU system: indeed, it merely begs the question. If the aim is to explain the EU system, single detailed studies would be of little use, since insights gained from such studies would contribute more to horizontal comparisons beyond the EU than to an explanation of the EU itself. Thus, if this were to become the exclusive 'raison d'être' of political science, works more widely concerned with European integration (Jachtenfuchs and Kohler-Koch, 2003) or the European Union, would seem anachronistic because of their adoption of a macroperspective. Studies of the EU would become redundant, as the components of single studies would not be able to advance an overall understanding of the system. While identifying EU-related topics for testing against particular cross-sectional theses is not to be discouraged in principle, my plea is, rather, that we should not lose sight of a dynamic macroperspective in our research efforts. Even if the EU should emerge as an n=1 case study, it would, for academic as well as normative reasons, be problematic *not* to continue to discuss the overall evolution of this *sui generis* system.

normative dimensions

In view of the rising political significance of the EU, another cleavage concerns contributions made by academics to the political debate. Does this mean that the normative foundations of the EU will have to be addressed to a greater extent in the future? My argument is that while fundamental political categories and evaluative yardsticks should continue to be identified and applied, contributions from the field of 'critical theory' should also be drawn from to a greater extent, so as to subject systematically those aspects of European integration that may have been taken for granted to closer scrutiny.

There are considerable hurdles in pursuing this kind of approach. Understanding the EU in terms of 'post-national constellations' (Zürn, 2002; Habermas, 1998; Beck, 1998), 'post modern integration' (European Commission 2001), or even a 'post communitarian Union', demands that the precise meanings of terms, such as 'constitution', 'identity', 'democracy' and 'state' must be clarified. This should not deter political scientists from seeking a deeper understanding of constitutional reform, or 'better governance' (European Commission, 2001), however – even if that often requires the application of a clear definition of legitimation.

Normative debate ought not to rest on an unreflected transfer of commonly used terms and concepts. The concept of 'democracy' provides a case in point. In defining and applying this concept, we can quite easily draw on a range of differing perspectives: from the well-known claim that there is a 'democratic deficit' in the EU, to its wholesale repudiation. While, for some, democracy is thought impossible as a matter of principle, in the absence of a real 'demos' or 'communicative sphere', for others, the EU is a prime example of 'consensus democracy'. However, the multitude of measures and yardsticks applied to normative debate must not be allowed to lead to a sense of apathy or indifference. The debate on the optimal form the EU might take as a political system will therefore continue until it is capable of living up to commonly accepted norms that reflect real-life conditions within the Union.

the pull from the eu-system: research objects and controversies

constitutionalization

For researchers, real life developments in the EU system remain of major importance. The deepening and widening of the Union represent key areas of interest within EU Studies, with the events of the last few years having led to a 'constitutional turn' in the field (Wiener and Diez, 2003, 238). While there will continue to be controversies about the most appropriate research focus and about key concepts, constitutional and institutional developments remain essential areas for examination. Even though the treaty amendments themselves may not always be particularly innovative, every 'history-making decision' (Peterson and Bomberg, 1999: 10–16) or 'critical juncture' (Pierson, 1996) agreed within the 'legal' constitution (Olsen, 2000, 7) forms a 'natural' object for in-depth political analysis. In undertaking this kind of research, a variety of theoretical and methodological approaches should always be adopted. This means that the research agenda, and its corresponding impact on teaching, will have to be broadly conceived. A perspective that differentiates between a 'written' or 'legal' constitution, on the one hand, and a 'living' or 'real' constitution, on the other, may offer a point of departure. Thus, first analysing norms in the Treaty or Constitution, and subsequently examining their practical application, is likely to be a particularly promising approach.

The cyclical or causal relationship existing between these two elements in the analysis demands careful methodological attention, however. Thus far, the vast majority of interest has been in elucidating how the amended treaty provisions might impact upon the 'living constitution' (Maurer and Wessels, 2003, 39; Olsen, 2000, 7). Yet, there is more work to be done on precisely how 'constitutional politics [determines the] opportunities and constraints of governance' (Jachtenfuchs and Kohler-Koch, 2003, 27–8) and how this flows back into the design of future treaties.

This kind of debate about constitutionalization is likely to gain in importance as a result of research on the Treaty Establishing a Constitution for Europe. It is also likely to encourage an exchange across disciplines and national research communities. Historical and legal contributions, for example, can offer important supplements to and elaborations of these kinds of political analyses.

Hence, quite independent of whether or not the Constitutional Treaty will eventually enter into force, it will continue to offer major points of reference and provide an important source of materials to be used in both traditional and more innovative research. By looking at the 'career patterns' followed by its central provisions, it is also possible to identify future areas of research interest. The Treaty not only allows for a review of sectoral developments, but it also paves the way for a wholesale examination of the EU system at large. The text and its origins can thus be used to test both basic theoretical currents and more novel approaches of a neoinstitutionalist and constructivist character. From a dynamic perspective, the Constitutional Treaty and the preceding rounds of Treaty revisions might even provide the researcher with indicators that could lead to the development of a macropolitical evolutionary theory of integration.

The normative debate about what the 'best' constitution for Europe might be is also given a boost by the Constitutional Treaty, not least through the detailed analysis of single provisions and paragraphs. While the institutional architecture of the EU may be a natural focus for research conducted within the political sciences, the distribution of competences, including the subsidiarity principle, and the application of procedural rules in specific policy fields, also provides a number of potentially fruitful research questions. Should the Treaty enter into force, a detailed research agenda during the implementation phase would need to be drawn up.

enlargement

The enlargement process offers another focus for converging research interests, with the new enlarged Union, post-2004, generating a multitude of fundamental research questions. For example, in the future, academics will have to monitor how existing rules are used to govern 25 or more member states, under circumstances where every state and non-state actor, old or new, must reposition itself within the EU system. Furthermore, the politics and policies of accession, and, in particular, the possibility of Turkish membership of the EU, is likely to increase the demand for deeper analyses of basic issues. In this vein, the dimensions of European 'identity' will need to be discussed, as much as the options for reform within key sectors, such as agriculture. Alongside research on enlargement, supplementary studies on *'Leitbilder'* (Maurer, 2003; Göler, 2003), 'basic understandings' (Schneider, 1998, 129–45), 'constitutional ideas' (Jachtenfuchs, 2002) and 'preferences' (Moravcsik, 1993), are likely to enrich academic discourse. To that end, the political debates in the new member states must be examined with care. Beyond the simple catchphrase of the 'return to Europe' (Lippert and Umbach, 2005, 16), political actors in the new member states are likely to formulate their ideas on European integration more assertively in the future. Indeed, firm positions have already been advanced by the new members in the Convention on the Future of Europe, and in the subsequent Intergovernmental Conferences, as well as in debates in the run up to the 2004 European Parliament elections.

Just how actors in the member states, regardless of their accession date, define their European policy will have to be scrutinized comprehensively in the future. One question of increasing relevance, which is both theoretical and political, concerns the extent to which these political actors will change their ideas about the Union, as a consequence of their experience of Europeanization. Should their constitutional ideas shift dramatically, the analytical narratives shaping the EU system might have to be written anew.

With regard to the kind of studies likely to be undertaken by researchers, a number of possibilities present themselves. It may be that the discourse on European integration will follow a traditional, albeit slightly modified, western European canon. In this scenario, the *acquis académique* would assert itself, not least because of the Anglo-American dominance of teaching materials. Another possibility is that current dividing lines between large and small, or old and new, member states might translate into a new public or academic discourse. This fragmentation might be further amplified by an increase in euroscepticism, whether on the left or the right of the political spectrum. The consequence of this could be a more intense and fundamental debate over the character of the Union which, might ultimately lead to the emergence of a 'core Europe', composed of states sharing similar understandings of the European project. A third scenario points to a deeper paradigm shift, in which the political and academic discourse adjusts to the 'new Europe', forging a 'post-community' Europe. Considering that our observations are time-bound and that we find ourselves in the midst of several simultaneous political currents, identifying possible trends requires a finely-tuned and differentiated set of instruments, which academics researching the EU are able to provide.

catchphrases from the political debate: common challenges

As this review of the *acquis académique* indicates, political science as an academic discipline, has picked up a number of catchphrases from the political realm. Unconventional approaches that promise new perspectives have always been popular with academics. Debates frequently erupt around the use of terms such as 'multi-tier integration' (Tindemans, 1975), 'Europe à la carte' (Dahrendorf, 1973), 'core Europe' (Schäuble and Lamers, 1994), 'Europe à plusieurs vitesses' ('multi-speed Europe') (Wallace and Wallace, 1995, 55), 'pioneering Europe' (Chirac, 2001), and 'enhanced cooperation'. Similarly, the term 'open method of coordination' has recently attracted a great deal of attention.

Academic and, more often, think-tank contributions, sometimes risk being swept away on a political wave. Clearly, the limits of these politically attractive concepts also need to be discussed. A general prognosis on the use of 'fashionable' terms in political science cannot possibly be provided here. However, we ought to expect the political debate to continue delivering captivating key phrases of this kind, which political scientists will adopt and discuss on their own terms.

the push from general political theory-building

Theoretical perspectives on the EU cannot be sketched simply by examining the growth and the differentiation of the EU, but must also be viewed as a sort of mirror image of the evolution of disciplines. EU-focused academia has not fostered interest in European integration in a vacuum, but reflects, to a considerable degree, prevalent theoretical and methodological priorities in the political sciences, both in Europe and the United States. Even neofunctionalism, which can be understood as the child of European integration, can only be thoroughly comprehended in a context of the political science environment of the 1950s.

Within the field of political science, for a long time the study of European integration occupied a rather marginal position. While this topic was often confined to the sidelines, or viewed as an offshoot of international politics, it has more recently been absorbed into the 'mainstream' (H. Wallace, 2000b, 68). The political system of the EU, or specific aspects of the integration process, are now often drawn on as test cases in research, and are embedded in general theories (see, for example, Tsebelis, 2002; Lijphart, 1999). As a consequence, one might anticipate closer ties with and feedback into general political theory-building and methods. Moreover, novel currents in political science have led to stimulating new directions in integration theory. Neoinstitutionalist schools (Schneider and Aspinwall, 2001; Peters, 1999; Pierson, 1996; Bulmer, 1994a) have influenced the focus and the choice of methodological tools, as have more recent constructivist developments (Christiansen *et al.*, 2002; Risse, 2000). Labels such as 'governance' and 'Europeanization' are closely linked to general trends in political science. The development of political science is therefore likely to persist as an essential determinant of discussions on European integration. Applying innovative approaches and scientific methods to the ever-changing reality of the EU offers a fertile ground for experimentation. Proceeding in this way promises to provide insights, not only into this subject area, but also into the discipline as a whole.

controversies on methods: in search of an optimal mix

As is the case in every community of researchers, controversies about the appropriate use of conventional and innovative methods of research remain a central issue in the field of EU Studies. There is an increasing amount of quantitative research undertaken in this field, which sits alongside case studies and other forms of qualitative work. The accessibility of data which covers a long period (compiled by the EC organs themselves, albeit for other purposes) has facilitated quantitative studies of this kind, on topics such as Council decisions (Maurer and Wessels, 2003; Sandholtz and Stone Sweet, 1998), votes in the European Parliament (Wessels, 2000), as well as in patterns of attendance and participation of Members of the European Parliament (Wessels, 2000). This literature also includes statistics produced by Eurobarometer that capture the attitudes of the Community's citizens since 1973, as well as those of Central and Eastern Europe from 1990 onwards. Despite some concerns about the validity of indicators and the reliability of the collected data, this approach offers considerable research potential.

Other empirical information can sometimes be gathered more directly to address specific research questions; but there are problems of reliability and viability. These data tend not to invite long-term analyses, but rather present a static view of the EU, offering little potential for dynamic, diachronic comparisons. Analysing trends is of great importance to the study of the EU, allowing 'laws of integrative motion' to be identified, whilst delivering explanations of the EU's evolution that go beyond the mere charting of its status quo characteristics. This is not to say that a 'comparative static method' – such as an assessment of Treaty changes – is not an appropriate starting point for capturing developments in the 'living constitution' however (Maurer and Wessels, 2003).

In doing research on the EU, methodological monism is far from a promising approach. Instead, comparing results obtained through different methods is much more likely to generate far-reaching insights. In demanding this kind of methodological mix, we should be aware of controversies surrounding the use of so-called 'accompanying observations' in collecting information that might be used to guide the design of hypotheses. This practice draws on conversations and open interviews with actors involved in EU politics. It is not quite the same as participatory observation or the use of ethnographic methods (Bryman, 2001, 289), but is nonetheless based on similar premises: that we can understand and explain a chain of events and the arguments advanced by key actors, and gain a deeper understanding of EU affairs through targeted questioning much closer in time to the actual event.[13] The collection and analysis of 'anecdotal evidence' or 'mini case studies' can provide revelations that can probably not be replicated at a later stage – or only with considerable difficulty. Thus, while direct contact with political events in Brussels and in European arenas within the member states are a desirable component of any study of the EU, its weakness is that other academics rarely have access to exactly the same sources.

Academic research often leads to discussions with practitioners, and in the field of EU Studies this is particularly cultivated by think-tanks. In this context, academics, politicians and civil servants exchange views and discuss possible options or solutions. Academic participants are able to collect new inputs for their research and are, at the same time, induced to produce theoretical reflections of some practical value. While both groups, the 'ivory tower' and the 'diplomatic club', learn by interacting in these arenas, they all too often learn different lessons from the experience. For academic teachers, anecdotal evidence can be used to good effect in the classroom – a particular advantage of this working method.

Nevertheless, there are disadvantages, too. For example, there is a considerable risk of losing one's critical distance for the object in question. Personal proximity can quickly result in an identification with the interests and viewpoints of the actors being researched. Becoming involved in 'epistemic communities' (Haas, 1992) can lead to a narrowing of an academic's own perspectives on a question. This kind of 'cocooning' might be reduced by the opening up of academic networks, to allow academics to break out of narrow discursive contexts.

conclusion

Thus, to conclude: reviewing the *acquis académique* allows us to identify several blurred lines of cleavage, controversy and convergence. Despite all the uncertainty that exists in defining and delineating core subjects, approaches and methods in EU Studies, one prospect seems evident: in light of the EU itself acting as a 'pull' factor, and the academic disciplines, notably political science, as 'push' factors, we can expect anything but academic boredom in this relatively new field of European Union Studies.

notes

*   This chapter is based on ideas developed in: Wessels, Wolfgang (2005), 'Theoretischer Pluralismus und Integrationsdynamik: Herausforderungen für der "acquis académique"', in H.-J. Bieling and M. Lerch (eds), *Theorien europäischer Integration* (V.S. Wiesbaden), pp. 427–57.

1.   For helpful recent overviews, see Rosamond (2000a); and Wiener and Diez (2003). For a transdisciplinary typology, see Loth and Wessels (2001, 11), and also Bieling and Lerch (2005, forthcoming).

2. See, among others, *Journal of Common Market Studies* (JCMS), *Journal of European Public Policy*; *European Union Politics*; *Zeitschrift für Internationale Beziehungen*; and *Internationale Politik*.
3. See also the European Consortium for Political Research (ECPR), European Community studies Association (ECSA), EPSNET, and the Jean Monnet Network.
4. See <www.cordis.lu/improving>.
5. See <www.cordis.lu/era/fp7.htm>.
6. See <www.volkswagen-stiftung.de>.
7. For example, the *Bertelsmann Stiftung* and the *Centrum für Angewandte Politikforschung* in Munich.
8. See numerous efforts by the EU to establish centres of excellence all over the world: <http://europa.eu.int/comm/education/programmes/ajm/ajm/directory_en.html>.
9. See for example the relevant chapters in Wiener and Diez (2003); and Cini (2003); Chryssochoou (2001); and Rosamond (2000a).
10. For the difficulties this author has in grasping the ongoing debates, see Wessels (1986).
11. See for example Hix's study (2004b).
12. For this kind of exercise on enlargement, see the contributions in Wiener and Diez (2003).
13. See works on Common Foreign and Security Policy, such as Nuttall (2000); and Regelsberger *et al.*, (1997).

references

Aalberts, T. (2004) 'The Future of Sovereignty in Multi-level Governance Europe: A Constructivist Reading', *Journal of Common Market Studies*, XLII 23–46.

Abbott, K. and Snidal, D. (1998) 'Why States Act Through Formal International Organizations', *Journal of Conflict Resolution*, XLII 3–32.

Abélès, Marc, Irène Bellier, Maryon McDonald (1993) 'Approche Anthropologique de la Commission Européenne'. Unpublished Report for the European Commission, Brussels.

Abizadeh, A. (2002) 'Does Liberal Democracy Presuppose a Cultural Nation? Four Arguments', *American Political Science Review*, XCVI 495–509.

Abromeit, H. (1998) *Democracy in Europe: Legitimising Politics in a Non-State Polity* (New York: Berghahn Books).

Adcock, R. and Collier, D. (2001) 'Connecting Ideas with Facts: The Validity of Measurement', *American Political Science Review*, XCV 529–46.

Adshead, M. (2002) *Developing European Regions: Comparative Governance, Policy Networks and European Integration* (Aldershot: Ashgate).

Aggestam, L. (1999) 'Role Conceptions and the Politics of Identity in Foreign Policy', ARENA Working Paper 8.

Aggestam, L. (2000a) 'A Common Foreign and Security Policy: Role Conceptions and the Politics of Identity in the EU', in L. Aggestam and A. Hyde Price (eds), *New Perspectives on Security and Identity in Europe* (London: Macmillan).

Aggestam, L. (2000b) 'Europe Puissance: French Influence and European Independence', in H. Sjursen (ed.), *Redefining Security? The role of the European Union in European Security Structures*, ARENA Report 7.

Alesina, A., Roubini, N. and Cohen, G. (1997) *Political Cycles and the Macroeconomy* (Cambridge MA: The MIT Press).

Allen, D. (1998) 'Who Speaks for Europe? The Search for an Effective and Coherent External Policy', in J. Peterson and H. Sjursen (eds), *A Common Foreign Policy for Europe? Competing Visions of the CFSP* (London: Routledge).

Allen, D. and Smith, M. (1991) 'Western Europe's Presence in the Contemporary International Arena', in M. Holland (ed.), *The Future of European Political Cooperation, Essays on Theory and Practice* (Basingstoke: Macmillan).

Almond, G. and Verba, S. (1963) *The Civic Culture: Political Attitudes and Democracy in Five Nations* (Princeton NJ: Princeton University Press).

Almond, M. (1994) *Europe's Backyard War: The War in the Balkans*, revised edn (London: Mandarin).

Alt, J. and Shepsle, K. (1990) *Perspectives on Positive Political Economy*, Political Economy *of Institutions and Decisions* (Cambridge: Cambridge University Press).

Althusius, J. (1995 [1603/14]) *Politica Methodice Digesta*, trans. by F. Carney (Indianapolis: Liberty Press).

Andersen, S. and Burns, T. (1996) 'The European Union and the Erosion of Parliamentary Democracy: A Study of Post-Parliamentary Governance', in S. Andersen and K. Eliassen (eds), *The European Union: How Democratic Is It?* (London: Sage).

Anderson, P. (1991) 'Nation-States and National Identity', *London Review of Books*, 9 May.

Anderson, P. (1998) *The Origins of Postmodernity* (London: Verso).

Andonova, L. (2003) *Transnational Politics of the Environment. The EU and Environmental Policy in Central and Eastern Europe* (Cambridge MA: MIT Press).

Angerer, T. (1998) 'Exklusivität und Selbstausschließung: Frankreich, Österreich und die Erweiterungsfrage in der europäischen Integrationsgeschichte', *Revue d'Europe Centrale*, VI 25–54.

Aoun, E. (2003) 'European Foreign Policy and the Arab-Israeli Dispute: Much Ado About Nothing?' *European Foreign Affairs Review*, VIII 289–312.

Armstrong, K. and Bulmer, S. (1998) *The Governance of the Single European Market* (London: Palgrave Macmillan).

Arrow, Kenneth J. (1951) *Social Choice and Individual Values* (New York: Wiley & Sons).

Aspinwall, M. and Schneider, G. (2000) 'Same Menu, Separate Tables: The Institutionalist Turn in Political Science and the Study of European Integration', *European Journal of Political Research*, XXXVIII 1–36.

Avery, G. (2004) 'The Enlargement Negotiations', in F. Cameron (ed.), *The Future of Europe: Integration and Enlargement* (London: Routledge).

Axelrod, R. (1984) *The Evolution of Cooperation* (New York: Basic Books).

Bache, I. (1998) *The Politics of European Union Regional Policy: Multi-level Governance or Flexible Gatekeeping?* (Sheffield: Sheffield Academic Press).

Bache, I. (2003) 'Europeanisation: A Governance Approach', Paper presented at the EUSA 8th International Biennial Conference, Nashville, March 27–29.

Bache, I. and Flinders, M. (2004) 'Conclusions and Implications', in I. Bache and M. Flinders (eds), *Multi-level Governance* (Oxford: Oxford University Press).

Bailer, S. and Schneider, G. (2000) 'The Power of Legislative Hot Air: Informal Rules and the Enlargement Debate in the European Parliament', *Journal of Legislative Studies*, VI 19–44.

Balassa (1961) *The Theory of Economic Integration* (London: Allen and Unwin).

Ballmann, A., Epstein, D. and O'Halloran, S. (2002) 'Delegation, Comitology, and the Separation of Powers in the European Union', *International Organization*, LVI 551–74.

Banchoff, T. and Smith, M. (1999) 'Introduction: Conceptualizing Legitimacy in a Contested Polity', in T. Banchoff and M. Smith (eds), *Legitimacy and the European Union* (London: Routledge).

Barnett, M. and Finnemore, M. (1999) 'The Politics, Power, and Pathologies of International Organizations', *International Organization*, LIII 699–732.

Barry, B. (1991) 'Is Democracy Special?', in B. Brian (ed.), *Democracy and Power: Essays in Political Theory*, Vol.1 (Oxford: Oxford University Press).

Barysch, K. (2004) *The EU and Russia: Strategic Partners or Squabbling Neighbours?* (London: Centre for European Reform).

Bates, R. (1997) 'Area Studies and the Discipline: A Useful Controversy?', *Political Science and Politics*, XXX 166–9.

Bauer, M. (2002) 'Limitations to Agency Control in European Union Policy-Making: The Commission and the Poverty Programmes', *Journal of Common Market Studies*, XL 381–400.

Beck, U. (ed.) (1998) *Politik der Globalisierung* (Frankfurt-a-M: Suhrkamp).

Beetham, D. (1991) *The Legitimation of Power* (London: Macmillan).

Beetham, D. and Lord, C. (1998) *Legitimacy and the European Union* (London: Longman).

Begg. I and Grimwade, N. (1998) *Paying for Europe* (Sheffield: Sheffield Academic Press).

Bellamy, R. (1995) 'The Constitution of Europe: Rights or Democracy?', in R. Bellamy, V. Bufacchi and D. Castiglione (eds), *Democracy and Constitutional Culture in the Union of Europe* (London: Lothian Foundation Press).

Bellamy, R. (1999) *Liberalism and Pluralism* (London: Routledge).

Bellamy, R. and Castiglione, D. (2003) 'Legitimizing the Euro-Polity and Its Regime: The Normative Turn in EU Studies', *European Journal of Political Theory*, II 7–34.

Bellamy, R. and Warleigh, A. (eds) (2001) *Citizenship and Governance in the European Union* (London: Continuum).

Bendle, M. (2002) 'The Crisis of "Identity" in High Modernity', *British Journal of Sociology*, LIII 1–18.

Bennett, A., Barth, A. and Rutherford, K. (2003) 'Do We Preach What We Practice? A Survey of Methods in Political Science Journals and Curricula', *PS: Political Science and Politics*, XXXVI 373–8.

Berger, F. (1997) 'Les Sidérurgistes Français et Allemands face à l'Europe: Convergences et Divergences de Conception et d'Intérêts 1932–1952', *Journal of European Integration History*, III 35–52.

Berger, P. and Luckmann, T. (1966) *The Social Construction of Reality, A Treatise on the Sociology of Knowledge* (London: Penguin).

Berghahn, V. (2001) *America and the Intellectual Cold Wars in Europe: Shepard Stone between Philanthrophy, Academy, and Diplomacy* (Princeton: Princeton University Press).

Bernhard, W., Broz, J. and Clark, W. (2002) 'The Political Economy of Monetary Institutions', *International Organization*, LVI 693–723.

Bertozzi, F. and Bonoli G. (2002) 'Europeanisation and the convergence of national social and employment policies: What can the open method of coordination achieve?', Paper prepared for the ECPR joint sessions of workshops, Turin, 22–27 March 2002.

Beyers, J. and Dierickx, G. (1998) 'The Working Groups of the Council of the European Union: Supranational or Intergovernmental Negotiations?', *Journal of Common Market Studies*, XXXVI 289–317.

Bieler, A. (2000) *Globalisation and Enlargement of the European Union. Austrian and Swedish Social Forces in the Struggle over Membership* (London: Routledge).

Bieling, H.-J. and Lerch, M. (2005) *Theorien der europaïschen Integration* (Stuttgart: UTB).

Biersteker, Thomas and Weber, Cynthia (eds) (1996) *State Sovereignty as Social Construct* (Cambridge: Cambridge University Press).

Billig, M. (1995) *Banal Nationalism* (London: Sage).

Bitsch, M.-T. (2001) *Histoire de la construction européenne* (Paris: Editions Complexe).

Bitsch, M.-T., Loth, W. and Poidevin, R. (eds) (1998) *Institutions Européennes et Identités Européennes* (Brussels: Bruylant).

Black, Duncan (1958) *The Theory of Committees and Elections* (London and New York: Cambridge University Press).

Boli, J. and Thomas, G. (eds) (1999) *Constructing World Culture: International Nongovernmental Organizations since 1875* (Stanford: Stanford University Press).

Borras, S. and Greve, B. (eds) (2004) 'The Open Method of Coordination in the European Union', *Journal of European Public Policy*, XI 185–208.

Börzel, T. (1999) 'Towards Convergence in Europe? Institutional Adaptation to Europeanization in Germany and Spain', *Journal of Common Market Studies*, XXXVII 573–96.

Börzel, T. (2001) 'Non-Compliance in the European Union: Pathology or Statistical Artefact?', *Journal of European Public Policy*, VIII 803–24.

Börzel, T. (2002) 'Pace-Setting, Foot-Dragging, and Fence-Sitting: Member State Responses to Europeanization', *Journal of Common Market Studies*, XL 193–214.

Börzel, T. (2004) 'How the European Union Interacts with its Member States', in C. Lequesne and S. Bulmer (eds), *Members States and the European Union* (Oxford: Oxford University Press).

Börzel, T. and Hosli, M. (2002) 'Brussels between Bern and Berlin: Comparative Federalism meets the European Union', Constitutionalism Web-papers, ConWEB 2.

Börzel, T. and Risse, T. (2003) 'Conceptualising the Domestic Impact of Europe', in K. Featherstone and C. Radaelli (eds), *The Politics of Europeanisation* (Oxford: Oxford University Press).

Bretherton, C. and Vogler, J. (1999) *The European Union as a Global Actor* (London: Routledge).

Broad, R. and Preston, V. (eds) (2001) *Moored to the Continent? Britain and European Integration* (London: IHR/University of London Press).

Brubaker, R. and Cooper, F. (2000) 'Beyond "identity"', *Theory and Society*, XXIX 1–47.

Brusis, M. (2002) 'Between EU Requirements, Competitive Politics, and National Traditions: Re-creating Regions in the Accession Countries of Central and Eastern Europe', *Governance*, XV 531–59.

Bryman, A. (2001) *Sociological Research Methods* (Oxford: Oxford University Press).

Buchanan, J. (1965) 'An Economic Theory of Clubs', *Economica*, XXXII 1–14.

Bührer, W. (1999) *Ruhrstahl und Europa. Die Wirtschaftsvereinigung Eisen- und Stahlindustrie und die Anfänge der Europäischen Integration 1945–1952* (Munich: Oldenbourg).

Bull, H. (1977) *The Anarchical Society: A Study of Order in World Politics* (Basingstoke: Macmillan).

Bull, H. (1982) 'Civilian Power Europe: A Contradiction in Terms?', *Journal of Common Market Studies*, XXI 149–64.

Bull, M. and Baudner, J. (2004) 'Europeanisation and Italian policy for the Mezzogiorno', *Journal of European Public Policy*, XI 1058–78.

Buller, J. and Gamble, A. (2002) 'Conceptualising Europeanisation', *Public Policy and Administration*, XVII No.2: 4–24.

Bulmer, S. (1994a) 'Institutions and Policy Change in the European Communities: The Case of Merger Control', *Public Administration*, LXXII 423–44.

Bulmer, S. (1994b) 'The Governance of the European Union: A New Institutionalist Approach', *Journal of Public Policy*, XIII 351–80.

Bulmer, S. and Radaelli, C. (2005) 'The Europeanisation of Public Policy', in S. Bulmer and C. Lequesne (eds), *Member States and the European Union* (Oxford: Oxford University Press).

Burgess, M. (2004) 'Federalism', in A. Wiener and T. Diez (eds), *Theories of European Integration: Past, Present and Future* (Oxford: Oxford University Press).

Burley, A.-M. and Mattli, W. (1993) 'Europe Before the Court: A Political Theory of Legal Integration', *International Organization*, XLVII 41–76.

Busch, A. (2004) 'National Filters: Europeanisation, Institutions, and Discourse in the case of Banking Regulation', *West European Politics*, XXVII, 2 310–33.

Buti, M. and Giudice, G. (2002) 'Maastricht's Fiscal Rules at Ten: An Assessment', *Journal of Common Market Studies*, XL, 823–48.

Buzan, B., Waever, O. and de Wilde, J. (1998) *Security: A New Framework of Analysis* (Boulder, CO: Lynne Rienner).

Cafruny, A. and Ryner, M. (eds) (2003) *A Ruined Fortress? Neoliberal Hegemony and Transformation in Europe* (Lanham, MD, Boulder: Rowman & Littlefield).

Calhoun, C. (2001) 'The Virtues of Inconsistency: Identity and Plurality in the Conceptualization of Europe', in L.-E. Cederman (ed.), *Constructing Europe's Identity, The External Dimension* (Boulder/London: Lynne Rienner).

Calhoun, C. (2003) 'European Studies: Always Already There and Still In Formation', *Comparative European Politics*, I 5–20.

Cameron, F. (2002) 'The European Union's Growing International Role: Closing the Capability – Expectations Gap?', National Europe Centre Paper 14, Australian National University, Canberra.

Campbell, D. (1969) 'Ethnocentrism of Disciplines and the Fish-Scale Model of Omniscience', in M. Sherif and C. Sherif (eds), *Interdisciplinary Relationships in the Social Sciences* (Chicago: Aldine Publishing).

Caporaso, J. (1996) 'The European Union and Forms of the State: Westphalian, Regulatory or Post-Modern?', *Journal of Common Market Studies*, XXXIV 29–52.

Caporaso, J. (1997) 'Across the Great Divide: Integrating Comparative and International Politics', *International Studies Quarterly*, XLI 563–92.

Caporaso, J. (1998) 'Regional Integration Theory: Understanding Our Past and Anticipating Our Future', in W. Sandholz and A. Stone Sweet (eds), *European Integration and Supranational Governance* (Oxford: Oxford University Press).

Caporaso, J. and Keeler J. (1995) 'The European Union and Regional Integration Theory', in C. Rhodes and S. Mazey (eds), *State of the European Union, vol. 3, Building a European Polity?* (Boulder, CO: Lynne Rienner).

Castells, M. (1997) *The Power of Identity* (London: Blackwell).

Cederman, L.-E. (1997) *Emergent Actors in World Politics: How States and Nations Develop and Dissolve* (Princeton: Princeton University Press).

Cederman, L.-E. (2001) 'Nationalism and Bounded Integration: What Would it Take to Construct a European Demos?' *European Journal of International Relations*, VII 139–74.

Chayes, A. and Chayes, A.H. (1995) *The New Sovereignty: Compliance with International Regulatory Regimes* (Cambridge and London: Harvard University Press).

Checkel, J. (1998) 'The Constructivist Turn in International Relations Theory', *World Politics*, L 324–48.

Checkel, J. (1999a) 'Norms, Institutions, and National Identity in Contemporary Europe', *International Studies Quarterly*, XLIII 83–114.

Checkel, J. (1999b) 'Social Construction and Integration', *Journal of European Public Policy*, VI 545–60.

Checkel, J. (2001a) 'The Europeanization of Citizenship?', in M.G. Cowles, J. Caporaso and T. Risse (eds), *Transforming Europe: Europeanization and Domestic Change* (Ithaca: Cornell University Press).

Checkel, J. (2001b) 'Why Comply? Social Norms Learning and European Identity Change', *International Organization*, LV 553–88.

Checkel, J. and Moravcsik, A. (2001) 'A Constructivist Research Program in EU Studies?', Forum debate, *European Union Politics*, II 219–49.

Chirac, J. (2001) 'Notre Europe: Rede vor dem Deutschen Bundestag, Berlin 27 June 2000', in H. Marhold (ed.), *Die Neue Europadebatte* (Bonn: Leitbilder das Europa der Zukunft).

Choudhry, S. (2001) 'Citizenship and Federations: Some Preliminary Reflections', in K. Nicolaidis and R. Howse (eds), *The Federal Vision: Legitimacy and Levels of Governance in the US and the EU* (Oxford: Oxford University Press).

Christiansen, T. and Kirchner, E. (ed.) (2000) *Administering the New Europe: Inter-Institutional Relations and Comitology in the European Union* (Manchester: Manchester University Press).

Christiansen, T. and Piattoni, S. (eds) (2003) *Informal Governance in the European Union* (Aldershot: Edward Elgar).

Christiansen, T., Falkner, G. and Jørgensen, K.-E. (2002) 'Theorizing EU Treaty Reform: Beyond Diplomacy and Bargaining', *Journal of European Public Policy*, IX 12–33.

Christiansen, T., Jørgensen, K.-E. and Wiener, A. (1999) 'The Social Construction of Europe', *Journal of European Public Policy*, VI 528–44.

Christiansen, T., Jørgensen, K.-E. and Wiener, A. (eds) (2001) *The Social Construction of Europe* (London: Sage).

Chryssochoou, D. (1995) 'European Union and the Dynamics of Confederal Consocation: Problems and Prospects for a Democratic Future', *Journal of European Integration*, XVIII 279–305.

Chryssochoou, D. (2001) *Theorising European Integration* (London: Sage).

Chwieroth, J. (2003) 'A Capital Idea: The Role of Neoliberalism in the Liberalization of Finance in Emerging Markets', Unpublished Ph.D. dissertation (Santa Barbara: Department of Political Science, University of California).

Cini, M. (ed.) (2003) *European Union Politics* (Oxford: Oxford University Press).

Citrin, J. (2004) 'Critical Review of Survey Data on European Identity', in R. Herrmann, T. Risse and M. Brewer (eds), *Europeanization: Institutions and the Evolution of Social Identities* (Lanham MD: Rowman & Littlefield).

Citrin, J. and Sides, J. (2004) 'More than Nationals: How Identity Choice Matters in the New Europe', in R. Hermann, T. Risse and M. Brewer (eds), *Identities in Europe and the Institutions of the European Union* (London: Rowman & Littlefield).

Clark, I. (1994) *Nuclear Diplomacy and the Special Relationship: Britain's Deterrent and America, 1957–1962* (Oxford: Clarendon Press).

Closa, C. (2003) 'Improving EU Constitutional Politics? A Preliminary Assessment of the Convention', Constitutionalism Web-papers, ConWEB, 1/2003.

Cocks, P. (1980) 'Towards a Marxist Theory of European Integration', *International Organization*, XXXIV 1–40.

Cohen, J. and Rogers, J. (1995) *Associations and Democracy* (London: Verso).

Cole, J. and Cole, F. (1997) *A Geography of the European Union*, 2nd edn (London: Routledge).

Coleman, W. and Chiasson, C. (2002) 'State Power, Transformative Capacity and Adapting to Globalization: An Analysis of French Agricultural Policy', *Journal of European Public Policy*, IX 168–85.

Collins, S. (2002) *German Policy-Making and Eastern Enlargement of the European Union During the Kohl Era: Managing the Agenda?* (Manchester: Manchester University Press).

Connor, W. (1994) *Ethnonationalism: The Quest for Understanding* (Princeton: Princeton University Press).

Cooke, P. (1996) 'Policy Networks, Innovation Networks and Regional Policy – A Review of the Literature and an Example from South Wales', in H. Heinelt and R. Smith (eds), *Policy Networks and European Structural Funds* (Aldershot: Ashgate).

Corbett, R. (2000) 'Academic Modelling of the Co-decision Procedure: A Practitioner's Puzzled Reaction', *European Union Politics*, I 373–9.

Cortell, A. and Davis, J. (2000) 'Understanding the Domestic Impact of International Norms: A Research Agenda', *International Studies Review*, II 65–87.

Cowles, M.G., Caporaso, J. and Risse, T. (eds) (2001) *Transforming Europe: Europeanization and Domestic Change* (Ithaca NY: Cornell University Press).

Cowles, M.G. and Curtis, S. (2004) 'Developments in European Integration Theory: The EU as "Other"', in M.G. Cowles and D. Dinan (eds), *Developments in the European Union* (Basingstoke: Palgrave Macmillan).

Cox, R. (1981) 'Social Forces, States and World Orders: Beyond International Relations Theory', *Millennium Journal of International Studies*, X N° 2, 126–55.

Cox, R. (1983) 'Gramsci, Hegemony and International Relations: An Essay in Method', *Millennium*, XII 162–75.

Cox, R. (1995) 'Critical Political Economy,' in B. Hettne (ed.), *International Political Economy: Understanding Global Disorder* (Halifax: Fernwood Books).

Craig, P. (2001) 'Constitutions, Constitutionalism, and the European Union', *European Law Journal*, VII 125–50.

Craig, P. (2003) 'What Constitution Does Europe Need? The House That Giscard Built: Constitutional Rooms With a View', Constitutional Online Paper 26/03, The Federal Trust, London.

Cram, L. (1996) 'Integration Theory and the Study of the European Policy Process', in J. Richardson (ed.), *European Union: Power and Policymaking* (London: Routledge).

Cram, L. (1997) *Policy-making in the EU: Conceptual Lenses and Integration Process* (London: Routledge).

Crowley, P. (2001) 'The Institutional Implications of EMU', *Journal of Common Market Studies*, XXXIX 385–404.

Daddow, O. (ed.) (2003) *Harold Wilson and European Integration. Britain's Second Application to join the EEC* (London: Frank Cass).

Dahrendorf, R. (1973) *Plädoyer für die Europäische Union* (Munich; Zurich: Piper).

Dalton, R. (1999) 'Political Support in Advanced Industrial Democracies', in P. Norris (ed.), *Critical Citizens: Global Support for Democratic Government* (Oxford: Oxford University Press)

de Grauwe, P. (2003) *Economics of Monetary Union*, 5th edn (Oxford: Oxford University Press).

De Haan, J., Inklaar, R. and Sleijpen, O. (2002) 'Have Business Cycles Become More Synchronized?', *Journal of Common Market Studies*, XL 23–42.

de la Fuente, A. and Doménech, R. (2001) 'The Redistributive Effects of the EU Budget: An Analysis and Proposal for Reform', *Journal of Common Market Studies*, XXXIX 307–30.

De la Porte, C. and Pochet, P. (eds) (2002) *Building Social Europe through the Open Method of Coordination* (Brussels: Peter Lang).

Dehousse, R. (ed.) (1994) *Europe After Maastricht: An Ever Closer Union?* (Munich: Law Books in Europe).

Dehousse, R. (1999) 'Towards a Regulation of Transitional Governance? Citizen's Rights and the Reform of Comitology Procedures', in C. Joerges and E. Vos (eds), *EU Committees: Social Regulation, Law and Politics* (Oxford: Hart).

Deighton, A. and Milward, A. (eds) (1999) *Widening, Deepening and Acceleration: The European Economic Community 1957–1963* (Baden-Baden: Nomos).

Dell, E. (1995) *The Schuman Plan and the British Abdication of Leadership in Europe* (Oxford: Oxford University Press).

Delors, J. (2000) 'Reuniting Europe: Our Historic Mission', Speech at the 'Wallensberg Conference' at the Aspen Institute, 14 November 1999, in *Agence Europe* Nr. 7625, 3/4 January 2000, and *Agence Europe* Nr. 7626, 5 January.

Dessler, D. (1999) 'Constructivism within a Positivist Social Science', *Review of International Studies*, XXV 123–37.

Deutsch, K.W. (1954) *Political Community at the International Level* (Garden City, NY: Doubleday).

Deutsch, K. *et al.* (1957) *Political Community and the North Atlantic Area: International Organization in the Light of Historical Experience* (Princeton: Princeton University Press).

Deutsch, K. *et al.* (1970) *Political Community at the International Level: Problems of Definition and Measurement* (New York: Doubleday, 1954; Garden City NY: Archon Books).

Diez, T. (1997) 'International Ethics and European Integration: Federal State or Network Horizon?', *Alternatives*, XXII 287–312.

Diez, T. (1999a) 'Speaking "Europe": The Politics of Integration Discourse', *Journal of European Public Policy*, VI 598–613.

Diez, T. (1999b) *Die EU Lesen: Diskursive Knotenpunkte in der britischen Europadebatte* (Opladen: Leske & Budrich).

Diez, T. (2001) 'Europe as a Discursive Battleground: Discourse Analysis and European Integration Studies', *Cooperation and Conflict*, XXXVI 5–38.

Diez, T. and Whitman, R. (2002) 'Analysing European Integration: Reflecting on the English School – Scenarios for an Encounter', *Journal of Common Market Studies*, XL 43–67.

Diez, T. and Wiener, A. (2003) 'Introducing the Mosaic of Integration Theory: Its Past, Present and Future', in A. Wiener and T. Diez (eds), *European Integration Theory* (Oxford: Oxford University Press).

Dimitrova, A. (2002) 'Enlargement, Institution Building and the EU's Administrative Capacity Requirement', *West European Politics*, XXV No.4: 171–90.

Dinan, D. (2004) *Europe Recast: A History of European Union* (Basingstoke: Palgrave Macmillan).

Dobson, L. (2004) 'Conceptions of Freedom and the European Constitution', in L. Dobson and A. Føllesdal (eds), *Political Theory and the European Constitution* (London: Routledge).

Dobson, L. and Føllesdal, A. (eds) (2004) *Political Theory and the European Constitution* (London: Routledge).

Dosenrode, S. and Stubkjaer, A. (2002) *The European Union and the Middle East* (Sheffield: Sheffield Academic Press).

Doty, R.L. (1997) 'Aporia: A Critical Exploration of the Agency-Structure Problematique in International Relations Theory', *European Journal of Political Research*, III N° 3, 365–92.

Downs, A. (1957) *An Economic Theory of Democracy* (New York: Harper and Row).

Dryzek, J. (1990) *Discursive Democracy: Politics, Policy, and Political Science* (Cambridge: Cambridge University Press, 1990).

Dryzek, J. (1996) 'Strategies of Ecological Democratization', in W. Lafferty and J. Meadowcroft (eds), *Democracy and the Environment: Problems and Prospects* (Cheltenham: Edward Elgar).

Duchêne, F. (1972) 'Europe's Role in World Peace', in R. Mayne (ed.), *Europe Tomorrow: Sixteen Europeans Look Ahead* (London: Fontana).

Duchêne, F. (1973) 'The European Communities and the Uncertainties of Interdependence', in M. Kohnstamm and W. Hager (eds), *A Nation Writ Large? Foreign-Policy Problems Before the Community* (London: Macmillan).

Duchêne, F. (1994) *Jean Monnet: The First Statesman of Interdependence* (New York: Norton).

Dumoulin, M. (ed.) (1995) *Wartime Plans for Postwar Europe* (Baden-Baden: Nomos).

Dumoulin, M. and Dutrieue, A.-M. (1993) *La Ligue Européenne de Coopération Économique (1946–1981): Un Group d'Etude et de Pression dans la Construction Européenne* (Berne: Peter Lang).

Dyson, K. (ed.) (2002) *European States and the Euro: Europeanization, Variation and Convergence* (Oxford: Oxford University Press).

Dyson, K. and Featherstone, K. (1999) *The Road to Maastricht: Negotiating Economic and Monetary Union* (Oxford: Oxford University Press).

Dyson, K. and Goetz, K.H. (eds) (2003) *Germany, Europe and the Politics of Constraint* (Oxford University Press).

Easton, D. (1965) *A Systems Analysis of Political Life* (New York: Wiley).

Egeberg, M. (1999) 'Transcending Intergovernmentalism: Identity and Role Perceptions of National Officials in EU Decision-making', *European Journal of Public Policy*, VI 456–74.

Eising, R. (2002) 'Policy Learning in Embedded Negotiations: Explaining EU Electricity Liberalization', *International Organization*, LVI 85–120.

El-Agraa, A.M. (1990) *Economics of the European Community*, 3rd ed. (Basingstoke: Macmillan).

Elazar, D. (1987) *Federalism As Grand Design: Political Philosophers and the Federal Principle* (Lanham, MD: University Press of America).

Elgie, R. (2002) 'The Politics of the European Central Bank; Principal-Agent Theory and the Democratic Deficit', *Journal of European Public Policy*, IX 201–18.

Eliassen, K. (ed.) (1998) *Foreign and Security Policy in the European Union* (London: Sage).

Ellison, J. (2000) *Threatening Europe. Britain and the Creation of the European Community, 1955–58* (London: Macmillan).

Elster, J. and Slagstad, R. (1988) *Constitutionalism and Democracy* (Cambridge: Cambridge University Press).

Elster, J. (1989a) *Nuts and Bolts for the Social Sciences* (Cambridge: Cambridge University Press).

Elster, J. (1989b) *The Cement of Society: A Study of Social Order, Studies in Rationality and Social Change* (Cambridge: Cambridge University Press).

Elster, J. (1998) 'Deliberation and Constitution Making', in J. Elster (ed.), *Deliberative Democracy* (Cambridge: Cambridge University Press).

Epstein, D. and O'Halloran, S. (1999) *Delegating Powers: A Transaction Cost Politics Approach to Policy Making under Separate Powers* (Cambridge: Cambridge University Press).

Epstein, R. (2002) 'International Institutions and the Depoliticization of Economic Policy in Postcommunist Poland: Central Banking and Agriculture Compared', *RSCAS Working Paper* No.2002/69 (Florence: European University Institute).

Eriksen, E. (2000) 'Deliberative Supranationalism in the EU', in E. Eriksen and J. Fossum (eds), *Democracy in the European Union: Integration Through Deliberation?* (London: Routledge).

European Commission (1996) *'Eurobarometer': Top Decision Makers Survey* (Brussels: Commission DG X).

European Commission (2001) *Europäisches Regieren: Ein Weißbuch* [European Governance: A White Paper] COM (2001) 438 final (Brussels: European Commission).

Everts, S. (2003) *The EU and the Middle East* (London: Centre for European Reform).

Falkner, G. (2000) 'How Pervasive are Euro-Politics? Effects of EU Membership on a New Member State', *Journal of Common Market Studies*, XXXVIII 223–50.

Falkner, G. (2003) 'Comparing Europeanisation Effects: From Metaphor to Operationalisation', European Integration On-line Papers (EIoP), VII N° 13, at <http://eiop.or.at/eiop/texte/2003-013a.htm>.

Featherstone, K. (2003) 'In the Name of Europe', in K. Featherstone and C. Radaelli (eds), *The Politics of Europeanization* (Oxford: Oxford University Press).

Featherstone, K. and Radaelli, C. (eds) (2003) *The Politics of Europeanization* (Oxford: Oxford University Press).

Femia, J. (1996) 'Complexity and Deliberative Democracy', *Inquiry*, XXXIX 359–97.

Ferrera, M., Matsaganis, M. and Sacchi, S. (2002) 'Open Coordination against Poverty: The New EU Social Inclusion Process', *Journal of European Social Policy*, XII 227–39.

Fierke, K. (1998) *Changing Games, Changing Strategies* (Manchester: Manchester University Press, 1998).

Fierke, K. and Wiener, A. (1999) 'Constructing Institutional Interests: EU and NATO Enlargement', *Journal of European Public Policy*, VI 721–42.

Filtenborg, M., Gänzle, S. and Johansson, E. (2002) 'An Alternative Approach to EU Foreign Policy: Network Governance and the Case of the Northern Dimension Initiative', *Cooperation and Conflict*, XXXVII 387–404.

Finnemore, M. (1996) *National Interests in International Society* (Ithaca: Cornell University Press).

Finnemore, M. and Sikkink, K. (1998) 'International Norm Dynamics and Political Change', *International Organization*, LII 887–917.

Fioretos, K.-O. (1997) 'The Anatomy of Autonomy: Interdependence, Domestic Balances of Power, and European Integration', *Review of International Studies*, XXIII 293–320.

Fiorina, M. (1996) 'Rational Choice, Empirical Contributions and the Scientific Enterprise', in J. Friedman (ed.), *The Rational Choice Controversy: Economic Models of Politics Reconsidered* (New Haven: Yale University Press).

Fisher, R. and Ury, W. (1987) *Getting to Yes* (Boston: Penguin).

Fligstein, N. and Merand, F. (2001) 'Globalization or Europeanization? Evidence on the European Economy Since 1980', Working Paper WPS-2001-02m Center for Culture, Organizations and Politics, University of California, Berkeley.

Føllesdal, A. (1997) 'Democracy and Federalism in the EU: A Liberal Contractualist Perspective', in A. Føllesdal and P. Koslowski (eds), *Democracy and the European Union: Studies in Economic Ethics and Philosophy* ARENA Reprint 98/9 (Berlin: Springer).

Føllesdal, A. (1998a) 'Democracy, Legitimacy and Majority Rule in the EU', in A. Weale and M. Nentwich (eds), *Political Theory and the European Union: Legitimacy, Constitutional Choice and Citizenship* ARENA Reprint 99/2 (London: Routledge).

Føllesdal, A. (1998b) 'Subsidiarity', *Journal of Political Philosophy*, VI 231–59.

Føllesdal, A. (2000) 'The Future Soul of Europe: Nationalism or Just Patriotism? On David Miller's Defence of Nationality', *Journal of Peace Research*, XXXVII 503–18.

Føllesdal, A. (2001) 'Federal Inequality Among Equals: A Contractualist Defense', *Metaphilosophy*, 236–55.

Føllesdal, A. (2003) 'Federalism', in E. Zalta (ed.), *Stanford Encyclopedia of Philosophy* <http://plato.stanford.edu/>.

Føllesdal, A. (2005) 'The Legitimacy Deficits of the European Union', *Journal of Political Philosophy* XIII.

Fossum, J. (2001) 'Identity-politics in the European Union', *ARENA Working Papers*, WP 01/17.

Franchino, F. (2000) 'Control of the Commission's Executive Functions: Uncertainty, Conflict and Decision-Rules', *European Union Politics*, I 63–92.

Frieden, J. (2002) 'Real Sources of European Currency Policy: Sectoral Interests and European Monetary Integration', *International Organization*, LVI 831–60.

Friedman, J. (ed.) (1996) *The Rational Choice Controversy* (New Haven: Yale University Press).

Friis, L. (1998a) 'Approaching the "Third Half" of EU Grand Bargaining – the Post-negotiation Phase of the "Europe Agreement" Game', *Journal of European Public Policy*, V 322–38.

Friis, L. (1998b) '... And Then They Were 15: The EU's EFTA-Enlargement Negotiations', *Cooperation and Conflict*, XXXIII 81–107.

Friis, L. (1998c) '"The End of the Beginning" of Eastern Enlargement – Luxembourg Summit and Agenda-setting', *European Integration online Papers*, 2/7.

Friis, L. and Murphy, A. (1999) 'The European Union and Central and Eastern Europe: Governance and Boundaries', *Journal of Common Market Studies*, XXXVII 211–32.

Galtung, J. (1973) *The European Community: A Superpower in the Making* (London: George Allen and Unwin).

Garman, J. and Hilditch, L. (1998) 'Behind the Scenes: An Examination of the Importance of the Informal Processes at Work in Conciliation', *Journal of European Public Policy*, V 271–84.

Garrett, G. (1992) 'International Cooperation and Institutional Choice: The European Community's Internal Market', *International Organization*, XLVI 533–60.

Garrett, G. and Tsebelis, G. (1996) 'An Institutional Critique of Intergovernmentalism', *International Organization*, L 269–99.

Garrett, G. and Tsebelis, G. (2001) 'The Institutional Determinants of Intergovernmentalism and Supranationalism in the EU', *International Organization*, LV 357–90.

Garrett, G. and Weingast, B. (1993) 'Ideas, Interests, and Institutions: Constructing the European Community's Internal Market', in J. Goldstein and R. Keohane (eds), *Ideas & Foreign Policy. Beliefs, Institutions and Political Change* (Ithaca: Cornell University Press).

Gasiorek, M., Smith, A. and Venables, A. (2002) 'The Accession of the UK to the EC: A Welfare Analysis', *Journal of Common Market Studies*, XL 425–47.

Gaspari, O. (2002) 'Cities against States? Hopes, Dreams and Shortcomings of the European Municipal Movement, 1900–1960', *Contemporary European History*, XI 597–621.

Gehler, M. (2002) *Der lange Weg nach Europa: Österreich vom Ende der Monarchie bis zur EU* (Innsbruck: Studienverlag).

Gehler, M. and Kaiser, W. (2001a) 'Transnationalism and Early European Integration: The Nouvelles Equipes Internationales and the Geneva Circle, 1947–1957', *The Historical Journal*, XLIV 773–98.

Gehler, M. and Kaiser, W. (2004) *Transnationale Parteienkooperation der europäischen Christdemokraten 1945–1965* (Munich: K.G. Saur).

Gellner, E. (1983) *Nations and Nationalism* (London: Blackwell).

German Constitutional Court 'Brunner v European Union Treaty', *BVerfGE*, 89: 155 (1993).

Giddens, A. (1979) 'Agency, Structure', in A. Giddens (ed.), *Central Problems in Social Theory* (Berkeley: University of California Press).

Giddens, A. (1991) *Modernity and Self-Identity: Self and Society in the Late Modern Age* (Cambridge: Polity Press).

Giesen, B. and Eisenstadt, S. N (1995) 'The Construction of Collective Identity', *Archives Européenne de Sociologies*, XXXVI 72–102.

Gillespie, P. (1996) 'Diversity in the Union', in B. Laffan (ed.), *The Governance of the Union: Towards a New Architecture of Statehood?*, Paper presented to the COST A7 workshop, organized by the National Economic and Social Council, on Negotiated Economic and Social Governance and European Integration, Dublin.

Gillespie, P. (2001) 'Enhanced Cooperation', in J. Dooge and P. Keatinge (eds), *What the Treaty of Nice Means* (Dublin: Institute of European Affairs).

Gillingham, J. (1991) *Coal, Steel and the Rebirth of Europe, 1945–1955: The Germans and French from Ruhr Conflict to Economic Community* (Cambridge: Cambridge University Press).

Gillingham, J. (2003) *European Integration 1950–2003: Superstate or New Market Economy?* (Cambridge: Cambridge University Press).

Giuliani, M. (2001) 'Europeanization and Italy: A Bottom-up Process?', in K. Featherstone and G. Kazamias (eds), *Europeanization and the Southern Periphery* (London: Frank Cass).

Giuliani, M. (2003) 'Europeanization in Comparative Perspective: Institutional Fit and National Adaptation', in K. Featherstone and C. Radaelli (eds), *The Politics of Europeanization* (Oxford: Oxford University Press).

Giuliani, M. (2004) 'Europeizzazione come istituzionalizzazione: questioni definitorie e di metodo', *Rivista Italiana di Politiche Pubbliche*, I 141–61.

Gleason, P. (1983) 'Identifying Identity: A Semantic History', *Journal of American History*, LXIX 910–31.

Glenny, M. (1993) *The Fall of Yugoslavia: The Third Balkan War* (London: Penguin).

Goetz, K. (ed.) (2001) 'Executive Governance in Central and Eastern Europe', *Journal of European Public Policy*, VIII 863–1051.

Goetz, K. (2002) 'Four Worlds of Europeanisation', Paper prepared for the ECPR Joint Sessions of Workshops, Turin, Italy, 22–27 March.

Goldsmith, M. (2003) 'Variable Geometry, Multi-level Governance: European Integration and Sub-national Government in the New Millenium', in K. Featherstone and C. Radaelli (eds), *The Politics of Europeanization* (Oxford: Oxford University Press).

Goldstein, Judith and Keohane, Robert O. (1993) 'Ideas and Foreign Policy: An Analytical Framework', in Judith Goldstein and Robert O. Keohane (eds), *Ideas and Foreign Policy* (Ithaca: Cornell University Press).

Göler, D. (2003) 'Between Deliberation and Bargaining: The Influence of the Institutional Setting of the Convention on the Mode of Interaction', Paper presented at the CIDEL Conference 'Deliberative Constitutional Politics in the EU', Albarracín, Zaragoza, 19–22 June. <www.arena.uio.no/cidel/workshopZaragoza/goelercidel.pdf>.

Gomez, R. (2003) *Negotiating the Euro-Mediterranean Partnership: Strategic Action in EU Foreign Policy?* (London: Ashgate).

Goodin, R.E. (1993) 'Democracy: Preferences and Paternalism', *Policy Sciences*, XXVI N° 3, 229–47.

Goodin, Robert E. (2003) 'Input Democracy' in O. Østerud and F. Engelstad (eds), *Power and Democracy* (Aldershot: Ashgate).

Grabbe, H. (2003) 'Europeanization Goes East', in K. Featherstone and C. Radaelli (eds), *The Politics of Europeanization* (Oxford: Oxford University Press).

Grabbe, H. (2005) 'Regulating the Flow of People across Europe', in F. Schimmelfennig and U. Sedelmeier (eds), *The Europeanization of East Central Europe* (Ithaca: Cornell University Press).

Granell, F. (1995) 'The European Union's Enlargement Negotiations with Austria, Finland, Norway, and Sweden', *Journal of Common Market Studies*, XXXIII 117–42.

Grant, W. (2005) 'The Common Agriculture Policy: Challenges in the Wake of Eastern Enlargement', in A. Verdun and O. Croci (eds), *Institutional and Policy-making Challenges to the European Union in the Wake of Eastern Enlargement* (Manchester: Manchester University Press).

Green, D. (2000) 'The End of Identity? The Implications of Postmodernity for Political Identification', *Nationalism and Ethnic Politics*, VI 68–90.

Green, D.P. and Shapiro, I. (1994) *Pathologies of Rational Choice: A Critique of Applications in Political Science* (New Haven: Yale University Press).

Green-Pedersen, C., Van Kersbergen, K. and Hemerijck, A. (2001) 'Neo-liberalism, the "third way" or what? Recent social democratic welfare policies in Denmark and the Netherlands', *Journal of European Public Policy*, VIII 307–25.

Greilsammer, I. and Weiler, J. (1987) *Europe's Middle East Dilemma: The Quest for a Unified Stance* (Boulder: Westview Press).

Grieco, J. (1995) 'The Maastricht Treaty, Economic and Monetary Union and the Neorealist Research Programme', *Review of International Studies*, XXI N° 1, 21–40.

Grimm, D. (1995) 'Does Europe Need a Constitution?', *European Law Journal*, I 282–302.

Gstöhl, S. (2002) *Reluctant Europeans: Norway, Sweden, and Switzerland* (Boulder, CO.: Lynne Rienner).

Gualini, E. (2003) *Multi-level Governance and Institutional Change: The Europeanization of Regional Policy in Italy* (Aldershot: Ashgate).

Guerrina, R. (2002) *Europe, History, Ideas and Ideologies* (London: Hodder).

Guggenbuhl, A. (1995) 'The Political Economy of Association with Eastern Europe', in F. Laursen (ed.), *The Political Economy of European Integration* (The Hague: Kluwer).

Guirao Pineyro, F. (1998) *Spain and the Reconstruction of Western Europe, 1945–57* (London: Macmillan).

Gustavsson, S. (1997) 'Double Assymmetry As Normative Challenge', in A. Føllesdal and P. Koslowski (eds), *Democracy and the European Union* (Berlin: Springer).

Haas, E. (1958) *The Uniting of Europe: Political, Economic and Social Forces, 1950–1957* (London: Stevens, 1958; and Stanford: Stanford University Press).

Haas, E. (1961) 'International Integration: The European and the Universal Process', *International Organization*, IV 607–46.

Haas, E. (1968) *The Uniting of Europe: Political, Social, and Economic Forces 1950–1957*, 2nd edn. (Berkeley: University of California Press, 1968; Stanford: Stanford University Press).

Haas, P. (1992) 'Introduction: Epistemic Communities and International Policy Co-ordination', *International Organization*, XLVI 1–35.

Habermas, J. (1981) *Theorie Des Kommunikativen Handelns*, Zwei Bände (Frankfurt a.M.: Suhrkamp).

Habermas, J. (1992) 'Citizenship and National Identity: Some Reflections on the Future of Europe', *Praxis International*, XII 1–19.

Habermas, J. (1995) 'Reconciliation Through the Public use of Reason: Remarks on John Rawls's Political Liberalism', *The Journal of Philosophy*, XCII 109–31.

Habermas, J. (1998) 'Does Europe Need a Constitution? Remarks on Dieter Grimm', in J. Habermas, *The Inclusion of the Other: Studies in Political Theory* (Cambridge MA: MIT Press, 1998). First printed as 'Remarks on Dieter Grimm's "Does Europe need a Constitution?"', *European Law Journal*, I 303–7.

Habermas, J. (2001) *The Postnational Constellation, Political Essays* (London: Polity Press).

Habermas, J. and Derrida, J. (2003) 'Unsere Erneuerung', *Frankfurter Allgemeine Zeitung*, 31 May.

Haggard, S., Levy, M., Moravcsik, A. and Nicolaidis, K. (1993) 'Integrating the Two Halves of Europe: Theories of Interests, Bargaining, and Institutions', in Robert Keohane, J. Nye and S. Hoffmann (eds), *After the Cold War* (Cambridge MA: Harvard University Press).

Hajer, M. and Wagenaar, H. (2003) 'Introduction', in M. Hajer and H. Wagenaar (eds), *Deliberative Policy Analysis* (Cambridge: Cambridge University Press).

Hall, P. and Soskice, D. (2001) *Varieties of Capitalism: The Institutional Foundations of Comparative Advantage* (Oxford: Oxford University Press).

Hall, P. and Taylor, R. (1996) 'Political Science and the Three New Institutionalisms', *Political Studies*, XLIV 936–57.

Hall, S. (1996) 'Introduction: Who needs "Identity"?', in S. Hall and P. du Gay (eds), *Questions of Cultural Identity* (London: Sage).

Hallerberg, M. (2002) 'Veto Players and the Choice of Monetary Institutions', *International Organization*, LVI 775–802.

Hallstein, W. (1969) *Der unvollendete Bundesstaat* (Düsseldorf: Econ-Verl., 1969); English translation: *Europe in the Making* (London: Allen and Unwin, 1972); afterwards published as: *Die Europäische Gemeinschaft* (Düsseldorf & Vienna: Econ-Verl.).

Hamilton, A., Madison, J. and Jay, J. (1961 [1787–88]) 'The Federalist', in J. Cooke (ed.), *The Federalist* (Middletown, CT: Wesleyan Univ. Press).

Handler, R. (1994) 'Is "Identity" a Useful Cross-Cultural Concept?', in J. Gilles (ed.), *Commemorations: The Politics of National Identity* (Princeton: Princeton University Press).

Hardin, G. (1968) 'The Tragedy of the Commons', *Science*, CLXII 1243–8.

Hartley, T. (1998) *The Foundation of European Community Law*, 4th edn (Oxford: Clarendon Press).

Hassenteufel, P. and Surel, Y. (2000) 'Des Politiques Publiques comme les Autres? Construction de l'Objet et Outils d'Analyse des Politiques Européennes', *Politique Européenne*, I 8–24.

Haupt, H.-G., Müller, M. and Wolff, S. (1998) *Regional and National Identities in Europe in the 19th and 20th Centuries* (Leiden: Kluwer).

Hay, C. (2002) *Political Analysis. A Critical Introduction* (New York: Palgrave Macmillan).

Hay, C. and Rosamond, B. (2002) 'Globalisation, European Integration and the Discursive Construction of Economic Imperatives', *Journal of European Public Policy*, IX 147–67.

Heinelt, H. and Smith, R. (1996a) 'Introduction', in H. Heinelt and R. Smith (eds), *Policy Networks and European Structural Funds* (Aldershot: Ashgate).

Heinelt, H. and Smith, R. (eds) (1996b) *Policy Networks and European Structural Funds* (Aldershot: Ashgate).

Heipertz M. and Verdun, A. (2004) 'The Dog that Would Never Bite? On the Origins of the Stability and Growth Pact', *Journal of European Public Policy*, XI, 5 765–80.

Heisenberg, D. and Richmond, A. (2002) 'Supranational Institution-building in the European Union: A Comparison of the European Court of Justice and the European Central Bank', *Journal of European Public Policy*, IX 201–18.

Hennis, M. (2001) 'Europeanization and Globalization: The Missing Link', *Journal of Common Market Studies*, XXXIX 829–50.

Héritier, A. (1999) 'Elements of Democratic Legitimation in Europe: an Alternative Perspective', *Journal of European Public Policy*, VI 269–82.

Héritier, A. (2001) 'Market Integration and Social Cohesion: The Politics of Public Services in European Regulation', *Journal of European Public Policy*, VIII 825–52.

Héritier, A. and Thatcher, M. (eds) (2002) 'Regulatory Reform in Europe', special issue, *Journal of European Public Policy*, IX No.6: 859–1025.

Héritier, A., Kerwer, D., Knill, C., Lehmkuhl, D., Teutsch, M. and Douillet, A.-C. (2001) *Differential Europe: The European Union Impact on National Policymaking* (Lanham, MD: Rowman & Littlefield).

Herrmann, R., Risse, T. and Brewer, M. (eds) (2004) *Identities in Europe and the Institutions of the European Union* (Lanham MD: Rowman & Littlefield).

Hill, C. (1993) 'The Capability-Expectations Gap, or Conceptualising Europe's International Role', *Journal of Common Market Studies*, XXXI 305–28.

Hill, C. and Wallace, W. (1996) 'Introduction: Actors and Actions', in C. Hill (ed.), *The Actors in Europe's Foreign Policy* (London: Routledge).

Hirschman, A. (1970) *Exit, Voice, and Loyalty* (Cambridge MA: Harvard University Press).

Hirst, P. (1994) *Associative Democracy* (Cambridge: Polity Press).

Hix, S. (1994) 'The Study of the European Community: The Challenge to Comparative Politics', *West European Politics*, XVII 1–30.

Hix, S. (1996) 'CP, IR, and the EU! A Rejoinder to Hurrell and Menon', *West European Politics*, XIX No.4: 802–4.

Hix, S. (1998) 'The Study of the European Union II: The "New Governance" Agenda and Its Rival', *Journal of European Public Policy*, V 38–65.

Hix S. (1999) *The Political System of the European Union* (Basingstoke: Macmillan).

Hix, S. (2001) 'Legislative Behaviour and Party Competition in the European Parliament: An Application', *Journal of Common Market Studies*, XXXIX 663–88.

Hix, S. (2002) 'Parliamentary Behaviour with Two Principals: Preferences, Parties and Voting in the European Parliament', *American Journal of Political Science*, XLVI 688–98.

Hix, S. (2004a) 'Electoral Systems and Legislative Behaviour: Explaining Voting Defection in the European Parliament', *World Politics*, LVI 194–223.

Hix, S. (2004b) 'European Universities in a Global Ranking of Political Science Departments', *European Political Science*, III No.2: 5–23.

Hix, S. (2005) *The Political System of the European Union*, 2nd edn (London: Palgrave Macmillan).

Hix, S. and Goetz, K. (eds) (2001) *Europeanised Politics? European Integration and National Political Systems* (London: Frank Cass).

Hix, S., Noury, A. and Roland, G. (2002) 'A Normal Parliament? Party Cohesion and Competition.in the European Parliament, 1979- 2001', EPRG Working Paper No. 9 at <www.lse.ac.uk/Depts/eprg/pdf/Working%20Paper%209.pdf>.

Hodson, D. and Maher, I. (2001) 'The Open Method as a New Mode of Governance', *Journal of Common Market Studies*, XXXIX 719–46.

Hodson, D. and Maher, I. (2002) 'Economic and Monetary Union: Balancing Credibility and Legitimacy in an Asymmetric Policy-mix', *Journal of European Public Policy*, IX 391–407.

Hoffmann, S. (1966) 'Obstinate or Obsolete? The Fate of the Nation State and the Case of Western Europe', *Daedalus*, XCV 862–915.

Hoffmann, S. (2000) 'Towards a Common Foreign and Security Policy', *Journal of Common Market Studies*, XXXVIII 189–98.

Hogan, M. (1987) *The Marshall Plan: America, Britain, and the Reconstruction of Western Europe, 1947–1952* (Cambridge: Cambridge University Press).

Holland, M. (1988) *The European Community and South Africa: European Political Co-Operation Under Strain* (London; New York: Continuum Books).

Holland, M. (1995) *European Union Foreign Policy: From EPC to CFSP Joint Action and South Africa* (Basingstoke: Macmillan).

Hooghe, L. (1996a) 'Building a Europe With the Regions: The Changing Role of the European Commission', in L. Hooghe (ed.), *Cohesion Policy and European Integration: Building Multi-level Governance* (Oxford: Clarendon Press).

Hooghe, L. (ed.) (1996b) *Cohesion Policy and European Integration: Building Multi-level Governance* (Oxford: Clarendon Press).

Hooghe, L. (1996c) 'Introduction: Reconciling EU-Wide Policy With National Diversity', in L. Hooghe (ed.), *Cohesion Policy and European Integration: Building Multi-level Governance* (Oxford: Clarendon Press).

Hooghe, L. and Marks, G. (2001a) *Multi-level Governance and European Integration* (Oxford: Rowman & Littlefield).

Hooghe, L. and Marks, G. (2001b) 'Types of Multi-Level Governance', *European Integration online Papers* (EIoP), V at <http://eiop.or.at/eiop/texte/2001-011.htm>.

Hooghe, L. and Marks, G. (2003) 'Unravelling the Central State, but How? Types of Multi-Level Governance', *American Political Science Review*, XCVII 233–43.

Höreth, M. (1999) 'No Way Out for the Beast? The Unsolved Legitimacy Problem of European Governance', *Journal of European Public Policy*, VI 249–68.

Hosli, M.O. (1996) 'Coalitions and Power: Effects of Qualified Majority Voting in the Council of the European Union', *Journal of Common Market Studies*, XXXII N° 2, 255–73.

Hosli, M.O. (1997) 'Voting Strength in the European Parliament: The Influence of National and of Partisan Actors', *European Journal of Political Research*, XXXI 351–66.

Howarth, J. (2000) *European Integration and Defence: The Ultimate Challenge?*, Chaillot Paper, 43, WEU Institute for Security Studies, Paris.

Huelsse, R. (2003) *Metaphern Der EU-Erweiterung Als Konstruktionen Europäischer Identität* (Baden-Baden: Nomos).

Hume, D. (1960 [1739]) *A Treatise of Human Nature*, edited by L. Selby-Bigge and P. Nidditch (Oxford: Clarendon Press).

Hume, D. (1992 [1754]) 'Idea of a Perfect Commonwealth', in D. Hume, *Essays Moral, Political and Literary* (London: Longmans, Green).

Huntingdon, S. (1997) *The Clash of Civilisations and the Remaking of World Order* (New York: Touchstone).

Hurrell, A. and Menon, A. (1996) 'Politics Like Any Other? Comparative Politics, International Relations, and the Study of the EU', *West European Politics*, XIX 2: 386–402.

Huysmans, J. (1998) 'Security! What Do You Mean? From Concept to Thick Signifier', *European Journal of International Relations*, IV 226–55.

Huysmans, J. (2005) *What is Politics?* (Edinburgh: Edinburgh University Press).

Hyde-Price, A. (2000) *Germany and European Order: Enlarging NATO and the EU* (Manchester: Manchester University Press).

Hyde-Price, A. and Jeffery, C. (2001) 'Germany in the European Union: Constructing Normality', *Journal of Common Market Studies*, XXXIX 689–717.

Ifestos, P. (1987) *European Political Cooperation: Towards a Framework of Supranational Diplomacy?* (Aldershot: Avebury).

Ignatieff, M. (2000) *Virtual War: Kosovo and Beyond* (New York: Picador).

Ingebritsen, C. (1998) *The Nordic States and European Unity* (Ithaca: Cornell University Press).

Inglehart, R. (1999a) 'Trust, Well-being and Democracy', in M. Warren (ed.), *Democracy and Trust* (Cambridge: Cambridge University Press).

Inglehart, R. (1999b) 'Postmodernization Erodes Respect for Authority, but Increases Support for Democracy', in P. Norris (ed.), *Critical Citizens: Global Support for Democratic Government* (Oxford: Oxford University Press).

Irondelle, B. (2003) 'Europeanization without the European Union? French Military Reforms 1991–1996', *Journal of European Public Policy*, X 208–26.

Jachtenfuchs, M. (1995) 'Theoretical Perspectives on European Governance', *European Law Journal*, I 115–33.

Jachtenfuchs, M. (2001) 'The Governance Approach to European Integration', *Journal of Common Market Studies*, XXXIX 245–64.

Jachtenfuchs, M. (2002) *Die Konstruktion Europas: Verfassungsideen und institutionelle Entwicklung* (Baden-Baden: Nomos).

Jachtenfuchs, M., Diez, T. and Jung, S. (1998) 'Which Europe? Conflicting Models of Legitimate Political Order', *European Journal of International Relations*, IV 409–45.

Jachtenfuchs, M. and Kohler-Koch, B. (2003) 'Regieren und Institutionenbildung', in M. Jachtenfuchs and B. Kohler-Koch, *Europäische Integration*, 2nd edn (Opladen: Leske & Budrich).

Jacoby, W. (2000) *Imitation and Politics: Redesigning Modern Germany* (Ithaca: Cornell University Press).

Jacoby, W. (2004) *Ordering from the Menu in Central Europe: The Enlargement of the EU and NATO* (Cambridge: Cambridge University Press).

Jacoby, W. (2005) 'External Incentives and Lesson-drawing in Regional Policy and Health Care in Central Europe', in F. Schimmelfennig and U. Sedelmeier (eds), *The Europeanisation of East Central Europe* (Ithaca: Cornell University Press).

Jacquot, S. and Woll, C. (2003) 'Usage of European Integration: Europeanisation from a Sociological Perspective', *European Integration online Papers* (EioP), VII N° 12 at <http://eiop.or.at/eiop/pdf/2003-012.pdf>.

Jeffery, C. (ed.) (1997) *The Regional Dimension of the European Union: Towards a Third Level in Europe?* (London: Frank Cass).

Jeffery, C. (2000) 'Sub-national Mobilisation in the European Union: Does It Make Any Difference?', *Journal of Common Market Studies*, XXXVIII 1–23.

Joao Rodrigues, M. (2004) *European Policies for a Knowledge Economy* (Cheltenham: Edward Elgar).

Joergensen, K.E. (1997) *Reflective Approaches to European Governance* (Basingstoke: Macmillan).

Joerges, C. (1999) '"Good Governance" Through Comitology?', in C. Joerges and E. Vos (eds), *EU Committees: Social Regulation, Law and Politics* (Oxford: Hart).

Joerges, C. (2002) 'The Law in the Process of Constitutionalizing Europe'. Paper prepared for the annual ARENA Conference, Oslo. Mimeo.

Joerges, C., Mény, Y. and Weiler, J.H.H. (eds) (2001) 'Responses to the European Commission's White Paper on Governance', The Robert Schuman Centre for Advanced Studies, Symposium, 2001.

Joerges, C. and Neyer, J. (1997a) 'From Intergovernmental Bargaining to Deliberative Political Process: The Constitutionalization of Comitology', *European Law Journal*, III 273–99.

Joerges, C. and Neyer, J. (1997b) 'Transforming Strategic Interaction into Deliberative Problem-Solving: European Comitology in the Foodstuffs Sector', *Journal of European Public Policy*, IV 609–25.

Johannson, K. (2002) 'Another Road to Maastricht: The Christian Democrat Coalition and the Quest for European Union', *Journal of Common Market Studies*, XL 871–93.

Jones, E. (2003) 'Idiosyncrasy and Integration: Suggestions from Comparative Political Economy', *Journal of European Public Policy*, X 140–58.

Jones, E. and Verdun, A. (eds) (2003) 'Political Economy and the Study of European Integration', special issue, *Journal of European Public Policy*, X 1 81–158.

Jones, E. and Verdun, A. (2005) 'Introduction', in Erik Jones and Amy Verdun (eds), *The Political Economy of European Integration: Arguments and Analysis* (London; New York: Routledge).

Jordan, A. (2003) *The Europeanization of British Environmental Policy* (Basingstoke: Palgrave Macmillan).

Jørgensen, K.-E. (ed.) (1997) *Reflective Approaches to European Governance* (Basingstoke: Macmillan).

Jospin, L. (2001) 'On the Future of an Enlarged Europe', Speech on 28 May, at <http://www.premier-ministre.gouv.fr/en/p.cfm?ref=24924>.

Jupille, J. and Caporaso, J. (1999) 'Institutionalism and the European Union: Beyond International Relations and Comparative Politics, *Annual Review of Political Science*, II 409–25.

Jupille, J., Caporaso, A. and Checkel, J. (2003) 'Integrating Institutions: Rationalism, Constructivism, and the Study of the European Union', *Comparative Political Studies*, XXXVI 7–41.

Kaelble, H. (2002) 'The Historical Rise of a European Public Sphere?', *Journal of European Integration History*, VIII 9–22.

Kagan, R. (2003) *Paradise and Power: America and Europe in the New World Order* (London: Atlantic Books).

Kaiser, W. (1995) 'The Bomb and Europe. Britain, France, and the EEC Entry Negotiations, 1961–1963', *Journal of European Integration History*, I 65–85.

Kaiser, W. (1999) *Using Europe, Abusing the Europeans. Britain and European Integration, 1945–63* (London: Macmillan).

Kaiser, W. (2001a) 'Culturally Embedded and Path-Dependent: Peripheral Alternatives to ECSC/EEC "Core Europe" since 1945', *Journal of European Integration History*, VII 11–36.

Kaiser, W. (2001b) '"Une bataille est perdue, mais la guerre reste à gagner" – Das Scheitern der Europäischen Verteidigungsgemeinschaft 1954 und der Durchbruch zur horizontalen Wirtschaftsintegration', in R. Kirt (ed.), *Die Europäische Union und ihre Krisen* (Baden-Baden: Nomos).

Kaiser, W. (2001c) 'The Successes and Limits of Industrial Market Integration: The European Free Trade Association 1963–1969', in W. Loth (ed.), *Crises and Compromises: The European Project 1963–1969* (Baden-Baden: Nomos).

Kaiser, W. (2002) '"Überzeugter Katholik und CDU-Wähler": Zur Historiography der Integrationsgeschichte am Beispiel Walter Lipgens', *Journal of European Integration History*, VIII 119–28.

Kaiser, W. (2005) 'Transnational Western Europe since 1945', in W. Kaiser and P. Starie (eds), *Transnational European Union: Towards a Common Political Space*, 17–35 (London: Routledge).

Kaiser, W. and Elvert, J. (eds) (2004) *European Union Enlargement: A Comparative History* (London: Routledge).

Kallestrup, M. (2002) 'Europeanisation as a Discourse: Domestic Policy Legitimization through the Articulation of a Need for Adaptation', *Public Policy and Administration*, XVII 110–24.

Kaltenthaler, K. (2002) 'German Interests in European Monetary Integration', *Journal of Common Market Studies*, XL 69–88.

Karlsson, C. (2001) *Democracy, Legitimacy and the European Union* (Uppsala: Acta Universitatis Upsaliensis).

Kassim, H. (1994) 'Policy Networks, Networks and European Union Policy-Making: A Sceptical View', *West European Politics*, XVII, 4 15–27.

Katzenstein, P. (ed.) (1996) *The Culture of National Security: Norms and Identity in World Politics* (New York: Columbia University Press).

Katzenstein, P. (1993) 'Coping with Terrorism: Norms and Internal Security in Germany and Japan', in J. Goldstein and R.O. Keohane (eds), *Ideas and Foreign Policy* (Ithaca: Cornell University Press).

Katzenstein, P. (1997) 'United Germany in an Integrating Europe', in P. Katzenstein (ed.), *Tamed Power: Germany in Europe* (Ithaca: Cornell University Press).

Keck, M.E. and Sikkink, K. (1998) *Activities Beyond Borders* (Ithaca and London: Cornell University Press).

Keeler, J.T.S. (2005) 'Mapping EU Studies: From Boutique to Boom Field 1960–2000' *Journal of Common Market Studies* LVIII, 551–82.

Kelemen, R. (2004) *The Rules of Federalism: Institutions and Regulatory Politics in the EU and Beyond* (Cambridge MA: Harvard University Press).

Keohane, R. (1984) *After Hegemony* (Princeton: Princeton University Press).

Keohane, R. (ed.) (1986) *Neorealism and its Critics* (New York: Columbia University Press).

Keohane, R. (2000) 'Ideas Part-Way Down', *Review of International Studies*, XXVI 125–30.

Keohane, R. and Hoffmann, S. (1991) 'Institutional Change in Europe in the 1980s', in R. Keohane and S. Hoffmann (eds), *The New European Community: Decisionmaking and Institutional Change* (Boulder CO: Westview Press).

Keohane, R., Nye, J. and Hoffmann, S. (eds) (1993) *After the Cold War: International Institutions and State Strategies in Europe, 1989–1991* (Cambridge MA: Harvard University Press).

Kerremans, B. (1998) 'The Political and Institutional Consequences of Widening: Capacity and Control in an Enlarged Council', in P.-H. Laurent and M. Maresceau (eds), *The State of the European Union: Deepening and Widening* (Boulder: Lynne Rienner).

Key, V. Jr. (1961) *Public Opinion and American Democracy* (New York: Alfred A. Knopf).

King, G., Verba, S. and Keohane, R. (1994) *Designing Social Inquiry: Scientific Inference in Qualitative Research* (Princeton: Princeton University Press).

Klotz, Audie (2001) 'Can We Speak a Common Constructivist Language?', in K.M. Fierke and K.E. Jørgensen (eds), *Constructing International Relations. The Next Generation* (Armonk NY and London: M.E. Sharpe).

Knill, C. (2001a) *The Transformation of National Administrations in Europe. Patterns of Change and Persistence* (Cambridge: Cambridge University Press).

Knill, C. (2001b) 'Private Governance across Multiple Arenas: European Integration Associations as Interface Actors', *Journal of European Public Policy*, VIII 227–46.

Knill, C. and Lehmkuhl, D. (1999) 'How Europe Matters: Different Mechanisms of Europeanization', European Integration online Papers (EIoP), III N° 7 at <http://eiop.or.at/eiop/texte/1999-007.htm>.

Knill, C. and Lehmkuhl, D. (2002) 'The National Impact of European Union Regulatory Policy: Three Europeanization Mechanisms', *European Journal of Political Research*, XLI 255–80.

Knudsen, A.-C. (2001a) 'Defining the Policies of the Common Agricultural Policy. A Historical Study', unpublished PhD thesis, European University Institute, Florence.

Knudsen, A.-C.(2001b) 'Creating the Common Agricultural Policy. Story of the Cereals Prices', in W. Loth (ed.), *Crises and Compromises: The European Project 1963–1969* (Baden-Baden: Nomos).

Kohler-Koch, B. (1996) 'Catching Up With Change: The Transformation of Governance in the European Union', *Journal of European Public Policy*, III 359–80.

Kohler-Koch, B. (1999) 'The Evolution and Transformation of European Governance', in B. Kohler-Koch and R. Eising (eds), *The Transformation of Governance in the European Union* (London/New York: Routledge).

Kohler-Koch, B. (2000) 'Framing: The Bottleneck of Constructing Legitimate Institutions', *Journal of European Public Policy*, VII 513–31.

Kohler-Koch, B. and Eising, R. (eds) (1999) *The Transformation of Governance in the European Union* (London: Routledge).

Koslowski, R. and Kratochwil, F. (1994) 'Understanding Change in International Politics: The Soviet Empire's Demise and the International System', *International Organization* XXXXVIII N° 2, 215–47.

Krasner, S. (2000) 'Wars, Hotel Fires, and Plane Crashes', *Review of International Studies*, XXVI 131–6.

Kratochwil, F. (1989) *Rules, Norms, and Decisions: On the Conditions of Practical and Legal Reasoning in International Relations and Domestic Affairs* (Cambridge: Cambridge University Press).

Kratochwil, F. and Ruggie, J. (1986) 'International Organization: A State of the Art on an Art of the State', *International Organization*, XL 753–75.

Kreppel, A. (2002) *The European Parliament and Supranational Party System: A Study in Institutional Development* (Cambridge: Cambridge University Press).

Kuhn, T. (1988) *Die Struktur wissenschaftlicher Revolutionen* (Frankfurt a.M.: Suhrkamp).

Kuper, R. (2000) 'Democratization: A Constitutionalizing Process', in C. Hoskyns and M. Newman (eds), *Democratizing the European Union: Issues for the 21st Century* (Manchester: Manchester University Press).

Kurzer, P. (2001) *Markets and Moral Regulation: Cultural Change in the European Union* (Cambridge: Cambridge University Press).

Küsters, H. (1982) *Die Gründung der Europäischen Wirtschaftsgemeinschaft* (Baden-Baden: Nomos).

Kymlicka, W. (1995) *Multicultural Citizenship: A Liberal Theory of Minority Rights* (Oxford: Oxford University Press).

Ladrech, R. (2002) 'Europeanization and Political Parties', *Party Politics*, VIII 389–403.

Laffan, B. (2001) 'The European Union Polity: A Union of Regulative, Normative and Cognitive Pillars', *Journal of European Public Policy*, VIII 709–27.

Laffan, B. (2004) 'The European Union and its Institutions as Identity Builders', in R. Herrmann, T. Risse and M. Brewer (eds), *Europeanization: Institutions and the Evolution of Social Identities* (Lanham MD: Rowman & Littlefield).

Laffan, B., O'Donnell, R. and Smith, M. (2000) *Europe's Experimental Union, Rethinking Integration* (London/New York: Routledge).

Lakatos, I. (1978) *The Methodology of Scientific Research Programmes: Philosophical Papers*, Vol. 1, ed. by J. Worrall and G. Currie (Cambridge: Cambridge University Press).

Lamb, R. (1995) *The Macmillan Years: The Emerging Truth* (London: John Murray).

Landfried, C. (1999) 'The European Regulation of Biotechnology by Polycratic Governance', in C. Joerges and E. Vos (eds), *EU Committees: Social Regulation, Law and Politics* (Oxford; Portland: Hart Publishing).

Landfried, C. (2004) 'Difference as a Potential for European Constitution Making', Paper presented at the European Forum, Robert Schumann Centre, European University Institute, 18 March.

Landuyt, A., and Preda, D. (eds) (2000) *I Movimenti per l'Unità Europea 1970–1986*, 2 vols (Bologna: il Mulino).

Landy, M. and Teles, S. (2001) 'Beyond Devolution: From Subsidiarity to Mutuality', in K. Nicolaidis and R. Howse (eds), *The Federal Vision: Legitimacy and Levels of Governance in the US and the EU* (Oxford: Oxford University Press).

Larsen, H. (1997) *Foreign Policy and Discourse Analysis: France, Britain and Europe* (London: Routledge).

Lavenex, S. (2001) 'Migration and the EU's New Eastern Border: Between Realism and Liberalism', *Journal of European Public Policy*, VIII 24–42.

Lawton, T., Rosenau, J. and Verdun, A. (eds) (2000) *Strange Power: Shaping the Parameters of International Relations and International Political Economy* (London: Ashgate).

Lehning, P. (1997) 'Pluralism, Contractarianism and Europe', in P. Lehning and A. Weale (eds), *Citizenship, Democracy and Justice in the New Europe* (London: Routledge).

Lenaerts, K. and Desomer, M. (2002) 'New Models of Constitution-Making in Europe: The Quest for Legitimacy', *Common Market Law Review*, XXXIX 1217–53.

Levi, M. (1998a) *Consent, Dissent and Patriotism* (New York: Cambridge University Press).

Levi, M. (1998b) 'A State of Trust', in V. Braithwaite and M. Levi (eds), *Trust and Governance* (New York: Russell Sage).

Levi-Faur, D. (2004) 'On the Net Impact of Europeanization: The EU's Telecoms and Electricity Regimes between the Global and the National', *Comparative Political Studies*, XXXVII 3–29.

Levy, R. (2003) 'Critical Success Factors in Public Management Reform: The Case of the European Commission', *International Review of Administrative Sciences*, LXIX 553–66.

Lieshout, R.S., Segers, M.L.L. and van der Vleuten, A.M. (2004) 'De Gaulle, Moravcsik and *The Choice for Europe*: Soft Sources, Weak Evidence', *Journal of Cold War Studies*, VI N° 4, 89–139.

Lieven, A. (2002) 'The End of the West?', *Prospect*, September, 20–25.

Lijphart, A. (1999) *Patterns of Democracy: Government Forms and Performance in Thirty-Six Countries* (New Haven: Yale University Press).

Lindberg, L. and Scheingold, S. (1970) *Europe's Would-Be Polity: Patterns of Change in the European Community* (Englewood Cliffs: Prentice Hall).

Lipgens, W. (1968) *Europa-Förderationspläne der Widerstandsbewegungen, 1940–1945: eine Dokumentation* (Munich: Oldenbourg).

Lipgens, W. (1982 [1977]) *A History of European Integration*, vol. 1: 1945–47 (Oxford: Clarendon Press).

Lipgens, W. (1983) 'Der Zusammenschluß Westeuropas: Leitlinien für den historischen Unterricht', *Geschichte in Wissenschaft und Unterricht*, XXXIV 345–72.

Lipgens, W. (ed., partly with W. Loth) (1984–91) *Documents on the History of European Integration*, 4 vols (Berlin: De Gruyter).

Lippert, B. and Umbach, G. (2005) *Pressures of Europeanisation. From Post-Communist State Administrations towards Normal Players in the EU system* (Baden-Baden: Nomos).

Lodge, J. (1994) 'Transparency and Democratic Legitimacy', *Journal of Common Market Studies*, XXXII 343–68.

Lodge, J. (1996) 'The European Parliament', in S. Andersen and K. Eliassen (eds), *The European Union: How Democratic Is It?* (London: Sage).

Long, D. (1997) 'Multilateralism in the CFSP', in M. Holland (ed.), *Common Foreign and Security Policy: The Record and Reforms* (London: Pinter).

Longman, C. (2002) 'The Political Mobilisation of Cultural Identity: Catalonia and Wales in the Matrix of European Integration', unpublished PhD thesis, University of Reading.

Lord, C. (1993) *British Entry to the European Community Under the Heath Government of 1970–74* (Aldershot: Dartmouth).

Lord, C. (1998) *Democracy in the European Union* (Sheffield: Sheffield University Press).

Lord, C. and Beetham, D. (2001) 'Legitimizing the EU: Is There a "Post-Parliamentary Basis" for Its Legitimation?', *Journal of Common Market Studies*, XXXIX 443–62.

Lord, C. and Magnette, P. (2004) 'E Pluribus Unum? Creative Disagreement About Legitimacy in the EU', *Journal of Common Market Studies*, XLII 183–202.

Loth, W. (1996) *Der Weg nach Europa. Geschichte der europäischen Integration 1939–1957* (Göttingen: Vandenhoeck & Ruprecht).

Loth, W. (ed.) (2001a) *Crises and Compromises: The European Project 1963–1969* (Baden-Baden: Nomos).

Loth, W. (2001b) 'Beiträge der Geschichtswissenschaft zur Deutung der Europäischen Integration', in W. Loth and W. Wessels (eds), *Theorien europäischer Integration* (Opladen: Leske and Budrich).

Loth, W. and Wessels, W. (2001) 'Auf dem Weg zur Integrationswissenschaft', in W. Loth and W. Wessels (eds), *Theorien europäischer Integration* (Opladen: Leske & Budrich).

Lübbe, H. (1994) *Abschied vom Superstaat: Vereinigte Staaten von Europa wird es nicht geben* (Berlin: Siedler Verlag).

Ludlow, P. (1997) *Dealing with Britain. The Six and the First UK Application to the EEC* (Cambridge: Cambridge University Press).

Ludlow, P. (1999) 'Challenging French Leadership in Europe: Germany, Italy and the Netherlands and the Empty Chair Crisis of 1965–6', *Contemporary European History*, VIII 231–48.

Ludlow, P. (2001) 'The Eclipse of the Extremes. Demythologising the Luxembourg Compromise', in W. Loth (ed.), *Crises and Compromises: The European Project 1963–1969* (Baden-Baden: Nomos).

Luhman, N. (1969) *Legitimation Durch Verfahren* (Darmstadt: Luchterhand).

Lundestad, G. (1998) *"Empire" by Integration: The United States and European Integration, 1945–1997* (Oxford: Oxford University Press).

MacCormick, N. (1999) *Questioning Sovereignty: Law, State, and Nation in the European Commonwealth* (Oxford: Oxford University Press).

Madison, J. (1967 [1787]) 'Vices of the Political System of the United States', *The Papers of James Madison*, Papers 9: 348–57 (Chicago: University of Chicago Press).

Maes, I. and Verdun, A. (2005) 'Small States and the Creation of EMU: Belgium and the Netherlands, Pacesetters and Gate-keepers', *Journal of Common Market Studies*, Vol. 43, 2, 327–48.

Magnette, P. (2000) 'Towards "Accountable Independence"? Parliamentary Controls of the European Central Bank and the Rise of a New Democratic Model', *European Law Journal*, VI 326–40.

Magnette, P. (2001) 'European Governance and Civic Participation: Can the European Union Be Politicised?', in C. Joerges, Y. Meny and J. Weiler (eds), *Symposium: Responses to the European Commission's White Paper on Governance* (Florence: EUI, RSC/Jean Monnet Programme).

Mair, P. (2000) 'The Limited Impact of Europe on National Party Systems', *West European Politics*, XXIII No. 4: 27–51.

Mair, P. (2004) 'The Europeanisation Dimension', *Journal of European Public Policy*, XI 337–48.

Mair, P. and Zielonka, J. (2000) 'Introduction: Diversity and Adaptation in the Enlarged European Union', special issue on 'The Enlarged European Union, Diversity and Adaptation' edited by P. Mair and J. Zielonka, *West European Politics*, XXV No. 2: 1–18.

Mair, P. and Zielonka, J. (2002) *The Enlarged EU: Diversity and Adaptation* (London: Frank Cass).

Majone, G. (1990) 'Preservation of Cultural Diversity in a Federal System: The Role of the Regions', in M. Tushnet (ed.), *Comparative Constitutional Federalism. Europe and America* (New York: Greenwood Press).

Majone, G. (1994) 'The Rise of the Regulatory State in Europe', *West European Politics*, XVII No. 3: 77–101.

Majone, G. (1998a) 'Europe's "Democratic Deficit": The Question of Standards', *European Law Journal*, IV 5–28.

Majone, G. (1998b) 'State, Market and Regulatory Competition: Lessons for the Integrating World Economy', in A. Moravcsik (ed.), *Centralization or Fragmentation? Europe Facing the Challenges of Deepening, Diversity, and Democracy* (New York: Council on Foreign Relations).

Majone, G. (2001) 'Regulatory Legitimacy in the United States and the European Union', in K. Nicolaidis and R. Howse (eds), *The Federal Vision: Legitimacy and Levels of Governance in the US and the EU* (Oxford: Oxford University Press).

Malmborg, M. (1995) *Den Ståndaktiga Nationalstaten. Sverige och den västeuropeiska Integrationen 1945–1959* (Lund: Lund University Press).

Malmborg, M. and Laursen, J. (1995) 'The Creation of EFTA', in T. Olesen (ed.), *Interdependence versus Integration. Denmark, Scandinavia and Western Europe, 1945–1960* (Odense: Odense University Press).

Malmborg, M. and Stråth, B. (eds) (2002) *The Meaning of Europe. Variety and Contention within and among Nations* (Oxford: Berg).

Mancini, G. (1991) 'The Making of the Constitution of Europe', in R. Keohane and S. Hoffmann (eds), *The New European Community* (Boulder: Westview Press).

Manin, B.(1987) 'On Legitimacy and Political Deliberation', *Political Theory*, XV 338–68.

Mann, M. (1993) 'Nation-states in Europe and Other Continents: Diversifying, Developing, not Dying', *Daedalus*, CXXII 115–40.

Mann, M. (1996) 'Nation-states in Europe and Other Continents: Diversifying, Developing, not Dying', in G. Balakrishnan (ed.), *Mapping the Nation* (London: Verso).

Manners, I. (2002) 'Normative Power Europe: A Contradiction in Terms?', *Journal of Common Market Studies*, XL 235–58.

Manners, I. and Whitman, R. (2003) 'The "Difference Engine": Constructing and Representing the International Identity of the European Union', *Journal of European Public Policy*, X 380–404.

March, J. and Olsen, J. (1989) *Rediscovering Institutions: The Organizational Basis of Politics* (New York: The Free Press).

March, J. and Olsen, J. (1998) 'The Institutional Dynamics of International Political Orders', *International Organization*, LII 943–70.

Marcussen, M. (2000) *Ideas and Elites: The Social Construction of Economic and Monetary Union* (Aalborg: Aalborg University Press).

Marcussen, M., Risse, T., Engelmann-Martin, D., Knopf, H. and Roscher, K. (1999) 'Constructing Europe? The Evolution of French, British and German Nation State Identities', *European Journal of Public Policy*, VI 614–33.

Maresceau, M. and Lannon, E. (2001) *The EU's Enlargement and Mediterranean Strategies: A Comparative Analysis* (Basingstoke/New York: Palgrave Macmillan).

Marks, G. (1996) 'An Actor-centred Approach to Multi-level Governance', *Regional and Federal Studies*, VI 20–38.

Marks, G. and Hooghe, L. (2000) 'Optimality and Authority: A Critique of Neoclassical Theory', *Journal of Common Market Studies*, XXXVIII 795–816.

Marks, G. and Hooghe, L. (2001) *Multi-level Governance and European Integration* (Boulder, CO: Rowman & Littlefield).

Marks, G. and Hooghe, L. (2004). 'Contrasting Visions of Multi-level Governance', in I. Bache and M. Flinders (eds), *Multi-level Governance* (Oxford: Oxford University Press).

Marks, G., Hooghe, L. and Blank, K. (1996) 'European Integration Since the 1980s: State-centric Versus Multi-level Governance', *Journal of Common Market Studies*, XXXIV 341–78.

Marlowe, L. (2001) 'US and them', *The Irish Times Magazine*, 14 July.

Marsh, D. (1998) 'The Utility and Future of Policy Network Analysis', in D. Marsh (ed.), *Comparing Policy Networks* (Buckingham: Open University Press).

Martin, A. and Ross, G. (eds) (2004) *Euros and Europeans: Monetary Integration and the European Model of Society* (Cambridge: Cambridge University Press).

Matlary, J. (2002) *Intervention for Human Rights in Europe* (London: Palgrave Macmillan).

Mattli, W. (1999) *The Logic of Regional Integration. Europe and Beyond* (Cambridge: Cambridge University Press).

Maurer, A. (2003) 'Die Methode des Konvents – ein Modell deliberativer Demokratie?', *Integration*, II 130–40.

Maurer, A. and Wessels, W. (2003) 'The European Union Matters: Structuring Self-made Offers and Demands', in W. Wessels, A. Maurer and J. Mittag (eds), *Fifteen into One? The European Union and its Member States* (Manchester: Manchester University Press).

McDonald, M. (2005) 'EU Policy and Destiny', *Anthropology Today*, XXI 3–4.

McKelvey, Richard D. (1976) 'Intransitivities in Multidimensional Voting Models and Some Implications for Agenda Control', *Journal of Economic Theory*, XII 472–82.

McKenzie, W. (1978) *Political Identity* (London: Penguin).

McLean, I. (2003) 'Two Analytic Narratives about the History of the EU', *European Union Politics*, IV 499–506.

Megie, A. and Ravinet, P. (2004) 'Contrainte de Coopération Intergouvernementale et Processus d'Européanisation: La Construction des Espaces Européens de l'Enseignement Supérieur et de la Justice', Paper delivered to the conference on Europeanization of Public Policies and European Integration, Institut d'Etudes Politiques, Paris, 13 February.

Menéndez, A. (2002) 'Chartering Europe', *Journal of Common Market Studies*, XXXX N° 3, 471–90.

Merkel, W. (1999) 'Die Europäische Integration und das Elend der Theorie', *Geschichte und Gesellschaft*, XXV 302–38.

Merlingen, M. (2001) 'Identity, Politics and Germany's Post-TEU Policy on EMU', *Journal of Common Market Studies*, XXXIX 463–83.

Merlingen, M., Mudde, C. and Sedelmeier, U. (2000) 'Constitutional Politics and the "Embedded Acquis Communautaire": The Case of the EU Fourteen against the Austrian Government', Constitutionalism Web-papers, ConWEB, no. 4/2000.

Michelman, F. (2000) 'W(h)ither the Constitution?', *Cardozo Law Review*, XXI 1063–83.

Mill, J. (1958 [1861]) *Considerations on Representative Government* (New York: Liberal Arts Press).

Miller, A. and Listhaug, O. (1999) 'Political Performance and Institutional Trust', in P. Norris (ed.), *Critical Citizens: Global Support for Democratic Government* (Oxford: Oxford University Press).

Miller, D. (1995) *On Nationality* (Oxford: Oxford University Press).

Miller, D. (2000) *Citizenship and National Identity* (London: Blackwell).

Milliken, J. (1999) 'The Study of Discourse in International Relations: A Critique of Research and Methods', *European Journal of International Relations*, V 225–54.

Milward, A. (1984) *The Reconstruction of Western Europe 1945–1951* (London: Methuen).

Milward, A. (1992) *The European Rescue of the Nation-State* (London: Routledge).

Milward, A. (1995) 'Allegiance. The Past and the Future', *Journal of European Integration History*, I 7–19.

Milward, A. (2002a) *The United Kingdom and the European Community, vol. 1: The Rise and Fall of a National Strategy 1945–1963* (London: Frank Cass).

Milward, A. (2002b) 'Historical Teleologies', in M. Farrell, S. Fella and M. Newman (eds), *European Integration in the 21st Century: Unity in Diversity?* (London: Sage).

Milward, A. and Sørensen, V. (1993) 'Interdependence or Integration? A National Choice', in A. Milward *et al.* (eds), *The Frontier of National Sovereignty. History and Theory 1945–1992* (London: Routledge).

Moberg, A. (2002) 'The Nice Treaty and Voting Rules in the Council', *Journal of Common Market Studies*, XL 259–82.

Moe, T. (1984) 'The New Economics of Organization', *American Journal of Political Science*, XXVIII 739–77.

Moravcsik, A. (1991) 'Negotiating the Single European Act: National Interests and Conventional Statecraft in the European Community', *International Organization*, XLV 19–56.

Moravcsik, A. (1993) 'Preferences and Power in the European Community: A Liberal Intergovernmentalist Approach', *Journal of Common Market Studies*, XXXI 473–524.

Moravcsik, A. (1994) 'A Liberal Intergovernmentalist Approach to the EC', in S. Bulmer and A. Scott (eds), *Economic and Political Integration in Europe: Internal Dynamics and Global Context* (London: Blackwell).

Moravcsik, A. (1998a) *The Choice for Europe: Social Purpose and State Power from Messina to Maastricht* (Ithaca: Cornell University Press and London: UCL Press).

Moravcsik, A. (ed.) (1998b) *Centralization or Fragmentation? Europe Facing the Challenges of Deepening, Diversity, and Democracy* (New York: Council on Foreign Relations).

Moravcsik, A. (1999) 'A New Statecraft: Supranational Entrepreneurs and International Cooperation', *International Organization*, LIII 267–306.

Moravcsik, A. (2000a) 'De Gaulle Between Grain and Grandeur: The Political Economy of French EC Policy 1958–1970 (Part 1)', *Journal of Cold War Studies*, II No. 2 3–43.

Moravcsik, A. (2000b) 'De Gaulle Between Grain and Grandeur: The Political Economy of French EC Policy 1958–1970 (Part 2)', *Journal of Cold War Studies*, II No. 3 4–68.

Moravcsik, A. (2000c) 'In Defence of the "Democratic Deficit": Reassessing Legitimacy in the European Union', *Journal of Common Market Studies*, XL 603–24.

Moravcsik, A. (2003a) 'Reassessing Legitimacy in the European Union', in J. Weiler, I. Begg and J. Peterson (eds), *Integration in an Expanding European Union: Reassessing the Fundamentals* (Oxford: Blackwell).

Moravcsik, A. (2003b) 'Europe comes of age', *Newsweek*, 16 June.

Moravcsik, A. and Vachudova, M. '(2003) National Interests, State Power, and EU Enlargement', *East European Politics and Societies*, XVII 42–57.

Morgenthau, H. (1946) *Man vs. Power Politics* (Chicago: University of Chicago Press).

Morris, C. (2004) 'The Modern State', in G. Gaus and C. Kukathas (eds), *Handbook of Political Theory* (London: Sage).

Mörth, U. (2003) 'Europeanization as Interpretation, Translation, and Editing of Public Policies', in K. Featherstone and C. Radaelli (eds), *The Politics of Europeanization* (Oxford: Oxford University Press).

Moser, P. (1996) 'The European Parliament as a Conditional Agenda Setter. What are the Conditions? A Critique of Tsebelis (1994)', *American Political Science Review*, XC 834–8.

Moser, P., Schneider, G. and Kirchgassner, G. (eds) (2000) *Decision Rules in the European Union A Rational Choice Perspective* (London: Palgrave Macmillan).

Mueller, H. (2004) 'Arguing, Bargaining, and All That: Reflections on the Relationship of Communicative Action and Rationalist Theory in Analysing International Negotiation', *European Journal of International Relations*, X 395–495.

Muller, P. (1995) 'Les Politiques Publiques comme Construction d'un Rapport au Monde', in A. Faure, G. Pollet and W. Philippe (eds), *La Construction du Sens dans les Politiques Publiques, Débats autour de la Notion de Référentiel* (Paris: L'Harmattan).

Muller, P. (2000) 'L'Analyse Cognitive des Politiques Publiques: vers une Sociologie Politique de l'Action Publique', *Revue Française de Science Politique*, L 189–207.

Muller P. and Rouault, S. (1997) 'La Mise en Oeuvre de l'Initiative Emploi, une Grammaire Européenne de l'Expérimentation Sociale', *Cultures et Conflits* Autumn.

Mundell, R. (1961) 'A Theory of Optimal Currency Areas', *American Economic Review*, LI 657–65.

Mundell, R. (1973) 'Uncommon Arguments for Common Currencies', in H. Johnson and A. Swoboda (eds), *The Economics of Common Currencies* (London: Allen and Unwin).

Murphy, D. (2004) *The Structure of Regulatory Competition* (Oxford: Oxford University Press).

Neal, L. and Barbezat, D. (1998) 'The Common Agricultural Policy: Economic Efficiency vs Self-sufficiency', in L. Neal and D. Barbezat (eds), *The Economics of the European Union and the Economics of Europe* (Oxford: Oxford University Press).

Neunreither, K. (1994) 'The Democratic Deficit of the European Union: Towards Closer Cooperation Between the European Parliament and the National Parliaments', *Government and Opposition*, XXIX 299–314.

Neuss, B. (2000) *Geburtshelfer Europas? Die Rolle der Vereinigten Staaten im Europäischen Integrationsprozeß* (Baden-Baden: Nomos).

Nino, C. (1996) *The Constitution of Deliberative Democracy* (New Haven, CT: Yale University Press).

Norman, W. (1994) 'Towards a Philosophy of Federalism', in J. Baker (ed.), *Group Rights* (Toronto: University of Toronto Press).

Norris, P. (ed.) (1999a) *Critical Citizens: Global Support for Democratic Government* (Oxford: Oxford University Press).

Norris, P. (1999b) 'Institutional Explanations for Political Support', in P. Norris (ed.), *Critical Citizens: Global Support for Democratic Government* (Oxford: Oxford University Press).

North, D. (1990) 'The Path of Institutional Change', in D. North (ed.), *Institutions, Institutional Change and Economic Performance* (Cambridge: Cambridge University Press).

Nuttall, S. (1992) *European Political Cooperation* (Oxford: Clarendon Press).

Nuttall, S. (2000) *European Foreign Policy* (Oxford: Oxford University Press).

Nyikos, S. and Pollack, M. (2003) 'Researching the European Union: Qualitative and Quantitative Approaches', in T. Börzel and R. Chichowski (eds), *State of the European Union, vol. 6: Law, Politics and Society* (Oxford: Oxford University Press).

Ojanen, H. (2000) 'The EU and its Northern Dimension: An Actor in Search of a Policy or a Policy in Search of an Actor?', *European Foreign Affairs Review*, V 359–76.

Olsen, J. (2000) 'Organising European Institutions of Governance. A Prelude to an Institutional Account of Political Integration', *ARENA Working Papers*, WP 00/2, ARENA, Oslo.

Olsen, J. (2002) 'The Many Faces of Europeanization', *Journal of Common Market Studies*, XL 921–52.

Olsen, T. (2004) 'United Under God? Or Not?', in L. Dobson and A. Føllesdal (eds), *Political Theory and the European Constitution* (London: Routledge).

Olson, M. (1965) *The Logic of Collective Action* (Cambridge: Cambridge University Press).

O'Neill, M. (1996) *The Politics of European Integration: A Reader* (London: Routledge)

Onuf, N. (1989) *World of Our Making: Rules and Rule in Social Theory and International Relations* (Columbia: University of South Carolina Press).

Onuf, N. (2002) 'Institutions, Intentions and International Relations', *Review of International Studies*, XXVIII 211–28.

Oppermann, T. (1993) 'Der Maastrichter Unionsvertrag – Rechtspolitische Wertung', in R. Hrbek (ed.), *Der Vertrag von Maastricht in der wissenschaftlichen Kontroverse* (Baden-Baden: Nomos).

Orchard, V. (2002) 'Culture as Opposed to What? Cultural Belonging in the Context of National and European Identity', *European Journal of Social Theory*, V 419–33.

Ostrom, E. (1991) *Governing the Commons: The Evolution of Institutions for Collective Action* (Cambridge: Cambridge University Press).

Overton, W. (1998) 'Metatheory and Methodology in Developmental Psychology' (Philadelphia, PA: Temple University).

Özkirimli, U. (2000) *Theories of Nationalism, A Critical Introduction* (London: Macmillan).

Padoan, P. (1997) 'Regional Arrangements as Clubs: The European Case', in E. Mansfield and H. Milner (eds), *The Political Economy of Regionalism* (New York: Columbia University Press).

Page, E. (2003) 'Europeanization and the Persistence of Administrative Systems', in J. Hayward and A. Menon (eds), *Governing Europe* (Oxford: Oxford University Press).

Palan, R. (1992) 'The Second Structuralist Theories of International Relations: A Research Note', *International Studies Notes*, XVII 22–9.

Papadimitriou, D. (2002) *Negotiating the New Europe: The European Union and Eastern Europe* (Aldershot: Ashgate).

Parsons, C. (2002) 'Showing Ideas as Causes: The Origins of the European Union', *International Organization*, LVI 47–84.

Parsons, C. (2003) *A Certain Idea of Europe* (Ithaca: Cornell University Press).

Pasture, P. (2001) 'The Interwar Origins of the International Labour's European Commitment (1919–1934)', *Contemporary European History*, X 221–37.

Pateman, C. (1970) *Participation and Democratic Theory* (Cambridge: Cambridge University Press).

Persson, T., Roland, G. and Tabellini, G. (2000) 'Comparative Politics and Public Finance', *Journal of Political Economy*, MVIII 1121–61.

Peters, B.G. (1999) *Institutional Theory in Political Science. The 'New Institutionalism'* (New York: Pinter).

Peters, B.G. and Pierre, J. (2004) 'Multi-level Governance and Democracy: A Faustian Bargain?', in I. Bache and M. Flinders (eds), *Multi-level Governance* (Oxford: Oxford University Press).

Peterson, J. (1995) 'Decision-making in the EU: Towards a Framework for Analysis', *Journal of European Public Policy*, II 69–93.

Peterson, J. (2001) 'The Choice for EU Theorists: Establishing a Common Framework for Analysis', *European Journal of Political Research*, XXXIX 289–318.

Peterson, J. (2004) 'Policy Networks', in A.Wiener and T. Diez (eds), *European Integration Theory* (Oxford: Oxford University Press).

Peterson, J. and Bomberg, E. (1999) *Decision-Making in the European Union* (Basingstoke: Macmillan).

Pettit, P. (1997) *Republicanism: A Theory of Freedom and Government* (Oxford: Clarendon Press).

Phinnemore, D. (1999) *Association: Stepping-Stone or Alternative to EU Membership?* (Sheffield: Sheffield Academic Press).

Pierson, P. (1996) 'The Path to European Integration: A Historical Institutionalist Analysis', *Comparative Political Studies*, XXIX 123–63.

Pijpers, A.(1990) *The Vicissitudes of European Political Cooperation: Towards a Realist Interpretation of the EC's Collective Diplomacy* (Gravenhage: CIP Gegevens Koninklijke Bibliotheek).

Pijpers, A. (1991) 'European Political Cooperation and the Realist Paradigm', in M. Holland (ed.), *The Future of European Political Cooperation* (London: Macmillan).

Pijpers, A. (1996) 'The Netherlands: The Weakening Pull of Atlanticism', in C. Hill (ed.), *The Actors in Europe's Foreign Policy* (London: Routledge).

Pinder, J. (1968) 'Positive Integration and Negative Integration: Some Problems of Economic Union in the EEC', *The World Today*, XXIV 89–110.

Pinker, S. (1999) *How the Mind Works* (London: Penguin).

Pion-Berlin, D. and Cleary, D. (2005 forthcoming) 'Methodological Bias in the APSR', in K. Monroe (ed.), *Perestroika: Methodological Pluralism, Governance, and Diversity in Contemporary American Political Science* (New Haven, CT: Yale University Press).

Pistone, S. (ed.) (1992) *I Movimenti per l'Unità Europea 1945–1954* (Milan: Jaca).
Pistone, S. (ed.) (1996) *I Movimenti per l'Unità Europea 1954–1969* (Pavia: University of Pavia Press).
Pogge, T. (2002) *World Poverty and Human Rights* (Cambridge: Polity Press).
Poidevin, R. (ed.) (1986) *Origins of the European Integration* (Baden-Baden: Nomos).
Poidevin, R. (1989) *Robert Schuman: Homme d'Etat 1886–1963* (Paris: Imprimerie Nationale).
Pollack, M. (2001) 'International Relations Theory and European Integration', *Journal of Common Market Studies*, XXXIX 221–44.
Pollack, M. (2003a) *The Engines of European Integration: Delegation, Agency and Agenda-Setting in the EU* (Oxford: Oxford University Press).
Pollack, M. (2003b) 'The New Institutionalisms and European Integration', in A. Wiener and T. Diez (eds), *European Integration Theory* (Oxford: Oxford University Press).
Poole, R. (1999) *Nations and Identity* (London; New York: Routledge).
Powell, W. and DiMaggio, P. (1991) *The New Institutionalism in Organizational Analysis* (Chicago: University of Chicago Press).
Preston, C. (1997) *Enlargement and Integration in the European Union* (London: Routledge).
Przeworski, A. (1998) 'Deliberation and Ideological Domination', in J. Elster (ed.), *Deliberative Democracy* (Cambridge: Cambridge University Press).
Puchala, D. (1972) 'Of Blind Men, Elephants, and European Integration', *Journal of Common Market Studies*, X 267–84.
Puchala, D. (1999) 'Institutionalism, Intergovernmentalism and European Integration: A Review Article', *Journal of Common Market Studies*, XXXVII 317–31.
Putnam, R. (1993) *Making Democracy Work: Civic Traditions in Modern Italy* (Princeton: Princeton University Press).
Putnam, R. (1995) 'Bowling Alone: America's Declining Social Capital', *Journal of Democracy*, VI 65–78.
Quermonne, J.-L. (2001) *Le Système Politique de l'Union Européen* (Paris: Montchrestien).
Radaelli, C. (1999) 'Harmful Tax Competition in the European Union: Policy Narratives and Advocacy Coalitions', *Journal of Common Market Studies*, XXXVII 661–82.
Radaelli, C. (2003a) 'The Europeanization of Public Policy', in K. Featherstone and C. Radaelli (eds), *The Politics of Europeanization* (Oxford: Oxford University Press).
Radaelli, C. (2003b) 'The Open Method of Coordination: A New Governance Architecture for the European Union?', Report No.1 (Stockholm: Swedish Institute of European Policy Studies).
Radaelli, C. (2003c) 'The Code of Conduct in Business Taxation: Open Method of Coordination in Disguise', *Public Administration*, LXXXI 513–31.
Radaelli, C. (ed.) (2004) 'The Puzzle of Regulatory Competition', *Journal of Public Policy*, XXIV 1–23.
Raunio, T. and Wiberg, M. (1998) 'Winners and Losers in the Council: Voting Power Consequences of EU Enlargements', *Journal of Common Market Studies*, XXXVI 549–62.
Rawls, J. (1971) *Theory of Justice* (Cambridge, MA: Harvard University Press).
Rawls, J. (1993) *Political Liberalism* (New York: Columbia University Press).
Regelsberger, E., de Schoutheete de Tervarent, P. and Wessels, W. (eds) (1997) *Foreign Policy of the European Union: From EPC to CFSP and Beyond* (Boulder, CO: Lynne Rienner).
Rhenisch, T. (1999) *Europäische Integration und industrielles Interesse. Die deutsche Industrie und die Gründung der Europäischen Wirtschaftsgemeinschaft* (Stuttgart: Franz Steiner Verlag).

Rhodes, R. (1997) *Understanding Governance. Policy Networks, Governance, Reflexivity and Accountability* (Buckingham; Philadelphia: Open University Press).

Rhodes, R. and Marsh, D. (1992) 'New Directions in the Study of Policy Networks', *European Journal of Political Research*, XXI 181–205.

Rhodes, R., Bache, I. and George, S. (1996) 'Policy Networks and Policy-Making in the European Union: A Critical Appraisal', in L. Hooghe (ed.), *Cohesion Policy and European Integration: Building Multi-level Governance* (Oxford: Clarendon Press).

Richardson, J. (2001) 'Policy-Making in the EU: Interests, Ideas and Garbage Cans of Primeval Soup', in J. Richardson (ed.), *European Union Power and Policy-Making*, 2nd edn (London: Routledge).

Rieger, E. (2000) 'The Common Agricultural Policy: Politics against Markets', in H. Wallace and W. Wallace (eds), *Policy-Making in the European Union*, 4th edn (Oxford: Oxford University Press).

Riker, W. (1982) 'The Two-Party System and Duverger's Law: An Essay on the History of Political Science', *American Political Science Review*, LXXVI 753–66.

Riker, W. (1990) 'Political Science and Rational Choice', in J. Alt and K. Shepsle (eds), *Perspectives on Positive Political Economy* (Cambridge: Cambridge University Press).

Riker, W. (2003) 'Social Choice Theory and Constitutional Democracy', in T. Christiano (ed.), *Philosophy and Democracy* (Oxford: Oxford University Press).

Riondel, B. (1998) 'Affirmation du Parlement européen et émergence d'une identité européenne, des années soixante à nos jours', in M.-T. Bitsch *et al.* (eds), *Institutions Européennes et Identités Européennes* (Brussels: Bruylant).

Risse, T. (2000) 'Let's Argue!: Communicative Action in World Politics', *International Organization*, LIV 1–40.

Risse, T., Caporaso, J. and Cowles, M.G. (2001) 'Europeanization and Domestic Change. Introduction', in M. Cowles, J. Caporaso and T. Risse (eds), *Transforming Europe: Europeanization and Domestic Change* (Ithaca: Cornell University Press).

Risse, T. and Maier, M. (2003) *Europeanization, Collective Identities and Public Discourses*, IDNET project (Florence: EUI, Robert Schuman Centre for Advanced Studies).

Risse, T., Ropp, S. and Sikkink, K. (eds) (1999) *The Power of Human Rights: International Norms and Domestic Change* (Cambridge: Cambridge University Press).

Risse-Kappen, T. (1996) 'Exploring the Nature of the Beast: International Relations Theory and Comparative Policy Analysis Meet the European Union', *Journal of Common Market Studies*, XXXIV 53–80.

Rittberger, B. (2000) 'Impatient Legislators and New Issue-Dimensions: A Critique of the Garrett and Tsebelis "Standard Version" of Legislative Politics', *Journal of European Public Policy*, VII 554–75.

Rittberger, B. (2003) 'The Creation and Empowerment of the European Parliament', *Journal of Common Market Studies*, XLI 203–26.

Roberson, B. (1998) *The Middle East and Europe. The Power Deficit* (London: Routledge).

Rodriguez-Pose, A. (2002) *The European Union: Economy, Security and Polity* (Oxford: Oxford University Press).

Rometsch, D. and Wessels, W. (eds) (1996) *The EC and Its Member States: Towards Institutional Fusion?* (Manchester: Manchester University Press).

Rosamond, B. (2000a) *Theories of European Integration* (Basingstoke: Macmillan).

Rosamond, B. (2000b) 'Theorising the European Union Past, Present and Future: On Knowledge, Disciplines and "Thinking Thoroughly" About Integration Theory', *Current Politics and Economics of Europe*, IX 147–63.

Rose, R. (2002) 'Ten Steps in Lesson-Drawing: A Guide to Learning from Abroad', RSCAS Working Paper 2002/05, European University Institute, Florence.

Rosenau, J. (2004) 'Strong Demand, Huge Supply: Governance in an Emerging Epoch', in I. Bache and M. Flinders (eds), *Multi-level Governance* (Oxford: Oxford University Press).

Rosencrance, R. (1998) 'The European Union: A New Type of International Actor', in J. Zielonka (ed.), *Paradoxes of European Foreign Policy* (The Hague: Kluwer Law International).

Rothstein, B. (1998) *Just Institutions Matter: The Moral and Political Logic of the Universal Welfare State* (Cambridge: Cambridge University Press).

Rousseau, J.-J. (1978 [1762]) *On the Social Contract*, ed. by R. Masters, transl. by J. Masters (New York: St Martin's Press).

Ruano, L. (2002) 'Origins and Implications of the European Union's Enlargement Negotiations Procedure', RSC Working Paper, 2002/62, European University Institute, Florence.

Ruano, L. (2005) 'Institutions, Policy Communities, and Enlargement: British, Spanish and Central European Accession Negotiations in the Agricultural Sector', in F. Schimmelfennig, and U. Sedelmeier (eds), *The Politics of European Union Enlargement: Theoretical Approaches* (London: Routledge).

Ruggie, J.G. (1975) 'Responses to Technology: Concepts and Threats', *International Organization*, XXIX N° 3, 557–83.

Ruggie, J.G. (1998) 'What Makes the World Hang Together? Neo-Utilitarianism and the Social Constructivist Challenge', *International Organisation*, LII N° 4, 855–85.

Rumford, C. (2002) *The European Union: A Political Sociology* (Oxford: Blackwell).

Rumford, C. and Murray, P. (2003) 'Do We Need a Core Curriculum in European Studies?', *European Political Science*, III 85–92.

Sabatier, P. (1998) 'The Advocacy Coalition Framework: Revisions and Relevance for Europe', *Journal of European Public Policy*, V 98–130.

Sabatier, P. (2000) 'Clear Enough to be Wrong', *Journal of European Public Policy*, VII 135–40.

Salgado, R. and Woll, C. (2004) 'L'Européanisation et les acteurs non-Etatiques', paper delivered at the Conference on 'Europeanisation of Public Policies and European Integration', Institut d'Etudes Politique de Paris, Paris, 13 February.

Sandholtz, W. and Stone Sweet, A. (1998) *European Integration and Supranational Governance* (Oxford: Oxford University Press).

Sandholtz, W. and Zysman, J. (1989) '1992: Recasting the European Bargain', *World Politics*, XLII 95–128.

Sandler, T., Loehr, W. and Cauley, J. (1978) *The Political Economy of Public Goods and International Cooperation* (Denver: University of Denver).

Sassatelli, M. (2002) 'Imagined Europe: The Shaping of a European Cultural Identity through EU Cultural Policy', *European Journal of Social Theory*, V 435–51.

Sbragia, A. (1993) 'The European Community: A Balancing Act', *Publius*, XXIII 3–38.

Sbragia, A. (1999) 'Politics in the European Union', in G. Almond, R. Dalton and G. Powell, Jr. (eds), *European Politics Today* (New York: Longman).

Scanlon, T. (1998) *What We Owe to Each Other* (Cambridge MA: Harvard University Press).

Schäfer, A. (2004) 'A New and Effective Form of Governance? Comparing the OMC to Multi-lateral Surveillance by the IMF and the OECD', Paper presented at the 2004 Conference of Europeanists, Chicago, 11–13 March.

Scharpf, F. (1988) 'The Joint-Decision Trap: Lessons from German Federalism and European Integration', *Public Administration*, LXVI 239–78.

Scharpf, F. (1996) 'Negative and Positive Integration in the Political Economy of European Welfare States', in G. Marks, F. Scharpf, P. Schmitter and W. Streeck (eds), *Governance in the Emerging Euro-Polity* (London: Sage).

Scharpf, F. (1997) 'Economic Integration, Democracy and the Welfare State', *Journal of European Public Policy*, IV 18–36.

Scharpf, F. (1999) *Governing in Europe: Effective and Democratic?* (Oxford: Oxford University Press).

Scharpf, F. (2001) 'What Have We Learned? Problem-Solving Capacity of the Multilevel European Polity', *Max Planck Institute Working Papers Series*, MPIfG Working Paper 01/4, Max-Planck-Institute für Gesellschaftsforschung, Cologne.

Scharpf, F. (2002) 'The European Social Model: Coping with the Challenges of Diversity', *Journal of Common Market Studies*, XL 645–70.

Scharpf, F. and Schmidt, V. (eds) (2000) *Welfare and Work in the Open Economy: Volume I: From Vulnerability to Competitiveness* (Oxford: Oxford University Press).

Scharpf, F., Crowley, R. and Thompson, F. (1991) *Crisis and Choice in European Social Democracy*, Cornell Studies in Political Economy (Ithaca: Cornell University Press).

Schattschneider, E. (1960) *The Semi-Sovereign People: A Realist's View of Democracy in America* (New York: Holt, Rinehart and Winston).

Schäuble, W. and Lamers, K. (1994) 'Überlegungen zur europäischen Politik', [Schäuble/Lamers-Paper] (Bonn: CDU/CSU-Fraktion des Deutschen Bundestages) 1 September.

Schimmelfennig, F. (2001) 'The Community Trap: Liberal Norms, Rhetorical Action, and the Eastern Enlargement of the European Union', *International Organization*, LV 47–80.

Schimmelfennig, F. (2002) 'Liberal Community and Enlargement: An Event History Analysis', *European Journal of Public Policy*, IX 598–626.

Schimmelfennig, F. (2003a) 'Internationale Sozialisation: Von einem "erschöpften" zu einem produktiven Forschungsprogramm?', in G. Hellmann, K. Wolf and M. Zürn (eds), *Forschungsstand und Perspektiven der Internationalen Beziehungen in Deutschland* (Baden-Baden: Nomos).

Schimmelfennig, F. (2003b) 'Liberal Intergovernmentalism', in A. Wiener and T. Diez (eds), *European Integration Theory* (Oxford: Oxford University Press).

Schimmelfennig, F. and Sedelmeier, U. (2002) 'Theorising EU Enlargement: Research Focus, Hypotheses, and the State of Research', *Journal of European Public Policy*, IX 500–28.

Schimmelpfennig, F. and Sedelmeier, U. (2004) 'Governance by Conditionality: EU Rule Transfer to the Candidate Countries of Central and Eastern Europe', *Journal of European Public Policy*, X1 4 661–79.

Schimmelfennig, F. and Sedelmeier, U. (eds) (2005a) *The Europeanisation of Central and Eastern Europe. The Impact of the European Union on Candidate Countries* (Ithaca: Cornell University Press).

Schimmelfennig, F. and Sedelmeier, U. (eds) (2005b) *The Politics of European Union Enlargement: Theoretical Approaches* (London: Routledge).

Schimmelfennig, F., Engert, S. and Knobel, H. (2003) 'Costs, Commitments, and Compliance: The Impact of EU Democratic Conditionality on Latvia, Slovakia, and Turkey', *Journal of Common Market Studies*, XLI 495–517.

Schmidt, V. (2001) 'The Politics of Economic Adjustment in France and Britain; When Does Discourse Matter?', *Journal of European Public Policy*, VIII 247–64.

Schmidt, V. (2002) 'Does Discourse Matter in the Politics of Welfare Adjustment?', *Comparative Political Studies*, XXXV 168–93.

Schmidt, V. and Radaelli, C. (2004) 'Policy Change and Discourse in Europe: Conceptual and Methodological Issues', *West European Politics*, XXVII No.2: 183–210.

Schmitt, H. and Thomassen, J. (eds) (1999) *Political Representation and Legitimacy in the European Union* (Oxford: Oxford University Press).

Schmitter, P. (1969) 'Three Neo-Functional Hypotheses about International Integration', *International Organization*, XXIII 161–6.

Schmitter, P. (2000) *How to Democratize the European Union – and Why Bother?* (London: Rowman).

Schmitter, P. (2004) 'Neo-Functionalism', in A. Wiener and T. Diez (eds), *Theories of European Integration: Past, Present and Future* (Oxford: Oxford University Press).

Schneider, G. and Aspinwall, M. (eds) (2001) *The Rules of Integration: Institutionalist Approaches to the Study of Europe* (Manchester: Manchester University Press).

Schneider, H. (1977) *Leitbilder der Europapolitik 1: Der Weg zur Integration*, Europäische Studien des Instituts für Europäische Politik 9 (Bonn: Europa Union Verlag).

Schneider, H. (1998) 'Ein Wandel europapolitischer Grundverständnisse? Grundsatzüberlegungen, Erklärungsansätze und Konsequenzen für die politische Bildungsarbeit', in M. Jopp, A. Maurer and H. Schneider (eds), *Europapolitische Grundverständnisse im Wande: Analysen und Konsequenzen für die politische Bildung* (Bonn: Europa Union Verlag).

Schneider, H. and Hrbek, R. (1980) 'Die europaïschen Union in Werden', in H. von der Groeben and H. Möller (eds), *Die Europaïschen Union als Prozess* (Baden-Baden: Nomos).

Schuman, R. (1950) 'Declaration of 9 May 1950, at <www.robert-schuman.org/gb/robert-schuman/declaration2an.htm>.

Schumpeter, J. (1976 [1943]) *Capitalism, Socialism and Democracy* (London: Allen and Unwin).

Schwabe, K. (1988) *The Beginnings of the Schuman-Plan* (Baden-Baden: Nomos).

Schwarz, H.-P. (1986) *Adenauer: der Aufstieg 1876–1952* (Stuttgart: DVA).

Schwarz, H.-P. (1991) *Adenauer: der Staatsmann 1952–1967* (Stuttgart: DVA).

Schwellnus, G. (2005) 'The Adoption of Non-discrimination and Minority Protection Rules in Romania, Hungary and Poland', in F. Schimmelfennig and U. Sedelmeier (eds), *The Europeanisation of East Central Europe* (Ithaca: Cornell University Press).

Scully, R. (1997a) 'The European Parliament and the Co-Decision Procedure: A Re-Assessment', *Journal of Legislative Studies*, III 58–73.

Scully, R. (1997b) 'The European Parliament and Co-Decision: A Rejoinder to Tsebelis and Garrett', *Journal of Legislative Studies*, III 93–103.

Scully, R. (2005) *Becoming Europeans? Attitudes, Behaviour and Socialization in the European Parliament* (Oxford: Oxford University Press).

Sedelmeier, U. (2000) 'Eastern Enlargement: Risk, Rationality, and Role-Compliance', in M. G. Cowles and M. Smith (eds), *The State of the European Union: Risks, Reform, Resistance, and Revival* (Oxford: Oxford University Press).

Sedelmeier, U. (2002) 'Sectoral Dynamics of EU Enlargement: Advocacy, Access and Alliances in a Composite Policy', *Journal of European Public Policy*, IX 627–49.

Sen, A. (1967) 'Isolation, Assurance and the Social Rate of Discount', *Quarterly Journal of Economics*, LXXXI 112–24.

Serra, E. (ed.) (1989) *The Relaunching of Europe and the Treaties of Rome* (Baden-Baden: Nomos).

Shaw, J. (1999) 'Postnational Constitutionaism in the European Union', *Journal of European Public Policy*, VI 579–97.

Shaw, J. (2003) *What is a Convention?* *Process and Substance in the Project of European Constitution-Building*, Political Science Series 89, HIS, Vienna.

Shepsle, K. (1979) 'Institutional Arrangements and Equilibrium in Multidimensional Voting Models', *American Journal of Political Science*, XXIII 27–59.

Shore, C. (2000) *Building Europe, The Cultural Politics of European Integration* (London: Routledge).

Sikkink, Kathryn (1993) 'The Power of Principled Ideas: Human Rights Policies in the United States and Western Europe', in Judith Goldstein and Robert O. Keohane (eds), *Ideas and Foreign Policy* (Ithaca: Cornell University Press).

Simeon, R. and Conway, D.-P. (2001) 'Federalism and the Management of Conflict in Multinational Societies', in A.-G. Gagnon and J. Tully (eds), *Multinational Democracies* (Cambridge: Cambridge University Press).

Sissenich, B. (2002) 'State Building by a Nonstate: European Union Enlargement and the Diffusion of EU Social Policy in Poland and Hungary', PhD thesis (Ithaca: Cornell University).

Sissenich, B. (2005) 'The Transfer of EU Social Policy to Poland and Hungary', in F. Schimmelfennig and U. Sedelmeier (eds), *The Europeanisation of East Central Europe* (Ithaca: Cornell University Press).

Sjøsted, G. (1977) *The External Role of the European Community* (Farnborough: Saxon House).

Sjursen, H. (2000) 'Coping or Not Coping with Change: Norway in European Security', *European Foreign Affairs Review*, V 539–59.

Sjursen, H. (2002) 'Why Expand? The Question of Legitimacy and Justification in the EU's Enlargement Policy', *Journal of Common Market Studies*, XL 491–513.

Sjursen, H. (2003) 'Understanding the Common Foreign and Security Policy: Analytical Building Blocks', in M. Knodt and S. Princen (eds), *Understanding the European Union's External Relations* (London: Routledge).

Skålnes, L. (2005) 'Geopolitics and the Eastern Enlargement of the European Union', in F. Schimmelfennig and U. Sedelmeier (eds), *The Politics of European Union Enlargement: Theoretical Approaches* (London: Routledge).

Smith, A. (1992) 'National Identity and the Idea of European Unity', *International Affairs*, LXVIII 55–76.

Smith, A. (1998) *Nationalism and Modernism: A Critical Survey of Recent Theories of Nations and Nationalism* (London: Routledge).

Smith, D. and Ray, J. (1993) 'European Integration: Gloomy Theory Versus Rosy Reality', in D. Smith and J. Ray (eds), *The 1992 Project and the Future of Integration in Europe* (Armonk, NY: M.E. Sharpe).

Smith, H. (1995) *European Union Foreign Policy and Central America* (London: Macmillan).

Smith, K. (1998a) *The Making of EU Foreign Policy: The Case of Eastern Europe* (London: Macmillan).

Smith, K. (1998b) 'The Instruments of European Union Foreign Policy', in J. Zielonka (ed.), *Paradoxes of European Foreign Policy* (The Hague: Kluwer Law International).

Smith, K. (1999) *The Making of EU Foreign Policy: The Case of Eastern Europe* (London: Macmillan).

Smith, K. (2003) *European Union Foreign Policy in a Changing World* (Cambridge: Polity Press).

Smith, K. (2003) 'The Evolution and Application of EU Membership Conditionality', in M. Cremona (ed.), *The Enlargement of the European Union* (Oxford: Oxford University Press).

Smith, M. (1996) 'The EU as an International Actor', in J. Richardson (ed.), *European Union: Power and Policymaking* (London: Routledge).

Smith, M. (1998) 'Does the Flag Follow Trade? "Politicization" and the Emergence of a European Foreign Policy', in J. Peterson and H. Sjursen (eds), *A Common Foreign Policy for Europe: Competing Visions of the CFSP* (London: Routledge).

Smith, M. (2000) 'European Foreign and Security Policy', in S. Bromley (ed.), *The Governance of the European Union* (London: Sage).

Smith M. (2003) 'The Framing of European Foreign and Security Policy: Towards a Post-Modern Policy Framework?', *Journal of European Public Policy*, X 556–73.

Smith, M.E. (2001a) 'The Legalization of EU Foreign Policy', *Journal of Common Market Studies*, XXXIX 79–104.

Smith, M.E. (2001b) 'The Quest for Coherence: Institutional Dilemmas of External Action from Maastricht to Amsterdam', in A. Stone Sweet, W. Sandholtz and N. Fligstein (eds), *The Institutionalization of Europe* (Oxford: Oxford University Press).

Smith, M.P. (2001) 'In Pursuit of Selective Liberalization: Single Market Competition and its Limits', *Journal of European Public Policy*, VIII 519–40.

Smith, S. (1999) 'Social Constructivisms and European Studies: A Reflectivist Critique', *Journal of European Public Policy*, VI 682–91.

Smith, S. (2000) 'Wendt's World', *Review of International Studies*, XXVI 151–63.

Snyder, F. (1994) 'Soft Law and Institutional Practice in the European Community', in S. Martin (ed.), *The Construction of Europe: Essays in Honour of Emile Noël* (Dordrecht: Kluwer Academic Publishers).

Soetendorp, B. (2002) 'The EU's Involvement in the Israeli-Palestinian Peace Process: The Building of a Visible International Identity', *European Foreign Affairs Review*, VII 283–95.

Soutou, G.-H. (2000) 'Die französische Schule der Geschichte der internationalen Beziehungen', in W. Loth and J. Osterhammel (eds), *Internationale Geschichte. Themen – Ergebnisse – Aussichten* (Munich: Oldenbourg).

Spierenburg, D. and Poidevin, R. (1994) *The History of the High Authority of the European Coal and Steel Community* (London: Weidenfeld & Nicolson).

Stavridis, S. and Hill, C. (1996) *Domestic Sources of Foreign Policy: West European Reactions to the Falklands Conflict* (Oxford: Berg).

Stepan, A. (1999) 'Federalism and Democracy: Beyond the U.S. Model', *Journal of Democracy*, X 19–34.

Steunenberg, B. (ed.) (2002) *Widening the European Union: The Politics of Institutional Change and Reform* (London: Routledge).

Stone Sweet, A. and Brunell, T.L. (1998) 'Constructing a Supranational Constitution: Dispute Resolution and Governance in the European Community', *American Political Science Review*, XCII 63–82.

Stone Sweet, A. and Caporaso, J. (1998) 'From Free Trade to Supranational Polity: The European Court and Integration', in W. Sandholtz and A. Stone Sweet (eds), *European Integration and Supranational Governance* (Oxford: Oxford University Press).

Stone Sweet, A., Sandholtz, W., and N. Fligstein (eds) (2001) *The Institutionalization of Europe* (Oxford: Oxford University Press).

Streeck, W. (1996) 'Neo-Voluntarism: A New European Social Policy Regime?', in G. Marks, F. Scharpf, P. Schmitter and W. Streeck (eds), *Governance in the European Union* (London: Sage).

Strom, K. (1990) 'A Behavioral Theory of Competitive Political Parties', *American Journal of Political Science*, XXXIV 565–98.

Surel, Y. (2000) 'The Role of Cognitive and Normative Frames in Policy-Making', *European Journal of Public Policy*, VII 495–512.

Swenden, W. (2004) 'Is the European Union in Need of a Competence Catalogue? Insights from a Comparative Federalism', *Journal of Common Market Studies*, XXXXII 2 371–92.

Szczerbiak, Aleks and Taggart, Paul (2000) 'Opposing Europe: Party Systems and Opposition to the Union, the Euro and Europeanisation', *Opposing Europe Research Network Working Paper No.1* (Brighton: Sussex European Institute).

Tallberg, J. (2002) 'Paths to Compliance: Enforcement, Management, and the European Union', *International Organization*, LVI 609–43.

Tamborini, R. (2001) 'Living in EMU: Prices, Interest Rates and the Adjustment of Payments in a Monetary Union', *Journal of Common Market Studies*, XXXIX 123–46.

Taylor, C. (1993) 'To Follow a Rule ...', in C. Calhoun, E. LiPuma and M. Postone (eds), *Bourdieu: Critical Perspectives* (Cambridge: Polity Press).

Taylor, M. (1987) *The Possibility of Cooperation* (Cambridge: Cambridge University Press).

Taylor, P. (1975) 'The Politics of the European Communities: The Confederal Phase', *World Politics*, XXVII 336–60.

Taylor, P. (1991) 'The European Community and the State: Assumptions, Theories and Propositions', *Review of International Studies*, XVII 109–25.

Tewes, H. (1998) 'Between Deepening and Widening: Role Conflict in Germany's Enlargement Policy', *West European Politics*, XXI 2 117–33.

Thatcher, M. (2004) 'Winners and Losers in Europeanisation: Reforming the National Regulation of Telecommunications', *West European Politics*, XXVII 2 284–309.

Theiler T. (2004) *Political Symbolism and European Integration* (Manchester: Manchester University Press)

Thelen, K. and Steinmo, S. (1992) 'Historical Institutionalism in Comparative Politics', in S. Steinmo, K. Thelen and F. Longstreth (eds), *Structuring Politics – Historical Institutionalism in Comparative Analysis* (Cambridge: Cambridge University Press).

Thomas, G., Meyer, J., Ramirez, F. and Boli, J. (1987) *Institutional Structure: Constituting State, Society, and the Individual* (Beverly Hills, CA: Sage).

Thompson, D. and Gutmann, A. (1996) *Democracy and Disagreement* (Cambridge MA: Harvard University Press).

Tinbergen, J. (1965) *International Economic Integration* (Amsterdam: Elsevier).

Tindemans, L. (1975) 'Bericht von Leo Tindemans, Belgischer Premierminister, an den Europäischen Rat, 29.12.1975', *Bulletin der Europäischen Gemeinschaften, Luxemburg*, 1/76.

Tömmel, I. (1998) 'Transformation of Governance: The European Commission's Strategy for Creating a "Europe of the Regions"', *Regional and Federal Studies*, VIII 52–80.

Tonra, B. (1997) 'The Impact of Political Co-operation', in K. Jørgensen (ed.), *Reflective Approaches to European Governance* (London: Macmillan Press).

Tonra, B. (2001) *Europeanisation of National Foreign Policy: Dutch, Danish and Irish Foreign Policies in CFSP* (Aldershot: Ashgate).

Tonra, B. (2003) 'Constructing the Common Foreign and Security Policy: The Utility of a Cognitive Approach', *Journal of Common Market Studies*, XLII 731–56.

Torreblanca, J. (2001a) *The Reuniting of Europe. Promises, Negotiations and Compromise* (Aldershot: Ashgate).

Torreblanca, J. (2001b) 'Ideas, Preferences and Institutions: Explaining the Europeanisation of Spanish Foreign Policy', ARENA Working Paper 26.

Trachtenberg, M. (2000) 'De Gaulle, Moravcsik, and Europe', *Journal of Cold War Studies*, II 101–16.

Tranholm-Mikkelsen, J. (1991) 'Neo-functionalism: Obstinate or Obsolete? A Reappraisal in the Light of the New Dynamism of the EC', *Millennium: Journal of International Studies*, XX 1–21.

Trausch, G. (ed.) (1993) *The European Integration from the Schuman-Plan to the Treaties of Rome* (Baden-Baden: Nomos).

Treaty on European Union (1997) *Official Journal of the European Communities* C 340, 10.11.1997.

Trimidas, T. (1999) *The General Principles of EC Law* (Oxford: Oxford University Press).

Trondal, J. (2000) 'Multiple Institutional Embeddedness in Europe: The Case of Danish, Norwegian, and Swedish Government Officials', *Scandinavian Political Studies*, XIII 311–41.

Trondal, J. (2001) 'Is there any Social Constructivist-Institutionalist Divide? Unpacking Social Mechanisms Affecting Representational Roles among EU Decision-Makers', *European Journal of Public Policy*, VIII 1–23.

Trondal, J. (2002) 'Beyond the EU Membership–Non-Membership Dichotomy? Supranational Identities among National EU Decision-makers', *Journal of European Public Policy*, IX 468–87.

Tsebelis, G. (1990) *Nested Games: Rational Choice in Comparative Politics* (Berkeley: University of California Press).

Tsebelis, G. (1994) 'The Power of the European Parliament as a Conditional Agenda Setter', *American Political Science Review*, LXXXVIII 128–42.

Tsebelis, G. (2002) *Veto Players: How Political Institutions Work* (New York, NY: Russel Sage Foundation).

Tsebelis, G. and Garrett, G. (1996) 'An Institutional Critique of Intergovermentalism', *International Organization*, L 269–99.

Tsebelis, G. and Garrett, J. (2000) 'Legislative Politics in the European Union', *European Union Politics*, I, 9–36.

Tsebelis, G., Jensen, C., Kalandrakis, A. and Kreppel, A. (2001), 'Legislative Procedures in the European Union', *British Journal of Political Science*, XXXI, 573–99.

Tsebelis, G. and Yataganas, X. (2002) 'Veto Players and Decision-making in the EU After Nice: Policy Stability and Bureaucratic/Judicial Discretion', *Journal of Common Market Studies*, XL 283–307.

Tsoukalis, L. (1997) *The New European Economy Revisited* (Oxford: Oxford University Press).

Tully, J. (2002) 'The Unfreedom of the Moderns in Comparison to Their Ideals of Constitutionalism and Democracy', *Modern Law Review*, LXV, 204–28.

Ugland, T. (2003) 'Making Policy in the EU: The Case of the Council Recommendation on the Drinking of Alcohol by Young People', *Contemporary Drug Problems*, XXX, 739–55.

Umbach, G. (2003) 'Responding to the European Curricula Development: A "Teaching Companion" in EU Studies', *Kiosk Plus*, June.

Umbach, G. and Scholl, B. (2003) 'Towards a Core Curriculum in EU Studies', *European Political Science*, II, 2 71–80.

Urwin, D. (2002) *The Community of Europe. A History of European Integration since 1945* (London: Longman).

Usherwood, S. (2003) 'Beyond Party Politics: Opposition to the European Union in France and the UK, 1985–1999', PhD thesis, London School of Economics.

Vachudova, M. (2001) 'The Leverage of International Institutions on Democratising States: The European Union and Eastern Europe', RSCAS Working Paper, No. 2001/33 (Florence: European University Institute).

Vachudova, M. (2004) *Europe Undivided: Democracy, Leverage and Integration Since 1989* (Oxford: Oxford University Press).

Van Apeldoorn, B. (2002) *Transnational Capital and the Struggle over European Integration* (London: Routledge).

Van der Eijk, C. and Franklin, M. (eds) (1996) *Choosing Europe? The European Electorate and National Politics in the Face of Union* (Ann Arbor: University of Michigan Press).

Van der Pijl, K. (1998) *Transnational Classes and International Relations* (London: Routledge).

Varsori, A. (1988) *Il Patto di Bruxelles (1948): tra Integrazione Europea e Alleanza Atlantica* (Rome: Bonacci).

Vaubel, R. (1986) 'A Public Choice Approach to International Organization', *Public Choice*, LI 39–57.

Verdier, D. and Breen, R. (2001) 'Europeanization and Globalization: Politics against Markets', *Comparative Political Studies*, XXXIV 227–62.

Verdun, Amy (1998) 'The Institutional Design of EMU: A Democratic Deficit?, *Journal of Public Policy*, XVIII 2 107–32.

Verdun, A. (2000) *European Responses to Globalization and Financial Market Integration: Perceptions of EMU in Britain, France and Germany* (Basingstoke: Palgrave Macmillan).

Verdun, A. (2003) 'An American/European Divide in European Integration Studies – Bridging the Gap with International Political Economy', *Journal of European Public Policy*, X 84–101.

Verdun, A. and Christiansen, T. (2000) 'Policies, Institutions, and the Euro: Dilemmas of Legitimacy', in C. Crouch (ed.), *After the Euro – Shaping Institutions for Governance in the Wake of European Monetary Union* (Oxford: Oxford University Press).

Verwaal, E. and Cnossen, S. (2002) 'Europe's New Border Taxes', *Journal of Common Market Studies*, XL 309–30.

Viner, J. (1950) *The Customs Union Issue* (New York: Carnegie Endowment for International Peace).

Vogel, D. (1995) *Trading up: Consumer and Environmental Regulation in a Global Economy* (Cambrige MA: Harvard University Press).

Vos, E. (1999) 'EU Committees: The Evolution of Unforeseen Institutional Actors in European Product Regulation', in C. Joerges and E. Vos (eds), *EU Committees: Social Regulation, Law and Politics* (Oxford: Hart).

Wagner, W. (2003) 'Why the EU's Common Foreign and Security Policy will Remain Intergovernmental: A Rationalist Institutional Choice Analysis of European Crisis Management Policy', *Journal of European Public Policy*, X 576–95.

Waldron, J. (1987) 'Theoretical Foundations of Liberalism', *Philosophical Quarterly*, XXXVII 27–50.

Walker, N. (2001) 'The White Paper in Constitutional Context', in C. Joerges, Y. Meny and J. Weiler (eds), *Symposium: Responses to the European Commission's White Paper on Governance*, Jean Monnet Working Paper No 6/01.

Walker, R. (1989) 'History and Structure in the Theory of I.R.', *Millennium*, XVIII 163–83.

Wallace, H. (1993) 'Deepening and Widening: Problems of Legitimacy for the EC', in S. Garcia (ed.), *European Identity and the Search for Legitimacy* (London: Pinter).

Wallace, H. (2000a) 'EU Enlargement: A Neglected Subject', in M.G. Cowles and M. Smith (eds), *The State of the European Union: Risks, Reform, Resistance, and Revival* (Oxford: Oxford University Press).

Wallace, H. (2000b) 'Analysing and Explaining Policies', in H. Wallace and W. Wallace (eds), *Policy-Making in the European Union*, 4th edn (Oxford: Oxford University Press).

Wallace, H. (2002) 'Enlarging the European Union: Reflections on the Challenge of Analysis', *Journal of European Public Policy*, IX 658–65.

Wallace, H. and Wallace, W. (1995) 'Flying together in a larger and more diverse European Union', Working Documents (W87) of the Netherlands Scientific Council for Government Policy WRR, The Hague.

Wallace, H. and Wallace, W. (eds) (2000) *Policy-Making in the European Union*, 4th edn (Oxford: Oxford University Press).

Wallace, W. (1996) 'Government without Statehood', in H. Wallace and W. Wallace (eds), *Policy-Making in the European Union*, 3rd edn (Oxford: Oxford University Press).

Wallace, W. (2000) 'Collective Governance', in H. Wallace and W. Wallace (eds), *Policy-Making in the European Union*, 4th edn (Oxford: Oxford University Press).

Walt, S. (1987) *The Origins of Alliances* (Ithaca: Cornell University Press).

Waltz, K. (1979) *Theory of International Politics* (New York: Random House).

Walzenbach, G. (2000) 'The Doubtful Handshake: From International to Comparative Political Economy?', in T. Lawton, J. Rosenau and A. Verdun (eds), *Strange Power: Shaping the Parameters of International Relations and International Political Economy* (London: Ashgate).

Warleigh, A. (1998) 'Better the Devil You Know? Synthetic and Confederal Understandings of European Unification', *West European Politics*, XXI 3 1–18.

Warleigh, A. (2000a) 'History Repeating? Framework Theory and Europe's Multi-level Confederation', *Journal of European Integration*, XXII 173–200.

Warleigh, A. (2000b) 'The Hustle: Citizenship Practice, NGOs and "Policy Coalitions" in the EU – The Cases of Auto Oil, Drinking Water and Unit Pricing', *Journal of European Public Policy*, VII 229–43.

Warleigh, A. (2001) 'Europeanising Civil Society: NGOs As Agents of Political Socialisation', *Journal of Common Market Studies*, XXXIX 619–39.

Warleigh, A. (2002) *Flexible Integration, Which Model for the European Union?* (Sheffield: Sheffield Academic Press).

Warleigh, A. (2003a) *Democracy in the European Union: Theory, Practice and Reform* (London: Sage).

Warleigh, A. (2003b) 'Spinning Around: Rethinking a "Europe of the Regions" in the Light of Flexibility', *Comparative European Politics*, I 49–66.

Warleigh, A. and Fairbrass, J. (eds) (2003) *Influence and Interests in the European Union: The New Politics of Persuasion and Advocacy* (London: Europa).

Weale, A. (1989) 'The Limits of Democracy', in A. Hamlin and P. Pettit (eds), *The Good Polity* (Oxford: Blackwell).

Weale, A. (1999) *Democracy* (London: Macmillan).

Weber, K. and Hallerberg, M. (2001) 'Explaining Variation in Institutional Integration in the European Union: Why Firms may Prefer European Solutions', *Journal of European Public Policy*, VIII 171–91.

Weber, M. (1964 [1947]) *The Theory of Social and Economic Organization*, translated by A. Henderson and T. Parsons (New York: The Free Press).

Weiler, J. (1991) 'The Transformation of Europe', *Yale Law Review*, M 1–81.

Weiler, J. (1995a) 'Does Europe Need a Constitution? Reflections on Demos, Telos and the German Maastricht Decision', *European Law Journal*, I 219–58.

Weiler, J. (1995b) 'The State "Uber Alles" Demos and Telos in the German Maastricht Decision', Jean Monnet Working Paper Series 6/95 Harvard Law School, Cambridge MA.

Weiler, J. (1999a) 'A Constitution for Europe? Some Hard Choices', *Journal of Common Market Studies*, XL 563–80.

Weiler, J. (1999b) *The Constitution of Europe* (Cambridge: Cambridge University Press).

Weiler, J. (2001) 'Federalism and Constitutionalism: Europe's Sonderweg', in K. Nicolaidis and R. Howse (eds), *The Federal Vision: Legitimacy and Levels of Governance in the US and the EU* (Oxford: Oxford University Press).

Weiler, J., Haltern, U. and Mayer, F. (1995) 'European Democracy and Its Critique: Five Uneasy Pieces', RSC Working Paper No 95/11.

Weiler, J. and Wind, M. (2003) *European Constitutionalism Beyond the State* (Cambridge: Cambridge University Press).

Weingast, B. (2002) 'Rational-Choice Institutionalism', in I. Katznelson and H. Milner (eds), *Political Science: State of the Discipline* (New York: W.W. Norton).

Weithman, P. (1995) 'Contractualist Liberalism and Deliberative Democracy', *Philosophy and Public Affairs*, XXIV 14–43.

Wendt, A. (1998a) 'Der Internationalstaat: Identität und Strukturwandel in der internationalen Politik', in U. Beck (ed.) *Politik der Globalisierung* (Frankfurt-am-Main: Suhrkamp).

Wendt, A. (1998b) 'On Constitution and Causation in International Relations', *Review of International Studies*, XXIV 101–18.

Wendt, A. (1999) *Social Theory of International Politics* (Cambridge: Cambridge University Press).

Wendt, A. (2000) 'On the Via Media: A Response to the Critics', *Review of International Studies*, XXVI 165–80.

Wendt, A.E. (1987) 'The Agent-Structure Problem in International Relations Theory', *International Organisation*, XXXXI, 335–70.

Wendt, A. and Fearon, J. (2001) 'Rationalism vs. Constructivism: A Skeptical View', in W. Carlsnaes, T. Risse and B. Simmons (eds), *Handbook of International Relations* (London: Sage).

Wessels, W. (1997) 'An Ever Closer Fusion? A Dynamic Macro-political View on Integration Processes', *Journal of Common Market Studies*, XXXV 267–99.

Wessels, W. (1982) 'European Political Cooperation: Towards a Foreign Policy for Western Europe', in D. Allen, R. Rummel and W. Wessels (eds), *European Political Cooperation: Towards a Foreign Policy for Western Europe* (London: Butterworth).

Wessels, W. (1986) 'Die Europapolitik in der wissenschaftlichen Debatte', in W. Weidenfeld and W. Wessels (eds), *Jahrbuch der Europäischen Integration* (Bonn: Europa Union Verlag).

Wessels, W. (2000) *Die Öffnung des Staates: Modelle und Wirklichkeit grenzüberschreitender Verwaltungspraxis 1960–1995* (Opladen: Leske and Budrich).

Wessels, W. and Diedrichs, U. (1997) 'Zur Diskussion um eine Europäische Union nach Maastricht: Fragmente oder Bausteine einer Theorie mittlerer Reichweite?', PVS, 3/97 584–93.

Wessels, W. and Diedrichs, U. (1999) 'The European Parliament and EU Legitimacy', in T. Banchoff and M.P. Smith (eds), *Legitimacy and the European Union* (London: Routledge).

Wheeler, N. (2000) *Saving Strangers: Humanitarian Intervention in International Society* (Oxford: Oxford University Press).

White, B. (2001) *Understanding European Foreign Policy* (London: Palgrave).

Wiener, A. (1998) 'The Embedded Acquis Communautaire. Transmission Belt and Prism of New Governance', *European Law Journal*, IV 294–315.

Wiener, A. (2001) 'Zur Verfassungspolitik Jenseits Des Staates: Die Vermittlung Von Bedeutung Am Beispiel Der Unionsbürgerschaft', *Zeitschrift für Internationale Beziehungen*, VIII 73–104.

Wiener, A. (2003) 'Constructivism: The Limits of Bridging Gaps', *Journal of International Relations and Development*, VI N° 2, 253–76.

Wiener, A. (2003a) 'Citizenship', in M. Cini (ed.), *European Union Politics* (Oxford: Oxford University Press).

Wiener, A. (2003b) 'Constructivism: The Limits of Bridging Gaps', *Journal of International Relations and Development*, VI 253–76.

Wiener, A. (2003c) 'Finality Vs. Enlargement: Constitutive Practices and Opposing Rationales in the Reconstruction of Europe', J. Weiler and M. Wind (eds), *European Constitutionalism Beyond the State* (Cambridge: Cambridge University Press).

Wiener, A. (2004) 'Contested Compliance: Interventions on the Normative Structure in World Politics', *European Journal of International Relations*, X 189–234.

Wiener, A. (2005) 'Soft Institutions', in A. von Bogdandy (ed.), *Principles of European Constitutional Law* (Oxford: Hart Publishing).

Wiener, A. and Diez, T. (eds) (2003) *Theories of European Integration: Past, Present and Future* (Oxford: Oxford University Press).

Wiener, A. and Schwellnus, G. (2004) 'Contested Norms of European Enlargement', in G. Bermann and K.P. Pistor (eds), *Law and Governance in an Enlarged Europe* (Oxford: Hart).

Williamson, T. (2000) *Knowledge and Its Limits* (Oxford: Oxford University Press).

Winand, P. (1993) *Eisenhower, Kennedy, and the United States of Europe* (New York: St Martin's Press).

Wincott, D. (1995) 'Institutional Interaction and European Integration: Towards an Everyday Critique of Liberal Intergovernmentalism', *Journal of Common Market Studies*, XXXIII 597–610.

Wincott, D. (2003) 'The Idea of the European Social Model: Limits and Paradoxes of Europeanisation', in K. Featherstone and C. Radaelli (eds), *The Politics of Europeanization* (Oxford: Oxford University Press).

Winn, N. and Harris, E. (2003) 'Conclusion: The Story of a Death Foretold?', *Perspectives on European Politics and Society*, IV 167–70.

Wobbe, T. (2000) *Weltgesellschaft* (Bielefeld: Transcript Verlag).

Wolf, K. (1999) 'The New Raison d'Etat as a Problem for Democracy in World Society', *European Journal of International Relations*, V 333–63.

Woods, N. (2001) 'International Political Economy in an Age of Globalisation', in J. Baylis and S. Smith (eds), *The Globalization of World Politics: An Introduction to International Relations* (Oxford: Oxford University Press).

Wurm, C. (1995) 'Early European Integration as a Research Field: Perspectives, Debates, Problems', in C. Wurm (ed.), *Western Europe and Germany: The Beginnings of European Integration 1945–1960* (Oxford: Berg).

Young, J. (2000) *Britain and European Unity 1945–1999* (Basingstoke: Macmillan).

Zahariadis, N. (2004) 'European Markets and National Regulation: Conflict and Cooperation in British Competition Policy', *Journal of Public Policy*, XXIV 49–73.

Zielonka, J. (2001) 'How New Enlarged Borders will Reshape the European Union', *Journal of Common Market Studies*, XXXIX 507–36.

Zito, A. (2001) 'Epistemic Communities, Collective Entrepreneurship and European Integration', *Journal of European Public Policy*, VIII 585–603.

Zürn, M. (1999) 'The State in the Post-National Constellation – Societal Denationalization and Multi-Level Governance', *ARENA Working Papers*, WP 99/35.

Zürn, M. (2000) 'Democratic Governance Beyond the Nation-State: The EU and Other International Institutions', *European Journal of International Relations*, VI 183–221.

Zürn, M. (2002) 'From Interdependence to Globalization', in W. Carlsnaes, T. Risse and B. Simmons (eds), *Handbook of International Relations* (London: Sage).

index

accession process, 49, 52, 96, 98, 99,
   105, 106, 112, 114, 142
acquis académique, 233–6, 245
acquis communautaire, 54, 114, 223, 242
Adenauer, Konrad, 198
Afganistan, 118
African Union, 130
agency-structure debate, 37, 38, 39–41,
   44–5, 51, 57, 64, 75, 83, 126, 198,
   204, 210
agenda setting, 26, 67, 88
   conditional agenda setting, 29
Amsterdam Treaty, 48, 51, 118, 127
area studies, 7, 187
Arrow, Kenneth, 21
Aspinwall, Mark, 220
Association Agreements, 98, 99
Association of Southeast Asian Nations
   (ASEAN), 121–2, 130
Austria, 96, 111, 149, 195

Bache, Ian, 62
balance of power, 58, 103
Balassa, Bela, 180
Balkans, 49, 97, 98, 112, 118, 122, 133
Banchoff, Thomas, 153, 158
behaviouralism, 37, 52
Belgium, 23, 182, 193
Bellamy, Richard, 167, 168, 170
benchmarking, 67, 71, 87
Berger, Peter, 177
Berlusconi, Silvio, 131, 132
Bologna process, 235
Börzel, Tanya, 63–4, 72

Bourdieu, Pierre, 40
budget, 104, 105, 111, 112, 184
Bulgaria, 96
Bull, Hedley, 36, 128, 136, 150
bureaucracy, 36, 72, 115, 138, 145
Burley, Anne-Marie, 218

Campbell, Donald, 229–31
Caparaso, James, 213, 218
Cederman, Lars-Erik, 216
Charter of Fundamental Rights, 143,
   154, 167
Checkel, Jeffrey, 177, 185–6, 213
christianity, 139, 193
Christiansen, Thomas, 35, 238, 243
citizenship, 50–2, 55, 84, 133, 134, 138,
   140, 144, 148, 151
classical theories of European
   integration, 91, 93, 174
   early integovernmentalism, 4, 8,
      120–1, 132, 174, 199, 217–18, 235
   neofunctionalism, 1, 4, 8, 48, 58, 93,
      96, 119–21, 132, 174, 192, 199,
      217–18, 200, 235, 243
   transactionalism, 4, 96, 217–18
cohesion policy (including structural
   policy), 79, 81, 83, 90, 111
cold war, 96, 97, 110, 113, 119, 129, 133,
   135
College of Europe, 235
comitology, 26, 27, 145, 157, 170, 185
Common Agricultural Policy (CAP), 1,
   49, 111, 119, 180–1, 182, 184, 203

Common Foreign and Security Policy
(CFSP), 117–30, 158
    and EU as international actor, 118,
    119–21, 129
    and national foreign policies, 123–4
    and regional integration theory, 118,
    119–21, 121–4
    challenges for, and critiques of, 118,
    119, 122
    defence: European Security and
    Defence Policy (ESDP), 117, 118
    defence: European Rapid Reaction
    Force (ERRF), 117
    EU foreign minister, 127
    High Representative of CFSP, 127
    policy planning cell, 127
    see also transatlantic relations, foreign
    policy analysis, European Political
    Cooperation (EPC)
Comparative Politics, 6, 8, 48–9, 57, 61,
    62, 66, 74, 90, 175–4, 187, 199, 211,
    213, 214, 221, 239
competition policy, 66, 72, 73
compliance, 151, 153, 154–60
    contingent compliers, 161–4
    see also normative political theory
Connor, Walker, 137
constitutionalism, 48, 52, 142, 156, 158,
    240, 241
constitutional process in EU, 48–50,
    52–4, 154, 237, 238, 240–1, 244
Constitutional Treaty, 40, 52–4, 84, 87,
    92, 118, 127, 131–2, 139, 143, 157,
    165–71, 182, 203, 237
constructivism, 35–55, 51, 174, 177,
    185–6, 187, 200, 201, 204, 241,
    243
    and common foreign and security
    policy, 123, 126–9
    and enlargement, 97, 100, 101, 102,
    105–6, 107–8, 109, 110–15
    and Europeanization, 63
    and identities, 132, 140, 146, 177–8
    and multilevel governance, 82, 94
    and rationalism, 10–11, 41–3, 68,
    220–1
    and reflexivism, 41–5
    as metatheory, 221, 213, 215–16, 217,
    220, 226

    in evolution of EU studies, 8, 11, 48
    intersubjectivity 39–40, 43, 45
    modern and reflexive
    constitutionalism, 37, 39–41
    see also sociological institutionalism
    and identities
Convention on the Future of Europe,
    52–4, 84, 118, 127, 131, 138, 139,
    143, 153, 162, 203, 242
Council, 36, 152, 154, 183, 184, 185
    Committee of Permanent
    Representatives (COREPER), 36
    in legislative process, 28–30
    qualified majority voting, 27, 28, 103,
    121, 154, 161, 168, 170
    voting power of member states, 27,
    103, 214; see also methodology,
    under formal methods
Cowles, Maria, 26, 27
credible commitments, 24, 25–6, 156,
    157, see also delegation theory
Croatia, 97
customs union, 180, 203
Cyprus, 96, 97
Czech Republic, 96, 114

Davignon Report (1970), 127
'deepening', 100, 104, 107, 108, 133,
    134, 138
de Gaulle, Charles, 23, 202, 203–4
Dehousse, Renaud, 157, 163
delegation theory, 25–7
Dell, Edmund, 195
Delors, Jacques, 23
democracy, 48, 50, 151, 181, 219, 240
    and enlargement, 111, 113, 114
    and identities, 135, 137, 138, 140,
    142–3, 146, 149
    and legitimacy, 152, 154, 155, 157–6,
    162–4, 165–71
    and multilevel governance, 79, 85, 87,
    88, 94
Denmark, 87, 96, 146, 151, 159, 184,
    203
Deutsch, Karl, 174, 217, 235
discourse, 40–1, 43, 45, 59, 60, 65, 67,
    72, 75, 107, 126, 139, 149, 157,
    187, 205, 214
Dobson, Lynn, 168

domestic politics, 56–75, 129, 137, 176–7, 186, 213
  and enlargement 100, 104, 107, 108–9, 110–13, 114
  and multilevel governance, 78–81, 91, 92
Downs, Anthony, 22
Duchêne, Francois, 128, 198
Dyson, Kenneth, 178, 183

Economic and Monetary Union (EMU), 1, 66, 67, 86, 87, 133, 143, 151, 156, 158, 175, 179–81, 183–4, 184–5, 186
Economic Community of West African States, 130
Eising, Rainer, 63, 157
'empty chair' crisis (1965–66), 194, 203
Enlargement
  and Constitutional Treaty, 52–4
  and identities, 142–3, 133
  and regional integration theory, 96–9
  applicants' enlargement politics, 98–9, 103–6
  conditionality, 53, 98, 99, 108, 109, 114, 115, 142–3
  enlargement policy, 98, 99, 106–9
  Eastern enlargement, 96, 100, 109, 111–13, 114, 184
  EFTA enlargement, 96, 97, 99, 100, 109, 110–11, 200
  impact of, 98, 100, 103, 108–9, 113–15
  member state enlargement politics, 98, 99, 103–6, 110–11
  theoretical controversies, 109–13
environmental policy, 39, 72, 114
epistemology, 43, 45, 211, 212, 213, 215–16, 217, 220, 222, 226, 245
epistemic community, 109
Estonia, 96
Euratom, 181, 202
Eurobarometer, 144–7, 151, 244
Europe Agreements, 98
European Coal and Steel Community (ECSC), 23, 129, 130, 165, 180, 181, 190, 192, 193, 195, 203, 206
European Central Bank, 25, 156, 159, 183, 185
European Commission
  and common foreign and security policy, 120, 121, 127

  and enlargement, 107, 112,113
  and legitimacy, 158, 164, 169
  and multilevel governance, 79, 81, 84
  as supranational entrepreneur, 23
  in legislative process, 28
  in integration process, 23, 24–5, 36, 66, 144, 154, 185, 191, 194, 196, 203, 205
  Presidents, 23, 193, 203
European Community Liaison Committee of Historians, 191, 193
European Court of Justice, 24, 25–6, 36, 70, 152–3
European Defence Community (EDC), 159, 202
European Economic Area (EEA), 98, 114
European Economic Community (EEC), 180, 181, 190, 192, 193, 194, 195, 202–3
European Free Trade Area (EFTA), 142, 190, 193, 204, 205, 207, see also enlargement, under EFTA enlargement
Europeanization, 39, 47, 49, 50, 123, 141, 144, 184, 195, 201, 205, 207, 219, 235, 242, 243
  adaptation pressure, 58, 59–60, 63, 67, 70, 72, 108, 109
  and enlargement, 100, 108–9, 113–15
  and regional integration theory, 58, 59
  and institutionalization, 63–5
  and governance, 62–3
  'bottom up' approaches, 59, 60–2, 67, 68
  critiques, 60, 61, 62, 64
  definitions, 57–9
  facilitated coordination, 73
  'goodness of fit'(and policy and institutional 'misfit'), 61, 63–4, 67, 69, 70, 75, 108
  in evolution of EU studies, 56–7
  'top down' approaches, 59–60, 73
  'downloading' and 'uploading', 58, 69, 73
European Parliament, 36, 242
  and common foreign and security policy, 120, 121
  and enlargement, 107
  and identity formation, 205

European Parliament *continued*
  and multilevel governance, 79, 80, 81,
    84, 92
  in integration process, 24, 25–6, 200
  in legislative process, 28–30, 203
  political parties in, 30–1, 147, 151,
    153
  voting and MEPs, 30–31, 244
  see also legitimacy, under European
    Parliament
European Payments Union (EPU), 193
European Political Cooperation (EPC),
  120, 127
European Movement, 192, 193
European Studies, 1–2, 235
European Union Studies
  basic trends, 4, 8–12, 233–6, 237–45
  disciplines within, 3, 5–6, 243:
    anthropology, 5, 141, 174;
    economics, 5, 20, 22, 38, 175,
    179–81, 187, 190, 211; geography,
    3, 175; history, 5, 23, 141, 175,
    190–208, 239, 241; law, 5, 47,
    49–50, 54, 142, 175, 190, 241;
    sociology, 5, 35, 37, 38, 44–5, 47,
    141, 211, 175; politics, 3, 5 , 9, 35,
    47, 49, 50, 57, 75, 141, 174, 175,
    179, 181–3, 187, 190, 191, 200, 211,
    237, 239, 241, 243–4,(*see also*
    Comparative Politics and
    International Relations); political
    economy, 74, 175–6, 183–4, 184–8
  funding of, 234–5
  interdisciplinarity, 7–8, 35, 47, 57, 75,
    135, 141, 148, 175, 197, 201, 209
  multidisciplinarity, 7, 135
  normative debate in, 240–1
  teaching, 235, 237, 242
European University Institute, Florence,
  191, 235
Europessimism, 218
Euroscepticism, 141, 147–8, 242
eurosclerosis, 218
external relations policy, 117–18, 119,
  120, 127, 133

Featherstone, Kevin, 183
Federalism, 139–40, 141, 146, 165, 166,
  167, 170, 193, 218, 219, 235–6
Finland, 61, 66, 96, 110

Finnemore, Martha, 38, 44, 177
Fischer, Joschka, 53
fisheries policy, 110
flexibility, 86–7, 139
foreign policy analysis, 43, 118, 125
France, 24, 67, 70, 87, 117, 129, 149,
  152, 182, 184, 185, 187, 193, 194,
  195, 202, 203–4, 206
Frank, Robert, 204
free trade, 86, 175, 180, 184, 203

Garrett, Geoffrey, 11, 28–30, 38
Gellner, Ernst, 136
General Agreement on Tariffs and Trade
  (GATT), 121
Germany, 24, 53, 99, 129, 131, 152,
  159,182, 183, 184, 185, 186, 193,
  194, 195, 202, 203, 206
Giddens, Anthony, 40
Gillingham, John, 198, 199
Girault, René, 204
globalization, 65, 66, 67, 74, 125,
  129–30, 135, 184, 207, 235
Goetz, Klaus, 56
Goldstein, Judith, 43
governance, 50, 57, 58, 78, 88, 91, 92,
  123, 130, 135, 138, 157, 174, 181,
  219
  and Europeanization, 62–3, 68–71, 73,
    74
  supranational governance, 63, 138
Graf von Galen, Clemens August, 193
Greece, 96, 184
Gualini, Enrico, 62–3, 64

Haas, Ernst, 22, 174, 217–18, 192
Habermas, Jürgen, 39, 53, 140, 135, 156,
  157, 166, 240
Hague Congress (1948), 192
Haider, Joerg, 149
Hallstein, Walter, 23, 202, 203, 205
Hay, Colin, 65, 238
Hill, Christopher, 124
Hix, Simon, 27, 30–1, 56, 199, 213, 221,
  239
Hoffman, Stanley, 8, 100, 120–1, 174,
  194, 199, 217–18, 235
Hooghe, Leisbet, 78–81, 81–2, 84–8, 91,
  93, 137, 219, 238

human rights, 39, 44, 114, 128, 142–3, 146, 156, 162, 163, 165–8
Hungary, 96

Iceland, 110
ideas, 36, 39, 43–7, 62, 65, 72, 73, 78, 82, 105, 125, 126–9, 179, 183, 192, 195, 196, 200, 206, 207, 241
  beliefs, 43–4, 59, 105, 123, 124, 125, 126–9, 130, 183
  cognitive frame, 62, 65, 67, 68, 71, 142, 144, 149
  ideology, 157, 159, 160, 183, 202, 208
  principles, 40, 43, 49, 65, 160
  values, 39, 49, 65, 82, 105–6, 107–8, 123, 126–9, 130, 142, 143
identities, 25, 64, 85, 87,100, 102, 105, 107–8, 109,111, 113, 123, 126–9, 130, 150, 186, 221, 220, 240, 241
  and evolution of EU studies, 132
  and historical research, 204–6, 208
  and regional integration theory, 132, 135–41, 148–50
  Declaration on European identity (1974), 127, 133
  elite and mass identification, 144–5, 153–4
  European and national identities, 144–8
  EU and identity building, 142–4, 196
implementation, 52, 53, 60, 69, 73, 109, 115, 155, 162
institutions, 35, 36–41, 54–5, 62, 98, 101–2, 122, 125, 126, 151, 157–60, 160–4, 177, 185, 186, 203, 205
  soft institutions, 36, 43, 45, 50, 54
institutionalization, 48, 206–7, 243
  and Common Foreign Security Policy, 123
  and enlargement, 97, 98, 101
  and Europeanization, 63–5
  types of institution-building, 47–8
institutionalism, 48, 88, 132, 142, 149, 160, 174, 177, 183, 219, 241
  and Europeanization, 64, 65
  historical institutional, 140, 200, 201, 219
  'lock in' effects, 38
  'path dependency', 38, 55, 117
  rational institutionalism, 11, 21, 28, 100, 108, 115, 219

sociological institutionalism, 35–55, 82, 100, 109, 140, 219, see also constructivism
supranational institutionalism, 97, 100–102, 105, 106–7, 112
types of institutional analysis: agency-orientated, 37–8, 51; structure-orientated, 37, 38–9, 51; interactive approaches, 37, 39–41
interest (or pressure) groups, 23, 35, 51, 72, 79, 80, 84, 88, 90, 99, 100, 110, 111, 112, 129, 147, 157, 170–1, 182, 184, 185, 186, 187, 192, 196, 202–3, 204, 206, 207, 208, 237
interests (or preferences), 23–4, 25, 36–41, 43–4, 65, 78–81, 84, 99, 100–2, 103, 105, 106, 107, 112, 113, 119, 120–1, 122, 123, 126, 129, 130, 134, 176–7, 137–8, 168–9, 171, 185, 186, 187, 194, 200, 202, 208, 211, 220, 242
International Relations, 35, 36, 40, 57, 97, 101, 115, 118, 121–3, 141, 174–5, 176, 183, 187, 194, 199, 204, 211, 212, 213, 215, 217, 221, 229
  critical theory, 48, 178, 213, 235, 239
  liberalism (including neoliberalism), 43, 121–3, 126, 129–30, 175–6, 178
  realism (including neorealism), 37, 97, 100, 101, 102, 103–4, 106, 110–11, 121–3, 126, 129, 176–7, 177, 178, 183, 202–4, 207, 235
  impact on evolution of EU studies, 4, 6, 8, 11
  see also constructivism and institutionalism
Iraq, 118, 134
Ireland, 96, 152, 203
Italy, 66, 131, 132, 193

Japan, 129
Jeffery, Charlie, 84
journals, 234
  Comparative Politics, 221
  Comparative Political Studies, 221
  European Law Review, 5
  European Union Politics, 224–8
  International Organization, 176, 184, 217, 221, 224–8
  International Studies Quarterly, 221

journals *continued*
  Journal of Common Market Studies, 5,
    186, 217, 224–8
  Journal of European Public Policy, 186–7,
    224–8
  Journal of European Integration History,
    191, 200
  Journal of International Relations, 224–8

Kallestrup, Morten, 65
Kassim, Hussein, 90
Keohane, Robert, 43, 100, 177, 213, 235
Kohler-Koch, Beate, 63, 157, 238
Kratochwil, Friedrich, 35, 45, 56

Lakatos, Imre, 56–7
language, 43, 45–6, 65, 154, 202, 203,
    235
Latvia, 96
Legitimacy, 48, 50, 63, 94, 109, 137–8,
    151, 181, 182, 190, 196, 205, 207,
    240
  and European Parliament, 26, 152,
    153–4, 157, 164, 169, 170, 196
  'deficit' or 'crisis', 151, 152–60
  'permissive consensus', 152, 155
  trust, 151, 160–5
liberal intergovernmentalism
  and Common Foreign and Security
    Policy, 120–1
  and enlargement, 97, 100, 101, 106,
    110–13
  and identities, 137–8, 141
  core claims, 23–4
  critiques, 24–5, 198, 199
  influence on EU studies, 10, 11, 22–3,
    48, 194, 195
  see also Moravcsik, Andrew
liberalization, 68, 70, 185
Lipgens, Walter, 191–3, 195, 199
Lisbon agenda, 71
Lithuania, 96
Lord, Christopher, 158
Lowi, Theodor, 64
Luckman, Thomas, 177
Ludlow, Peter, 203
Luxembourg, 182, 193
Luxembourg compromise, 218

Maastricht Treaty, 29, 36, 48, 50, 51, 66,
    133, 146, 151, 152–3, 154, 155, 166,
    174, 182, 200, 206

MacCormick, Neil, 165, 167, 168
Mair, Peter, 75
Majone, Giandomenico, 158, 159, 171
Malta, 96
Manners, Ian, 128, 141
March, James, 11, 38, 44, 126, 142
Marks, Gary, 78–81, 82, 84–8, 91, 92,
    139, 219, 238
Marsh, David, 201
marxism, 176, 197, 213, 218
Mattli, Walter, 218
media, 153, 154, 162, 163, 196, 237
mercantilism, 176
metatheory
  and EU studies, 210–14, 214, 217–22
  definitions, 210
methodology, 11, 175
  and EU studies, 209–10, 215, 222–8
  case studies, 6, 81, 97, 100, 214, 218,
    244
  degenerative and progressive research
    programmes, 56–7, 74
  explanans and *explanandum*, 60, 61,
    62, 72
  formal, 214–15, 223–8, 244: game
    theory, 38, 161, 175, 184, 185, 214;
    spatial modelling, 28–30, 103, 215;
    see also Council, under voting power
  'grand' (or general) theory, 115, 174,
    212, 217–9, 238–9
  interviews, 244–5
  middle range theories, 83, 93, 94, 101,
    174, 238–9
  positivism, 43, 45, 81–3, 94, 126, 128,
    211, 213, 215, 220
  postpostivism, 118, 211, 213, 215–16,
    220, 226
  process tracing, 68
  qualitative, 214, 223–9, 244
  statistical, 214, 215, 216, 223–8, 244
  sui generis nature of EU, 63, 158, 165,
    175, 188, 238, 239
Middle East, 22, 49, 119, 123
Miller, David, 137, 166
Millward, Alan, 23, 138, 193–5, 199,
    200, 201
Monnet, Jean, 130, 180, 198
Moravcsik, Andrew, 10, 22–5, 106, 112,
    120–1, 138, 141, 194, 198, 200, 202,
    218

multilevel governance, 10, 48, 77–95, 138–9, 140, 166, 170, 199, 219
Mundell, Robert, 189

Nationalism, 131, 134–9, 196
negative integration, 70, 180, *compare* with positive integration
Netherlands, The, 182, 193
Nice Treaty, 48, 118
Nordic Customs Union, 193
normative political theory
  and Constitutional Treaty, 165–71
  and EU legitimacy, 153–64
  and trust, 160–4
  definition, 151
  see also compliance
norms, 36, 37, 38–41, 43–7, 50, 51, 52, 54, 55, 59, 62, 64, 65, 67, 68, 71, 78, 97, 100, 101, 105–6, 107–8, 109, 113, 123, 124, 126–9, 142, 145, 149, 159, 167, 183, 186, 192, 198, 200, 201, 220, 240
North American Free Trade Agreement (NAFTA), 130
North Atlantic Treaty Organisation (NATO), 87, 117, 133
Norway, 61, 87, 110–11, 142, 200, 203
Nye, Joseph, 100

Olsen, Johan, 11, 38, 44, 59, 126, 142
Olson, Mancur, 22
ontology, 42–3, 45, 210, 212, 213, 215–16, 217, 222, 238
open method of coordination, 71, 73, 87, 154, 243
optimal currency area, 180–1, 186
opt-outs, 87–7
Organisation for Economic Cooperation and Development (OECD), 121, 193

paradigms, 59, 66, 72, 73, 107, 112, 242
Parsons, Craig, 206
Peters, B. Guy, 92, 83
Peterson, John, 10
Pierre, Jon, 92, 83
Pinder, John, 10
Poland, 53, 96, 114
Poidevin, Reymond, 193, 203
policy analysis, 48, 57, 61, 62, 65, 74
policy networks, 10,
  advocacy coalitions, 98, 206

critiques, 90
definitions, 88–9
policy coalitions, 89
policy communities and issue networks, 88–9,
policy style, 59, 65
policy transfer, 71, 109
political culture, 109, 111, 166
political parties, 147, 154, 158, 164, 179, 185, 193, 196, 203, 206
Pollack, Mark, 25
Portugal, 96
positive integration, 71, 180, 184,
  compare with negative integration
postmodernism, 125, 132, 134, 149, 140, 148, 240
principal–agent relationship, 25, 27, 30,
  see also delegation theory
public opinion, 144–8, 152, 153, 191
Puchala, Donald, 9, 12

Rationalism, 194, 200, 208
  and Common Foreign and Security Policy, 118, 121–3, 125, 126, 130
  and enlargement, 100–2, 104–5, 103, 105, 106, 110, 114
  and liberal intergovernmentalism, 22
  and multilevel governance, 82–3
  and sociological approaches, 10–11, 68, 186, 220–1
  as metatheory, 211, 212, 213, 215, 217, 220
  controversies and critiques, 19–20, 32
  core claims, 20–2
  see also delegation theory, rational institutionalism
Rawles, John, 161, 167
Referenda, 106, 111, 147, 146, 152, 153, 157, 182
regions and local government, 72, 78–82, 84, 86, 92, 139, 170, 208, 237
regulatory competition, 77
resources, 60, 64, 65, 88–90, 92, 94, 109
Rhodes, Rod, 62, 88–90
Risse, Thomas, 39, 40, 44, 63–4, 72, 177, 243
Romania, 96
Rome Treaties, 48, 133, 202
Rosamond, Ben, 65

Ruggie, John, 35, 46, 56, 177, 213
Russia, 111, 130

Sandholtz, Wayne, 140, 218
Santer, Jacques, 193
Scharpf, Fritz, 158, 162, 166
Schengen, 49, 87, 115
Schimmelfennig, Frank, 39, 201
Schneider, Gerald, 220
Schuman, Robert, 180, 198
Schuman Declaration (or Plan), 142,
    191, 195
September 11 attacks, 48, 49
Single European Act, 28, 94, 120, 154,
    199, 218
single (common) market, 1, 4, 81, 86,
    87, 110, 133, 175, 180
Slovakia, 96
Slovenia, 96
Smith, Anthony, 137
Smith, Michael, 119, 125, 153, 158
social Europe (or social policy), 63, 87,
    159
socialization 31, 44, 52, 59, 62, 63, 66,
    67, 68, 69, 71, 106, 107, 109, 115,
    138, 145, 161, 162, 170, 177, 178,
    191, 201, 205, 207
social (or policy) learning, 39, 44, 64,
    67, 71, 75, 109, 114, 145, 171, 177,
    183, 186, 187
soft law, 71
South Africa, 119
sovereignty, 44–5, 152, 155, 165, 181
Spaak Report (1956), 202
Spain, 96, 99, 100
St Malo Declaration, 117
Stone Sweet, Alex, 63, 140, 218

structural policy, see cohesion policy
Sweden, 61, 67, 87, 96, 110–11
Switzerland, 87, 98, 111
subsidiarity, 167, 168, 241
symbols, 143–4

Tranholm Mikkelsen, Jeppe, 218
transatlantic relations, 118, 134, 194,
    195
transatlantic scholarly divide, 212,
    218–19, 217, 221, 226–8, 198
transnationalization, 206–7
Trausch, Gilbert, 193
Tsebelis, George, 28–30, 243
Tully, James, 50
Turkey, 96, 166

Ukraine, 186
United Kingdom, 24, 73, 80, 87, 88, 96,
    98, 99, 152, 195–6, 198, 203, 204,
    205, 206
United Nations, 121
United States of America, 117, 122, 129,
    149, 166 182, 191, 194, 195, 206

Wallace, William, 124
Waltz, Kenneth, 176–7
Weiler, Joseph, 140, 154, 155
Weingast, Barry, 11, 38
Wendt, Alexander, 35
White, Brian, 125
Whitman, Richard, 128, 141

Veto players, 64, 108, 109, 112, 114
Von der Groeben, Hans, 202

Zysman, John, 218